An Anthology of Nonviolence

An Anthology of Nonviolence

Historical and Contemporary Voices

Edited by Krishna Mallick and Doris Hunter

Foreword by Elise Boulding

An Oryx Book

GREENWOOD PRESS
Westport, Connecticut · London

Library of Congress Cataloging-in-Publication Data

An Anthology of nonviolence : historical and contemporary voices / edited by Krishna
Mallick and Doris Hunter ; foreword by Elise Boulding.
       p.   cm.
  Includes bibliographical references and index.
  ISBN 0–313–31879–4 (alk. paper)
   1. Nonviolence. 2. Nonviolence—History. 3. Nonviolence—Religious aspects. I.
Mallick Krishna, 1946– II. Hunter, Doris A., 1929–
HM1281.A5 2002
303.6′1—dc21   2002021622

British Library Cataloguing in Publication Data is available.

Library of Congress Catalog Card Number: 2002021622
ISBN: 0–313–31879–4

First published in 2002

Greenwood Press, 88 Post Road West, Westport, CT 06881
An imprint of Greenwood Publishing Group, Inc.
www.greenwood.com

Printed in the United States of America

The paper used in this book complies with the
Permanent Paper Standard issued by the National
Information Standards Organization (Z39.48–1984).

10 9 8 7 6 5 4 3 2 1

Excerpts from *Animal Liberation*, by Peter Singer. Harper Collins, rev. ed., 1975, 1990. Reprinted with permission of Peter Singer.

Excerpts from *Race Matters* by Cornel West. © 1975 by Cornell West. Reprinted by permission of Beacon Press, Boston.

Excerpts from *Globalization from Below: The Power of Solidarity* by Jeremy Brecher, Tim Costello, and Brendan Smith. South End Press, 2000. Reprinted with permission of the publisher.

Excerpts from *Ecofeminism: Women, Culture, Nature*, edited by Karen Warren. Bloomington: Indiana University Press, 1997. Reprinted with permission of the publisher.

Excerpts from *Women Healing Earth* by Vandana Shiva, edited by Rosemary Radford Reuther. Orbis Books, 1996.

Excerpts from "The Importance of Strategic Planning in Nonviolent Struggle," by Gene Sharp, in *Nonviolent Sanctions* (Spring 1995): 1–5. Reprinted with permission of Gene Sharp.

Excerpts from *The Eight Essential Steps to Conflict Resolution*, by Dudley Weeks. J. P. Tarcher, 1992. Reprinted with permission of Dudley Weeks.

Excerpts from "Visions of an Interfaith Future," by Marcus Braybrooke, edited by Aba and David Storey. International Interfaith Center, 1994. Reprinted with permission of Marcus Braybrooke.

Excerpts from "The 1989 Democratic Uprising in China: A Nonviolent Perspective," by Michael True. In *Legacy and Future of Nonviolence*, edited by Mahendra Kumar and Peter Low. Gandhi Peace Foundation, India, 1996. Reprinted with permission of Michael True.

Excerpts from "The Global Spread of Active Nonviolence," by Richard Deats, *Fellowship* (July/August, 1996): 5–12. Reprinted with permission of Richard Deats.

Excerpts from *Silence at the Brandenburg Gate*, by Maria Diefenbach. Pamphlet. Reprinted with permission of Maria Diefenbach.

Every reasonable effort has been made to trace the owners of copyright materials but in some instances this has proven impossible. The author and publisher will be glad to receive information leading to more complete acknowledgments in subsequent printings of the book and in the meantime extend their apologies for any omissions.

Contents

Acknowledgments

This project was made possible, in part, by a grant from the Faculty Research Support Fund at Salem State College. Thanks to all of the publishers and the authors of the articles included in this book for their help in making this anthology a reality. Our special thanks to Professor Michael True, Professor Emeritus of English, Assumption College for his valuable suggestions in selecting the articles for this book and Professor Elise Boulding for writing the Foreword. We would also like to thank Krishna Mallick's students at Salem State College— Katharine (Nell) Brimmer, Diona Fulton, Katrina Sealy, and Jenifer (Jen) Snow, who worked diligently in typing and editing the manuscript. Above all, without the help of Subir Mallick, who has spent endless hours at the computer formatting the chapters and verifying references of this manuscript, this project would not have been completed. Last, but not the least, thanks to our readers, who will find that nonviolence is a viable alternative for anyone in any part of the world.

Foreword

History is full of incongruities. Emerging from a violent century destructive of many forms of life, the United Nations General Assembly has declared the first decade of the twenty-first century to be the Decade for Education for a Culture of Peace and Nonviolence. Is there any basis for thinking that the citizens of this new century will have any interest in, and capacity for, nonviolence? Since humans are a diverse lot with diverse interests and needs, conflict is a core fact of human experience. But does it have be violent? Humans also have a core need for relationship, for bonding. Noting this, peace researchers optimistically note a paradigm shift in the perception of conflict, away from the concept of power struggles in which the strongest wins and toward a concept of cooperative problem solving and the seeking of mutual advantage. In fact, most conflicts have throughout history been solved peacefully, though history books tend to focus on wars won or lost.

What about the peace stories in history? What is the basis for choosing nonviolent responses to the ever-present reality of human difference and unjust appropriation of resources? This anthology provides a valuable selection of readings from many different cultural traditions and social perspectives that point to a persistent human search for relationship with all living things, even in situations of serious oppression and evil. What determines the choice of nonviolence in the face of evil? This is a very complex question. The editors have chosen to highlight a series of heroes of nonviolence, from the highly intellectual advocate of civil disobedience, Henry David Thoreau, to the inspired practitioner of conflict transformation, Nelson Mandela—but also to devote several sections of the anthology to both principled and strategic nonviolence in dealing with the major social abuses of our time.

The opening selections may startle the reader. They consist of passages from the *Bhagavad-Gita*, Plato, and the Sermon on the Mount, supplemented by peace prayers from many different faith traditions. These selections are very important in conveying the intensity of the perennial spiritual search for a way of being in the world so that outward action is rooted in a deep inwardness. This search goes so far beyond the ordinary human activities of "getting and spending" that the reader is led into serious reflection about human purposes and human possibilities. Here are the deep sources of the capacity for love, joy, compassion, forgiveness, and voluntary suffering. These readings are an important background for understanding Gandhi, Martin Luther King, the Dalai Lama, and Nelson Mandela. Each of these exemplars combines a deep spiritual capacity with a gift for the practical strategies that are needed for social movements to coalesce and be effective for social change. (In a future edition I would hope to see added voices such as Sushila Nayar, Muriel Lester, and Dorothy Day, for women, too, have walked this path.)

The readings on contemporary social issues begin very appropriately with a powerful exposition of speciesism. Peter Singer focuses primarily on our need to be in relationship with all animal species. I would add plants which have taught us as much or more than animals have, and we "moderns" forget that nature was the human species' first teacher. Cornel West writes of another set of teachers— our African American brothers and sisters. We have a broken society to repair and qualities of relationship to develop. Strong traditional community values still exist in both white and black communities and need to be rediscovered, honored, and shared.

An interesting nonviolent approach to the evils generated by the ruthless globalization of the world economy is Jeremy Brecher, Tim Costello, and Brendan Smith's proposal for a Global Economy Truth Commission. Truth commissions represent one of the most creative nonviolent strategies for dealing with the genocidal impact of authoritarian regimes, and certainly the corporate global economy can be thought of as an authoritarian regime. While it is a leap from corporate violence to Doris Hunter's incisive account of the violence inflicted by primitive attitudes toward sexuality and by the refusal to recognize the rich and diverse types of relationships that exist among women, among men, and between women and men, there is a truth-seeking that ties these disparate themes together. We need a Truth Commission on Sexuality!

The call for the rediscovery of the right relationship between humans and nature made earlier by Brecher et al. returns with the presentation by Karen J. Warren of ecofeminism—one of contemporary feminism's most important contributions to a holistic understanding of the environmental crisis that threatens life as we know it on planet earth. Woman's special knowledge and skills in relation to earth—its soil, plants, forests, waters—as farmer and gatherer, and her complete exclusion from policy making due to crude stereotypes about women and nature, have set the stage for today's ecocatastrophe. A basic culture change in regard to the ways in which women are present in society and their social, economic, and political roles is essential. Vandana Shiva spells this out further in "Let Us Survive," an eloquent statement of how "development" has increasingly displaced women even from those earlier recognized food production roles in the

Two-Thirds World, leading to impoverishment of families, soils, and society. Shiva describes women's creativity in regaining their traditional roles through the nonviolent Chipko (tree-hugging) movement but gives a sober assessment of the extent of the task of undoing the harm that "development" based on faulty science and religion based on fanaticism, have done in her part of the world.

Part V, the closing section of the anthology, moves from social issues that call for nonviolence to specific examples of nonviolence in action, beginning with a strong statement by Gene Sharp, today's foremost scholar in the field, about the key role of strategic thinking in nonviolent action. This is followed by a summary analysis by experienced conflict resolution facilitator Dudley Weeks of steps in the conflict resolution process. Since religious teachings in every faith have called believers to experience the oneness of the human family and to love one another, it is very helpful to have Marcus Braybrooke's account of the century-old international interfaith movement. He also presents the current activities of the World Conference on Religion and Peace, which affirms the peace witness and commitment to nonviolence of at least some sectors of each faith community, though unfortunately not all. While much nonviolent action today is, in fact, secular, the continuing presence of the spiritual affirmation of one people "under heaven," as the Chinese tradition puts it, provides a solid grounding for a variety of nonviolent practices and actions. Michael True's vivid eyewitness account of the very secular 1989 nonviolent student uprising in China cannot be fully appreciated without an awareness of the "under heaven" teachings, even though the student generation itself was sadly lacking in familiarity with either Buddhist or Taoist practice.

No one is better equipped than Richard Deats of the International Fellowship of Reconciliation to describe the "global spread of active nonviolence"—the uprisings that have occurred in recent decades in the Philippines, Chile, Haiti, China, Burma, Israel-Palestine, South Africa, and former states of the Soviet bloc. These uprisings are the more striking in that none of them could have been predicted in advance. They confirm the existence of a social movement that at one and the same time is local in its manifestations and yet has profound ramifications for the international community. How nonviolent practicee as satyagraha, developed by Gandhi during India's independence struggle, was applied to the Chipko movement to save the forests, in a "forest satyagraha," is described by Krishna Mallick in an illuminating analysis of the principles of satyagraha and is very suggestive of ways that those principles can be applied in a wide variety of settings.

Fittingly, this section closes with a brief, but powerful, analysis by Maria Diefenbach of how the creation of a special space for silence and reflection in a setting linked to high levels of conflict—whether in the Room of Silence at the Brandenburg Gate in Berlin or the room for meditation at the United Nations building in New York—provides the grounding for creative nonviolent action in the halls of international diplomacy. This completes the journey of the reader of this anthology from the great spiritual teachings of nonviolence, through its practice as a strategy to deal with injustice and oppression in a great variety of settings and by a great variety of practitioners. The subject being very complex, many new questions will arise in the mind of the reader during the journey. An excellent bibliography is included that enables both further study and, equally important, the possibility of the actual practice of nonviolence in the real world.

Elise Boulding
Professor Emeritus, Dartmouth College

Introduction

This book of readings is designed to confront the reader with the puzzling questions that are faced when a course of action that is chosen will have consequences not only for the individual but for other persons and perhaps society. Some of these questions have already been encountered when a decision for action has been necessary:

When should one choose to act?

What are the appropriate motives for one's action?

How can one predict the consequences of action or of a particular range of actions?

One response to these questions involves a commitment to nonviolence. This book is about such a response—nonviolence as a choice, or position, for action. In order to understand this position, one needs to consider these basic questions:

What is "nonviolence"—a belief? an attitude? a tactic? a strategy?

What has motivated (and motivates) people to decide in favor of a nonviolent approach to life's dilemmas?

What is the relationship between nonviolent and violent action in one's experience?

What are the various ways of viewing nonviolence?

In the following paragraphs we present some of the language and some of the historical perspective connected with the tradition of nonviolence as a choice for action in order to give a background for examining these complex questions. The readings that follow the introduction are intended to help the reader understand the reasons behind the choice for or against nonviolent action and become more critical in one's thinking about an ethic of action.

As heaven and earth are not afraid, and never suffer loss or harm,
Even so, my spirit, fear not thou.

As day and night are not afraid, nor ever suffer loss or harm,
Even so, my spirit, fear not thou.
As sun and moon are not afraid, nor ever suffer loss or harm,
Even so, my spirit, fear not thou.
As Brahmanhood and princely power fear not, nor suffer loss or harm,
Even so, my spirit, fear not thou.
As what hath been and what shall be fear not, nor suffer loss or harm,
Even so, my spirit, fear not thou.

—*Atharva-Veda*[1]

In the literature of world religions, we find that nonviolence as a way of life has a very ancient history. Long before the Christians thought about loving the enemy, the Hindus chanted hymns of praise to the spiritual Oneness of all things. These hymns reflect a deep reverence for life, which the Hindu tradition defines as *ahimsa*, the refusal to do harm to life. *Ahimsa* is the ideal for Jainism, a major religious sect in India whose strict adherents cover their mouths and softly sweep the path before their feet in order not to kill inadvertently one of creation's tiny insects. As a son of Hindu tradition, Gautama the Buddha developed this intense sense of reverence for all life into a feeling of compassion for human life. More than 500 years before the birth of Jesus, Buddha told his friends:

All that we are is the result of what we have thought; it is founded on our thoughts, is made up of our thoughts. If a man speaks or acts with a pure thought, happiness follows him, like a shadow that never leaves him.
"He abused me, he beat me, he defeated me, he robbed me"—in those who harbour such thoughts hatred will never cease.
"He abused me, he beat me, he defeated me, he robbed me"—in those who do not harbor such thoughts hatred will cease.
For hatred does not cease by hatred at any time: hatred ceases by love—this is an old rule.
Let a man overcome anger by love, let him overcome evil by good, let him overcome the greedy by liberality, the liar by truth!
Speak the truth, do not yield to anger; give, if thou are asked for little; by these three steps thou wilt go near the gods.

—*Dhammapada*[2]

In the Far East the tradition of Taoism express a similar nonviolent approach to life. A legend relates the story of an old man affectionately called Lao Tzu, "Old Philosopher," who, seeing the corruption of Chinese civilization, decided to find his own "Walden" beyond the walls of the state. Before leaving, he wrote a document of about 5,000 characters, the *Tao-Te-Ching*, which became the basic scripture for Taoism. The *Tao* (the divine principle of the universe), innate in all persons, makes possible the nonviolent act for those sensitive to its *Te* (power). The *Tao*—the way of harmony—and the *Te*—the power—enable us to return love for hatred.

Return love for great hatred.
Otherwise, when a great hatred is reconciled, some of it will surely remain.
How can this end in goodness?
Therefore the sage holds to the left half of an agreement but does not exact what the other holder ought to do.
The virtuous resort to agreement;
the virtueless resort to exaction.
"The Tao of heaven shows no partiality;
It abides always with good men."
—*Tao-Te-Ching*[3]

About the same time in China (during the last decades of the sixth century B.C.) when Lao Tzu was leaving civilization on his water-buffalo, Master Kung (Confucius) was editing the ancient ethical principles of Chinese life and attempting to apply these principles to everyday life. In the *Analects*,[4] he was asked by one of his students, "Is there one word which may serve as a rule of practice for all one's life?" The Great Teacher responded, "Is not Reciprocity such a word? What do you not want done to yourself, do not do to others."

Confucius' emphasis on the ethical implications of the harmonious life rather than on any abstract speculation about heaven parallels the ethical concerns of Judaism. The prophets of Israel saw a direct and realistic relationship between the religious life of obedience, and the possibility for nonviolence as a way of life for all persons. They continually reminded the people that violence (and God's judgment) ends only when they give their absolute obedience to God.

Come, let us go up to the mountain of the Lord,
to the house of the God of Jacob;
that he may teach us his ways
and we may walk in his paths.
For out of Zion shall go forth the law,
and the word of the Lord from Jerusalem,
He shall judge between many peoples,
and shall decide for strong nations afar off;
And they shall beat their swords into plowshares,
and their spears into pruning hooks;
Nations shall not lift up sword against nation,
neither shall they learn war any more;
but they shall sit every man under his vine
and under his fig tree,
and none shall make them afraid;
for the mouth of the Lord of hosts
has spoken.
—*Book of Micah*[5]

The Judaism of early Christian times turned away from this difficult demand of the prophets to "walk in his paths" and became, in many respects, a legalistic system of rituals performed by the priests for the people. Jesus opposed this type of external religion and emphasized a return to that personal and difficult relationship between human beings and God stressed by the prophets. When the Christians began writing their own literature, they used the Greek word *agape* to indicate the unique quality of this relationship. *Agape* means in Greek a love that is self-giving, which asks nothing in return for its goodwill. This type of self-giving love is different from self-fulfilling love represented by the two other Greek words for love, *eros* and *philos*. *Eros* is aesthetic or romantic (erotic) love, which desires intellectual or physical fulfillment. *Philos*, the other Greek word for love, describes the love of friend for friend, brotherly and sisterly love. The early Christians hoped, by using these Greek words, to help us see the distinction between self-giving love, *agape*, which is God's love for us, which motivates, in turn, our unselfish love for others, and a self-fulfilling love (*eros* and *philos*), which is our love for certain types of personal desire.[6]

The Christian idea of nonviolence is based on this belief in *agape*. The Christians believe that by acting nonviolently toward the enemy (by loving the enemy), they are transmitting God's power and self-giving love into human life, and by being the transmitter, they have the power of *agape* to change the enemy into a friend. Martin Luther King Jr., a twentieth-century Christian, expressed this belief to his congregation when he told them that together, by practicing *agape,* they tell the enemy:

> We shall match your capacity to inflict suffering by our capacity to endure suffering. We will meet your physical force with soul force. Do to us what you will and we will still love you . . . . Bomb our homes and threaten our children, and, as difficult as it is, we will still love you. Send your hooded perpetrators of violence into our communities at the midnight hour and drag us out on some wayside road and leave us half-dead as you beat us, and we will still love you. Send you propaganda agents around the country, and make it clear that we are not fit, culturally and otherwise, for integration, and we'll still love you. But be assured that we'll wear you down by our capacity to suffer, and one day we will win our freedom. We will not only win freedom for ourselves; we will so appeal to your heart and conscience that we will win you in the process, and our victory will be a double victory.[7]

For Hindus the act of nonviolence is also a matter of belief. Their refusal to do harm to life, including human life, comes from a conviction that all life is one in *Brahman* (Spiritual Oneness of all things). Gandhi makes this spiritual premise of nonviolence clear when he says,

"Destruction (*himsa*) does not need to be taught. Man as animal is violent, but as Spirit is non-violent. The moment he awakes to the Spirit within, he cannot remain violent. Either he progresses toward *ahimsa* or rushes to his doom."[8]

The notion that everyone needs to "wake up to the Spirit within" conveys the perspective, found in all religions, that a commitment to nonviolence requires spiritual discipline. In the Hindu tradition the practice of nonviolence is involved in special disciplines or *yogas*. Gandhi illustrated this when he combined the concepts of *ahimsa* and *agape* into the word *satyagraha* meaning the "power of truth" or "love force." We cannot exemplify satyagraha unless we practice the demanding requirements of *ahimsa* in our daily life. When we practice nonviolence as a discipline, we discover the force (*graha*) or truth (*satya*) as universally true for everyone. *Agape*, in a similar fashion, requires a life of discipline from the Christian. Although the methods are not similar, the conviction is basically the same: without a disciplined life that is committed to a belief in *ahimsa* or *agape*, all our own efforts to be consistently nonviolent in attitude and behavior are futile.

Nonviolence is, therefore, not a passive concept to these religious traditions. *Ahimsa, agape*, the *Tao* involve the power of Truth to their adherents. Acting nonviolently is demonstrating the Truth; thus, no advocate of nonviolence can retreat in cowardice from any situation. Gandhi tells us:

> My non-violence does not admit of running away from danger and leaving dear ones unprotected. Between violence and cowardly flight, I can only prefer violence to cowardice. I can no more preach non-violence to a coward than I can tempt a blind man to enjoy healthy scenes. Non-violence is the summit of bravery. And in my own experience, I have had no difficulty in demonstrating to men trained in the school of violence the superiority of non-violence. As a coward, which I was for years, I harboured violence. I began to prize non-violence only when I began to shed cowardice.[9]

The power of nonviolence as Truth, to all its advocates, is too dynamic to be used as a tactic, a technique for manipulating people and situations; nor does it turn anyone into a human punching bag or into a tactical technician. A person of nonviolence is rather "*a witness* testifying to the power of love by deeds of truth and thereby fostering his just cause, inviting the opponent both singly and en masse to join him in it."[10] The words and actions of Gandhi and Martin Luther King illustrate the power, not the passivity, of a commitment to nonviolence.

One will also discover that the religious concept of nonviolence as the power of Truth involves a belief that nonviolence is not an abstract principle that can be applied in an identical manner to every problem. The advocate of *ahimsa, agape*, or *satyagraha* cannot put this truth into a formula, which if taken by the following directions, brings instant success. One rather makes a total commitment to a belief that confronts the problems and asks the questions. Socrates, who practiced nonviolence in his attitude toward the Greek state, reminded his friends that the unexamined life is not worth living. Nonviolence is precisely this appeal to examine the meaning of life in the ultimate sense, which, in turn, demands a dynamic response to every new situation.

The complexity of life itself makes a life "dedicated" to nonviolence a difficult one. As Gandhi indicated in his discussions about *ahimsa*, it is impossible for us to be nonviolent as long as we are engaged in the basic activities of life—breathing, eating, drinking. To be alive is to be violent. However, if we are sensitive to the paradoxes of life, then we are able to realize the reasons behind our decisions regarding both the violence and nonviolence in life. For example, we are aware that violence ranges from brutal physical and mental destructiveness, to more "civilized" uses of force.[11] We all use such "civilized" force when we employ persuasion, pressure, and coercion for our purposes. Even persons committed to nonviolence as a religious way of life use persuasion to emphasize to others firmness to its principles. They attempt by their example (and many times these are very persuasive examples) to influence another person's point of view. A familiar model is the "friendly persuasion" used by the Quakers in their historical efforts to find peaceful solutions to violent problems. Their unique response to the violence of the Vietnam War was to sail into Hanoi's harbor with a shipment of medical supplies. The use of pressure, on the other hand, is a moderate position between persuasion and coercion, since coercion involves the extreme to which force can be applied to any situation and to any person! Coercion could range from a social threat (strike), to a physical use of force by the law (police). The subtlety among these uses of force is very obvious when we attempt to make clear distinctions among the tactics used by their proponents. When do the tactics of persuasion become the tactics of pressure or the tactics of pressure become those of coercion? These difficulties become even more apparent when the tactics of modified force are seen by others in the activities of the advocates for nonviolence!

As there are alternatives regarding the way we modify our violence, so there are alternatives in the way we understand and modify nonviolence. First approach is to view nonviolence as nonresistance. This approach is directly related to the traditions of the world religions and is the one that we have been describing at considerable length in this Introduction in order to demonstrate some of its ancient sources and religious-philosophical beliefs. Nonresistance is a matter of faith and discipline, and, for this reason, its adherents identify the truth of nonviolence with eternal principles—*Tao* for the Taoist, *ahimsa* for the Hindu, *agape* for the Christian. Persons committed to nonresistance for a religious reason never measure Truth by any consequences resulting from their actions for Truth—whether they succeed or fail. Instead, nonviolence is to them a way of life that willingly involves suffering for others and for their belief, and they willingly sacrifice life itself for that belief:

> "I saw that nations like individuals could only be made through the agony of the Cross and in no other way. Joy comes not out of infliction of pain on others but out of pain voluntarily borne by oneself."[12]

Passive resistance is the second interpretation of nonviolence. Historically, passive resistance has been used by oppressed people who desire immediate justice and immediate human rights. They are concerned with social and legal change rather than with truth as an eternal principle. Passive resisters take an ethical position that demands results—pragmatic results that correct a social or political injustice. They are concerned with the success or failure of their actions! The method that they use to obtain change is noncooperation such as the use of the walkout or the boycott. If nonresistance means "going the second mile," passive resistance means refusing to go the first mile.[13]

A third way of viewing nonviolence is defined by the terms "nonviolent direct action." Obviously, the words "direct action" indicate the basic distinction between passive resistance and non-resistance. The proponents of this approach take the initiative and move into the problem area rather than withdrawing from it. Ideally, they challenge their opponents in order to make them change their minds *or* to make them take an active stand against the direct nonviolent action and resist it. Such resistance, the challengers sometimes hope, will cause the opponents to respond emotionally and thereby make them feel the physical reality of the resister. Hate is closer to love than indifference. This type of action is called civil disobedience, and, as such, it entails all the difficulties associated with legal and moral issues. The dramatic confrontation of civil rights marches and war protest marches—with or without marching permits—illustrates this type of nonviolent direct action.

Again, the distinctions among these various views regarding nonviolence and the tactics employed (as with those regarding force) are often difficult to make. Martin Luther King was committed to *agape* as a religious way of life, and yet this commitment led him to an ethical position that demanded social change and involved him in acts of civil disobedience. The following articles in this book will involve such questions as: Is nonviolence possible only when it is motivated by spiritual discipline? Can it be an action based on ethical commitment without faith in nonviolence as truth—as the eternal principle of *ahimsa* or *agape?* What techniques would various advocates of nonviolence consider legitimate? How do these techniques relate to a person's commitments to nonviolence? In answering these questions, one will become involved in asking oneself the more personal questions: Should I choose to act nonviolently? What are the appropriate motives for my nonviolent action if and when I do become involved in this choice? What issues will I confront in making the choice of nonviolence under various conditions?

In the Socratic spirit we would remind ourselves that the unexamined life is not worth living, and certainly that unexamined violence is not worth doing, while—and this is the issue—unexamined nonviolence is not worth having.

NOTES

1. *World Bible*, edited by Robert O. Ballou (New York: Viking Press, 1944), p. 36.

2. *World Bible*, p. 135.

3. *World Bible*, pp. 551–552.

4. *World Bible*, p. 508.

5. *World Bible*, p. 336.

6. W. R. Miller, *Nonviolence, A Christian Interpretation* (New York: Schocken Books, 1966), p. 26 and following. Excellent source for a more detailed study of the Christian concept of nonviolence.

7. Martin Luther King Jr., *The Trumpet of Conscience* (New York: Harper and Row, 1968), pp. 74–75.

8. Gandhi, *All Men Are Brothers* (New York: Columbia University Press, 1958), p. 87.

9. Gandhi, *All Men Are Brothers*, p. 102.

10. Miller, *Nonviolence*, p. 45

11. Miller, *Nonviolence*, p. 45. For a thorough study of the variations regarding the use of force see pages 37-61.

12. Gandhi, *All Men Are Brothers*, p. 86.

13. Miller, *Nonviolence*, p. 54.

Part I

Historical Sources
of Nonviolence

1

Bhagavad Gita

*Translated by Swami Prabhavananda and
Christopher Isherwood*

The *Bhagavad-Gita* (literally meaning the Song of God) is found in the middle
section of one of Indian's great epics, *Mahabharata*. Most scholars of the *Gita*
believe that it was written between the fifth and second centuries B.C., and they
agree that it was not originally a part of the *Mahabharata* itself. However, as a
separate piece of Hindu literature, the *Gita* has made a greater impact on Western
thought than either of the two classic epics, the *Mahabharata* or the *Ramayana*.
In the *Bhagavad-Gita* the relationship between human beings and their reasons
for action are considered. Although the primary emphasis here is on right action
for the sake of the probability of escape from the "wheel of life and rebirth," on
achieving enlightenment, there is also mention of the wise person's serving as a
model for those less wise. The selection from the *Gita* that follows is a dialogue
between the two central speakers, Krishna and Arjuna. Sri Krishna (Sri meaning
Lord, a title of reverence) is the divine incarnation of Vishnu, one of the important Gods of the Hindu religion. But more essential to the message of the *Gita*,
Krishna is *Brahman*, the ultimate Reality. *Brahman* is the source of ultimate Oneness to which everything returns. Arjuna, the other principal character, is mortal.
He is a famous warrior confronted with the task of performing his caste duty
even if it means killing his relatives in a civil war. The conversation in the *Gita*
between Krishna and Arjuna presents to the reader various possibilities for interpretation, which range from a literal reading—Arjuna and his problems regarding
his caste duty—to a spiritual, reading—everyone's search for a way for achieving
oneness with *Brahman*.

I have explained to you the true nature of the Atman. Now listen to the
method of Karma Yoga.[1] If you can understand and follow it, you will be able to
break the chains of desire which bind you to your actions.

In this yoga, even the abortive attempt is not wasted. Nor can it produce a
contrary result. Even a little practice of this yoga will save you from the terrible
wheel of rebirth and death.

In this yoga, the will is directed singly toward one ideal. When a man lacks this discrimination, his will wanders in all directions, after innumerable aims. Those who lack discrimination may quote the letter of the scripture, but they are really denying its inner truth. They are full of worldly desires, and hungry for the rewards of heaven. They use beautiful figures of speech. They teach elaborate rituals which are supposed to obtain pleasure and power for those who perform them. But, actually, they understand nothing except the law of Karma, that chains men to rebirth.

Those whose discrimination is stolen away by such talk grow deeply attached to pleasure and power. And so they are unable to develop that concentration of the will which leads a man to absorption in God.

The Vedas[2] teach us about the three gunas[3] and their functions. You, Arjuna, must overcome the three gunas. You must be free from the pairs of opposites.[4] Poise your mind in tranquility. Take care neither to acquire nor to hoard. Be established in the consciousness of the Atman, always.

When the whole country is flooded, the reservoir becomes superfluous. So, to the illumined seer, the Vedas are all superfluous.

You have the right to work, but for the work's sake only. You have no right to the fruits of work. Desire for the fruits of work must never be your motive in working. Never give way to laziness, either.

Perform every action with your heart fixed on the Supreme Lord. Renounce attachment to the fruits. Be even-tempered in success and failure; for it is this evenness of temper which is meant by yoga.

Work done with anxiety about results is far inferior to work done without such anxiety, in the calm of self-surrender. Seek refuge in the Knowledge of Brahman.[5] They who work selfishly for results are miserable.

In the calm of self-surrender you can free yourself from the bondage of virtue and vice during this very life. Devote yourself, therefore, to reaching union with Brahman. To unite the heart with Brahman and then to act: that is the secret of non-attached work. In the calm of self-surrender, the seers renounce the fruits of their actions, and so reach enlightenment. Then they are free from the bondage of rebirth, and pass to that state which is beyond all evil.

When your intellect has cleared itself of its delusions, you will become indifferent to the results of all action, present or future. At present, your intellect is bewildered by conflicting interpretation of the scriptures. When it can rest, steady and undistracted, in contemplation of the Atman, then you will reach union with the Atman.

Arjuna:

Krishna, how can one identify a man who is firmly established and absorbed in Brahman? In what manner does an illumined soul speak? How does he sit? How does he walk?

Sri Krishna:

> He knows bliss in the Atman
> And wants nothing else.
> Cravings torment the heart;
> He renounces cravings.
> I call him illumined.
>
> Not shaken by adversity,
> Not hankering after happiness:
> Free from fear, free from anger,
> Free from the things of desire.
> I call him a seer, and illumined.
> The bonds of his flesh are broken.
> He is lucky, and does not rejoice:
> He is unlucky, and does not weep.
> I call him illumined.
>
> The tortoise can draw in his legs:
> The seer can draw in his senses.
> I call him illumined.
>
> The abstinent run away from what they desire
> But carry their desires with them:
> When a man enters Reality,
> He leaves his desires behind him.
>
> Even a mind that knows the path
> Can be dragged from the path:
> The senses are so unruly.
> But he controls the senses
> And recollects the mind
> And fixes it on me.
> I call him illumined.
>
> Thinking about sense-objects
> Will attach you to sense-objects:
> Grow attached, and you become addicted;
> Thwart your addiction, it turns to anger;
> Be angry, and you confuse your mind;
> Confuse your mind; you forget the lesson of experience;
> Forget experience, you lose discrimination;
> Lose discrimination, and you miss life's only purpose.
> When he has no lust, no hatred,

A man walks safely among the things of lust and hatred.
To obey the Atman
Is his peaceful joy:
Sorrow melts
Into that clear peace:
His quiet mind
Is soon established in peace.

The uncontrolled mind
Does not guess that the Atman is present:
How can it meditate?
Without meditation; where is peace?
Without peace, where is happiness?

The wind turns a ship
From its course upon the waters:
The wandering winds of the senses
Cast man's mind adrift
And turn his better judgment from its course.
When a man can still the senses
I call him illumined.
The recollected mind is awake
In the knowledge of the Atman
Which is dark night to the ignorant:
The ignorant are awake in their sense-life

Which they think is daylight:
To the seer it is darkness.

Water flows continually into the ocean
But the ocean is never disturbed:
Desire flows into the mind of the seer
But he is never disturbed.
The seer knows peace:
The man who stirs up his own lusts
Can never know peace.
He knows peace who has forgotten desire.
He lives without craving:
Free from ego, free from pride.

This is the state of enlightenment in Brahman:
A man does not fall back from it
Into delusion.
Even at the moment of death

He is alive in that enlightenment:
Brahman and he are one.

Arjuna:

But, Krishna, if you consider knowledge of Brahman superior to any sort of action, why are you telling me to do these terrible deeds?

Your statements seem to contradict each other. They confuse my mind. Tell me one definite way of reaching the highest good.

Sri Krishna:

I have already told that, in this world, aspirants may find enlightenment by two different paths. For the contemplative is the path of knowledge: for the active is the path of selfless action.

Freedom from activity is never achieved by abstaining from action. Nobody can become perfect by merely ceasing to act. In fact, nobody can ever rest from his activity[6] even for a moment. All are helplessly forced to act, by the gunas.

A man who renounces certain physical actions but still lets his mind dwell on the objects of his sensual desire, is deceiving himself. He can only be called a hypocrite. The truly admirable man controls his senses by the power of his will. All his actions are disinterested. All are directed along the path of union with Brahman.

Activity is better than inertia. Act, but with self-control. If you are lazy, you cannot even sustain your own body.

The world is imprisoned in its own activity, except when actions are performed as worship of God. Therefore you must perform every action sacramentally, and be free from all attachments to results.

In the beginning
The Lord of beings
Created all men,
To each his duty.
"Do this," He said,
"And you shall prosper.
Duty well done
Fulfills desire
Like Kamadhenu[7]
The wish-fulfiller."
"Doing of duty
Honours the devas:[8]
To you the devas
In turn will be gracious:

Each honoring other,
Man reaches the Highest.
Please the divas:
Your prayer will be granted."
But he who enjoys the devas' bounty
Showing no thanks,
He thieves from the devas.
Pious men eat
What the gods leave over
After the offering:
Thus they are sinless.
But those ungodly
Cooking good food
For the greed of their stomachs
Sin as they eat it.
Food quickens the life-sperm:
Food grows from the rainfall
Called down out of heaven
By sacrifice offered;
Sacrifice speaks
Through the act of the ritual.
This is the ritual
Taught by the sacred
Scriptures that spring
From the lips of the Changeless:
Know therefore that Brahman
The all-pervading
Is dwelling for ever
Within this ritual.

If a man plays no part
In the acts thus appointed
His living is evil
His joy is in lusting.
Know this, O Prince:
His life is for nothing.

But when a man has found delight and satisfaction and peace in the Atman,
then he is no longer obliged to perform any kind of action. He has nothing to gain
in this world by action, and nothing to lose by refraining from action. He is independent of everybody and everything. Do your duty, always; but without attachment. That is how a man reaches the ultimate Truth; by working without anxiety
about results. In fact, Janaka[9] and many others reached enlightenment, simply

because they did their duty in this spirit. Your motive in working should be to set others, by your example, on the path of duty.

Whatever a great man does, ordinary people will imitate; they follow his example. Consider me: I am not bound by any sort of duty. There is nothing, in all the three worlds, which I do not already possess; nothing I have yet to acquire. But I go on working, nevertheless. If I did not continue to work untiringly as I do, mankind would still follow me, no matter where I led them. Suppose I were to stop? They would all be lost. The result would be caste-mixture and universal destruction.

> The ignorant work
> For the fruit of their action:
> The wise must work also
> Without desire
> Pointing man's feet
> To the path of his duty.

> Let the wise beware
> Lest they bewilder
> The minds of the ignorant
> Hungry for action:
> Let them show by example
> How work is holy
> When the heart of the worker
> Is fixed on the Highest.

Every action is really performed by the gunas. Man, deluded by his egoism, thinks: "I am the doer." But he who has the true insight into the operations of the gunas and their various functions, knows that when senses attach themselves to objects, gunas are merely attaching themselves to gunas. Knowing this, he does not become attached to his actions.

The illumined soul must not create confusion in the minds of the ignorant by refraining from work. The ignorant, in their delusion, identify the Atman with the gunas. They become tied to the senses and the action of the senses.

Shake off this fever of ignorance. Stop hoping for worldly rewards. Fix your mind on the Atman. Be free from the sense of ego. Dedicate all your actions to me. Then go forward and fight.

If a man keeps following my teaching with faith in his heart, and does not make mental reservations, he will be released from the bondage of his karma. But those who scorn my teaching, and do not follow it, are lost. They are without spiritual discrimination. All their knowledge is a delusion.

Even a wise man acts according to the tendencies of his own nature. All living creatures follow their tendencies. What use is any external restraint? The attraction and aversion which the senses feel for different objects are natural. But you must not give way to such feelings; they are obstacles.

It is better to do your own duty, however imperfectly, than to assume the duties of another person, however successfully. Prefer to die doing your own duty: the duty of another will bring you into great spiritual danger.

Arjuna:

Krishna, what is it that makes a man do evil, even against his own will; under compulsion, as it were?

Sri Krishna:

The rajo-guna has two faces,
Rage and lust: the ravenous, the deadly:
Recognize these: they are your enemies.

Smoke hides fire,
Dust hides a mirror,
The womb hides the embryo:
By lust the Atman is hidden.

Lust hides the Atman in its hungry flames,
The wise man's faithful foe.
Intellect senses and mind
Are fuel to its fire:
Thus it deludes
The dweller in the body,
Bewildering his judgment.

Therefore, Arjuna, you must first control your senses, then kill this evil thing which obstructs discriminative knowledge and realization of the Atman.

The senses are said to be higher than the sense-objects. The mind is higher than the senses. The intelligent will is higher than the mind. What is higher than the intelligent will? The Atman Itself.

You must know Him who is above the intelligent will. Get control of the mind through spiritual discrimination. Then destroy your elusive enemy, who wears the form of lust.

AFTERWORD

Henry Canby in his biography of Thoreau writes, "It is not too much to say that Thoreau was made by two books, Emerson's *Essay on Nature* and the *Bhagavad-Gita*."[10] It is not too much, either, to believe that Ralph Waldo Emerson influenced the thinking of Thoreau, but in what way did that ancient Hindu literature, the *Bhagavad-Gita*, with its background of violent civil war, affect the mind of the Concord poet? The answer is found in the way that Thoreau understood this literature. If this is the case, then it is necessary for us to be aware of some of these interpretations of the *Gita* and to see the relationship of these interpretations to the concept of *ahimsa* (nonviolence), which developed out of this literature.

The opening lines of the *Gita* present to us the spectacle of Arjuna, the great military leader, hesitating to kill his relatives in a civil war. Krishna, his charioteer, who is really the Hindu God Vishnu, tells him to stop trembling, to pick up his bow, and to do his duty as a warrior. Is this the message of the *Gita*—a lesson from God instructing us not to be cowards but to do our duty without fear? It is possible to answer yes after a superficial reading of the first two chapters. However, if one reads the *Gita* more carefully and completely, one finds that cowardice is not the essential issue concerning the warrior Arjuna or the God Krishna. Arjuna's reluctance to fight is a very serious matter because he has an obligation to perform this duty as a member of the warrior (Kshatriyas) caste in Hindu society. Being a member of this caste, Arjuna must fight to perform his caste duty in order to escape repeating that duty all over again in a next rebirth or, worse, to be reborn into a lower caste position. Is the meaning of the *Gita,* then, a divine command to do the caste duty so that the next rebirth brings to the faithful follower a more advanced spiritual stage in the long series of rebirths? Again, the answer may be yes. Orthodox Hindu thought interprets the *Gita* precisely in this way—a divine summons to caste obligation, and yet one may ask, Certainly Henry David Thoreau did not interpret the *Gita* in terms of caste duty and how that duty related to a series of rebirths? Indeed, he did not. Thoreau, along with Gandhi and other scholars from both East and West, found that this type of interpretation of the *Gita* omits its most important concern. The *Gita*, they believe, deals with the ultimate issue in our life, how we are to *be* and to *act* in harmony with our real self. Arjuna exemplifies not only a man who fails to do his caste duty but also a man who is attached to his duty with a sense of selfish ego-involvement. It is *my* duty, he believes, even though I choose not to do it. The Gita's main task is to remove from Arjuna's mind—and all minds—this sense of ego-attachment, this sense of *mine*! Krishna knows from his endless incarnations that it is precisely this attitude of possession that causes a man to be selfish, jealous, and violent. This is *my* right! This is *my* wife! This is *my* land! On the other hand, the way of Truth for man is the way of detachment (detached from all ego-desires and attached to the life of the spirit). A man committed to Truth is unselfish, open-minded, and nonviolent. He has moved from *himsa* to *ahimsa.*

This type of interpretation of the *Gita* appealed to both Gandhi and Thoreau. In *Walden*, Thoreau attempted to find his own unique lifestyle inspired by these principles described in the *Gita*. He sensed, in the power of "living deliberately" the influence of its spirit.[11]

I went to the woods because I wished to live deliberately, to front only the essential facts of life, and see if I could not learn what it had to teach, and not, when I came to die, discover that I had not lived. I did not wish to live what was not life, living is so dear; nor did I wish to practice resignation, unless it was quite necessary. I wanted to live deep and suck out all the marrow of life, to live so sturdily and Spartan-like as to put to rout all that was not life, to cut a broad swath and shave close, to drive life into a corner, and reduce it to its lowest terms, and, if it proved to be mean, why then to get the whole and genuine meanness of it, and publish its meanness to the world; or if it were sublime, to know it by experience, and be able to give a true account of it in my next excursion.[12]

Gandhi, in his own original response to the *Gita,* understood this literature as an allegory in which the battlefield is the soul, Arjuna is a person's higher impulses struggling against evil, and Krishna is the Dweller within, ever whispering in a pure heart:

I venture to submit that the Bhagavad Gita is a gospel of non-cooperation between the forces of darkness and those of light. . . . I do not believe that the *Gita* teaches violence for doing good. It is pre-eminently a description of the duel that goes on in our own hearts. The divine author has used a historical incident for inculcating the lesson of doing one's duty even at the peril of one's life. It inculcates performance of duty irrespective of the consequences, for, we mortals, limited by our physical frames, are incapable of controlling actions save our own. The *Gita* distinguishes between the powers of light and darkness and demonstrates their incompatibility.[13]

If the essential meaning of the *Gita* is to teach us to "live deliberately" and to do our duty without fear, then how are we to learn this lesson? The entire text of the *Gita* is concerned with this question, but, basically, we can understand its answer as a commitment to the belief that any sense of "mine" in regard to any aspect of life is an illusion! Perhaps by thinking about our physical bodies, we can begin to understand the meaning of this illusion. The body, which sees, smells, tastes, feels, hears, is not *real* but is only a garment that will be thrown away when it is worn out.

Worn-out garments
Are shed by the body:
Worn-out bodies
Are shed by the dweller
Within the body.
New bodies are donned
By the dweller, like garments.[14]

Your real self, which the *Gita* calls Atman (spirit), will continue to live and will eventually find another body for its physical expression. Thus, the first lesson to learn is that your body is not the *real* you but that you are spirit (*Atman*), deathless, indivisible, and one with God (*Brahman-Atman*).

Know this Atman,
Unborn, undying,
Never ceasing,
Never beginning,
Deathless, birthless,
Unchanging for ever.
How can It die
The death of the body?[15]

The importance of this lesson is to realize that the concerns of the body are secondary and that the concerns of the spirit (*Atman*) are primary. The *Gita* states that only a person who has this perspective on life can live without attachment to the body, a family, a home, a nation. However, it takes a lifetime of rigorous discipline for a believer to acquire this sense of detachment. In fact, many Hindus believe in the theory of reincarnation because they know that it takes many rebirths (many lives) in order for the spirit to fulfill this idea and not to allow itself to be seduced by the lower concerns of the body and its possessions.

The *Gita* points out that there are several ways to discipline your life away from the illusion of attachment. There are the way of action (*Karma Yoga*), the way of love (*Bhakti Yoga*), the way of knowledge (*Jnana Yoga*), and the way of psychological exercises (*Raja Yoga*). The first way, yoga of action (*Karma*), is the most relevant to our study of nonviolence since the person of action (such as Gandhi, Thoreau, Martin Luther King) has the greatest impact upon our understanding of what is involved in a commitment to nonviolence.

Gandhi, who called the *Gita* "Mother" because it nourished his spirit, took the way of Karma Yoga as his personal discipline. Temperamentally, he was a man of action rather than a man of wisdom (scholar) or a man of devotion (priest), although both wisdom and devotion were essential aspects of his life. The section of the *Gita* cited previously was his favorite section. He memorized it and used it as a constant reminder of the ideal that he should meet in his attempt to use the means (*ahimsa*) to attain the end (Truth). This section specifically described the one discipline that Gandhi and all its adherents need to develop—selflessness in action.

"You have the right to work, but for the work's sake only. You have no right to the fruits of work. Desire for the fruits of work must never be your motive in working."[16]

The ideal of Karma Yoga, therefore, is to take action for a just cause without thought of any personal advantage. This does not mean that persons of action are indifferent to the results of just action or that they refuse to act out of frustration (this was Arjuna's problem). The *Gita* commands us to act and to act in the way of Truth, *but* we cannot brood over the results. Gandhi described the reason for this demand: "He who is ever brooding over results often loses nerve in the performance of his duty. He becomes impatient and then gives vent to anger and begins to do unworthy things; he jumps from action to action, never remaining faithful to any. He who broods over results is like a man given to objects of senses; he is ever distracted, he says goodbye to all scruples, everything is right in his estimation and he therefore resorts to means fair and foul to attain his end."[17] To renounce attachment to the "fruits" of action is to discover, Gandhi believed, the ideal of desirelessness. To the Hindu devotee of Karma Yoga this type of renunciation gives to a person that inner peace and poise necessary to achieve real lasting results, even material results, untainted by ugly means.[18]

In this way the *Gita* becomes the inspiration for a life committed to nonviolence (*ahimsa*). If one is able through discipline to detach oneself from the results of one's action, an action that one believes is right, then one is able to perform this action again no matter how distorted the truth of this action or the motive behind this action becomes because of the misunderstanding of other people who are judging its validity by the consequences alone. It is very difficult to understand the motive behind someone's action. How difficult it is, then, for us to expect other people to understand completely our intentions and not to understand our actions by the way the results of those actions work out in public life. We become angry when our truth is misunderstood and abused by other people. However, the *Gita* points out that this attitude occurs when we are attached to the consequences of our "just" action with a selfish concern. Consequences are sensory reflections of truth, and as sense-objects, they present to different people a limited view of Truth.

> Thinking about sense-objects
> Will attach you to sense-objects;
> Grow attached, and you become addicted;
> Thwart your addiction, it turns to anger;
> Confuse your mind, you forget the lesson of experience;
> Forget experience, you lose discrimination;
> Lose discrimination, and you miss life's only purpose.[19]

If we have no selfish involvement in our actions, if we don't make a one-to-one relationship between the consequences of our action and Truth, if we believe that Truth still survives even when it appears to be destroyed in the outcome of our actions, then there will be no opportunity for us to feel angry or violent. From the perspective of the *Gita*, the power of Truth makes even the thought of anger and violence unthinkable. The only alternative possible for a person who holds this perspective is an inward and outward life committed to nonviolence (*ahimsa*) as the essential way to Truth.

> He knows bliss in the Atman
> And wants nothing else.
> Cravings torment the heart;
> He renounces cravings.

I call him illumined.
Not shaken by adversity,
Not hankering after happiness:
Free from fear, free from anger,
Free from the things of desire.
I call him a seer, and illumined.
The bonds of his flesh are broken.
He is lucky, and does not rejoice:
He is unlucky, and does not weep.
I call him illumined.[20]

NOTES

1. *Karma*: (1) work, deed; (2) effect of a deed; (3) law of causation governing action and its effects in the physical and psychological plane. *Yoga*: (1) union with God; (2) a prescribed path of spiritual life. The various yogas are, therefore, different paths to union with God. Karma Yoga is the path of selfless, God-dedicated action. *Yogi*: one who practices yoga.

2. Revealed scriptures of the Hindus. The reference here is to the ritualistic portion of the Vedas.

3. The three forces or substances composing the universe of mind and matter. They are *sattwa*, *rajas*, and *tamas*.

4. Heat and cold, pleasure and pain, etc. The seeming contradictions of the relative world.

5. The Godhead.

6. Here "activity" includes mental action, conscious and sub-conscious.

7. A legendary cow, mentioned in the *Mahabharata*.

8. The inhabitants of heaven.

9. A royal saint mentioned in the *Upanishads*.

10. Henry Canby, *Thoreau* (Boston: Beacon Press, 1939), p. 97.

11. Canby, *Thoreau*, pp. 202-203; see also Thoreau, *A Week on the Concord and Merrimack Rivers* (New York: Thomas Crowell), p. 166; Thoreau said, "The Reader is nowhere raised into and sustained in a higher, purer, or rarer region of thought than in the Bhagavat-Geeta."

12. Thoreau, *Walden* (New York: Holt, Rienhart, and Winston, 1961), p. 74.

13. Gandhi, *Gita the Mother* (Lahore, India: Free India Publications), pp. 172, 155, 160.

14. *The Song of God, Bhagavad-Gita*, hereafter *Gita*, translated by Swami Prabhavananda and Christopher Insherwood, New American Library, 1944, p. 37.

15. *Gita*, Ibid.

16. See above, p. 5.

17. Gandhi, *Gita the Mother*, p. 10.

18. Louis Fischer, *Gandhi; His Life and Messages for the World* New York: Mentor Books, 1954, pp. 14-20. This is an excellent biography of Gandhi's life and commitment to nonviolence.

19. *Gita*, p. 42.

20. *Gita*, pp. 41-42.

2

Crito

Plato

This selection, the Dialogue of Plato, usually called *Crito*, deals with the relationship between a person and the laws of the state and examines the possibilities of action by certain kinds of people in order to achieve certain ends. The *Crito* is one of the many dialogues written by Plato (427-347 B.C.) in honor of his famous teacher, Socrates (470 -399 B.C.). Along with the *Apology* and *Phaedo*, it forms a trilogy, which is Plato's biography of Socrates' final days—his trial, imprisonment, and death. The literary method used by Plato is the dialectic—the investigation of concepts by question and answer—a method used by Socrates himself in his daily conversation with the Athenians. Since Socrates and Plato were both philosophers, they were more concerned with ethical principles than scientific facts. Knowledge is virtue, not merely scientific conclusions, and the good (virtue) is the true. Plato, the student, enhances the ethical concerns of his teacher with his own ideas concerning the immortality of the soul and his brilliant theory of "forms" or ideas. Scholars will always be at work attempting to discover where the historical Socrates ends and the philosophical Plato begins in these celebrated dialogues. However, if genuine respect for a teacher is fundamental to his student's faithful recording of his ideas, then it is certain that the authentic spirit of Socrates comes through in Plato's *Crito*.

PERSONS OF DIALOGUE: SOCRATES/ CRITO

Scene: The Prison of Socrates

Socrates: Why have you come at this hour, Crito? It must quite early.

Crito: Yes, certainly.

Socrates: What is the exact time?

Crito: The dawn is breaking.

Socrates: I wonder the keeper of the prison would let you in.

Crito: He knows me because I often come, Socrates; moreover, I have done him a kindness.

Socrates: And have you only just come?

Crito: No, I came some time ago.

Socrates: Then why did you sit and say nothing, instead of awaking me at once?

Crito: Why, indeed, Socrates, I myself would rather not have all this sleeplessness and sorrow. But I have been wondering at your peaceful slumbers, and that was the reason why I did not awaken you, because I wanted you to be out of pain. I have always thought you happy in the calmness of your temperament; but never did I see the like of the easy, cheerful way in which you bear this calamity.

Socrates: Why, Crito, when a man has reached my age he ought not to be repining at the prospect of death.

Crito: And yet other old men find themselves in similar misfortunes, and age does not prevent them from repining.

Socrates: That may be. But you have not told me why you come at this early hour.

Crito: I come to bring you a message which is sad and painful; not, as I believe, to yourself, but to all of us who are your friends, and saddest of all to me.

Socrates: What! I suppose that the ship has come from Delos, on the arrival of which I am to die?

Crito: No the ship has not actually arrived, but she will probably be here today, as persons who have come from Sunium tell me that they have left her there; and therefore tomorrow, Socrates, will be the last day of your life.

Socrates: Very well, Crito; if such is the will of God, I am willing; but my belief is that there will be a delay of a day.

Crito: Why do you say this?

Socrates: I will tell you. I am to die on the day after the arrival of the ship?

Crito: Yes; that is what the authorities say.

Socrates: But I do not think that the ship will be here until tomorrow; this I gather from a vision, which I had last night, or rather only just now, when you fortunately allowed me to sleep.

Crito: And what was the nature of the vision?

Socrates: There came to me the likeness of a woman, fair and comely, clothes in white raiment, who called to me and said: O Socrates — "The third day hence, to Phthia shalt thou go?"

Crito: What a singular dream, Socrates!

Socrates: There can be no doubt about the meaning Crito, I think.

Crito: Yes: the meaning is only too clear. But, O! My beloved Socrates, let me entreat you once more to take my advice and escape. For if you die I shall not only lose a friend who can never be replaced, but there is another evil: people who do not know you and me will believe that I might have saved you if I had been willing to give money, but that I did not care. Now, can there be a worse disgrace than this—that I should be thought to value money more than the life of a friend? For the many will not be persuaded that I wanted you to escape, and that you refused.

Socrates: But why, my dear Crito, should we care about the opinion of the many? Good men, and they are the only persons who are worth considering, will think of these things truly as they happened.

Crito: But do you see, Socrates, that the opinion of the many must be regarded, as is evident in your own case, because they can do the very greatest evil to anyone who has lost their good opinion?

Socrates: I only wish, Crito, that they could: for then they could also do the greatest good, and that would be well. But the truth is, that they can do neither good nor evil: they cannot make a man wise or make him foolish; and whatever they do is the result of chance.

Crito: Well, I will not dispute about that; but please tell me, Socrates, whether you are not acting out of regard to me and your other friends: are you not afraid that if you escape hence we may get into trouble with the informers for having stolen you away, and lose either the whole or a great part of our property; or that even a worse evil may happen to us? Now, if this is your fear, be at ease; for in order to save you, we ought surely to run this or even a greater risk; be persuaded, then, and do as I say.

Socrates: Yes, Crito, that is one fear, which you mention, but by no means the only one.

Crito: Fear not. There are persons who at no great cost are willing to save you and bring you out of prison; and as for the informers, you may observe that they are far from being exorbitant in their demands; a little money will satisfy them. My means, which, as I am sure, are ample, are at your service, and if you have a scruple about spending all mine, here are strangers who will give you the use of theirs; and one of them, Simmias the Theban, has brought a sum of money for this very purpose; and Cebes and many others are willing to spend their money too. I say, therefore, do not on that account hesitate about making your escape, and do not say, as you did in the court, that you will have a difficulty in knowing what to do with yourself if you escape. For men will love you in other places to which you may go, and not in Athens only; there are friends of mine in Thessaly, if you like to go to them, who will value and protect you, and no Thessalian will give you trouble. Nor can I think that you are justified, Socrates, in betraying your own life when you might be saved; this is playing into the hands of your enemies and destroyers; and moreover I should say that you were betraying your children; for you might bring them up and educate them; instead of which you go away and leave them, and they will have to take their chance; and if they do not meet with the usual fate of orphans, there will be small thanks to you. No man should bring children into the world who is unwilling to persevere to the end in their nurture and education. But you are choosing the easier part, as I think, not the better and manlier, which would rather have become one who professes virtue in all his actions, like yourself. And, indeed, I am ashamed not only of you, but of us who are your friends, when I reflect that this entire business of yours will be attributed to our want of courage. The trial need never have come on, or might have been brought to another issue; and the end of all, which is the crowning absurdity, will seem to have been permitted by us, through cowardice and baseness, who might have saved you, as you might have saved yourself, if we had been good for anything (for there was no difficulty in escaping); and we did not see how disgraceful, Socrates, and also miserable all this will be to us as well as to you. Make your mind up then, or rather have your mind already made up, for the time of deliberation is over, and there is only one thing to be done, which must be done, if at all, this very night, and which any delay will render all but impossible; I beseech you therefore, Socrates, to be persuaded by me, and to do as I say.

Socrates: Dear Crito, your zeal is invaluable, if a right one; but if wrong, the greater the zeal the greater the evil; and therefore we ought to consider whether these things shall be done or not. For I am and always have been one of those natures who must be guided by reason, whatever the reason may be which upon reflections appears to me to be the best; and now that this fortune has come upon me, I cannot put away the reasons which I have before given: the principles which I have hitherto honored and revered I still honor, and unless we can find other and better principles on the instant, I am certain not to agree with you; no, not even if the power of the multitude could inflict many more imprisonments, confiscations, deaths, frightening us like children with hobgoblin terrors. But what will be the fairest way of considering the question? Shall I return to your old argument about the opinions of men, some of which are to be regarded, and others, as we were saying, are not to be regarded? Now were we right in maintaining this before I was condemned? And has the argument which was once good now proved to be talk for the sake of talking; in fact an amusement only, and altogether vanity? That is what I want to consider with your help, Crito: whether, under my present circumstances, the argument appears to be in any way different or not; and is to be allowed by me or disallowed. That argument, which, as I believe, is maintained by many who assume to be authorities, was to the effect, as I was saying, that the opinions of some men are to be regarded, and of other men not to be regarded. Now you, Crito, are a disinterested person who are not going to die to-morrow—at least, there is no human probability of this, and you are therefore not liable to be deceived by the circumstances in which you are placed. Tell me, then, whether I am right in saying that some opinions, and the opinions of some men only, are to be valued, and other opinions, and the opinions of other men, are not to be valued. I ask you whether I was right in maintaining this?

Crito: Certainly.

Socrates: The good are to be regarded, and not the bad?

Crito: Yes.

Socrates: And the opinions of the wise are good, and the opinions of the unwise are evil?

Crito: Certainly.

Socrates: And what was said about another matter? Was the disciple in gymnastics supposed to attend to the praise and blame and opinion of every man, or of one man only—his physicians or trainer, whoever that was?

Crito: Of one man only.

Socrates: And he ought to fear the censure and welcome the praise of that one only and not of the many?

Crito: That is clear.

Socrates: And he ought to live and train, and eat and drink in the way, which seems good to his single master who has understanding, rather than according to the opinion of all other men put together?

Crito: True.

Socrates: And if he disobeys and disregards the opinion and approval of the one, and regards the opinion of the many who have no understanding, will he not suffer evil?

Crito: Certainly he will.

Socrates: And what will the evil be, whither tending and what affecting, in the disobedient person?

Crito: Clearly, affecting the body; that is what is destroyed by the evil.

Socrates: Very good, and is not this true, Crito, of other things which we need not separately enumerate? In the matter of just and unjust, fair and foul, good and evil, which are the subjects of our present consultation, ought we to follow the opinion of the many and to fear them; or the opinion of the one man who has understanding, and whom we ought to fear and reverence more than all the rest of the world: and whom deserting we shall destroy and injure that principle in us which may be assumed to be improved by justice and deteriorated by injustice; is there not such a principle?

Crito: Certainly there is, Socrates.

Socrates: Take a parallel instance; if, acting under the advice of men who have no understanding, we destroy that which is improvable by health and deteriorated by disease—when that has been destroyed, I say, would life be worth having? And that is—the body?

Crito: Yes.

Socrates: Could we live having an evil and corrupted body?

Crito: Certainly not.

Socrates: And will life be worth having, if that higher part of man be depraved, which is improved by justice and deteriorated by injustice? Do we suppose that principle, whatever it may be in man, which has to do with justice and injustice, to be inferior to the body?

Crito: Certainly not.

Socrates: More honored, then?

Crito: Far more honored.

Socrates: Then, my friend, we must not regard what the many say of us: but what he, the one man who has understanding of just and unjust, will say, and what the truth will say. And therefore you begin in error when you suggest that we should regard the opinion of the many about just and unjust, good and evil, honorable and dishonorable. Well, someone will say, " But the many can kill us."

Crito: Yes, Socrates; that will clearly be the answer.

Socrates: That is true; but still I find with surprise that the old argument is, as I conceive, unshaken as ever. And I should like to know whether I may say the same of another proposition— that not life, but a good life, is to be chiefly valued?

Crito: Yes, that also remains.

Socrates: And a good life is equivalent to a just and honorable one— that holds also?

Crito: Yes, that holds.

Socrates: From these premises I proceed to argue the question whether I ought or ought not to try to escape without the consent of the Athenians: and If I am clearly right in escaping, then I will make the attempt; but if not, I will abstain. The other considerations which you mention, of money and loss of character, and the duty of educating children, are, I fear, only the doctrines of the multitude, who would be as ready to call people to life, if they were able, as they are to put them to death—and with as little reason. But now, since the argument has thus far prevailed, the only question which remains to be considered is, whether we shall do rightly either in escaping or in suffering others to aid in our escape and paying them in money and thanks, or whether we shall not do rightly; and if the latter, then death or any other calamity which may ensue on my remaining here must not be allowed to enter into the calculation.

Crito: I think that you are right, Socrates; how then shall we proceed?

Socrates: Let us consider the matter together, and do you either refute me if you can, and I will be convinced; or else cease, my dear friend, from repeating to me that I ought to escape against the wishes of the Athenians: for I am extremely desirous to be persuaded by you, but not against my own better judgment. And now please to consider my first position, and do your best to answer me.

Crito: I will do my best.

Socrates: Are we to say that we are never intentionally to do wrong, or that in one way we ought and in another way we ought not to do wrong, or is doing wrong always evil and dishonorable, as I was just now saying, and as has been already acknowledged by us? Are all our former admissions which were made within a few days to be thrown away? And have we, at our age, been earnestly discoursing with one another all our life long only to discover that we are no better than children? Or are we to rest assured, in spite of the opinion of the many, and in spite of consequences whether better or worse, of the truth of what was then said, that injustice is always an evil and dishonor to him who act unjustly? Shall we affirm that?

Crito: Yes.

Socrates: Then we must do no wrong?

Crito: Certainly not.

Socrates: Nor when injured injure in return, as the many imagine; for we must injure no one at all?

Crito: Clearly not.

Socrates: Again, Crito, may we do evil?

Crito: Surely not, Socrates.

Socrates: And what of doing evil in return for evil, which is the morality of the many—is that just or not?

Crito: Not just.

Socrates: For doing evil to another is the same as injuring him?

Crito: Very true.

Socrates: Then we ought not to retaliate or render evil for evil to anyone, whatever evil we may have suffered from him. But I would have you consider, Crito, whether you really mean what you are saying. For this opinion has never been held, and never will be held, by any considerable number of persons; and those who are agreed and those who are not agreed upon this point have no common ground, and can only despise one another, when they see how widely they differ. Tell me, then, whether you agree with and assent to my first principle, that neither injury nor retaliation nor warding off evil by evil is ever right.

And shall that be the premise of our agreement? Or do you decline and dissent from this? For this has been of old and is still my opinion; but, if you are of another opinion, let me hear what you have to say. If, however, you remain of the same mind as formerly, I will proceed to the next step.

Crito: You may proceed, for I have not changed my mind.

Socrates: Then I will proceed to the next step, which may be put in the form of a question: Ought a man to do what he admits to be right, or ought he to betray the right?

Crito: He ought to do what he thinks is right.

Socrates: But if this is true, what is the application? In leaving the prison against the will of the Athenians, do I wrong any? Or rather do I not wrong those whom I ought least to wrong? Do I not desert the principles, which were acknowledged by us to be just? What do you say?

Crito: I cannot tell, Socrates, for I do not know.

Socrates: Then consider the matter in this way: Imagine that I am about to play truant (you may call the proceeding by any name which you like), and the laws and the government come and interrogate me: "Tell us, Socrates," they say; "what are you about? Are you going by an act of yours to overturn us—the laws and the whole State, as far as in your lies? Do you imagine that a State can subsist and not be over-thrown, in which the decisions of law have no power, but are set aside and overthrown by individuals?" What will be our answer, Crito, to these and the like words? Anyone, and especially a clever rhetorician, will have a good deal to urge about the evil of setting aside the law which requires a sentence to be carried out; and we might reply, "Yes; but the State has injured us and given an unjust sentence." Suppose I say that?

Crito: Very good Socrates.

Socrates: "And was that our agreement with you?" the law would say; "or were you to abide by the sentence of the State?" And if I were to express astonishment at their saying this, the law would probably add: "Answer, Socrates, instead of opening your eyes: you are in the habit of asking and answering questions. Tell us what complaint you have to make against us which justifies you in attempting to destroy us and the State? In the first place did we not bring you into existence? Your father married your mother by our aid and begat you. Say whether you have any objection to urge against those of us who regulate marriage?" None, I should reply, "Or against those of us who regulate the system of nurture and education of children in which you were trained? Were not the laws, who have the charge of this, right in commanding your father to train you in music and gymnastic?" Right, I should reply. "Well, then, since you were brought into the world and nurtured and educated by us, can you deny in the first place that you are our child and slave, as your fathers were before you? And if this is true you are not on equal terms with us; nor can you think that you have a right to do to us what we are doing to you. Would you have any right to strike or revile or do any other evil to a father or to your master, if you had one, when you have been struck or reviled by him, or received some other evil at his hands?—you would not say this? And because we think right to destroy you, do you think that you have any right to destroy us in return, and your country as far as in you lies? And will you, O professor of true virtue, say that you are justified in this? Has a philosopher like you failed to discover that our country is more to be valued and higher and holier far than mother or father or any ancestor, and more to be regarded in the eyes of the gods and of men of understanding? Also to be soothed, and gently and reverently entreated when angry, even more than a father, and if not persuaded, obeyed? And when we are punished by her, whether with imprisonment or stripes, the punishment is to be endured in silence; and if she leads us to wounds or death in battle, thither we follow as is right; neither may anyone yield or retreat or leave his rank, but whether in battle or in a court of law, or in any other place, he must do what his city and his country order him; or he must change their view of what is just: and if he may do no violence to his father or mother, much less may he do violence to his country." What answer shall we make to this, Crito? Do the laws speak truly, or do they not?

Crito: I think that they do.

Socrates: Then the laws will say: "Consider, Socrates, if this is true, that in your present attempt you are going to do us wrong. For, after having brought you into the world, and nurtured and educated you, and given you and every other citizen a share in every good that we had to give, we further proclaim and give the right to every Athenian, that if he does not like us when he has come of age and has seen the ways of the city, and made our acquaintance, he may go where he pleases and take his goods with him; and none of us laws will forbid him or interfere with him. Any of you who does not like us and the city, and who wants to go to a colony or to any other city, may go where he likes, and take his goods with him. But he who has experience of the manner in which we order justice and administer the State, and still remains, has entered into an implied contract that he will do as we command him. And he who disobeys us is, as we maintain, thrice wrong: first, because in disobeying us he is disobeying his parents; secondly, because we are the authors of his education; thirdly, because he has made an agreement with us that he will duly obey our commands; and he neither obeys them nor convinces us that our commands are wrong; and we do not rudely impose them, but give him the alternative of obeying or convincing us; that is what we offer, and he does neither. These are the sort of accusations to which, as we were saying, you, Socrates, will be exposed if you accomplish your intentions; you, above all other Athenians." Suppose, I ask, why is this? they will justly retort upon me that I above all other men have acknowledged the agreement. "There is clear proof," they will say, "Socrates, that we and the city were not displeasing to you. Of all Athenians you have been the most constant resident in the city, which as you never leave, you may be supposed to love. For you never went out of the city either to see the games, except once when you went to Isthmus, or to any other place unless when you were on military service; nor did you travel as other men do. Nor had you any curiosity to know other States or their laws: your affections did not go beyond us and our State; we were your especial favorites, and you acquiesced in our government of you; and this is the State in which you begat your children, which is a proof of your satisfaction. Moreover, you might, if you had liked, have fixed the penalty at banishment in the course of the trial—the State which refuses to let you go now would have let you go then. But you pretended that you preferred death to exile, and that you were not grieved at death. And now you have forgotten these fine sentiments, and pay no respect to us, the laws, of whom you are the destroyer; and are doing what only a miserable slave would do, running away and turning your back upon the compacts and agreements which you made as a citizen. And first of all answer this very question: Are we right in saying that you agreed to be governed according to us in deed, and not in word only? Is that true or not?" How shall we answer that, Crito? Must we not agree?

Crito: There is no help, Socrates.

Socrates: Then will they not say: "You, Socrates, are breaking the covenants and agreements which you made with us at your leisure, not in any haste or under any compulsion or deception, but having had seventy years to think of them, during which time you were at liberty to leave the city, if we were not to your mind, or if our covenants appeared to you to be unfair. You had your choice, and might have gone either to Lacedaemon or Crete, which you often praise for their good government, or to some other Hellenic or foreign State. Whereas you, above all other Athenians, seemed to be so fond of the State, or, in other words, of us her laws (for who would like a State that has no laws?), that you never stirred out of her: the halt, the blind, the maimed, were not more stationary in her than you were. And now you run away and forsake your agreements. Not so, Socrates, if you will take our advice; do not make yourself ridiculous by escaping out of the city.

"For just consider, if you transgress and err in this sort of way, what good will you do, either to yourself or to your friends? That your friends will be driven into exile and deprived of citizenship, or will lose their property, is tolerably certain; and you yourself, if you fly to one of the neighboring cities, as, for example, Thebes or Megara, both of which are well-governed cities, will come to them as an enemy, Socrates, and their government will be against you, and all patriotic citizens will cast an evil eye upon you as a subverter of the laws, and you will confirm in the minds of the judges the justice of their own condemnation of you. For he who is a corrupter of the laws is more than likely to be corrupter of the young and foolish portion of mankind. Will you then flee from well-ordered cities and virtuous men? And is existence worth having on these terms? Or will you go to them without shame, and talk to them, Socrates? And what will you say to them? What you say here about virtue and justice and institutions and laws being the best things among men? Would that be decent of you? Surely not. But if you go away from well-governed States to Crito's friends in Thessaly, where there is great disorder and license, they will be charmed to have the tale of your escape from prison, set off with ludicrous particulars of the manner in which you were wrapped in a goatskin or some other disguise, and metamorphosed as the fashion of runaways is—that is very likely; but will there be no one to remind you that in your old age you violated the most sacred laws from a miserable desire of a little more life? Perhaps not, if you keep them in a good temper; but if they are out of temper you will hear many degrading things; you will live, but how? —as the flatterer of all men, and the servant of all men; and doing what? —eating and drinking in Thessaly, having gone abroad in order that you may get a dinner. And where will be your fine sentiments about justice and virtue then? Say that you wish to live for the sake of your children that you may bring them up and educate them—will you take them into Thessaly and deprive them of Athenian citizenship? Is that the benefit, which you would confer upon them? Or are you under the impression that they will be better cared for and educated here if you are still alive, although absent from them; for that your friends will take care of them? Do you fancy that if you are an inhabitant of Thessaly they will take care of them, and if you are an inhabitant of the other world they will not take care of them? Nay; but if they who call themselves friends are truly friends, they surely will.

"Listen, then, Socrates, to us who have brought you up. Think not of life and children first and of justice afterwards, but of justice first, that you may be justified before the princes of the world below. For neither will you nor any that belong to you be happier or holier or juster in this life, or happier in another, if you do as Crito bids. Now you depart in innocence, a sufferer and not a doer of evil; a victim, not of the laws, but of men. But if you go forth, returning evil for evil, and injury for injury, breaking the covenants and agreements which you have made with us, and wronging those whom you ought least to wrong, that is to say, yourself, your friends, your country, and us, we shall be angry with you while you live, and our brethren, the laws in the world below, will receive you as an enemy; for they will know that you have done your best to destroy us. Listen, then, to us and not to Crito."

This is the voice, which I seem to hear murmuring in my ears, like the sound of the flute in the ears of the mystic; that voice, I say, is humming in my ears, and prevents me from hearing any other. And I know that anything more which you will say will be in vain. Yet speak, if you have anything to say.

Crito: I have nothing to say, Socrates.

Socrates: Then let me follow the intimations of the will of God.

AFTERWORD

A just person cannot act violently against the laws of the state: this is the belief that Socrates expresses in the *Crito* with his life as well as with his words. In this final conversation with Crito, Socrates insists that there is a relationship between the idea of justice as an eternal principle and his nonviolent acceptance of the justice of the state, which sentenced him to death. There is no doubt in Socrates' mind or in the mind of his friend Crito about the injustice of this sentence. Political expedience, not the impiety or corruption of youth, really condemns Socrates to drink the hemlock. Yet Socrates does not spend his last hours in self-pity. He spends these moments trying to convince Crito that the belief in the idea of justice as an eternal principle has a dynamic effect on all attitudes and actions. We can believe that Socrates experienced this dynamic relationship between belief and action, but for our study of the ethics of action, especially the dynamics of nonviolent action, we need to ask some questions about this relationship. What did Socrates mean by a belief in justice as an eternal principle? How did he develop his intense commitment to the concept of justice as an eternal principle?

We know, first of all, from historical accounts that the influential Athenians of Socrates' time were not at all interested in a belief in justice as an abstract ideal. They preferred the more attractive and practical positions of either the scientists or the Sophists. Both positions agreed (they agreed on nothing else!) that a discussion of abstract notions such as justice, virtue, wisdom, and goodness was a complete waste of time. The scientists indicated that they were too busy dealing with important issues to bother with such meaningless terms. The immediate need for humanity is for the scientists to resolve the problem of final authority for scientific truth. Was it to be physics with its notion that matter is real or logic with its view that structure is real? Socrates, although greatly influenced by science, especially scientific formalism, felt that this concern was secondary to the question, Is justice real?

The Sophists, who favored human problems rather than scientific theories, considered the idea of justice in terms of expediency—how to manipulate "justice" for gaining personal success and prestige. All abstract ideas (justice, truth, virtue, and goodness) were to the Sophists merely tools that we should learn how to utilize in order to attain materialistic and political goals. It pays to be practical, and one could pay the Sophists to teach one how to survive in the cutthroat competition of everyday life, and everyday life had its practical demands for the Athenians.

> One authority has estimated that the average Athenian businessman could expect to appear in court for one breach of contract suit a year; and, under the local laws, he had to present his own case. A small group of petty operators made a living from threatening lawsuits with nuisance value against important citizens, and settling out of courts. Charges of treason or impiety were brought on occasion as political maneuvers. (An illustration of this is Socrates' trial.) Not only success, but sometimes effective survival, made skill in law something to be desired.[1]

The Sophists were delighted to be on hand with the necessary skills in rhetoric and logic to teach the wealthy how to survive and to succeed very effectively.

Socrates disagreed vehemently with these Sophistic views. He not only condemned the amoralism and cheap instrumentalism, which degraded justice by using it as a means and not as an end, but also denounced its moral relativism. All ethical principles, such as justice, virtue, truth, and goodness, a moral relativist believes to be relative to the situation involved—the morals of Athens have nothing to do with the morals of Sparta. The Athenian has different sensory, intellectual, cultural experiences which do not relate in any absolute or universal way with the experiences of the man from Sparta. "Man is the measure of all things, of things that are that they are, and of things that are not that they are not." In protest against the moral relativism, Socrates would reverse its maxim. The "things" of justice, virtue, goodness, and truth measure us, and, more often than not, these principles find us failing to measure up to the minimal standards of judgment. Our life is relative, Socrates believed, only in the sense that it is transient and not in the sense that we cannot know principles to direct our life that are absolute and universal.

What motivated Socrates to take this unique position, which placed scientific interests secondary to moral concerns and which condemned the popular view of moral relativism held by the prominent citizens of his day? Tradition answers this question by suggesting that Socrates was fascinated all his life by two thoughts that originated from the oracle at Delphi: by the motto "Know Thyself" inscribed on the temple at Delphi and the statement made by the oracle to one of his friends that Socrates was the wisest of all men.

The motto "Know Thyself" revealed to Socrates that the search for self-knowledge was more essential than the search for scientific truth. The search for scientific knowledge is restricted by the very vastness of the universe and the finitude of our minds, but the search for self-knowledge is not limited because we have the "built-in" equipment, our mind, to accomplish the task. To Socrates, the mind is not an agent of mental activities that passively reacts to sensory stimuli; he defined it as the *psyche* (soul), which directs and causes the behavior of the body. Our soul's unique function is seen in the normative judgments that we make, that is, when we recognize and examine the discrepancy between what we are and what we ought to be, what we do and what we ought to do. This activity of the soul, making normative judgments, makes us *human*. We do not depend, Socrates discovered, in this human search for self-knowledge on the changing and relative facts in the world outside our soul, but we rely on ideas, which occur within. These ideas are those absolute principles of justice, virtue, goodness, and truth that set the standard for normative judgments.

From the second statement, that he was the wisest of all men, Socrates discovered that the source of authentic wisdom is found in the realization that comes when we know that we do *not* know. Taking this insight as a divine directive, Socrates began a lifetime of engaging in conversation with everyone whom he met in order to reveal to that poor soul the ignorance that supported his "wisdom." Naturally, this was not an entertaining experience. It is similar to a back-against-the-wall-encounter with an instructor who questions a student about a problem in this rapid-fire manner: What is your answer? How do you define these terms you use? How could you clarify this answer? Do you notice your contradictions? Now can you ask a new and penetrating question about the problem? Clearly, this use of the dialectical method by Socrates in conversations with his contemporaries was not at all popular. Still, his "inner voice" commanded him to seek out all ignorance in himself and in others by applying these probing instruments of inductive surgery to any intellectual illness. The discovery of ignorance by this operation (dialectical method) is only one factor in the search for truth. The most important insight for Socrates was the realization that every person has the ability to examine intellectually any opinion; therefore (and this is Socrates' claim), there is an intelligible order operating behind the visible world that makes possible all intellectual activity. When our soul is aware of this intelligible order, and it responds to the "ideas" (Plato called these ideas "forms"), then we have begun the search to "Know Thyself."

Believing in this intelligible order and everyone's ability to be aware of this order and to relate to it, Socrates held his ground against his enemies at the trial and against his friends when they came to prison with the offer of escape. He told both enemies and friends that the soul is more important than the body because it is able to *know* truths that are unchanging and to *feel* the attraction of these truths. Wisdom, courage, goodness, justice, truth are intrinsic values, and as eternal principles they give to human life both dignity and meaning. How could he exchange dignity and meaning for anything as fleeting as political gain, prestige, or even personal safety? For this reason Socrates saw the issue of his escape as a matter of principle, not as a matter of practicality. All of the arguments of his friend Crito for escape are sensible—yet isn't this the appeal of the Sophists? "Now be practical! Protect your immediate interests! Gain for yourself security, pleasure, power, prestige, wealth!" To Socrates these appeals to the concerns of the body are meaningless. A life that is not directed by the interests of the soul is a life of ignorance, a life without any valid direction. It is a life of chaos filled with the *emotions* of anger, envy, greed, fear and the *actions* of injustice and violence!

Socrates applied the same straightforward reasoning to his relationship with the State. All his life Athens had nurtured him—as a parent nurtures a child—from childhood to manhood, giving him the opportunity for the search for truth. It provided protection, education, and citizenship—all the necessities of life itself. How could he, the child, respond in anger to the state, his parent, for one mistake made against him during his seventy years of life as a citizen? In addition, Socrates saw the Athenian city-state with its laws and court system as an expression of the concept of justice. To be sure, this system of law and order is frail and fallible—Crito doesn't need to remind him of this—but to Socrates this was no excuse not to obey its laws. He saw the logical consequences of such an act of disobedience against the state. In true Socratic style, he would ask the question: How could a just man exemplify by his actions a precedent that, if followed by others, would overturn all law and justice in a state? Certainly the structure of law and justice is frail and fallible but it is a structure necessary for human relationships. How could Socrates, with his claim of being a just man, direct his violence against this structure of justice and not expect others to do the same in the name of some personal justice?

If you are going to give the Socratic answer to this question, then notice what the implications are for any violent behavior against injustice. Violence to Socrates (even the minor violence against the State by escaping from its sentence) is an action that is concerned with the body, not with the soul. In this sense, all violence is evil because it is behavior directed by physical, not spiritual, interests. The first spiritual interest, Socrates reminds Crito, of the just man is this: We ought not to retaliate or render evil for evil to anyone, whatever evil we may have suffered from him. Therefore, a just man cannot act violently against injustice. This principle is especially true for Socrates, not only in regard to his behavior toward the state but also in view of the influence that he has on other men who believe that he is a just man. Again, in Socratic style, he would ask, If a man's life is to another person an objective "idea" of justice, then would not his act of violence against the law of the state destroy that "idea" and cause that person to do violence to his own ideals and to the laws of the State?

In the *Crito* the Socratic search for truth comes to a predictable conclusion in view of these commitments. People of justice express and live nonviolently their belief in the idea of justice as an eternal principle. They obey the laws of the State because they are a temporal, necessary, and human expression of the idea of justice. By this obedience the people of justice can present their case rationally to all people: life is human only when there is a dynamic relationship between a belief in the universality of the ideas of justice, truth, goodness, and wisdom and a commitment to action that personifies this belief. Socrates rests his case for our judgment. Leave me then, Crito, to fulfill the will of God, and to follow whither He leads.

NOTE

1. Robert S. Brumbaugh, *Plato for the Modern Age* (London: Collier Books, 1962), 27.

3

The Sermon on the Mount

The New English Bible, New Testament

The Sermon on the Mount is unlike the two preceding chapters in that it is apt to be somewhat familiar to many readers and in that there is only one speaker. The two articles that precede the Sermon are dialogues, although the main speakers carry almost all of the message; one might say that Arjuna and Crito serve as straight men for the main speakers. However, the ideas considered here are far from comic; they deal directly with the deepest reasons for action that human beings have reached yet—those of religion and law. The question of the relation between spiritual and secular views of action or nonaction, violence or nonviolence is central in many of the readings that follow this part. It seems suitable to introduce the question with these ancient and powerful views.

The teachings of Jesus called The Sermon on The Mount are found in Chapters 5, 6, 7 in the section of the New Testament titled The gospel according to Matthew. The "author" of this Gospel was an early Christian teacher who prepared these writings as a teaching manual for Christians sometime during the last third of the first century. He probably used as one of his sources a collection of Jesus' sayings that the apostle Matthew is said to have made. Other sources that the author collected were the oral traditions and written accounts of Jesus' life and words. In time a title containing Matthew's name was given to the collection by the unknown compiler of these materials. Matthew's name gave the collection the special authority that comes from an apostle who was a firsthand witness to the life of Jesus, and it also indicated the unique interpretation that the apostle Matthew gave to his life and teachings. The theme of the gospel revolves around this interpretation. Jesus is the Messiah (Anointed One) sent by God to the Jewish people to fulfill the promises of their Scriptures. He brings to the Jews and to all people who understand him an urgent and divine message telling them to prepare for the coming of God and His Judgment into human history. Chapter 5 of the New Testament presents some of these teachings, which demand from everyone a radical way of living in order to be ready and to be accepted into God's Kingdom when it comes on earth.

5   When he saw the crowds he went up the hill. There he took his

2   seat, and when his disciples had gathered round him he began to address them. And this is the teaching he gave:

3   'How blest are those who know that they are poor;
          the kingdom of Heaven is theirs.

4   How blest are the sorrowful;
          they shall find consolation.

5   How blest are those of a gentle spirit;
          they shall have the earth for their possession.

6   How blest are those who hunger and thirst to see right prevail;[1]
          they shall be satisfied.

7   How blest are those who show mercy;
          mercy shall be shown to them.

8   How blest are those whose hearts are pure;
          they shall see God.

9   How blest are the peacemakers;
          God shall call them his sons.

10   How blest are those who have suffered persecution for the cause of right:
          the kingdom of Heaven is theirs.

11   'How blest you are, when you suffer insults and persecution

12   and every kind of calumny for my sake. Accept it with gladness and exultation, for you have a rich reward in heaven; in the same way they persecuted the prophets before you.

13   'You are salt to the world. And if salt becomes tasteless, how is its saltness to be restored? It is now good for nothing but to be thrown away and trodden underfoot.

14   'You are light for all the world. A town that stands on a hill

15   cannot be hidden. When a lamp is lit, it is not put under the meal-tub, but on the lamp-stand, where it gives light to everyone

16   in the house. And you, like the lamp, must shed light among your fellows, so that, when they see the good you do, they may give praise to your Father in heaven.

17   'DO NOT SUPPOSE that I have come to abolish the Law and the

18   prophets: I did not come to abolish, but to complete. I tell you this: so long as heaven and earth endure, not a letter, not a stroke, will disappear from the Law until all that must happen

19   has happened.[2] If any man therefore sets aside even the least of the Law's demands, and teaches others to do the same, he will have the lowest place in the kingdom of Heaven, whereas anyone who keeps the Law and teaches others so will stand high

20 in the kingdom of Heaven. I tell you, unless you show yourselves far better men than the Pharisees and the doctors of the law, you can never enter the kingdom of Heaven.

21 'You have learned that our forefathers were told, "Do not commit murder; anyone who commits murder must be brought

22 to judgment." But what I tell you is this: Anyone who nurses anger against his brother³ must be brought to judgment. If he abuses his brother he must answer for it to the court; if he sneers at him he will have to answer for it in the fires of hell.

23 'If, when you are bringing your gift to the altar, you suddenly remember that your brother has a grievance against you, leave

24 your gift where it is before the altar. First go and make your peace with your brother, and only then come back and offer your gift.

25 'If someone sues you, come to terms with him promptly while you are both on your way to court; otherwise he may hand you over to the judge, and the judge to the constable, and you will

26 be put in jail. I tell you, once you are there you will not be let out till you have paid the last farthing.

27 'You have learned that they were told, "Do not commit

28 adultery." But what I tell you is this: If a man looks on a woman with a lustful eye, he has already committed adultery with her in his heart.

29 'If your right eye leads you astray, tear it out and fling it away; it is better for you to lose one part of your body than for the

30 whole of it to be thrown into hell. And if your right hand is your undoing, cut it off and fling it away; it is better for you to lose one part of your body than for the whole of it to go to hell.

31 'They were told, "A man who divorces his wife must give her

32 a note of dismissal." But what I tell you is this: If a man divorces his wife for any cause other than unchastity he involves her in adultery; and anyone who marries a woman so divorced commits adultery.

33 'Again, you have learned that they were told, "Do not break

34 your oath." and, "Oaths sworn to the Lord must be kept." But what I tell you is this: You are not to swear at all—not by heaven,

35 for it is God's throne, nor by earth, for it is his footstool, nor

36 by Jerusalem, for it is the city of the great King, nor by your

37 own head, because you cannot turn one hair of it white or black. Plain "Yes" or "No" is all you need to say; anything beyond that comes from the devil.

38 'You have learned that they were told, "An eye for an eye, and

39 a tooth for a tooth." But what I tell you is : Do not set yourself against the man who wrongs you. If someone slaps you

40 on the right cheek, turn and offer him your left. If a man wants

41 to sue you for your shirt, let him have your coat as well. If a man in authority makes you go one mile, go with him two.

42 Give when you are asked to give; and do not turn your back on a man who wants to borrow.

43 'You have learned that they were told, "Love your neighbor,

44 hate your enemy." But what I tell you is this: Love your

45 enemies[4] and pray for your persecutors;[5] only so can you be children of your heavenly Father, who makes his sun rise on good and bad alike, and sends the rain on the honest and the

46 dishonest. If you love only those who love you, what reward can you expect? Surely the tax-gatherers do as much as that.

47 And if you greet only your brothers, what is there extraordinary

48 about that? Even the heathen do as much. You must therefore be all goodness, just as your heavenly Father is all good.

6 'BE CAREFUL not to make a show of your religion before men; if you do, no reward awaits you in your Father's house in heaven.

2 'Thus, when you do some act of charity, do not announce it with a flourish of trumpets, as the hypocrites do in synagogue and in the streets to win admiration from men. I tell you this:

3 they have their reward already. No; when you do some act of

4 charity, do not let your left hand know what your right is doing; your good deed must be secret, and your Father who sees what is done in secret will reward you.[6]

5 'Again, when you pray, do not be like the hypocrites; they love to say their prayers standing up in synagogue and at the street-corners, for everyone to see them. I tell you this: they

6 have their reward already. But when you pray, go into a room by yourself, shut the door, and pray to your Father who is there in the secret place; and your Father who sees what is secret will reward you.[7]

7 'In your prayers do not go babbling on like the heathen, who imagine that the more they say the more likely they are to be

8 heard. Do not imitate them. Your Father knows what your needs are before you ask him.

9 'This is how you should pray:
> "Our Father in heaven
> Thy name be hallowed;
> Thy kingdom come,

10 Thy will be done,
> On earth as in heaven.

11 Give us today our daily bread.[8]

12 Forgive us the wrong we have done,
> As we have forgiven those who have wronged us.

13 And do not bring us to the test,
> But save us from the evil one."[9]

14 For if you forgive others the wrongs they have done, your heavenly Father will also forgive you; but if you do not forgive

15 others, then the wrongs you have done will not be forgiven by your Father.

16 'So too when you fast, do not look gloomy like the hypocrites; they make their faces unsightly so that other people may see that they are fasting. I tell you this: they have their reward already.

17 But when you fast, anoint your head and wash your face , so that

18 men may not see that you are fasting, but only your Father who is in the secret place: and your Father who sees what is secret will give you your reward.

19 'DO NOT STORE up for yourselves treasures on earth, where it grows rusty and moth-eaten, and thieves break in to steal it.

20 Store up treasure in heaven, where there is no moth and no rust

21 to spoil it, no thieves to break in and steal. For where your wealth is, there will your heart be also.

22 'The lamp of the body is the eye. If your eyes are sound, you will have light for your whole body; if the eyes are bad, your

23 whole body will be in darkness. If then the only light you have is darkness, the darkness is doubly dark.

24 'No servant can be slave to two masters; for either he will hate the first and love the second, or he will be devoted to the first and think nothing of the second. You cannot serve God and Money.'

AFTERWORD

After reading the Sermon on the Mount, the reader is probably wondering how it is possible to live up to such impossible demands. Immediately after these teachings became religious literature (around A.D. 80), this question was asked by the followers of Jesus. The author of the *Gospel According to St. Matthew* gave the first answer to this very ancient and contemporary inquiry. He understood these teachings of Jesus as the New Law, which is delivered by the new Moses (Jesus) on the Mountain (as the Law was given to Moses on a mountain by God). Jesus was the new Law-Giver and the long-awaited Messiah from God.

When Christianity spread from its Jewish homeland to the West, its followers no longer needed to see Jesus' teachings as a New Law that replaced the Old Law of the Hebrew tradition. They understood the Sermon on the Mount as a *demand* coming from God through Jesus to them to live a life of perfection. They knew that only under the best conditions could they attempt such a life. Certainly, any Christian involved in the secular life of money, politics, and violence found the Sermon on the Mount an impossible teaching to follow. Thus, these particular teachings of Jesus became the guideline for Christian monastic orders—a call to the disciplined life of poverty, chastity, and obedience behind the walls of the monastery or nunnery.

Martin Luther, the leader of the Protestant Reformation, gave another interpretation to the Sermon on the Mount. Although he was a monk himself, he understood the teachings as a means used by God to destroy our confidence in ourselves whether we were inside or outside the monastic walls. No one could be perfect without divine help. How could someone love one's enemies unless God changed her or his attitude toward them? How could someone be happy when other people were cursing and hurting this person unless this person believed God was with her or him? How could one turn one's cheek to one's opponent and not be angry unless one had divine aid? Martin Luther believed that all fail to live up to the teachings in the Sermon on the Mount, but more important, that one must *know* that one fails in order to be willing to accept God's help (salvation).

In the nineteenth century other Christian thinkers gave yet another meaning to the Sermon on the Mount. They attempted to lift the awesome burden of failure (sin) from Christians by saying that these teachings are not absolute laws but guiding principles that indicate to people what they should *be* and not what they should *do*. People need God's help, yet as individuals they live by their own existential interpretation of Jesus' teaching, sometimes experiencing failure and sometimes experiencing success. Gandhi's deep appreciation of the Sermon on the Mount reflects this type of interpretation when he says that the teachings went straight to his heart. The Sermon on the Mount, in addition to the *Bhagavad-Gita*, gave to him guiding principles for his own spiritual life. Gandhi remarked, "The Sermon on the Mount gives the same law (law of love and man's abandon to God as he found it also expressed in the *Gita*) in wonderful language. The *New Testament* gave me comfort and boundless joy. . . .Today supposing I was deprived of the *Gita* and forgot all its contents but had a copy of the Sermon, I should derive the same joy from it as I do from the *Gita*."[10]

In this country, Albert Schweitzer, the famous medical missionary to Africa, believed that Jesus gave these teachings to his disciples as a warning in order to prepare them for the immediate coming to earth of God, who would then judge everyone according to his or her response to Jesus' teachings. The sky would open, the heavenly trumpets would sound, and the angels would descend announcing the arrival of God. Jesus demanded a radical obedience to his teachings from his followers, but only for a short time, since the day of God's terrible and Final Judgment was coming in their life-time. Schweitzer described the Sermon on the Mount as part of an "interim ethics," teachings for everyone to obey absolutely between now and the immediate future, when God would bring human history to an end.

Many contemporary thinkers agree with Schweitzer regarding Jesus' belief in the immediate coming of the Kingdom of God to earth, but they still emphasize—and Schweitzer would agree—that the Sermon on the Mount demands from everyone the same type of radical obedience today. These teachings are not obsolete because they developed out of a particular historical period nor because Jesus' literal belief in the coming of the Kingdom of God was wrong. The Sermon on the Mount is still painfully relevant because it has its source in truth, which is absolute and never changing in its ultimate meaning. As suggested in the Introduction, many advocates of "resist not evil," "return anger with love," and "love your enemies,"are believers in nonviolence because they are certain that nonviolence has its source in truth as an eternal principle. Socrates, the author of the *Gita*, and Jesus all responded in their own unique way to a belief in truth. Therefore, whether you interpret the Sermon on the Mount as Jesus' attempt to revitalize the Judaism of his day, as a call to the monastic life, and as a way to make us more sensitive to our need for divine help or whether you understand it as an "interim ethic" applicable for only a short time, it is still essential to remember that this literature comes out of a religious tradition that involves faith in God. It is this faith (a belief in God, a conviction in *ahimsa* as part of truth, a commitment to truth as an eternal principle) that one needs to examine in order to understand the reasons for the demands placed upon us found in the Sermon on the Mount, in the *Gita*, and in the Socratic search for truth—and placed upon anyone committed to the truth of nonviolence.

NOTES

1. *Or* to do what is right.
2. *Or* before all that it stands for is achieved.
3. *Some witnesses insert* without good cause.
4. *Some witnesses insert* bless those who curse you, do good to those who hate you.
5. *Some witnesses insert* and those who treat you spitefully.

6. *Some witnesses add* openly.

7. *Some witnesses add* openly.

8. *Or* our bread for the morrow.

9. *Some witnesses add* For thine is the kingdom and the power and the glory, forever. Amen.

10. Gandhi, *Gita the Mother*, p. 51.

4

A Jain Prayer

This selection includes prayers from the religious tradition of Jainism. Jainism emerged out of Brahmanic Hinduism in India in the sixth century B.C. According to the Jain tradition, these teachings go back into the prehistory of the cosmic age through a series of twenty-four Tirthankaras ("makers of the river crossing"), whose lifetimes collectively stretch over a period of nearly 9 million years. These teachings relate to the Hindu religion but stress the importance of nonviolence, *ahimsa* (no harm), with a complete devotion to a life of nonviolence toward all living beings. The Jain community is focused on forms of monastic life supported by laypersons. Monks, and in some sects, nuns take five vows to abstain from violence, deceit, theft, attachments to material things, and sex. Laypersons accept a modified version of the monastic vows in addition to practicing meditation, fasting twice a lunar month, and publicly confessing their faults. It is, however, the Jain tradition of nonviolence that relates to this section, reminding the reader of this religious tradition totally dedicated to the way of nonviolence.

1. May my thoughts and feeling be such that I may always act in a simple and straightforward manner. May I ever, so far as I can, do good in this life to others.

2. May I never hurt and harm any living being; may I never speak a lie. May I never be greedy of wealth or wife of another. May I ever drink the nectar of contentment!

3. May I always have a friendly feeling towards all living beings of the world and may the stream of compassion always flow from my heart towards distressed and afflicted living beings.

4. May I never entertain an idea of egotism; nor may I be angry with anybody! May I never become jealous on seeing the worldly prosperity of other people.

5. May I never become fretful towards bad, cruel and wicked persons. May I keep tolerance towards them. May I be so disposed!

6. May I ever have the good company of learned ascetics and may I ever keep them in mind. May my heart be always engrossed and inclined to adopt the rules of conduct which they observe.

7. May my heart be overflowing with love at the sight of the virtuous, and may I be happy to serve them so far as possible.

8. May I never be ungrateful (towards anybody); nor may I revolt (against anybody). May I ever be appreciating the good qualities of other persons and may I never look at their faults.

9. May my mind neither be puffed up with joy, nor may it become nervous in pain and grief. May it never be frightened even if I am in a terrible forest or strange places of cremation or graveyards.

10. May my mind remain always steady and firm, unswerving and unshaken; may it become stronger every day. May I bear and endure with patience the deprivation of dear ones and occurrences of undesired evils.

11. May all living beings of the world be happy! May nobody ever feel distressed! May the people of the world renounce enmity, sin, pride, and sing the songs of joy every day.

12. May Dharma (truth) be the topic of house-talk in every home! May evil be scarce! May (people) increase their knowledge and conduct and thereby enjoy the blessed fruit of human birth.

13. May disease and pestilence never spread, may the people live in peace, may the highest religion of Ahimsa (non-injury) pervade the whole world and may it bring about universal good!

14. May universal love pervade the world and may ignorance of attachment remain far away. May nobody speak unkind, bitter and harsh words!

15. May all become "heroes of the age" heartily and remain engaged in elevating the Cause of Righteousness. May all gain the sight of Truth called Vastuswarupa (Reality of substance) and may they bear with pleasure, trouble and misfortunes!

5

Peace Seeds

Prayers for Peace, Prayed in Assisi, Italy

Peace Seeds represent the twelve prayers for peace prayed in Assisi, Italy, on the Day of Prayer for World Peace during the United Nations International Year of Peace, 1986. The prayers were brought to the United States and entrusted to the care of the children at The Life Experience School and Peace Abbey in Sherborn, Massachusetts.

Like the bee gathering honey from the different flowers, the wise person accepts the essence of the different scriptures and sees only the good in all religions.

Mahatma Gandhi

HINDU PRAYER FOR PEACE

Oh God, lead us from the unreal to the Real. Oh God, lead us from darkness to light. Oh God, lead us from death to immortality. Shanti, Shanti, Shanti unto all. Oh Lord God almighty, may there be peace in celestial regions. May there be peace on earth. May the waters be appeasing. May herbs be wholesome, and may trees and plants bring peace to all. May all beneficent beings bring peace to us. May the Vedic Law propagate peace all through the world. May all things be a source of peace to us. And may thy peace itself, bestow peace on all, and may that peace come to me also.

BUDDHIST PRAYER FOR PEACE

May all beings everywhere plagued with sufferings of body and mind quickly be freed from their illnesses. May those frightened cease to be afraid, and may those bound be free. May the powerless find power, and may people think of befriending one another. May those who find themselves in trackless, fearful wildernesses—the children, the aged, the unprotected—be guarded by beneficent celestials, and may they swiftly attain Buddhahood.

JAIN PRAYER FOR PEACE

Peace and Universal Love is the essence of the Gospel preached by all the Enlightened Ones. The Lord has preached that equanimity is the Dharma. Forgive do I creatures all, and let all creatures forgive me. Unto all have I amity, and unto none enmity. Know that violence is the root cause of all miseries in the world. Violence, in fact, is the knot of bondage. "Do not injure any living being." This is the eternal, perennial, and unalterable way of spiritual life. A weapon howsoever powerful it may be, can always be superseded by a superior one; but no weapon can, however, be superior to non-violence and love.

MUSLIM PRAYER FOR PEACE

In the name of Allah, the beneficent, the merciful. Praise be to the Lord of the Universe who has created us and made us into tribes and nations, that we may know each other, not that we may despise each other. If the enemy incline towards peace, do thou also incline towards peace, and trust in God, for the Lord is the one that heareth and knoweth all things. And the servants of God, Most Gracious are those who walk on the Earth in humility, and when we address them, we say "PEACE."

SIKH PRAYER FOR PEACE

God adjudges us according to our deeds, not the coat that we wear: that Truth is above everything, but higher still is truthful living. Know that we attaineth God when we loveth, and only that victory endures in consequence of which no one is defeated.

BAHAI' PRAYER FOR PEACE

Be generous in prosperity, and thankful in adversity. Be fair in thy judgement, and guarded in thy speech. Be a lamp unto those who walk in darkness, and a home to the stranger. Be eyes to the blind, and a guiding light unto the feet of the erring. Be a breath of life to the body of humankind, a dew to the soil of the human heart, and a fruit upon the tree of humility.

SHINTO PRAYER FOR PEACE

Although the people living across the ocean surrounding us, I believe, are all our brothers and sisters, why are there constant troubles in this world? Why do winds and waves rise in the ocean surrounding us? I only earnestly wish that the wind will soon puff away all the clouds which are hanging over the tops of the mountains.

NATIVE AFRICAN PRAYER FOR PEACE

Almighty God, the Great Thumb we cannot evade to tie any knot; the Roaring Thunder that splits mighty trees: the all-seeing Lord up on high who sees even the footprints of an antelope on a rock mass here on Earth. You are the one who does not hesitate to respond to our call. You are the cornerstone of peace.

NATIVE AMERICAN PRAYER FOR PEACE

O Great Spirit of our Ancestors, I raise my pipe to you. To your messengers the four winds, and to Mother Earth who provides for your children. Give us the wisdom to teach our children to love, to respect, and to be kind to each other so that they may grow with peace in mind. Let us learn to share all the good things that you provide for us on this Earth.

ZOROASTRIAN PRAYER FOR PEACE

We pray to God to eradicate all the misery in the world: that understanding triumph over ignorance, that generosity triumph over indifference, that trust triumph over contempt, and that truth triumph over falsehood.

JEWISH PRAYER FOR PEACE

Come let us go up to the mountain of the Lord, that we may walk the paths of the Most High. And we shall beat our swords into ploughshares, and our spears into pruning hooks. Nation shall not lift up sword against nation—neither shall they learn war any more. And none shall be afraid, for the mouth of the Lord of Hosts has spoken.

CHRISTIAN PRAYER FOR PEACE

Blessed are the PEACEMAKERS, for they shall be known as the Children of God. But I say to you that hear, love your enemies, do good to those who hate you, bless those who curse you, pray for those who abuse you. To those who strike you on the cheek, offer the other also, and from those who take away your cloak, do not withhold your coat as well. Give to everyone who begs from you, and of those who take away your goods, do not ask them again. And as you wish that others would do to you, do so to them.

Part II

Historical Voices of Nonviolence

6

Civil Disobedience

Henry David Thoreau

Henry David Thoreau's essay, composed first as a lecture titled "The Rights and Duties of the Individual in Relation to Government" and later retitled to "Resistance to Civil Government" for publication in the *Aesthetic Papers*, May 1849, and later, "Civil Disobedience," has been taken as an expression of the appropriate position for an individual to hold when he or she is morally certain of his or her stance in opposition to a legal or governmental policy. Thoreau (1817–1862), sometimes called "the first American hippie," was a Harvard College graduate, a naturalist, a poet, a surveyor, a pencil maker, an early student of the American Indian, a bachelor (probably not by choice), and a prose stylist. But this list of labels does not in any manner sum up Thoreau. How could anyone summarize the life of a man who speaks about not keeping pace with his companions because he hears a different drummer and writes in *Walden* that "the true harvest of my daily life is somewhat as intangible and indescribable as the tints of morning or evening. It is a little stardust caught, a segment of the rainbow which I have clutched."

It is intriguing to think that Thoreau's arrest for not paying his Massachusetts poll tax and his subsequent one-night stay in jail may have caused him to write his most famous essay, "Civil Disobedience." However, we know that the reasons for writing the essay go much deeper into the convictions of the man than the influence of an arrest and one night in jail.

Being a peace-loving citizen and an abolitionist, Thoreau refused to support the Mexican War, which in his mind was not only the government's interference with an individual's personal liberty but also a war of expansionism that threatened to add new slave states to the Union. He proclaimed, therefore, his one-man, nonviolent rebellion against the government by refusing to pay his tax. His protest did not go unnoticed. One story—perhaps not totally reliable—relates that Ralph Waldo Emerson went to jail and asked Thoreau, "Henry, why are you here?" The reply was immediate, "Why are you not here?" Many contemporary followers of this type of civil disobedience ask the same question of observers who watch as they fill the jails for a cause of conscience. Thus, it is apparent that although Thoreau's protest was a particular one in its reference to the Mexican War and slavery, it is still universal in its meaning and application to other persons, in other places, and at other times in history. The most outstanding example of this is Gandhi, who when asked whether he had read Thoreau, responded with bright eyes and a chuckle, "Why, of course I read Thoreau."

I heartily accept the motto "That government is best which governs least"; and I should like to see it acted up to more rapidly and systematically. Carried out, it finally amounts to this, which also I believe, "That government is best which governs not at all"; and when men are prepared for it, that will be the kind of government which they will have. Government is at best but an expedient; but most governments are usually, all governments are sometimes, inexpedient. The objections which have been brought against a standing army, and they are many and weighty, and deserve to prevail, may also at last be brought against a standing government. The standing army is only an arm of the standing government. The government itself, which is only the mode which the people have chosen to execute their will, is equally liable to be abused and perverted before the people can act through it. Witness the present Mexican war, the work of comparatively a few individuals using the standing government as their tool; for, in the outset, the people would not have consented to this measure.

This American government—what is it but a tradition, though a recent one, endeavoring to transmit itself unimpaired to posterity, but each instant losing some of its integrity? It has not the vitality and force of a single living man; for a single man can bend it to his will. It is a sort of wooden gun to the people themselves. But it is not the less necessary for this; for the people must have some complicated machinery or other, and hear its din, to satisfy that idea of government which they have. Governments show thus how successfully men can be imposed on, even impose on themselves, for their own advantage. It is excellent, we must all allow. Yet this government never of itself furthered any enterprise, but by the alacrity with which it got out of its way. *It* does not keep the country free. *It* does not settle the West. *It* does not educate. The character inherent in the American people has done all that has been accomplished; and it would have done somewhat more, if the government had not sometimes got in its way. For government is an expedient by which men would fain succeed in letting one another alone; and, as has been said, when it is most expedient, the governed are most let alone by it. Trade and commerce, if they were not made of India-rubber, would never manage to bounce over the obstacles which legislators are continually putting in their way; and, if one were to judge these men wholly by the effects of their actions and not partly by their intentions, they would deserve to be classed and punished with those mischievous persons who put obstructions on the railroads.

But, to speak practically and as a citizen, unlike those who call themselves no-government men, I ask for, not at once no government, but *at once* a better government. Let every man make known what kind of government would command his respect, and that will be one step toward obtaining it.

After all, the practical reason why, when the power is once in the hands of the people, a majority are permitted, and for a long period continue, to rule, is not because they are most likely to be in the right, nor because this seems fairest to the minority, but because they are physically the strongest. But a government in which the majority rule in all cases cannot be based on justice, even as far as men understand it. Can there not be a government in which majorities do not virtually decide right and wrong, but conscience?—In which majorities decide only those questions to which the rule of expediency is applicable? Must the citizen ever for a moment, or in the least degree, resign his conscience to the legislator? Why has every man a conscience, then? I think that we should be men first, and subject afterward. It is not desirable to cultivate a respect for the law, so much as for the right. The only obligation which I have a right to assume is to do at any time what I think right. It is truly enough said that a corporation has no conscience; but a corporation of conscientious men is a corporation *with* a conscience. Law never made men a whit more just; and, by means of their respect for it, even the well-disposed are daily made the agents of injustice. A common and natural result of an undue respect for law is, that you may see a file of soldiers, colonel, captain, corporal, privates, powder-monkeys, and all, marching in admirable order over hill and dale to the wars, against their wills, ay, against their common sense and consciences, which makes it very steep marching indeed, and produces a palpitation of the heart. They have no doubt that it is a damnable business in which they are concerned; they are all peaceably inclined. Now, what are they? Men at all? Or small movable forts and magazines, at the service of some unscrupulous man in power? Visit the Navy Yard, and behold a marine, such a man as an American government can make, or such as it can make a man with its black arts—a mere shadow and reminiscence of humanity, a man laid out alive and standing, and already, as one may say, buried under arms with funeral accompaniments, though it may be,

Not a drum was heard, not a funeral note,
As his corpse to the rampart we hurried;
Not a soldier discharged his farewell shot
O'er the grave where our hero we buried.

The mass of men serve the state thus, not as men mainly, but as machines, with their bodies. They are the standing army, and the militia, jailors, constables, posse comitatus, etc. In most cases there is no free exercise whatever of the judgment or of the moral sense; but they put themselves on a level with wood and earth and stones; and wooden men can perhaps be manufactured that will serve the purpose as well. Such command no more respect than men of straw or a lump of dirt. They have the same sort of worth only as horses and dogs. Yet such as these even are commonly esteemed good citizens. Others—as most legislators,

politicians, lawyers, ministers, and office-holders—serve the state chiefly with
their heads; and, as they rarely make any moral distinctions, they are as likely to
serve the Devil, without *intending* it, as God. A very few, as heroes, patriots,
martyrs, reformers in the great sense, and *men*, serve as the state with their consciences also, and so necessarily resist it for the most part; and they are commonly treated as enemies by it. A wise man will only be useful as a man, and
will not submit to be "clay," and "stop a hole to keep the wind away," but leave
that office to his dust at least:

> I am too high-born to be propertied,
> To be a secondary at control,
> Or useful serving-man and instrument
> To any sovereign state throughout the world.

He who gives himself entirely to his fellow-men appears to them useless
and selfish; but he who gives himself partially to them is pronounced a benefac-
tor and philanthropist.

How does it become a man to behave toward this American government
today? I answer, that he cannot without disgrace be associated with it. I cannot
for an instant recognize that political organization as *my* government which is the
slave's government also.

All men recognize the right of revolution; that is, the right to refuse allegiance to, and to resist, the government, when its tyranny or its inefficiency are
great and unendurable. But almost all say that such is not the case now. But such
was the case, they think, in the Revolution of '75. If one were to tell me that this
was a bad government because it taxed certain foreign commodities brought to its
ports, it is most probable that I should not make an ado about it, for I can do without them. All machines have their friction; and possibly this does enough good
to counterbalance the evil. At any rate, it is a great evil to make a stir about it.
But when the friction comes to have its machine, and oppression and robbery are
organized, I say, let us not have such a machine any longer. In other words,
when a sixth of population of a nation which has undertaken to be the refuge of
liberty are slaves, and a whole country is unjustly overrun and conquered by a
foreign army, and subjected to military law, I think that it is not too soon for honest men to rebel and revolutionize. What makes this duty the more urgent is the
fact that the country so overrun is not our own, but ours is the invading army. . . .

> A drab of state, a cloth-o-silver slut,
> To have her train borne up, and her soul trail in the dirt.

Practically speaking, the opponents to a reform in Massachusetts are not a
hundred thousand politicians at the South, but a hundred thousand merchants and
farmers here, who are more interested in commerce and agriculture than they are
in humanity, and are not prepared to do justice to the slave and to Mexico, *cost*

what it may. I quarrel not with far-off foes, but with those who, near at home, cooperate with, and do the bidding of, those far away, and without whom the latter would be harmless. We are accustomed to say, that the mass of men are unprepared; but improvement is slow, because the few are not materially wiser or better than the many. It is not so important that many should be as good as you, as that there be some absolute goodness somewhere; for that will leaven the whole lump. There are thousands who are *in opinion* opposed to slavery and to the war, who yet in effect do nothing to put an end to them; who, esteeming themselves children of Washington and Franklin, sit down with their hands in their pockets, and say that they know not what to do, and do nothing; who even postpone the question of freedom to the question of free trade, and quietly read the prices-current along with latest advices from Mexico, after dinner, and, it may be, fall asleep over them both. What is the price-current of an honest man and patriot today? They hesitate, and they regret, and sometimes they petition; but they do nothing in earnest and with effect. They will wait, well disposed, for others to remedy the evil, that they may no longer have it to regret. At most, they give only a cheap vote, and a feeble countenance and God-speed, to the right, as it goes by them. There are nine hundred and ninety-nine patrons of virtue to one virtuous man. But it is easier to deal with the real possessor of a thing than with the temporary guardian of it.

All voting is a sort of gaming, like checkers or backgammon, with a slight moral tinge to it, a playing with right and wrong, with moral questions; and betting naturally accompanies it. The character of the voters is not staked. I cast my vote, perchance, as I think right; but I am not vitally concerned that that right should prevail. I am willing to leave it to the majority. Its obligation, therefore, never exceeds that of expediency. Even voting *for the right is doing* nothing for it. It is only expressing to men feebly your desire that it should prevail. A wise man will not leave the right to the mercy of chance, nor wish it to prevail through the power of the majority. There is but little virtue in the action of masses of men. When the majority shall at length vote for the abolition of slavery, it will be because they are indifferent to slavery, or because there is but little slavery left to be abolished by their vote. *They* will then be the only slaves. Only *his* vote can hasten the abolition of slavery who asserts his own freedom by his vote.

I hear of a convention to be held at Baltimore, or elsewhere, for the selection of a candidate for the Presidency, made up chiefly of editors, and men who are politicians by professions; but I think, what is it to any independent, intelligent, and respectable man what decision they may come to? Shall we not have the advantage of his wisdom and honesty nevertheless? Can we not count upon some independent votes? Are there not many individuals in the country who do not attend conventions? But no: I find that the respectable man, so called, has immediately drifted from his position, and despairs of his country, when his country has more reason to despair of him. He forthwith adopts one of the candidates thus selected as the only *available* one, thus proving that he is himself *available* for any purpose of the demagogue. His vote is of no more worth than that of any unprincipled foreigner or hireling native, who may have been bought. O for a man who is a *man*, and, as my neighbor says, has a bone in his back which you cannot pass your hand through! Our statistics are at fault: the population has been returned too large. How many *men* are there to a square thousand miles in this country? Hardly one. Does not America offer any inducement for men to settle here? The American has dwindled into an Odd Fellow—one who may be known by the development of his organ of gregariousness, and a manifest lack of intellect and cheerful self-reliance; whose first and chief concern, on coming into the world, is to see that the Almshouses are in good repair; and, before yet he has lawfully donned the virile garb, to collect a fund for the support of the widows and orphans that may be; who, in short, ventures to live only by the aid of the Mutual Insurance company, which has promised to bury him decently.

It is not a man's duty, as a matter of course, to devote himself to the eradication of any, even the most enormous wrong; he may still properly have other concerns to engage him: but it is his duty, at least, to wash his hands of it, and, if he gives it no thought longer, not to give it practically his support. If I devote myself to other pursuits and contemplations, I must first see, at least, that I do not pursue them sitting upon another man's shoulders. I must get off him first, that he may pursue his contemplations too. See what gross inconsistency is tolerated. I have heard some of my townsmen say, "I should like to have them order me out to help put down an insurrection of the slaves, or to march to Mexico—see if I would go"; and yet these very men have each, directly by their allegiance, and so indirectly, at least, by their money, furnished a substitute. The soldier is applauded who refuses to serve in an unjust war by those who do not refuse to sustain the unjust government which makes the war; is applauded by those whose own act and authority he disregards and sets at naught; as if the state were penitent to that degree that it hired one to scourge it while it sinned, but not to that degree that it left off sinning for a moment. Thus, under the name of Order and Civil Government, we are all made at last to pay homage to and support our own meanness. After the first blush of sin comes its indifference; and from immoral it becomes, as it were, *un*moral, and not quite unnecessary to that life which we have made.

The broadest and most prevalent error requires the most disinterested virtue to sustain it. The slight reproach to which the virtue of patriotism is commonly liable, the noble are most likely to incur. Those who, while they disapprove of the character and measures of a government, yield to it their allegiance and support are undoubtedly its most conscientious supporters, and so frequently the most serious obstacles to reform. Some are petitioning the state to dissolve the Union, to disregard the requisitions of the President. Why do they not dissolve it themselves—the union between themselves and the state—and refuse to pay their quota into its treasury? Do not they stand in the same relation to the state and that the state does to the Union? And have not the same reasons prevented the state from resisting the Union which have prevented them from resisting the state?

How can a man be satisfied to entertain an opinion merely, and enjoy it? Is there any enjoyment in it, if his opinion is that he is aggrieved? If you are cheated out of a single dollar by your neighbor, you do not rest satisfied with knowing that you are cheated, or even with petitioning him to pay you your due; but you take effectual steps at once to obtain the full amount, and see that you are never cheated again. Action from principle, the perception and the performance of right, changes things and relations; it is essentially revolutionary, and does not consist wholly with anything which was. It not only divides states and churches, it divides families; ay, it divides the *individual*, separating the diabolical in him from the divine.

Unjust laws exist: shall we be content to obey them, or shall we endeavor to amend them, and obey them until we have succeeded, or shall we transgress them at once? Men generally, under such a government as this, think that they ought to wait until they have persuaded the majority to alter them. They think that, if they should resist, the remedy would be worse than the evil. But it is the fault of the government itself that the remedy is worse than the evil. *It* makes it worse. Why is it not more apt to anticipate and provide for reform? Why does it not cherish its wise minority? Why does it cry and resist before it is hurt? Why does it not encourage its citizens to be on the alert to point out its faults, and *do* better than it would have them? Why does it always crucify Christ, and excommunicate Copernicus and Luther, and pronounce Washington and Franklin rebels?

One would think, that a deliberate and practical denial of its authority was the only offense never contemplated by government; else, why has it not assigned its definite, its suitable and proportionate penalty? If a man who has no property refuses but once to earn nine shillings for the state, he is put in prison for a period unlimited by any law that I know, and determined only by the discretion of those who placed him there; but if he should steal ninety times nine shillings from the state, he is soon permitted to go at large again.

If the injustice is part of the necessary friction of the machine of government, let it go: perchance it will wear smooth—certainly the machine will wear out. If the injustice has a spring, or a pulley, or a rope, or a crank, exclusively for itself, then perhaps you may consider whether the remedy will not be worse that the evil; but if it is of such a nature that it requires you to be the agent of injustice to another, then, I say, break the law. Let your life be a counter friction to stop the machine. What I have to do is to see, at any rate, that I do not lend myself to the wrong which I condemn.

As for adopting the ways which the state has provided for remedying the evil, I know not of such ways. They take too much time, and a man's life will be gone. I have other affairs to attend to. I came into this world, not chiefly to make this a good place to live in, but to live in it, be it good or bad. A man has not everything to do, but something; and because he cannot do *everything*, it is not necessary that he should do *something* wrong. It is not my business to be petitioning the Governor or the Legislature any more than it is theirs to petition me; and if they should not hear my petition, what should I do then? But in this case the state has provided no way: its very Constitution is the evil. This may seem to be harsh and stubborn and unconciliatory; but it is to treat with the utmost kindness and consideration the only spirit that can appreciate or deserves it. So is all change for the better, like birth and death, which convulse the body.

I do not hesitate to say, that those who call themselves Abolitionists should at once effectually withdraw their support, both in person and property, from the government of Massachusetts and not wait till they constitute a majority of one, before they suffer the right to prevail through them. I think that it is enough if they have God on their side, without waiting for the other one. Moreover, any man more right than his neighbors constitutes a majority of one already.

I meet this American government, or its representative, the state government, directly, and face to face, once a year—no more—in the person of its taxgatherer; this is the only mode in which a man situated as I am necessarily meets it; and it then says distinctly, Recognize me; and the simplest, most effectual, and, in the present posture of affairs, the indipensablest mode of treating with it on this head, of expressing your little satisfaction with and love for it, is to deny it then. My civil neighbor, the tax-gatherer, is the very man I have to deal with— for it is, after all, with men and not with parchment that I quarrel—and he has voluntarily chosen to be an agent of the government. How shall he ever know well what he is and does as an officer of the government, or as a man, until he is obliged to consider whether he shall treat me, his neighbor, for whom he has respect, as a neighbor and well-disposed man, or as a maniac and disturber of the peace, and see if he can get over this obstruction to his neighborliness without a ruder and more impetuous thought or speech corresponding with his action. I know this well, that if one thousand, if one hundred, if ten men whom I could name—if ten *honest* men only—ay, if *one* HONEST man, in this State of Massachusetts, *ceasing to hold slaves*, were actually to withdraw from this copartnership, and be locked up in the county jail therefor, it would be the abolition of slavery in America. For it matters not how small the beginning may seem to be: what is once well done is done for ever. But we love better to talk about it: that we say is our mission. Reform keeps many scores of newspapers in its service, but not one man. If my esteemed neighbor, the State's ambassador, who will devote his days to the settlement of the question of human rights in the Council Chamber, instead of being threatened with the prisons of Carolina, were to sit down the prisoner of Massachusetts, that Sate which is so anxious to foist the sin of slavery upon her sister—though at present she can discover only an act of inhospitality to be the ground of a quarrel with her—the Legislature would not wholly waive the subject the following winter.

Under a government which imprisons any unjustly, the true place for a just man is also a prison. The proper place today, the only place which Massachusetts has provided for her freer and less desponding spirits, is in her prisons, to be put out and locked out of the State by her own act, as they have already put themselves out by their principles. It is there that the fugitive slave, and the Mexican prisoner on parole, and the Indian come to plead the wrongs of his race should find them; on that separate, but more free and honorable ground, where the State places those who are not *with* her, but *against* her—the only house in a slave State in which a free man can abide with honor. If any think that their influence would be lost there, and their voices no longer afflict the ear of the State, that they would not be as an enemy within its walls, they do not know by how much truth is stronger than error, nor how much more eloquently and effectively he can combat injustice who has experienced a little in his own person. Cast your whole vote, not a strip of paper merely, but your whole influence. A minority is power-less while it conforms to the majority; it is not even a minority then; but it is irre-sistible when it clogs by its whole weight. If the alternative is to keep all just men in prison, or give up war and slavery, the State will not hesitate which to choose. If a thousand men were not to pay their tax-bills this year, that would not be a violent and bloody measure, as it would be to pay them, and enable the State to commit violence and shed innocent blood. This is, in fact, the definition of a peaceable revolution, if any such is possible. If the tax-gatherer, or any other public officer, asks me, as one has done, "But what shall I do?" my answer is, "If you really wish to do anything, resign your office." When the subject has refused allegiance, and the officer has resigned his office, then the revolution is accom-plished. But even suppose blood should flow. Is there not a sort of blood shed when the conscience is wounded? Through this wound a man's real manhood and immortality flow out, and he bleeds to an everlasting death. I see this blood flowing now.

I have contemplated the imprisonment of the offender, rather than the sei-zure of his goods—though both will serve the same purpose—because they who assert the purest right, and consequently are most dangerous to a corrupt State, commonly have not spent much time in accumulating property. To such the State renders comparatively small service, and a slight tax is wont to appear exor-bitant, particularly if they are obliged to earn it by special labor with their hands. If there were one who lived wholly without the use of money, the State itself would hesitate to demand it of him. But the rich man—not to make any invidious comparison—is always sold to the institution which makes him rich. Absolutely speaking, the more money, the less virtue; for money comes between a man and his objects, and obtains them for him; and it was certainly no great virtue to obtain it. It puts to rest many questions which he would otherwise be taxed to answer; while the only new question which it puts is the hard but superfluous one, how to spend it. Thus his moral ground is taken from under his feet. The opportunities of living are diminished in proportion as what are called the "means" are increased. The best thing a man can do for his culture when he is rich is to endeavor to carry out those schemes which he entertained when he was poor. Christ answered the Herodians according to their condition. "Show me the tribute-money," said he—and one took a penny out of his pocket; if you use money which has the image of Caesar on it and which he had made current and valuable, that is, *if you are men of the State*, and gladly enjoy the advantages of Caesar's government, then pay him back some of his own when he demands it. "Render therefore to Caesar that which is Caesar's, and to God those things which are God's"—leaving them no wiser than before as to which was which; for they did not wish to know....

I have paid no poll-tax for six years. I was put into a jail once on this account, for one night, and, as I stood considering the walls of solid stone, two or three feet thick, the door of wood and iron, a foot thick, and the iron grating which strained the light, I could not help being struck with the foolishness of that institution which treated me as if I were mere flesh and blood and bones, to be locked up. I wondered that it should have concluded at length that this was the best use it could put me to, and had never thought to avail itself of my services in some way. I saw that, if there was a wall of stone between me and my townsmen, there was a still more difficult one to climb or break through before they could get to be as free as I was. I did not for a moment feel confined, and the walls seemed a great waste of stone and mortar. I felt as if I alone of all my townsmen had paid my tax. They plainly did knot know how to treat me, but behaved like persons who are underbred. In every threat and in every compliment there was a blunder; for they thought that my chief desire was to stand the other side of that stone wall. I could not but smile to see how industriously they locked the door on my meditations, which followed them out again without let or hindrance, and *they* were really all that was dangerous. As they could not reach me, they had resolved to punish my body; just as boys, if they cannot come at some person against whom they have a spite, will abuse his dog. I saw that the State was half-witted, that it was timid as a lone woman with her silver spoons, and that it did not know its friends from its foes, and I lost all my remaining respect for it, and pitied it.

Thus the State never intentionally confronts a man's sense, intellectual or moral, but only his body, his senses. It is not armed with superior wit or honesty, but with superior physical strength. I was not born to be forced. I will breathe after my own fashion. Let us see who is the strongest. What force has a multitude? They only can force me who obey a higher law than I. They force me to become like themselves. I do not hear of *men* being *forced* to live this way or that by masses of men. What sort of life were that to live? When I meet a government which says to me, "Your money or your life," why should I be in haste to give it my money? It may be in a great strait, and not know what to do: I cannot help that. It must help itself: do as I do. It is not worth the while to snivel about it. I am not responsible for the successful working of the machinery of the society. I am not the son of the engineer. I perceive that, when an acorn and a chestnut fall side by side, the one does not remain inert to make way for the other, but obey their own laws, and spring and grow and flourish as best they can, till one, perchance, over-shadows and destroys the other. If a plant cannot live according to its nature, it dies; and so a man....

When I came out of prison—for someone interfered, and paid that tax—I did not perceive that great changes had taken place on the common, such as he observed who went in a youth and emerged a tottering and gray-headed man; and yet a change had to my eyes come over the scene—the town, and State, and country—greater than any that mere time could effect. I saw yet more distinctly the State in which I lived. I saw to what extent the people among whom I lived could be trusted as good neighbors and friends; that their friendship was for summer weather only; that they did not greatly propose to do right; that they were a distinct race from me by their prejudices and superstitions, as the Chinamen and Malays are; that in their sacrifices to humanity they ran no risks, not even to their property; that after all they were not so noble but they treated the thief as he had treated them, and hoped by a certain outward observance and a few prayers, and by walking in a particular straight though useless path from time to time, to save their souls. This may be to judge my neighbors harshly; for I believe that many of them are not aware that they have such an institution as the jail in their village.

It was formerly the custom in our village, when a poor debtor came out of jail, for his acquaintances to salute him, looking through their fingers, which were crossed to represent the grating of a jail window. "How do ye do?" My neighbors did not thus salute me, but first looked at me, and then at one another, as if I had returned from a long journey. I was put into jail as I was going to the shoemaker's to get a shoe which was mended. When I was let out the next morning, I proceeded to finish my errand, and having put on my mended shoe, joined a huckleberry party, who were impatient to put themselves under my conduct; and in half an hour—for the horse was soon tackled—was in the midst of a huckleberry field, no one of our highest hills, two miles off, and then the State was nowhere to be seen....

I have never declined to pay the highway tax, because I am as desirous of being a good neighbor as I am of being a bad subject; and as for supporting schools, I am doing my part to educate my fellow countrymen now. It is for no particular item in the tax-bill that I refuse to pay it. I simply wish to refuse allegiance to the State, to withdraw and stand aloof from it effectually. I do not care to trace the course of my dollar, if I could, till it buys a man or a musket to shoot with—the dollar is innocent—but I am concerned to trace the effects of my allegiance. In fact, I quietly declare war with the State, after my fashion, though I will still make what use and get what advantage of her I can, as is usual in such cases.

If others pay the tax which is demanded of me, from a sympathy with the State, they do but what they have already done in their own case, or rather they abet injustice to a greater extent than the State requires. If they pay the tax from a mistaken interest in the individual taxed, to save his property, or prevent his going to jail, it is because they have not considered wisely how far they let their private feelings interfere with the public good.

This then is my position at present. But one cannot be too much on his guard in such a case, lest his action be biased by obstinacy or an undue regard for

the opinions of men. Let him see that he does only what belongs to himself and
to the hour.

I think sometimes, Why, this people mean well, they are only ignorant; they
would do better if they knew how: why give your neighbors this pain to treat you
as they are not inclined to? But I think again. This is no reason why I should do
as they do, or permit others to suffer much greater pain of a different kind.
Again, I sometimes say to myself, When many millions of men, without heat,
without ill will, without personal feeling of any kind, demand of you a few shillings only, without the possibility, such is their constitution, of retracting or altering their present demand, and without the possibility, on your side, of appeal to
any other millions, why expose yourself to this overwhelming brute force? You
do not resist cold and hunger, the winds and the waves, thus obstinately; you quietly submit to a thousand similar necessities. You do not put your head into the
fire. But just in proportion as I regard this as not wholly a brute force, but partly
a human force, and consider that I have relations to those millions as to so many
millions of men, and not of mere brute or inanimate things, I see that appeal is
possible, first and instantaneously, from them to the Maker of them, and secondly, from them to themselves. But if I put my head deliberately into the fire,
there is no appeal to fire or to the Maker of fire, and I have only myself to blame.
If I could convince myself that I have any right to be satisfied with men as they
are, and to treat them accordingly, and not according, in some respects, to my
requisitions and expectations of what they and I ought to be, then, like a good
Mussulman and fatalist, I should endeavor to be satisfied with things as they are,
and say it is the will of God. And above all, there is this difference between
resisting this and a purely brute or natural force, that I can resist this with some
effect; but I cannot expect, like Orpheus, to change the nature of the rocks and
trees and beasts.

I do not wish to quarrel with any man or nation. I do not wish to split hairs,
to make fine distinctions, or set myself up as better than my neighbors. I seek
rather, I may say, even an excuse for conforming to the laws of the land. I am but
too ready to conform to them. Indeed, I have reason to suspect myself on this
head; and each year, as the tax-gatherer comes round, I find myself disposed to
review the acts and position of the general and State governments, and the spirits
of the people, to discover a pretext for conformity.

> We must affect our country as our parents,
> And if at any time we alienate
> Our love or industry from doing it honor,
> We must respect effects and teach the soul
> Matter of conscience and religion,
> And not desire of rule or benefit.

I believe that the State will soon be able to take all my work of this sort out
of my hands, and then I shall be no better a patriot than my fellow-countrymen.

Seen from a lower point of view, the Constitution, with all its faults, is very good; the law and the courts are very respectable; even this State and this American government are, in may respects, very admirable, and rare things, to be thankful for, such as a great many have described them; but seen from a point of view a little higher, they are what I have described them; seen from a higher still, and the highest, who shall say what they are, or that they are worth looking at or thinking of at all?

However, the government does not concern me much, and I shall bestow the fewest possible thoughts on it. It is not many moments that I live under a government, even in this world. If a man is thought-free, fancy-free, imagination-free, that which is *not* never for a long time appearing *to be* to him, unwise rulers or reformers cannot fatally interrupt him.

I know that most men think differently from myself; but those whose lives are by profession devoted to the study of these or kindred subjects content me as little as any. Statesmen and legislators, standing so completely within the institution, never distinctly and nakedly behold it. They speak of moving society, but have no resting-place without it. They may be men of a certain experience and discrimination, and have no doubt invented ingenious and even useful systems, for which we sincerely thank them; but all their wit and usefulness lie within certain not very wide limits. They are wont to forget that the world is not governed by policy and expediency. Webster never goes behind government, and so cannot speak with authority about it. His words are wisdom to those legislators who contemplate no essential reform in the existing government; but for thinkers, and those who legislate for all time, he never once glances at the subject. I know of those whose serene and wise speculations on this theme would soon reveal the limits of his mind's range and hospitality. Yet, compared with the cheap professions of most reformers, and the still cheaper wisdom and eloquence of politicians in general, his are almost the only sensible and valuable words, and we thank Heaven for him. Comparatively, he is always strong, original, and above all, practical. Still, his quality is not wisdom, but prudence. The lawyer's truth is not Truth, but consistency or a consistent expediency. Truth is always in harmony with herself, and is not concerned chiefly to reveal the justice that may consist with wrong-doing. He well deserves to be called, as he has been called, the Defender of the Constitution. There are really no blows to be given by him but defensive ones. He is not a leader, but a follower. His leaders are the men of '87. "I have never made an effort," he says, "and never propose to make an effort; I have never countenanced an effort, and never mean to countenance an effort, to disturb the arrangement as originally made, by which the various States came into the Union." Still thinking of the sanction which the Constitution gives to slavery, he says, "Because it was a part of the original compact—let it stand." Notwithstanding his special acuteness and ability, he is unable to take a fact out of its merely political relations, and behold it as it lies absolutely to be disposed of by the intellect—what, for instance, it behooves a man to do here in America today with regard to slavery—but ventures, or is driven, to make some such desperate answer as the following while professing to speak absolutely, and as a private man—from which what new and singular code of social duties might be inferred? "The manner," says he, "in which the government of those States where slavery exists are to regulate it is for their own consideration, under their responsibility to their constituents, to the general laws of propriety, humanity, and justice, and to God. Associations formed elsewhere, springing from a feeling of humanity, or other cause, have nothing whatever to do with it. They have never received any encouragement from me, and they never will."

They who know of no purer sources of truth, who have traced up its stream no higher, stand, and wisely stand, by the Bible and the Constitution, and drink at it there with reverence and humility; but they who behold where it comes trickling into this lake or that pool, gird up their loins once more, and continue their pilgrimage toward its fountainhead.

No man with a genius for legislation has appeared in America. They are rare in the history of the world. There are orators, politicians, and eloquent men, by the thousand; but the speaker has not yet opened his mouth to speak who is capable of settling the much-vexed questions of the day. We love eloquence for its own sake, and not for any truth which it may utter, or any heroism it may inspire. Our legislators have not yet learned the comparative value of free-trade and of freedom, of union, and of rectitude, to a nation. They have no genius or talent for comparatively humble questions of taxation and finance, commerce and manufactures and agriculture. If we were left solely to the wordy wit of legislators in Congress for our guidance, uncorrected by the seasonable experience and the effectual complaints of the people, America would not long retain her rank among the nations. For eighteen hundred years, though perchance I have no right to say it, the New Testament has been written; yet where is the legislator who has wisdom and practical talent enough to avail himself of the light which it sheds on the science of legislation?

The authority of government, even such as I am willing to submit to—for I will cheerfully obey those who know and can do better than I, and in many things even those who neither know nor can do as well—is still an impure one: to be strictly just, it must have the sanction and consent of the governed. It can have no pure right over my person and property but what I concede to it. The progress from an absolute to a limited monarchy, from a limited monarchy to a democracy, is a progress toward a true respect for the individual. Even the Chinese philosopher was wise enough to regard the individual as the basis of the empire. Is a democracy, such as we know it, the last improvement possible in government? Is it not possible to take a step further toward recognizing and organizing the rights of man? There will never be a really free and enlightened State until the State comes to recognize the individual as a higher and independent power, from which all its own power and authority are derived, and treats him accordingly. I please myself with imagining a State at last which can afford to be just to all men, and to treat the individual with respect as a neighbor; which even would not think it inconsistent with its own repose if a few were to live aloof from it, not meddling with it, nor embraced by it, who fulfilled all the duties of neighbors and fel-low-men. A State which bore this kind of fruit, and suffered it to drop off as fast as it ripened, would prepare the way for a still more perfect and glorious State, which also I have imagined, but not yet anywhere seen.

7

Ahimsa or the Way of Nonviolence

Mohandas K. Gandhi

Mohandas K. Gandhi (1869–1948), like Thoreau, cannot be summed up in a list of occupations (although his profession was the law); for such a list could not account for the man or his impact in India, the British Empire, and the world. After successfully applying satyagraha campaigns against the South African government as early as 1907, he returned to India to become the spiritual leader of India's Hindus and a major political leader in the struggle for Indian independence. On January 30, 1948, he was assassinated by a Hindu, Nathuram Vinayak Godse, who was opposed to his political views, which attempted to reconcile the violent tensions between Hindus and Muslims in India. The following selection on the meaning of *ahimsa,* or the way of nonviolence, comes from Chapter 4 in Gandhi's book *All Men Are Brothers*. This is not a systematic treatment of the topic of *ahimsa*, but it is rather an impressionistic approach similar to a conversation with a friend, moving from one aspect to another regarding a specific subject. Note the relationship between Gandhi's concept of nonviolence and the religious tradition of Hinduism as stated in the selections from the *Bhagavad-Gita* in Part I.

Non-violence is the greatest force at the disposal of mankind. It is mightier than the mightiest weapon of destruction devised by the ingenuity of man. Destruction is not the law of the humans. Man lives freely by his readiness to die, if need be, at the hands of his brother, never by killing him. Every murder or other injury, no matter for what cause, committed or inflicted on another is a crime against humanity.

The first condition of non-violence is justice all around in every department of life. Perhaps, it is too much to expect of human nature. I do not, however, think so. No one should dogmatize about the capacity of human nature for degradation or exaltation.

Just as one must learn the art of killing in the training for violence, so one must learn the art of dying in the training for non-violence. Violence does not mean emancipation from fear, but discovering the means of combating the cause of fear. Non-violence, on the other hand, has no cause for fear. The votary of non-violence has to cultivate the capacity for sacrifice of the highest type in order to be free from fear. He recks not if he should lose his land, his wealth, and his life. He who has not overcome all fear cannot practice *ahimsa* to perfection. The votary of *ahimsa* has only one fear, that is of God. He who seeks refuge in God ought to have a glimpse of the *Atma* that transcends the body; and the moment one has a glimpse of the imperishable *Atma* one sheds the love of the perishable body. Training in non-violence is thus diametrically opposed to training in violence. Violence is needed for the protection of things external, non-violence is needed for the protection of the *Atma*, for the protection of one's honour.

It is no non-violence if we merely love those that love us. It is non-violence only when we love those that hate us. I know how difficult it is to follow this grand law of love. But are not all great and good things difficult to do? Love of the hater is the most difficult of all. But by the grace of God even this most difficult thing becomes easy to accomplish if we want to do it.

I have found that life persists in the midst of destruction and therefore there must be a higher law than that of destruction. Only under that law would a well-ordered society be intelligible and life worth living. And if that is the law of life, we have to work it out in daily life. Whenever there are wars, wherever you are confronted with an opponent conquer him with love. In this crude manner I have worked it out in my life. That does not mean that all my difficulties are solved. Only I have found that this law of love has answered as the law of destruction has never done.

It is not that I am incapable of anger, for instance, but I succeed on almost all occasions to keep my feelings under control. Whatever may be the result, there is always in me conscious struggle for following the law of non-violence deliberately and ceaselessly. Such a struggle leaves one stronger for it. The more I work at this law, the more I feel the delight in my life, the delight in the scheme of the universe. It gives me a peace and a meaning of the mysteries of nature that I have no power to describe.

If we turn our eyes to the time of which history has any record down to our own time, we shall find that man has been steadily progressing towards *ahimsa*. Our remote ancestors were cannibals. Then came a time when they were fed up with cannibalism and they began to live on chase. Next came a stage when man was ashamed of leading the life of a wandering hunter. He therefore took to agriculture and depended principally on mother earth for his food. Thus from being a nomad he settled down to civilized stable life, founded villages and towns, and from member of a family he became member of a community and a nation. All these are signs of progressive *ahimsa* and diminishing *himsa*. Had it been otherwise, the human species should have been extinct by now, even as many of the lower species have disappeared.

Prophets and *avatars* have also taught the lesson of *ahimsa* more or less. Not one of them has professed to teach *himsa*. And how should it be otherwise?

Himsa does not need to be taught. Man as animal is violent, but as Spirit is non-violent. The moment he awakes to the Spirit within, he cannot remain violent. Either he progresses towards *ahimsa* or rushes to his doom. That is why the prophets and *avatars* have taught the lesson of truth, harmony, brotherhood, justice, etc—all attributes of *ahimsa*.

In the application of *Satyagraha*, I discovered in the earliest stages that pursuit of truth did not admit of violence being inflicted on one's opponent but that he must be weaned from error by patience and sympathy. For, what appears to be truth to the one may appear to be error to another. And patience means self-suffering. So the doctrine came to mean vindication of truth, not by infliction of suffering on the opponent, but on one's self.

In this age of wonders no one will say that a thing or idea is worthless because it is new. To say it is impossible because it is difficult, is again not in consonance with the spirit of the age. Things undreamt of are daily being seen, the impossible is ever becoming possible. We are constantly being astonished these days at the amazing discoveries in the field of violence. But I maintain that far more undreamt of and seemingly impossible discoveries will be made in the field of non-violence.

Some friends have told me that truth and non-violence have no place in politics and worldly affairs. I do not agree. I have no use for them as a means of individual salvation. Their introduction and application in everyday life has been my experiment all along.

No man could be actively non-violent and not rise against social injustice no matter where it occurred.

Passive resistance is a method of securing rights by personal suffering; it is the reverse of resistance by arms. When I refuse to do a thing that is repugnant to my conscience, I use soul-force. For instance, the government of the day has passed a law which is applicable to me. I do not like it. If by using violence I force the government to repeal the law, I am employing what may be termed body-force. If I do not obey the law and accept the penalty for its breach, I use soul-force. It involves sacrifice of self.

Everybody admits that sacrifice of self is infinitely superior to sacrifice of others. Moreover, if this kind of force is used in a cause that is unjust, only the person using it suffers. He does not make others suffer for his mistakes. Men have before now done many things which were subsequently found to have been wrong. No man can claim that he is absolutely in the right or that a particular thing is wrong because he thinks so, but it is wrong for him so long as that is his deliberate judgment. It is therefore moot that he should not do that which he knows to be wrong, and suffer the consequence whatever it may be. This is the key to the use of soul-force.

A votary of *ahimsa* cannot subscribe to the utilitarian formula (of the greatest good of the greatest number). He will strive for the greatest good of all and die in the attempt to realize the ideal. He will therefore be willing to die, so that the others may live. He will serve himself with the rest, by himself dying. The greatest good of all inevitably includes the good of the greatest number, and, therefore, he and the utilitarian will converge in many points in their career but there does come a time when they must part company, and even work in opposite directions. The utilitarian to be logical will never sacrifice himself. The absolutist will even sacrifice himself.

You might of course say that there can be no non-violent rebellion and there has been none known to history. Well, it is my ambition to provide an instance, and it is my dream that my country may win its freedom through non-violence. And, I would like to repeat to the world times without number, that I will not purchase my country's freedom at the cost of non-violence. My marriage to non-violence is such an absolute thing that I would rather commit suicide than be deflected from my position. I have not mentioned truth in this connection, simply because truth cannot be expressed excepting by non-violence.

Up to the year 1906, I simply relied on appeal to reason. I was a very industrious reformer. I was a good draftsman, as I always had a close grip of facts which in its turn was the necessary result of my meticulous regard for truth. But I found that reason failed to produce an impression when the critical moment arrived in South Africa. My people were excited; even a worm will and does sometimes turn—and there was talk of wreaking vengeance. I had then to choose between allying myself to violence or finding out some other method of meeting the crisis and stopping the rot and it came to me that we should refuse to obey legislation that was degrading and let them put us in jail if they liked. Thus came into being the moral equivalent of war. I was then a loyalist, because I implicitly believed that the sum total of the activities of the British Empire was good for India and for humanity. Arriving in England soon after the outbreak of the war I plunged into it and later when I was forced to go to India as a result of the pleurisy that I had developed, I led a recruiting campaign at the risk of my life, and to the horror of some of my friends. The disillusionment came in 1919 after the passage of the Black Rowlatt Act and the refusal of the government to give the simple elementary redress of proved wrongs that we had asked for. And so, in 1920, I became a rebel. Since then the conviction has been growing upon me, that things of fundamental importance to the people are not secured by reason alone but have to be purchased with their suffering. Suffering is the law of human beings; war is the law of the jungle. But suffering is infinitely more powerful than the law of the jungle for converting the opponent and opening his ears, which are otherwise shut, to the voice of reason. Nobody has probably drawn up more petitions or espoused more forlorn causes than I and I have come to this fundamental conclusion that if you want something really important to be done you must not merely satisfy the reason, you must move the heart also. The appeal of reason is more to the head but the penetration of the heart comes from suffering. It opens up the inner understanding in man. Suffering is the badge of the human race, not the sword.

Perfect non-violence is impossible so long as we exist physically, for we would want some space at least to occupy. Perfect non-violence whilst you are inhabiting the body is only a theory like Euclid's point or straight line, but we have to endeavor every moment of our lives.

In its positive form, *ahimsa* means the largest love, greatest charity. If I am a follower of *ahimsa*, I *must love* my enemy. I must apply the same rules to the wrong-doer who is my enemy or a stranger to me, as I would to my wrong-doing father or son. This active *ahimsa* necessarily includes truth and fearlessness. As man cannot deceive the loved one, he does not fear or frighten him or her. Gift of life is the greatest of all gifts; a man who gives it in reality, disarms all hostility. He has paved the way for an honorable understanding. And none who is himself subject to fear can bestow that gift. He must therefore be himself fearless. A man cannot practice *ahimsa* and be a coward at the same time. The practice of *ahimsa* calls forth the greatest courage.

Non-violence is "not a resignation from all real fighting against wickedness." On the contrary, the non-violence of my conception is a more active and real fight against wickedness than retaliation whose very nature is to increase wickedness. I contemplate a mental and therefore a moral opposition to immoralities. I seek entirely to blunt the edge of the tyrant's sword, not by putting up against it a sharper edged weapon, but by disappointing his expectation that I would be offering physical resistance. The resistance of the soul that I should offer would elude him. It would first dazzle him and at least compel recognition from him, which recognition would not humiliate but would uplift him. It may be urged that this is an ideal state. And so it is.

Ahimsa is a comprehensive principle. We are helpless mortals caught in the conflagration of *himsa*. The saying that life lives on life has a deep meaning in it. Man cannot for a moment live without consciously or unconsciously committing outward *himsa*. The very fact of his living—eating, drinking and moving about— necessarily involves some *himsa*, destruction of life, be it ever so minute. A votary of *ahimsa* therefore remains true to his faith if the spring of all his actions is compassion, if he shuns to the best of his ability the destruction of the tiniest creature, tries to save it, and thus incessantly strives to be free from the deadly coil of *himsa*.

Then again, because underlying *ahimsa* is the unity of all life, the error of one cannot but affect all, and hence man cannot be wholly free from *himsa*. So long as he continues to be a social being, he cannot but participate in the *himsa* that the very existence involves. When two nations are fighting, the duty of a votary of *ahimsa* is to stop war. He who is not equal to that duty, he who has no power of resisting war, he who is not qualified to resist war, may take part in war, and yet whole-heartedly try to free himself, his nation and the world from war.

Non-violence to be a potent force must begin with the mind. Non-violence of the mere body without the co-operation of the mind is non-violence of the weak or the cowardly, and has therefore no potency. If we bear malice and hatred in our bosoms and pretend not to retaliate, it must recoil upon us and lead to our destruction. For abstention from mere bodily violence not to be injurious, it is at least necessary not to entertain hatred if we cannot generate active love.

He is no follower of *ahimsa* who does not care a straw if he kills a man by inches by deceiving him in a trade or who would protect by force of arms a few cows and make away with the butcher or who, in order to do a supposed good to his country, does not mind killing off a few officials. All these are actuated by hatred, cowardice, and fear.

I object to violence because when it appears to do good, the good is only temporary; the evil it does is permanent. I do not believe that the killing of even every Englishman can do the slightest good to India. The millions will be just as badly off as they are today, if someone made it possible to kill off every Englishman tomorrow. The responsibility is more ours than that of the English for the present state of things. The English will be powerless to do evil if we will but be good. Hence my incessant emphasis on reform from within.

History teaches one that those who have, no doubt with honest motives, ousted the greedy by using brute force against them, have in their turn become a prey to the disease of the conquered.

If I can have nothing to do with the organized violence of the government, I can have less to do with the unorganized violence of the people. I would prefer to be crushed between the two.

The strength to kill is not essential for self-defense; one ought to have the strength to die. When a man is fully ready to die, he will not even desire to offer violence. Indeed, I may put it down as a self-evident proposition that the desire to kill is in inverse proportion to the desire to die. And history is replete with instances of men who by dying with courage and compassion on their lips converted the hearts of their violent opponents.

It has become the fashion these days that society cannot be organized or run on non-violent lines. I join issue on that point. In a family, when a father slaps his delinquent child, the latter does not think of retaliating. He obeys his father not because of the deterrent effect of the slap but because of the offended love which he senses behind it. That, in my opinion, is an epitome of the way in which society is or should be governed. What is true of the family must be true of society which is but a larger family.

I am not opposed to the progress of science as such. On the contrary, the scientific spirit of the West commands my admiration and if that admiration is qualified, it is because the scientist of the West takes no note of God's lower creation. I abhor vivisection with my whole soul. I detest the unpardonable slaughter of innocent life in the name of science and humanity so-called, and all the scientific discoveries stained with innocent blood I count as of no consequence. If the circulation of blood theory could not have been discovered without vivisection, the human kind could well have done without it. And I see the day clearly dawning when the honest scientist of the West will put limitations upon the present methods of pursuing knowledge.

Jesus Christ, Daniel and Socrates represented the purest form of passive resistance or soul-force. All these teachers counted their bodies as nothing in comparison to their soul. Tolstoy was the best and brightest (modern) exponent of the doctrine. He not only expounded it, but lived according to it. In India, the doctrine was understood and commonly practiced long before it came into vogue in Europe. It is easy to see that soul-force is infinitely superior to body-force. If people in order to secure redress of wrongs resort to soul-force, much of the present suffering will be avoided.

Buddha fearlessly carried the war into the enemy's camp and brought down on its knees an arrogant priesthood. Christ drove out the money-changers from the temple of Jerusalem and drew down curses from Heaven upon the hypocrites and the Pharisees. Both were for intensely direct action. But even as Buddha and Christ chastised, they showed unmistakable gentleness and love behind every act of theirs. They would not raise a finger against their enemies, but would gladly surrender themselves rather than the truth for which they lived. Buddha would have died resisting the priesthood, if the majesty of his love had not proved to be equal to the task of bending the priesthood. Christ died on the cross with a crown of thorns on his head defying the might of a whole empire. And if I raise resistances of a non-violent character, I simply and humbly follow in the footsteps of the great teachers.

Ahimsa is soul-force and the soul is imperishable, changeless and eternal. The atom bomb is the acme of physical force and, as such, subject to the law of dissipation, decay and death that governs the physical universe. Our scriptures bear witness that when soul-force is fully awakened in us, it becomes irresistible. But the test and condition of full awakening is that it must permeate every pore of our being and emanate with every breath that we breathe.

But no institution can be made non-violent by compulsion. Non-violence and truth cannot be written into a constitution. They have to be adopted of one's own free will. They must sit naturally upon us like next-to-skin garments or else they become a contradiction in terms.

My non-violence does not admit of running away from danger and leaving dear ones unprotected. Between violence and cowardly flight, I can only prefer violence to cowardice. I can no more preach non-violence to a coward than I can tempt a blind man to enjoy healthy scenes. Non-violence is the summit of bravery. And in my own experience, I have had no difficulty in demonstrating to men trained in the school of violence the superiority of non-violence. As a coward, which I was for years, I harbored violence. I began to prize non-violence only when I began to shed cowardice.

Supposing I was a Negro, and my sister was ravished by a white or lynched by a whole community, what would be my duty? I ask myself. And the answer comes to me: I must not wish ill to these, but neither must I co-operate with them. It may be that ordinarily I depend on the lynching community for my livelihood. I refuse to co-operate with them, refuse even to touch the food that comes from them, and I refuse to co-operate with even my brother Negroes who tolerate the wrong. That is the self-immolation I mean. I have often in my life resorted to the plan. Of course, a mechanical act of starvation will mean nothing. One's own faith must remain undimmed whilst life ebbs out, minute by minute. But I am a very poor specimen of the practice of non-violence, and my answer may not convince you. But I am striving very hard, and even if I do not succeed fully in this life, my faith will not diminish.

8

Selections from Gandhi's Autobiography

Mohandas Karamchand Gandhi

Gandhi was the greatest moral force in Indian history. For the accomplishment of liberty, justice, and peace, he rediscovered the old techniques of ahimsa and saty-agraha. He revealed to the masses not a power of rifles and machine guns but the power innate in each individual that makes wars impossible. Gandhi's whole life was an experiment with truth. His creed was the service of God through his ser-vice of humanity. To him, God was Truth, and Truth was God. In 1908 Gandhi began his satyagraha campaign in South Africa and continued with it when he returned to India from South Africa in 1915. In 1913, South Africa repealed some of the discriminatory legislation against the Indian community. With his nonviolent method of satyagraha, Gandhi made India independent from British rule on August 15, 1947. In these selections, he writes about his experiment with the discipline of satyagraha, which literally means truth-force or soul-force, that is. holding on to Truth at any cost. Gandhi shows how the seeds of satyagraha were created in South Africa and came to fruition in India. Gandhi studied all religious scriptures and took from each of them what appealed to him. According to him, the perfect vision of Truth can follow only a complete realization of ahimsa, or nonviolence. Gandhi has proved to the world that ahimsa or nonvio-lence can actually be practiced by a country. It is important to note that from 1956 to 1965, fourteen African nations achieved independence. Except for Alge-ria and Rhodesia, all other twelve African nations achieved their independence by nonviolent means.

THE £3 TAX

Balasundaram's case brought me into touch with the indentured Indians. What impelled me, however, to make a deep study of their condition was the campaign for bringing them under special heavy taxation.

In the same year, 1894, the Natal Government sought to impose an annual tax of £25 on the indentured Indians. The proposal astonished me. I put the matter before the Congress for discussion, and it was immediately resolved to organize the necessary opposition.

At the outset I must explain briefly the genesis of the tax.

About the year 1860 the Europeans in Natal, finding that there was considerable scope for sugar-cane cultivation, felt themselves in need of labour. Without outside labour the cultivation of cane and the manufacture of sugar were impossible, as the Natal Zulus were not suited to this form of work. The Natal Government therefore corresponded with the Indian Government, and secured their permission to recruit Indian labour. These recruits were to sign an indenture to work in Natal for five years, and at the end of the term they were to be at liberty to settle there and to have full rights of ownership of land. Those were the inducements held out to them, for the whites then had looked forward to improving their agriculture by the industry of the Indian labourers after the term of their indentures had expired.

But the Indians gave more than had been expected of them. They grew large quantities of vegetables. They introduced a number of Indian varieties and made it possible to grow the local varieties cheaper. They also introduced the mango. Nor did their enterprise stop at agriculture. They entered trade. They purchased land for building, and many raised themselves from the status of labourers to that of owners of land and houses. Merchants from India followed them and settled there for trade. The late Sheth Abubakar Amad was first among them. He soon built up an extensive business.

The white traders were alarmed. When they first welcomed the Indian labourers, they had not reckoned with their business skill. They might be tolerated as independent agriculturists, but their competition in trade could not be brooked.

This sowed the seed of the antagonism to Indians. Many other factors contributed to its growth. Our different ways of living, our simplicity, our contentment with small gains, our indifference to the laws of hygiene and sanitation, our slowness in keeping our surroundings clean and tidy, and our stinginess in keeping our houses in good repair—all these combined with the difference in religion, contributed to fan the flame of antagonism. Through legislation this antagonism found its expression in the disfranchising bill to impose a tax on the indentured Indians. Independent of legislation a number of pinpricks had already been started.

The first suggestion was that the Indian labourers should be forcibly repatriated, so that the term of their indentures might expire in India. The Government of India was not likely to accept the suggestion. Another proposal was therefore made to the effect that

1. the indentured labourer should return to India on the expiry of his indenture; or that

2. he should sign a fresh indenture every two years, an increment being given at each renewal; and that

3. in the case of his refusal to return to India or renew the indenture he should pay an annual tax of £25.

A deputation composed of Sir Henry Binns and Mr. Mason was sent to India to get the proposal approved by the Government there. The Viceroy at that time was Lord Elgin. He disapproved of the £25 tax, but agreed to a poll tax of £3. I thought then, as I do even now, that this was a serious blunder on the part of the Viceroy. In giving his approval he had in no way thought of the interests of India. It was no part of his duty thus to accommodate the Natal Europeans. In the course of three or four years an indentured labourer with his wife and each male child over 16 and female child over 13 came under the impost. To levy a yearly tax of £12 from a family of four—husband, wife and two children—when the average income of the husband was never more than 14s. a month, was atrocious and unknown anywhere else in the world.

We organized a fierce campaign against this tax. If the Natal Indian Congress had remained silent on the subject, the Viceroy might have approved of even the £25 tax. The reduction from £ 25 to £3 was probably due solely to the Congress agitation. But I may be mistaken in thinking so. It may be possible that the Indian Government had disapproved of the £25 tax from the beginning and reduced it to £3, irrespective of the opposition from the Congress. In any case it was a breach of trust on the part of the Indian Government. As trustee of the welfare of India, the Viceroy ought never to have approved of this inhuman tax.

The Congress could not regard it as any great achievement to have succeeded in getting the tax reduced from £25 to £3. The regret was still there that it had not completely safeguarded the interests of the indentured Indians. It ever remained its determination to get the tax remitted, but it was twenty years before the determination was realized. And when it was realized, it came as a result of the labours of not only the Natal Indians but of all the Indians in South Africa. The breach of faith with the late Mr. Gokhale became the occasion of the final campaign, in which the indentured Indians took their full share, some of them losing their lives as a result of the firing that was resorted to, and over ten thousand suffering imprisonment.

But truth triumphed in the end. The sufferings of the Indians were the expression of that truth. Yet it would not have triumphed except for unflinching faith, great patience and incessant effort. Had the community given up the struggle, had the Congress abandoned the campaign and submitted to the tax as inevitable, the hated impost would have continued to be levied from the indentured Indians until this day, to the eternal shame of the Indians in South Africa and of the whole of India.

COMPARATIVE STUDY OF RELIGIONS

If I found myself entirely absorbed in the service of the community, the reason behind it was my desire for self-realization. I had made the religion of service my own, as I felt that God could be realized only through service. And service for me was the service of India, because it came to me without my seeking, because I had an aptitude for it. I had gone to South Africa for travel, for finding an escape from Kahiawad intrigues and for gaining my own livelihood. But as I have said, I found myself in search of God and striving for self-realization.

Christian friends had whetted my appetite for knowledge, which had become almost insatiable, and they would not leave me in peace, even if I desired to be indifferent. In Durban Mr. Spencer Walton, the head of the South Africa General Mission, found me out. I became almost a member of his family. At the back of this acquaintance was of course my contact with Christians in Pretoria. Mr. Walton had a manner all his own. I do not recollect his ever having invited me to embrace Christianity. But he placed his life as an open book before me, and let me watch all his movements. Mrs. Walton was a very gentle and talented woman. I liked the attitude of this couple. We knew the fundamental differences between us. Any amount of discussion could not efface them. Yet even differences prove helpful, where there are tolerance, charity and truth. I liked Mr. and Mrs. Walton's humility, perseverance and devotion to work, and we met very frequently.

This friendship kept alive my interest in religion. It was impossible now to get the leisure that I used to have in Pretoria for my religious studies. But what little time I could spare I turned to good account. My religious correspondence continued. Raycahndbhai was guiding me. Some friend sent me Narmadashanker's book *Dharma Vichar.* Its preface proved very helpful. I had heard about the Bohemian way in which the poet had lived, and a description in the preface of the revolution effected in his life by his religious studies captivated me. I came to like the book, and read it from cover to cover with attention. I read with interest Max Muller's book, *India—What Can It Teach Us?* and the translation of the *Upanishads* published by the Theosophical Society. All this enhanced my regard for Hinduism, and its beauties began to grow upon me. It did not, however, prejudice me against other religions. I read Washington Irving's *Life of Mahomet and His Successors* and Carlyle's panegyric on the Prophet. These books raised Muhammad in my estimation. I also read a book called *The Sayings of Zarathustra.*

Thus I gained more knowledge of the different religions. The study stimulated my self-introspection and fostered in me the habit of putting into practice whatever appealed to me in my studies. Thus I began some of the Yogic practices, as well as I could understand them from a reading of the Hindu books. But I could not get on very far, and decided to follow them with the help of some expert when I returned to India. The desire has never been fulfilled.

I made too an intensive study of Tolststoy's books. *The Gospels in Brief,* *What to Do?* and other books made a deep impression on me. I began to realize more and more the infinite possibilities of universal love.

About the same time I came in contact with another Christian family. At their suggestion I attended the Wesleyan church every Sunday. For these days I also had their standing invitation to dinner. The church did not make a favour-able impression on me. The sermons seemed to be uninspiring. The congrega-tion did not strike me as being particularly religious. They were not an assembly of devout souls; they appeared rather to be worldly-minded people, going to church for recreation and in conformity to custom. Here, at times, I would invol-untarily doze. I was ashamed, but some of my neighbors, who were in no better case, lightened the shame. I could not go on long like this, and soon gave up attending the service.

My connection with the family I used to visit every Sunday was abruptly broken. In fact it may be said that I was warned to visit it no more. It happened thus. My hostess was a good and simple woman, but somewhat narrow-minded. We always discussed religious subjects. I was then re-reading Arnold's *Light of* *Asia.* Once we began to compare the life of Jesus with that of Buddha. "Look at Gautama's compassion!" said I. "It was not confined to mankind, it was extended to all living beings. Does not one's heart overflow with love to think of the lamb joyously perched on his shoulders? One fails to notice this love for all living beings in the life of Jesus." The comparison pained the good lady. I could under-stand her feelings. I cut the matter short, and we went to the dining room. Her son, a cherub aged scarcely five, was also with us. I am happiest when in the midst of children, and this youngster and I had long been friends. I spoke deri-sively of the piece of meat on his plate and in high praise of the apple on mine. The innocent boy was carried away and joined in my praise of the fruit.

But the mother? She was dismayed.

I was warned. I checked myself and changed the subject. The following week I visited the family as usual, but not without trepidation. I did not see that I should stop going there, I did not think it proper either. But the good lady made my way easy.

"Mr. Gandhi," she said, "please don't take it ill if I feel obliged to tell you that my boy is none the better for your company. Every day he hesitates to eat meat and asks for fruit, reminding me of your arguement. This is too much. If he gives up meat, he is bound to get weak, if not ill. How could I bear it? Your dis-cussions should henceforth be only with us elders. They are sure to react badly on children."

"Mrs.,—" I replied, "I am sorry. I can understand your feelings as a parent, for I too have children. We can very easily end this unpleasant state of things. What I eat and omit to eat is bound to have a greater effect on the child than what I say. The best way, therefore, is for me to stop these visits. That certainly need not affect our friendship."

"I thank you," she said with evident relief.

RESULT OF INTROSPECTION

When, in 1893, I came in close contact with Christian friends, I was a mere novice. They tried hard to bring home to me, and make me accept, the message of Jesus, and I was a humble and respectful listener with an open mind. At that time I naturally studied Hinduism to the best of my ability and endeavoured to understand other religions.

In 1903 the position was somewhat changed. Theosophist friends certainly intended to draw me into their society, but that was with a view to getting something from me as a Hindu. Theosophical literature is replete with Hindu influence, and so these friends expected that I should be helpful to them. I explained that my Samskrit study was not much to speak of, that I had not read the Hindu scriptures in the original, and that even my acquaintance with the translations was of the slightest. But being believers in *samskara* (tendencies caused by previous births) and *punarjanma* (rebirth), they assumed that I should be able to render some help. And so I felt like a Triton among the minnows. I started reading Swami Vivekananda's *Rajayoga* with some of these friends and M. N. Dvivedi's *Rajayoga* with others. I had to read Patanjali's *Yoga Sutras* with one friend and the *Bhagavadgita* with quite a number. We formed a sort of Seekers' Club where we had regular readings. I already had faith in the *Gita*, which had a fascination for me. Now I realized the necessity of diving deeper into it. I had one or two translations, by means of which I tried to understand the original Samskrit. I decided also to get by heart one or two verses every day. For this purpose I employed the time of my morning ablutions. The operation took me thirty-five minutes, fifteen minutes for the tooth brush and twenty for the bath. The first I used to do standing in western fashion. So on the wall opposite I stuck slips of paper on which were written the *Gita* verses and referred to them now and then to help my memory. This time was found sufficient for memorizing the daily portion and recalling the verses already learnt. I remember having thus committed to memory thirteen chapters. But the memorizing of the *Gita* had to give way to other work and the creation and nurture of Satyagraha, which absorbed all my thinking time, as the latter may be said to be doing even now.

What effect this reading of the *Gita* had on my friends only they can say, but to me the *Gita* became an infallible guide of conduct. It became my dictionary of daily reference. Just as I turned to the English dictionary for the meanings of English words that I did not understand, I turned to this dictionary of conduct for a ready solution of all my troubles and trials. Words like *aparigraha* (non-possession) and *samabhava* (equability) gripped me. How to cultivate and preserve that equability was the question. How was one to treat alike insulting, insolent and corrupt officials, co-workers of yesterday raising meaningless opposition, and men who had always been good to one? How was one to divest oneself of all possessions? Was not the body itself possession enough? Were not wife and children possessions? Was I to destroy all the cupboards of books I had? Was I to give up all I had and follow Him? Straight came the answer: I could not follow Him unless I gave up all I had. My study of English law came to my help. Snell's discussion of the maxims of Equity came to my memory. I understood more clearly in the light of the *Gita* teaching the implication of the word "trustee." My regard for jurisprudence increased, I discovered in it religion. I understood the Gita teaching of non-possession to mean that those who desired salvation should act like the trustee who, though having control over great possessions, regards not an iota of them as his own. It became clear to me as daylight that non-possession and equability presupposed a change of heart, a change of attitude. I then wrote to Revashankarbhai to allow the insurance policy to lapse and get whatever could be recovered, or else to regard the premiums already paid as lost, for I had become convinced that God, who created my wife and children as well as myself, would take care of them. To my brother, who had been as father to me, I wrote explaining that I had given him all that I had saved up to that moment, but that henceforth he should expect nothing from me, for future savings, if any, would be utilized for the benefit of the community.

I could not easily make my brother understand this. In stern language he explained to me my duty towards him. I should not, he said, aspire to be wiser than our father. I must support the family as he did. I pointed out to him that I was doing exactly what our father had done. The meaning of "family" had but to be slightly widened and the wisdom of my step would become clear.

My brother gave me up and practically stopped all communication. I was deeply distressed, but it would have been a greater distress to give up what I considered to be my duty, and I preferred the lesser. But that did not affect my devotion to him, which remained as pure and great as ever. His great love for me was at the root of his misery. He did not so much want my money as that I should be well-behaved towards the family. Near the end of his life, however, he appreciated my viewpoint. When almost on his deathbed, he realized that my step had been right and wrote me a most pathetic letter. He apologized to me, if indeed a father may apologize to his son. He commended his sons to my care, to be brought up as I thought fit, and expressed his impatience to meet me. He cabled that he would like to come to South Africa and I cabled in reply that he could. But that was not to be. Nor could his desire as regards his sons be fulfilled. He died before he could start for South Africa. His sons had been brought up in the old atmosphere and could not change their course of life. I could not draw them to me. It was not their fault. "Who can say thus far, no further, to the tide of his own nature?" Who can erase the impressions with which he is born? It is idle to expect one's children and wards necessarily to follow the same course of evolution as oneself.

This instance to some extent serves to show what a terrible responsibility it is to be a parent.

THE BIRTH OF SATYAGRAHA

Events were so shaping themselves in Johannesburg as to make this self-purification on my part a preliminary as it were to Satyagraha. I can now see that all the principal events in my life, culminating in the vow of *brahmacharya*, were secretly preparing me for it. The principle called Satyagraha came into being before that name was invented. Indeed when it was born, I myself could not say what it was. In Gujarati also we used the English phrase "passive resistance" to describe it. When in a meeting of Europeans I found that the term "passive resistance" was too narrowly construed, that it was supposed to be a weapon of the weak, that it could be characterized by hatred, and that it could finally manifest itself as violence, I had to demur to all these statements and explain the real nature of the Indian movement. It was clear that a new word must be coined by the Indians to designate their struggle.

But I could not for the life of me find out a new name, and therefore offered a nominal prize through *Indian Opinion* to the reader who made the best suggestion on the subject. As a result Maganlal Gandhi coined the word "Sadagraha" (Sat = truth, Agraha = firmness) and won the prize. But in order to make it clearer I changed the word to "Satyagraha" which has since become current in Gujarati as a designation for the struggle.

The history of this struggle is for all practical purposes a history of the remainder of my life in South Africa and especially of my experiments with truth in that sub-continent. I wrote the major portion of this history in Yeravda jail and finished it after I was released. It was published in *Navajivan* and subsequently issued in book form. Sjt. Valji Govindji Desai has been translating it into English for *Current Thought*, but I am now arranging to have the English translation [since published by S. Ganesa, Triplicane, Madras] published in book form at an early date, so that those who will may be able to familiarize themselves with my most important experiments in South Africa. I would recommend a perusal of my history of Satyagraha in South Africa to such readers as have not seen it already. I will not repeat what I have put down there, but in my next few chapters will deal only with a few personal incidents of my life in South Africa which has not been covered by that history. And when I have done with these, I will at once proceed to give the reader some idea of my experiments in India. Therefore, anyone who wishes to consider these experiments in their strict chronological order will now do well to keep the history of Satyagraha in South Africa before him.

TRAINING OF THE SPIRIT

The spiritual training of the boys was a much more difficult matter than their physical and mental training. I relied little on religious books for the training of the spirit. Of course I believed that every student should be acquainted with the elements of his own religion and have a general knowledge of his own scriptures, and therefore I provided for such knowledge as best I could. But that, to my mind, was part of the intellectual training. Long before I undertook the education of the youngsters of the Tolstoy Farm I had realized that the training of the spirit was a thing by itself. To develop the spirit is to build character and to enable one to work towards a knowledge of God and self-realization. And I held that this was an essential part of the training of the young, and that all training without culture of the spirit was of no use, and might be even harmful.

I am familiar with the superstition that self-realization is possible only in the fourth stage of life, *i.e., sannyasa* (renunciation). But it is a matter of common knowledge that those who defer preparation for this invaluable experience until the last stage of life attain not self-realization but old age amounting to a second and pitiable childhood, living as a burden on this earth. I have a full recollection that I held these views even whilst I was teaching, *i.e.,* in 1911–12, though I might not then have expressed them in identical language.

How then was this spiritual training to be given? I made the children memorize and recite hymns, and read to them from books on moral training. But that was far from satisfying me. As I came into closer contact with them I saw that it was not through books that one could impart training of the spirit. Just as physical training was to be imparted through physical exercise, and intellectual through intellectual exercise, even so the training of the spirit was possible only through the exercise of the spirit. And the exercise of the spirit entirely depended on the life and character of the teacher. The teacher had always to be mindful of his p's and q's, whether he was in the midst of his boys or not.

It is possible for a teacher situated miles away to affect the spirit of the pupils by his way of living. It would be idle for me, if I were a liar, to teach boys to tell the truth. A cowardly teacher would never succeed in making his boys valiant, and a stranger to self-restraint could never teach his pupils the value of self-restraint. I saw, therefore, that I must be an eternal object-lesson to the boys and girls living with me. They thus became my teachers, and I learnt I must be good and live straight, if only for their sakes. I may say that the increasing discipline and restraint I imposed on myself at Tolstoy Farm was mostly due to those wards of mine.

One of them was wild, unruly, given to lying, and quarrelsome. On one occasion he broke out most violently. I was exasperated. I never punished my boys, but this time I was very angry. I tried to reason with him. But he was adamant and even tried to overreach me. At last I picked up a ruler lying at hand and delivered a blow on his arm. I trembled as I struck him. I dare say he noticed it. This was an entirely novel experience for them all. The boy cried out and begged to be forgiven. He cried not because the beating was painful to him; he could, if he had been so minded, have paid me back in the same coin, being a stoutly built youth of seventeen; but he realized my pain in being driven to this violent resource. Never again after this incident did he disobey me. But I still repent that violence resource. I am afraid I exhibited before him that day not the spirit, but the brute, in me.

I have always been opposed to corporal punishment. I remember only one occasion on which I physically punished one of my sons. I have therefore never until this day been able to decide whether I was right or wrong in using the ruler. Probably it was improper, for it was prompted by anger and a desire to punish. Had it been an expression only of my distress, I should have considered it justified. But the motive in this case was mixed.

This incident set me thinking and taught me a better method of correcting students. I do not know whether that method would have availed on the occasion in question. The youngster soon forgot the incident, and I do not think he ever showed great improvement. But the incident made me understand better the duty of a teacher towards his pupils.

Cases of misconduct on the part of the boys often occurred after this, but I never resorted to corporal punishment. Thus in my endeavour to impart spiritual training to the boys and girls under me, I came to understand better and better the power of the spirit.

A SPIRITUAL DILEMMA

As soon as the news reached South Africa that I along with other Indians had offered my services in the war, I received two cables. One of these was from Mr. Polak who questioned the consistency of my action with my profession of *ahimsa*.

I had to a certain extent anticipated this objection, for I had discussed the question in my *Hind Swaraj (Indian Home Rule)*, and used to discuss it day in and day out with friends in South Africa. All of us recognized the immorality of war. If I was not prepared to prosecute my assailant, much less should I be willing to participate in a war, especially when I knew nothing of the justice or otherwise of the cause of the combatants. Friends of course knew that I had previously served in the Boer War, but they assumed that my view had since undergone a change.

As a matter of fact the very same line of argument that persuaded me to take part in the Boer War had weighed with me on this occasion. It was quite clear to me that participation in war could never be consistent with *ahimsa*. But it is not always given to one to be equally clear about one's duty. A votary of truth is often obliged to grope in the dark.

Ahimsa is a comprehensive principle. We are helpless mortals caught in the conflagration of *himsa*. The saying that life lives on life has a deep meaning in it. Man cannot for a moment live without consciously or unconsciously committing outward *himsa*. The very fact of his living—eating, drinking and moving about—necessarily involves some *himsa*, destruction of life, be it ever so minute. A votary of *ahimsa* therefore remains true to his faith if the spring of all his actions is compassion, if he shuns to the best of his ability the destruction of the tiniest creature, tries to save it, and thus incessantly strives to be free from the deadly coil of *himsa.* He will be constantly growing in self-restraint and compassion, but he can never become entirely free from outward *himsa.*

Then again, because underlying *ahimsa* is the unity of all life, the error of one cannot but affect all, and hence man cannot be wholly free from *himsa.* So long as he continues to be a social being, he cannot but participate in the *himsa* that the very existence of society involves. When two nations are fighting, the duty of a votary of *ahimsa* is to stop the war. He who is not equal to that duty, he who has no power of resisting war, he who is not qualified to resist war, may take part in war, and yet whole-heartedly try to free himself, his nation and the world from war.

I had hoped to improve my status and that of my people through the British Empire. Whilst in England I was enjoying the protection of the British Fleet, and taking shelter as I did under its armed might, I was directly participating in its potential violence. Therefore, if I desired to retain my connection with the Empire and to live under its banner, one of three courses was open to me: I could declare open resistance to the war and, in accordance with the law of Satyagraha, boycott the Empire until it changed its military policy; or I could seek imprisonment by civil disobedience of such of its laws as were fit to be disobeyed; or I could participate in the war on the side of the Empire and thereby acquire the capacity and fitness for resisting the violence of war. I lacked this capacity and fitness, so I thought there was nothing for it but to serve in the war.

I make no distinction, from the point of view of *ahimsa,* between combatants and non-combatants. He who volunteers to serve a band of dacoits, by working as their carrier, or their watchman while they are about their business, or their nurse when they are wounded, is as much guilty of dacoity as the dacoits themselves. In the same way those who confine themselves to attending to the wounded in battle cannot be absolved from the guilt of war.

I had argued the whole thing out to myself in this manner, before I received Polak's cable, and soon after its receipt, I discussed these views with several friends and concluded that it was my duty to offer to serve in the war. Even today I see no flaw in that line of argument, nor am I sorry for my action, holding, as I then did, views favourable to the British connection.

I know that even then I could not carry conviction with all my friends about the correctness of my position. The question is subtle. It admits of differences of opinion, and therefore I have submitted my argument as clearly as possible to those who believe in *ahimsa* and who are making serious efforts to practise it in every walk of life. A devotee of Truth may not do anything in deference to convention. He must always hold himself open to correction, and whenever he discovers himself to be wrong he must confess it at all costs and atone for it.

MINIATURE SATYAGRAHA

Though I thus took part in the war as a matter of duty, it chanced that I was not only unable directly to participate in it, but actually compelled to offer what may be called miniature Satyagraha even at that critical juncture.

I have already said that an officer was appointed in charge of our training, as soon as our names were approved and enlisted. We were all under the impression that this Commanding Officer was to be our chief only so far as technical matters were concerned, and that in all other matters I was the head of our Corps, which was directly responsible to me in matters of internal discipline; that is to say, the Commanding Officer had to deal with the Corps through me. But from the first the officer left us under no such delusion.

Mr. Sorabji Adajania was a shrewd man. He warned me. "Beware of this man," he said. "He seems inclined to lord it over us. We will have none of his orders. We are prepared to look upon him as our instructor. But the youngsters he has appointed to instruct us also feel as though they had come as our masters."

These youngsters were Oxford students who had come to instruct us and whom the Commanding Officer had appointed to be our section leaders.

I also had not failed to notice the high-handedness of the Commanding Officer, but I asked Sorabji not to be anxious and tried to pacify him. But he was not the man to be easily convinced.

"You are too trusting. These people will deceive you with wretched words, and when at last you see through them, you will ask us to resort to Satyagraha, and so come to grief, and bring us all to grief along with you," said he with a smile.

"What else but grief can you hope to come to after having cast in your lot with me?" said I. "A Satyagrahi is born to be deceived. Let the Commanding Officer deceive us. Have I not told you times without number that ultimately a deceiver only deceives himself?"

Sorabji gave a loud laugh. "Well, then," said he, "continue to be deceived. You will some day meet your death in Satyagraha and drag poor mortals like me behind you."

These words put me in mind of what the late Miss Emily Hobhouse wrote to me with regard to non-cooperation: "I should not be surprised if one of these days you have to go to the gallows for the sake of truth. May God show you the right path and protect you."

The talk with Sorabji took place just after the appointment of the Commanding Officer. In a very few days our relations with him reached the breaking point. I had hardly regained my strength after the fourteen days' fast, when I began to take part in the drill, often walking to the appointed place about two miles from home. This gave me pleurisy and laid me low. In this condition I had to go week-end camping. Whilst the others stayed there, I returned home. It was here that an occasion arose for Satyagraha.

The Commanding Officer began to exercise his authority somewhat freely. He gave us clearly to understand that he was our head in all matters, military and non-military, giving us at the same time a taste of his authority. Sorabji hurried to me. He was not at all prepared to put up with his high-handedness. He said: "We must have all orders through you. We are still in the training camp and all sorts of absurd orders are being issued. Invidious distinctions are made between ourselves and those youths who have been appointed to instruct us. We must have it out with the Commanding Officer, otherwise we shall not be able to go on any longer. The Indian students and others who have joined our Corps are not going to abide by any absurd orders. In a cause which has been taken up for the sake of self-respect, it is unthinkable to put up with loss of it."

I approached the Commanding Officer and drew his attention to the complaints I had received. He wrote asking me to set out the complaints in writing, at the same time asking me "to impress upon those who complain that the proper direction in which to make complaints is to me through their section commanders, now appointed, who will inform me through the instructors."

To this I replied saying that I claimed no authority, that in the military sense I was no more than any other private, but that I had believed that as Chairman of the Volunteer Corps, I should be allowed unofficially to act as their representative. I also set out the grievances and requests that had been brought to my notice, namely, that grievous dissatisfaction had been caused by the appointment of section leaders without reference to the feeling of the members of the Corps; that they be recalled, and the Corps be invited to elect section leaders, subject to the Commander's approval.

This did not appeal to the Commanding Officer, who said it was repugnant to all military discipline that the section leaders should be elected by the Corps, and that the recall of appointments already made would be subversive of all discipline.

So we held a meeting and decided upon withdrawal. I brought home to the members the serious consequences of Satyagraha. But a very large majority voted for the resolution, which was to the effect that, unless the appointments of Corporals already made were recalled and the members of the Corps given an opportunity of electing their own Corporals, the members would be obliged to abstain from further drilling and week-end camping.

I then addressed a letter to the Commanding Officer telling him what a severe disappointment his letter rejecting my suggestion had been. I assured him that I was not fond of any exercise of authority and that I was most anxious to serve. I also drew his attention to a precedent. I pointed out that, although I occupied no official rank in the South African Indian Ambulance Corps at the time of the Boer War, there was never a hitch between Colonel Gallwey and the Corps, and the Colonel never took a step without reference to me with a view to ascertain the wishes of the Corps. I also enclosed a copy of the resolution we had passed the previous evening.

This had no good effect on the Officer, who felt that the meeting and the resolution were a grave breach of discipline.

Hereupon I addressed a letter to the Secretary of State for India, acquainting him with all the facts and enclosing a copy of the resolution. He replied explaining that conditions in South Africa were different, and drawing my attention to the fact that under the rules the section commanders were appointed by the Commanding Officer, but assuring me that in future, when appointing section commanders, the Commanding Officer would consider my recommendations.

A good deal of correspondence passed between us after this, but I do not want to prolong the bitter tale. Suffice it to say that my experience was of a piece with the experiences we daily have in India. What with threats and what with adroitness the Commanding Officer succeeded in creating a division in our Corps. Some of those who had voted for the resolution yielded to the Commander's threats or persuasions and went back on their promise.

About this time an unexpectedly large contingent of wounded soldiers arrived at the Netley Hospital, and the services of our Corps were requisitioned. Those whom the Commanding Officer could persuade went to Netley. The others refused to go. I was on my back, but was in communication with the members of the Corps. Mr. Roberts, the Under-Secretary of State, honoured me with many calls during those days. He insisted on my persuading the others to serve. He suggested that they should form a separate Corps and that at the Netley Hospital they could be responsible only to the Commanding Officer there, so that there would be no question of loss of self-respect, Government would be placated, and at the same time helpful service would be rendered to the large number of wounded received at the hospital. This suggestion appealed both to my companions and to me, with the result that those who had stayed away also went to Netley.

Only I remained away, lying on my back and making the best of a bad job.

FACE-TO-FACE WITH AHIMSA

My object was to inquire into the condition of the Champaran agriculturists and understand their grievances against the indigo planters. For this purpose it was necessary that I should meet thousands of the ryots. But I deemed it essential, before starting on my inquiry, to know the planters' side of the case and see the Commissioner of the Division. I sought and was granted appointments with both.

The Secretary of the Planters' Association told me plainly that I was an outsider and that I had no business to come between the planters and their tenants, but if I had any representation to make, I might submit it in writing. I politely told him that I did not regard myself as an outsider, and that I had every right to inquire into the condition of the tenants if they desired me to do so.

The Commissioner, on whom I called, proceeded to bully me, and advised me forthwith to leave Tirhut.

I acquainted my co-workers with all this, and told them that there was a likelihood of Government stopping me from proceeding further, and that I might have to go to jail earlier than I had expected, and that, if I was to be arrested, it would be best that the arrest should take place in Motihari or if possible in Bettiah. It was advisable, therefore, that I should go to those places as early as possible.

Champaran is a district of the Tirhut division and Motihari is its headquarters. Rajkumar Shukla's place was in the vicinity of Bettiah, and the tenants belonging to the *kothis* in its neighbourhood were the poorest in the district. Rajkumar Shukla wanted me to see them and I was equally anxious to do so.

So I started with my co-workers for Motihari the same day. Babu Gorakh Prasad harboured us in his home, which became a caravanserai. It could hardly contain us all. The very same day we heard that about five miles from Motihari a tenant had been ill-treated. It was decided that, in company with Babu Dharanidhar Prasad, I should go and see him the next morning, and we accordingly set off for the place on elephant's back. An elephant, by the way, is about as common in Champaran as a bullock-cart in Gujarat. We had scarcely gone half way when a messenger from the Police Superintendent overtook us and said that the latter had sent his compliments. I saw what he meant. Having left Dharanidharbabu to proceed to the original destination, I got into the hired carriage which the messenger had brought. He then served on me a notice to leave Champaran, and drove me to my place. On his asking me to acknowledge the service of the notice, I wrote to the effect that I did not propose to comply with it and leave Champaran till my inquiry was finished. Thereupon I received a summons to take my trial the next day for disobeying the order to leave Champaran.

I kept awake that whole night writing letters and giving necessary instructions to Babu Brajkishore Prasad.

The news of the notice and the summons spread like wildfire, and I was told that Motihari that day witnessed unprecedented scenes. Gorakhbabu's house and the court house overflowed with men. Fortunately I had finished all my work during the night and so was able to cope with the crowds. My companions proved the greatest help. They occupied themselves with regulating the crowds, for the latter followed me wherever I went.

A sort of friendliness sprang up between the officials—Collector, Magistrate, Police Superintendent—and myself. I might have legally resisted the notices served on me. Instead I accepted them all, and my conduct towards the officials was correct. They thus saw that I did not want to offend them personally, but that I wanted to offer civil resistance to their orders. In this way they were put at ease, and instead of harassing me they gladly availed themselves of my and my co-workers' co-operation in regulating the crowds. But it was an ocular demonstration to them of the fact that their authority was shaken. The people had for the moment lost all fear of punishment and yielded obedience to the power of love which their new friend exercised.

It should be remembered that no one knew me in Champaran. The peasants were all ignorant. Champaran, being far up north of the Ganges, and right at the foot of the Himalayas in close proximity to Nepal, was cut off from the rest of India. The Congress was practically unknown in those parts. Even those who had heard the name of the Congress shrank from joining it or even mentioning it. And now the Congress and its members had entered this land, though not in the name of the Congress, yet in a far more real sense.

In consultation with my co-workers I had decided that nothing should be done in the name of the Congress. What we wanted was work and not name, substance and not shadow. For the name of the Congress was the *bête noire* of the Government and their controllers—the planters. To them the Congress was a byword for lawyers' wrangles, evasion of law through legal loopholes, a byword for bomb and anarchical crime and for diplomacy and hypocrisy. We had to dis-illusion them both. Therefore we had decided not to mention the name of the Congress and not to acquaint the peasants with the organization called the Con-gress. It was enough, we thought, if they understood and followed the spirit of the Congress instead of its letter.

No emissaries had therefore been sent there, openly or secretly, on behalf of the Congress to prepare the ground for our arrival. Rajkumar Shukla was incapa-ble of reaching the thousands of peasants. No political work had yet been done amongst them. The world outside Champaran was not known to them. And yet they received me as though we had been age-long friends. It is no exaggeration, but the literal truth, to say that in this meeting with the peasants I was face to face with God, Ahimsa and Truth.

When I come to examine my title to this realization, I find nothing but my love for the people. And this in turn is nothing but an expression of my unshak-able faith in Ahimsa.

That day in Champaran was an unforgettable event in my life and a red-let-ter day for the peasants and for me.

According to the law, I was to be on my trial, but truly speaking Govern-ment was to be on its trial. The Commissioner only succeeded in trapping Gov-ernment in the net which he had spread for me.

THE KHEDA SATYAGRAHA

No breathing time was, however, in store for me. Hardly was the Ahmeda-bad mill-hands' strike over, when I had to plunge into the Kheda Satyagraha struggle.

A condition approaching famine had arisen in the Kheda district owing to a widespread failure of crops, and the Patidars of Kheda were considering the question of getting the revenue assessment for the year suspended.

Sjt. Amritlal Thakkar had already inquired into and reported on the situa-tion and personally discussed the question with the Commissioner, before I gave definite advice to the cultivators. Sjts. Mohanlal Pandya and Shankarlal Parikh had also thrown themselves into the fight, and had set up an agitation in the Bombay Legislative Council through Sjt. Vithalbhai Patel and the late Sir Gokuldas Kahandas Parekh. More than one deputation had waited upon the Governor in that connection.

I was at this time President of the Gujarat Sabha. The Sabha sent petitions and telegrams to the Government and even patiently swallowed the insults and threats of the Commissioner. The conduct of the officials on this occasion was so ridiculous and undignified as to be almost incredible now.

The cultivators' demand was as clear as daylight, and so moderate as to make out a strong case for its acceptance. Under the Land Revenue Rules, if the crop was four annas or under, the cultivators could claim full suspension of the revenue assessment for the year. According to the official figures the crop was said to be over four annas. The contention of the cultivators, on the other hand, was that it was less than four annas. But the Government was in no mood to listen, and regarded the popular demand for arbitration as *lèse majesté*. At last all petitioning and prayer having failed, after taking counsel with co-workers, I advised the Patidars to resort to Satyagraha.

Besides the volunteers of Kheda, my principal comrades in this struggle were Sjts. Vallabhbhai Patel, Shankarlal Banker, Shrimati Anasuyabehn, Sjts. Indulal Yajnik, Mahadev Desai and others. Sjt. Vallabhbhai, in joining the struggle, had to suspend a splendid and growing practice at the bar, which for all practical purposes he was never able to resume.

We fixed up our headquarters at the Nadiad Anathashram, no other place being available which would have been large enough to accommodate all of us.

The following pledge was signed by the Satyagrahis:

Knowing that the crops of our villages are less than four annas, we requested the Government to suspend the collection of revenue assessment till the ensuing year, but the Government had not acceded to our prayer. Therefore, we, the undersigned, hereby solemnly declare that we shall not, of our own accord, pay to the Government the full or the remaining revenue for the year. We shall let the Government take whatever legal steps it may think fit and gladly suffer the consequences of our non-payment. We shall rather let our lands be forfeited than that by voluntary payment we should allow our case to be considered false or should compromise our self-respect. Should the Government , however, agree to suspend collection of the second installment of the assessment throughout the district, such amongst us as are in a position to pay will pay up the whole or the balance of the revenue that may be due. The reason why those who are able to pay still withhold payment is that, if they pay up, the poorer ryots may in a panic sell their chattels or incur debts to pay their dues, and thereby bring suffering upon themselves. In these circumstances we feel that, for the sake of the poor, it is the duty even of those who can afford to pay to withhold payment of their assessment.

I cannot devote many chapters to this struggle. So a number of sweet recollections in this connection will have to be crowded out. Those who want to make fuller and deeper study of this important fight would do well to read the full and authentic history of the Kheda Satyagraha by Sjt. Shankarlal Parikh of Kathal, Kheda.

END OF KHEDA SATYAGRAHA

The campaign came to an unexpected end. It was clear that the people were exhausted, and I hesitated to let the unbending be driven to utter ruin. I was casting about for some graceful way of terminating the struggle which would be acceptable to a Satyagrahi. Such a one appeared quite unexpectedly. The Mamlatdar of the Nadiad Taluka sent me word that, if well-to-do Patridars paid up, the poorer ones would be granted suspension. I asked for a written undertaking to that effect, which was given. But as a Mamlatdar could be responsible only for his Taluka, I inquired of the Collector, who alone could give an undertaking in respect of the whole district, whether the Mamlatdar's undertaking was true for the whole district. He replied that orders declaring suspension in terms of the Mamlatdar's letter had been already issued. I was not aware of it, but if it was a fact, the people's pledge had been fulfilled. The pledge, it will be remembered, had the same things for its object, and so we expressed ourselves satisfied with the orders.

However, the end was far from making me feel happy, inasmuch as it lacked the grace with which the termination of every Satyagraha campaign ought to be accompanied. The Collector carried on as though he had done nothing by way of a settlement. The poor were to be granted suspension, but hardly any got the benefit of it. It was the people's right to determine who was poor, but they could not exercise it. I was sad that they had not the strength to exercise the right. Although, therefore, the termination was celebrated as a triumph of Satyagraha, I could not enthuse over it, as it lacked the essentials of a complete triumph.

The end of a Satyagraha campaign can be described as worthy only when it leaves the Satyagrahis stronger and more spirited than they are in the beginning.

The campaign was not, however, without its indirect results which we can see today and the benefit of which we are reaping. The Kheda Satygraha marks the beginning of an awakening among the peasants of Gujarat, the beginning of their true political education.

Dr. Besant's brilliant Home Rule agitation had certainly touched the peasants, but it was the Kheda campaign that compelled the educated public workers to establish contact with the actual life of the peasants. They learnt to identify themselves with the latter. They found their proper sphere of work, their capacity for sacrifice increased. That Vallabhbhai found himself during this campaign was by itself no small achievement. We could realize its measure during the flood relief operations last year and the Bardoli Satyagraha this year. Public life in Gujarat became instinct with a new energy and a new vigour. The Patidar peasant came to an unforgettable consciousness of his strength. The lesson was indelibly imprinted on the public mind that the salvation of the people depends upon themselves, upon their capacity for suffering and sacrifice. Through the Kheda campaign Satyagraha took firm root in the soil of Gujarat.

Although, therefore, I found nothing to enthuse over in the termination of the Satyagraha, the Kheda peasants were jubilant, because they knew that what they had achieved was commensurate with their effort, and they had found the true and infallible method for a redress of their grievances. This knowledge was enough justification for their jubilation.

Nevertheless the Kheda peasants had not fully understood the inner meaning of Satyagraha, and they saw it to their cost, as we shall see in the chapters to follow.

THE BIRTH OF KHADI

I do not remember to have seen a handloom or a spinning wheel when in 1908 I described it in *Hind Swaraj* as the panacea for the growing pauperism of India. In that book I took it as understood that anything that helped India to get rid of the grinding poverty of her masses would in the same process also establish Swaraj. Even in 1915, when I returned to India from South Africa, I had not actually seen a spinning wheel. When the Satyagraha Ashram was founded at Sabarmati, we introduced a few handlooms there. But no sooner had we done this than we found ourselves up against a difficulty. All of us belonged either to the liberal professions or to business; not one of us was an artisan. We needed a weaving expert to teach us to weave before we could work the looms. One was at last procured from Palanpur, but he did not communicate to us the whole of his art. But Maganlal Gandhi was not to be easily baffled. Possessed of a natural talent for mechanics, he was able fully to master the art before long, and one after another several new weavers were trained up in the Ashram.

The object that we set before ourselves was to be able to clothe ourselves entirely in cloth manufactured by our own hands. We therefore forthwith discarded the use of mill-woven cloth, and all the members of the Ashram resolved to wear hand-woven cloth made from Indian yarn only. The adoption of this practice brought us a world of experience. It enabled us to know, from direct contact, the conditions of life among the weavers, the extent of their production, the handicaps in the way of their obtaining their yarn supply, the way in which they were being made victims of fraud, and, lastly, their ever growing indebtedness. We were not in a position immediately to manufacture all the cloth for our needs. The alternative therefore was to get our cloth supply from handloom weavers. But ready-made cloth from Indian mill-yarn was not easily obtainable either from the cloth-dealers or from the weavers themselves. All the fine cloth woven by the weavers was from foreign yarn, since Indian mills did not spin fine counts. Even today the outturn of higher counts by Indian mills is very limited, whilst highest counts they cannot spin at all. It was after the greatest effort that we were at last able to find some weavers who condescended to weave Swadeshi yarn for us, and only on condition that the Ashram would take up all the cloth that they might produce. By thus adopting cloth woven from mill-yarn as our wear, and propagating it among our friends, we made ourselves voluntary agents of the Indian spinning mills. This in its turn brought us into contact with the mills, and enabled us to know something about their management and their handicaps. We saw that the aim of the mills was more and more to weave the yarn spun by them; their co-operation with the handloom weaver was not willing, but unavoidable and temporary. We became impatient to be able to spin our own yarn. It was clear that, until we could do this ourselves, dependence on the mills would remain. We did not feel that we could render any service to the country by continuing as agents of Indian spinning mills.

No end of difficulties again faced us. We could get neither a spinning wheel nor a spinner to teach us how to spin. We were employing some wheels for filling pearns and bobbins for weaving in the Ashram. But we had no idea that these could be used as spinning wheels. Once Kalidas Jhaveri discovered a woman who, he said, would demonstrate to us how spinning was done. We sent to her a member of the Asharam who was known for his great versatility in learning new things. But even he returned without wresting the secret of the art.

So the time passed on, and my impatience grew with the time. I plied every chance visitor to the Ashram who was likely to possess some information about handspinning with questions about the art. But the art being confined to women and having been all but exterminated, if there was some stray spinner still surviving in some obscure corner, only a member of that sex was likely to find out her whereabouts.

In the year 1917 I was taken by my Gujarati friends to preside at the Broach Educational Conference. It was here that I discovered that remarkable lady Gangabehn Majmundar. She was a widow, but her enterprising spirit knew no bounds. Her education, in the accepted sense of the term, was not much. But in courage and commonsense she easily surpassed the general run of our educated women. She had already got rid of the curse of untouchability, and fearlessly moved among and served the suppressed classes. She had means of her own, and her needs were few. She had a well-seasoned constitution, and went about everywhere without an escort. She felt quite at home on horseback. I came to know her more intimately at the Godhra Conference. To her I poured out my grief about the charkha, and she lightened my burden by a promise to prosecute an earnest and incessant search for the spinning wheel.

FOUND AT LAST!

At last, after no end of wandering in Gujarat, Gangabehn found the spinning wheel in Vijapur in the Baroda State. Quite a number of people there had spinning wheels in their homes, but had long since consigned them to the lofts as useless lumber. They expressed to Gangabehn their readiness to resume spinning, if someone promised to provide them with a regular supply of slivers, and to buy the yarn spun by them. Gangabehn communicated the joyful news to me. The providing of slivers was found to be a difficult task. On my mentioning the thing to the late Umar Sobani, he solved the difficulty by immediately undertaking to send a sufficient supply of slivers from his mill. I sent to Ganagbehn the slivers received from Umar Sobani, and soon yarn began to pour in at such a rate that it became quite a problem how to cope with it.

Mr. Umar Sobani's generosity was great, but still one could not go on taking advantage of it forever. I felt ill at ease, continuously receiving slivers from him. Moreover, it seemed to me to be fundamentally wrong to use mill-slivers. If one could use mill-slivers, why not use mill-yarn as well? Surely no mills supplied slivers to the ancients? How did they make their slivers then? With these thoughts in my mind I suggested to Gangabehn to find carders who could supply slivers. She confidently undertook the task. She engaged a carder who was prepared to card cotton. He demanded thirty-five rupees, if not much more, per month. I considered no price too high at the time. She trained a few youngsters to make slivers out of the carded cotton. I begged for cotton in Bombay. Sjt. Yashvantprasad Desai at once responded. Gangabehn's enterprise thus prospered beyond expectation. She found out weavers to weave the yarn that was spun in Vijapur, and soon Vijapur Khadi gained a name for itself.

While these developments were taking place in Vijapur, the spinning wheel gained a rapid footing in the Ashram. Maganlal Gandhi, by bringing to bear all his splendid mechanical talent on the wheel, made many improvements in it, and wheels and their accessories began to be manufactured at the Ashram. The first piece of khadi manufactured in the Ashram cost 17 annas per yard. I did not hesitate to commend this very coarse khadi at that rate to friends, who willingly paid the price.

I was laid up in bed at Bombay. But I was fit enough to make searches for the wheel there. At last I chanced upon two spinners. They charged one rupee for a seer of yarn, *i.e.*, 28 *tolas* or nearly three quarters of a pound. I was then ignorant of the economics of khadi. I considered no price too high for securing handspun yarn. On comparing the rates paid by me with those paid in Vijapur I found that I was being cheated. The spinners refused to agree to any reduction in their rates. So I had to dispense with their services. But they served their purpose. They taught spinning to Shrimatis Avantikabai, Ramibai Kamdar, the widowed mother of Sjt. Shankarlal Banker and Shrimati Vasumatibehn. The wheel began merrily to hum in my room, and I may say without exaggeration that its hum had no small share in restoring me to health. I am prepared to admit that its effect was more psychological than physical. But then it only shows how powerfully the physical in man reacts to the psychological. I too set my hand to the wheel, but did not do much with it at the time.

In Bombay, again, the same old problem of obtaining a supply of handmade slivers presented itself. A carder twanging his bow used to pass daily by Sjt. Revashanakar's residence. I sent for him and learnt that he carded cotton for stuffing mattresses. He agreed to card cotton for slivers, but demanded a stiff price for it, which, however, I paid. The yarn thus prepared I disposed of to some

Vaishnava friends for making from it the garlands for the *pavitra ekadashi*. Sjt
Shivji started a spinning class in Bombay. All these experiments involved considerable expenditure. But it was willingly defrayed by patriotic friends, lovers
of the motherland, who had faith in Khadi. The money thus spent, in my humble
opinion, was not wasted. It brought us a rich store of experience, and revealed to
us the possibilities of the spinning wheel.

I now grew impatient for the exclusive adoption of khadi for my dress. My
dhoti was still of Indian mill cloth. The course khadi manufactured in the
Ashram and at Vijapur was only 30 inches in width. I gave notice to Gangabehn
that, unless she provided me with a khadi *dhoti* of 45 inches width within a
month, I would do with coarse, short khadi *dhoti*. The ultimatum came upon her
as a shock. But she proved equal to the demand made upon her. Well within the
month she sent me a pair of khadi *dhotis* 45 inches width, and thus relieved me
from what would then have been a difficult situation for me.

At about the same time Sjt. Lakshmidas brought Sjt. Ramji, the weaver,
with his wife Gangabehn from Lathi to the Ashram and got khadi *dhotis* woven
at the Ashram. The part played by this couple in the spread of khadi was by no
means insignificant. They initiated a host of persons in Gujarat and also outside
into the art of weaving handspun yarn. To see Gangabehn at her loom is a stirring sight. When this unlettered but self-possessed sister plies at her loom she
becomes so lost in it that it is difficult to distract her attention, and much more
difficult to draw her eyes off her beloved loom.

FAREWELL

The time has now come to bring these chapters to a close.

My life from this point onward has been so public that there is hardly anything about it that people do not know. Moreover, since 1921 I have worked in
such close association with the Congress leaders that I can hardly describe any
episode in my life since then without referring to my relations with them. For
though Shraddhanandji, the Deshabandhu, Hakim Seheb and Lalji are no more
with us today, we have the good luck to have a host of other veteran Congress
leaders still living and working in our midst. The history of the Congress, since
the great changes in it that I have described above, is still in the making. And my
principal experiments during the past seven years have all been made through the
Congress. A reference to my relations with the leaders would therefore be
unavoidable, if I set about describing my experiments further. And this I may not
do, at any rate for the present, if only from a sense of propriety. Lastly, my conclusions from my current experiments can hardly as yet be regarded as decisive.
It therefore seems to me to be my plain duty to close this narrative here. In fact
my pen instinctively refuses to proceed further.

It is not without a wrench that I have to take leave of the reader. I set a high
value on my experiments. I do not know whether I have been able to do justice to
them. I can only say that I have spared no pains to give a faithful narrative. To

describe truth, as it has appeared to me, and in the exact manner in which I have arrived at it, has been my ceaseless effort. The exercise has given me ineffable mental peace, because, it has been my fond hope that it might bring faith in Truth and Ahimsa to waverers.

My uniform experience has convinced me that there is no other God than Truth. And if every page of these chapters does not proclaim to the reader that the only means for the realization of Truth is Ahimsa, I shall deem all my labour in writing these chapters to have been in vain. And, even though my efforts in this behalf may prove fruitless, let the readers know that the vehicle, not the great principle, is at fault. After all, however sincere my strivings after Ahimsa may have been, they have still been imperfect and inadequate. The little fleeting glimpses, therefore, that I have been able to have of Truth can hardly convey an idea of the indescribable lustre of Truth, a million times more intense than of the sun we daily see with our eyes. In fact what I have caught is only the faintest glimmer of that mighty effulgence. But this much I can say with assurance, as a result of all my experiments, that a perfect vision of Truth can only follow a complete realization of Ahimsa.

To see the universal and all-pervading Spirit of Truth face to face one must be able to love the meanest of creation as oneself. And a man who aspires after that cannot afford to keep out of any field of life. That is why my devotion to Truth has drawn me into the field of politics; and I can say without the slightest hesitation, and yet in all humility, that those who say that religion has nothing to do with politics do not know what religion means.

Identification with everything that lives is impossible without self-purification; without self-purification the observance of the law of Ahimsa must remain an empty dream; God can never be realized by one who is not pure of heart. Self-purification therefore must mean purification in all the walks of life. And purification being highly infectious, purification of oneself necessarily leads to the purification of one's surroundings.

But the path of self-purification is hard and steep. To attain to perfect purity one has to become absolutely passion-free in thought, speech and action; to rise above the opposing currents of love and hatred, attachment and repulsion. I know that I have not in me as yet that triple purity, in spite of constant ceaseless striving for it. That is why the world's praise fails to move me, indeed it very often stings me. To conquer the subtle passions seems to me to be harder far than the physical conquest of the world by the force of arms. Ever since my return to India I have had experiences of the dormant passions lying hidden within me. The knowledge of them has made me feel humiliated though not defeated. The experiences and experiments have sustained me and given me great joy. But I know that I have still before me a difficult path to traverse. I must reduce myself to zero. So long as a man does not of his own free will put himself last among his fellow creatures, there is no salvation for him. Ahimsa is the farthest limit of humility.

In bidding farewell to the reader, for the time being at any rate, I ask him to join me in prayer to the God of Truth that He may grant me the boon of Ahimsa in mind, word and deed.

9

Letter from Birmingham Jail

Martin Luther King Jr.

Martin Luther King Jr. (1927–1968) deliberately adapted Gandhi's idea of satya-graha to the civil rights movement in the United States. Educated at Morehouse College, Crozer Theological Seminary, and Boston University Graduate School, his primary occupation was that of minister, but his influence went far beyond his pastorate at Dexter Avenue Baptist Church in Montgomery, Alabama. He led many marches and appealed against legally supported segregation, the most prominent being the Montgomery bus boycott, 1955–1956. Founder and presi-dent of the Southern Christian Leadership Conference, he was a leader of the 1963 March on Washington. There he delivered to thousands of people his famous speech "I Have a Dream," a speech considered by many people to be one of the most powerful given in recent history. His leadership in the nonviolent cause for changing a segregated society won for him in 1964 the Nobel Peace Prize. In 1968, Martin Luther King Jr. was assassinated by a white man in Mem-phis, Tennessee.

In *Why We Can't Wait,* Martin Luther King describes in his own words the circumstances and the reasons for his letter to his fellow clergymen from Ala-bama:

This response to a published statement by eight fellow clergymen from Alabama . . . was composed under somewhat constricting circumstances. Begun on the margins of the newspaper in which the statement appeared while I was in jail, the letter was continued on scraps of writing paper supplied by a friendly Negro trusty, and concluded on a pad my attorneys were eventually permitted to leave me. Although the text remains in substance unaltered, I have indulged in the author's prerogative of polishing it for publication.[1]

Here is the public statement written by the eight Alabama clergymen. Fol-lowing it is Martin Luther King's reaction, "Letter from Birmingham Jail."

PUBLIC STATEMENT BY EIGHT ALABAMA CLERGYMEN APRIL 12, 1963

We, the undersigned clergymen are among those who, in January, issued "An Appeal for Law and Order and Common Sense," in dealing with racial problems in Alabama. We expressed understanding that honest convictions in racial matters could properly be pursued in the courts, but urged that decisions of those courts should in the meantime be peacefully obeyed.

Since that time there had been some evidence of increased forbearance and a willingness to face facts. Responsible citizens have undertaken to work on various problems which cause racial friction and unrest. In Birmingham, recent public events have given indication that we all have opportunity for a new constructive and realistic approach to racial problems.

However, we are now confronted by a series of demonstrations by some of our Negro citizens, directed and led in part by outsiders. We recognize the natural impatience of people who feel that their hopes are slow in being realized. But we are convinced that these demonstrations are unwise and untimely.

We agree rather with certain local Negro leadership which has called for honest and open negotiation of racial issues in our area. And we believe this kind of facing of issues can best be accomplished by citizens of our own metropolitan area, white and Negro, meeting with their knowledge and experience of the local situation. All of us need to face that responsibility and find proper channels for its accomplishment.

Just as we formerly pointed out that "hatred and violence have no sanction in our religious and political traditions," we also point out that such actions as incite to hatred and violence, however technically peaceful those actions may be, have not contributed to the resolution of our local problems. We do not believe that these days of new hope are days when extreme measures are justified in Birmingham.

We commend the community as a whole, and the local news media and law enforcement officials in particular, on the calm manner in which these demonstrations have been handled. We urge the public to continue to show restraint should the demonstrations continue, and the law enforcement officials to remain calm and continue to protect our city from violence.

We further strongly urge our own Negro community to withdraw support from these demonstrations, and to unite locally in working peacefully for a better Birmingham. When rights are consistently denied, a cause should be pressed in the courts and in negotiations among local leaders, and not in the streets. We appeal to both our white and Negro citizenry to observe the principles of law and order and common sense.

Signed by:

C.C J. CARPENTER, D.D., LL.D., Bishop of Alabama

JOSEPH A. DURICK, D.D, Auxiliary Bishop, Diocese of Mobile-Birmingham

Rabbi MILTON L. GRAFMAN, Temple Emanu-El, Birmingham, Alabama

Bishop PAUL HARDIN, Bishop of the Alabama-West Florida Conference of the Methodist Church

Bishop NOLAN B. HARMON, Bishop of the North Alabama Conference of the Methodist Church

GEORGE M. MURRAY, D.D., LL.D., Bishop Coadjutor, Episcopal Diocese of Alabama

EDWARD V. RAMAGE, Moderator, Synod of the Alabama Presbyterian Church in the United States

EARL STALLINGS, Pastor, First Baptist Church, Birmingham, Alabama

LETTER FROM BIRMINGHAM JAIL

> Martin Luther King Jr.:
> Birmingham City Jail,
> April 16, 1963,

Bishop C.C. J. Carpenter
Bishop Joseph A. Durick
Rabbi Milton L. Grafman
Bishop Paul Hardin
Bishop Nolan B. Harmon
The Rev. George M. Murray
The Rev. Edward V. Ramage
The Rev. Earl Stallings

My dear Fellow Clergymen,

While confined here in the Birmingham City Jail, I came across your recent statement calling our present activities "unwise and untimely." Seldom, if ever, do I pause to answer criticisms of my work and ideas. If I sought to answer all of the criticisms that cross my desk, my secretaries would be engaged in little else in the course of the day and I would have no time for constructive work. But since I feel that you are men of genuine good will and your criticisms are sincerely set forth, I would like to answer your statement in what I hope will be patient and reasonable terms.

I think I should give the reason for my being in Birmingham, since you have been influenced by the argument of "outsiders coming in." I have the honor of serving as president of the Southern Christian Leadership Conference, an organization operating in every Southern state with headquarters in Atlanta, Georgia. We have some eighty-five affiliate organizations all across the South— one being the Alabama Christian Movement for Human Rights. Whenever necessary and possible we share staff, educational, and financial resources with our affiliates. Several months ago our local affiliate here in Birmingham invited us to be on call to engage in a nonviolent direct action program if such were deemed necessary. We readily consented and when the hour came we lived up to our promises. So I am here, along with several members of my staff, because we were invited here. I am here because I have basic organizational ties here. Beyond this, I am in Birmingham because injustice is here. Just as the eighth century prophets left their little villages and carried their "thus saith the Lord" far beyond the boundaries of their home town, and just as the Apostle Paul left his little village of Tarsus and carried the gospel of Jesus Christ to practically every hamlet and city of the Graeco-Roman world, I too am compelled to carry the gospel of freedom beyond my particular home town. Like Paul, I must constantly respond to the Macedonian call for aid.

Moreover, I am cognizant of the interrelatedness of all communities and states. I cannot sit idly by in Atlanta and not be concerned about what happens in Birmingham. Injustice anywhere is a threat to justice everywhere. We are caught in an inescapable network of mutuality tied in a single garment of destiny. Whatever affects one directly affects all indirectly. Never again can we afford to live with the narrow, provincial "outside agitator" idea. Anyone who lives inside the United States can never be considered an outsider anywhere in this country.

You deplore the demonstrations that are presently taking place in Birmingham. But I am sorry that your statement did not express a similar concern for the conditions that brought the demonstrations into being. I am sure that each of you would want to go beyond the superficial social analyst who looks merely at effects, and does not grapple with underlying causes. I would not hesitate to say that it is unfortunate that so-called demonstrations are taking place in Birmingham at this time, but I would say in more emphatic terms that it is even more unfortunate that the white power structure of this city left the Negro community with no other alternative.

In any nonviolent campaign there are four basic steps: (1) collection of the facts to determine whether injustices are alive; (2) negotiation; (3) self-purification; and (4) direct action. We have gone through all of these steps in Birmingham. There can be no gainsaying of the fact that racial injustice engulfs this community. Birmingham is probably the most thoroughly segregated city in the United States. Its ugly record of police brutality is known in every section of this country. Its unjust treatment of Negroes in the courts is a notorious reality. There have been more unsolved bombings of Negro homes and churches in Birmingham than any city in this nation. These are the hard, brutal, and unbelievable facts. On the basis of these conditions Negro leaders sought to negotiate with the city fathers. But the political leaders consistently refused to engage in good faith negotiation.

Then came the opportunity last September to talk with some of the leaders of the economic community. In these negotiating sessions certain promises were made by the merchants—such as the promise to remove the humiliating racial signs from the stores. On the basis of these promises Rev. Shuttlesworth and the leaders of the Alabama Christian Movement for Human Rights agreed to call a moratorium on any type of demonstrations. As the weeks and months unfolded we realized that we were the victims of a broken promise. The signs remained. As in so many experiences of the past we were confronted with blasted hopes, and the dark shadow of a deep disappointment settled upon us. So we had no alternative except that of preparing for direct action, whereby we would present our very bodies as a means of laying our case before the conscience of the local and national community. We were not unmindful of the difficulties involved. So we decided to go through a process of self-purification. We started having workshops on nonviolence and repeatedly asked ourselves the questions, "Are you able to accept blows without retaliating?" "Are you able to endure the ordeals of jail?"

We decided to set our direct action program around the Easter season, realizing that with the exception of Christmas, this was the largest shopping period of the year. Knowing that a strong economic withdrawal program would be the by-product of direct action, we felt that this was the best time to bring pressure on the merchants for the needed changes. Then it occurred to us that the March election was ahead, and so we speedily decided to postpone action until after election day. When we discovered that Mr. Connor was in the run-off, we decided again to postpone action so that the demonstrations could not be used to cloud the issues. At this time we agreed to begin our non-violent witness the day after the run-off.

This reveals that we did not move irresponsibly into direct action. We too wanted to see Mr. Connor defeated; so we went through postponement after postponement to aid in this community need. After this we felt that direct action could be delayed no longer.

You may well ask, "Why direct action? Why sit-ins, marches, etc.? Isn't negotiation a better path?" You are exactly right in your call for negotiation. Indeed, this is the purpose of direct action. Nonviolent direct action seeks to create such a crisis and establish such creative tension that a community that has constantly refused to negotiate is forced to confront the issue. It seeks so to dramatize the issue that it can no longer be ignored. I just referred to the creation of tension as a part of the work of the nonviolent resister. This may sound rather shocking. But I must confess that I am not afraid of the word tension. I have earnestly worked and preached against violent tension, but there is a type of constructive nonviolent tension that is necessary for growth. Just as Socrates felt that it was necessary to create a tension in the mind so that individuals could rise from the bondage of myths and half-truths to the unfettered realm of creative analysis and objective appraisal, we must see the need of having nonviolent gad-flies to create the kind of tension in society that will help men rise from the dark depths of prejudice and racism to the majestic heights of understanding and brotherhood. So the purpose of the direct action is to create a situation so crisis-packed that it will inevitably open the door to negotiation. Too long has our beloved Southland been bogged down in the tragic attempt to live in monologue rather than dialogue.

One of the basic points in your statement is that our acts are untimely. Some have asked, "Why didn't you give the new administration time to act?" The only answer that I can give to this inquiry is that the new administration must be prodded about as much as the outgoing one before it acts. We will be sadly mistaken if we feel that the election of Mr. Boutwell will bring the millennium to Birmingham. While Mr. Boutwell is much more articulate and gentle than Mr. Connor, they are both segregationists dedicated to the task of maintaining the sta-tus quo. The hope I see in Mr. Boutwell is that he will be reasonable enough to see the futility of massive resistance to desegregation. But he will not see this without pressure from the devotees of civil rights. My friends, I must say to you that we have not made a single gain in civil rights without determined legal and nonviolent pressure. History is the long and tragic story of the fact that privi-leged groups seldom give up their privileges voluntarily. Individuals may see the moral light and voluntarily give up their unjust posture; but as Reinhold Niebuhr has reminded us, groups are more immoral than individuals.

We know through painful experience that freedom is never voluntarily given by the oppressor; it must be demanded by the oppressed. Frankly I have never yet engaged in a direct action movement that was "well timed," according to the timetable of those who have not suffered unduly from the disease of segre-gation. For years now I have heard the word "Wait!" It rings in the ear of every Negro with a piercing familiarity. This "wait" has almost always meant "never." It has been a tranquilizing thalidomide, relieving the emotional stress for a moment, only to give birth to an ill-formed infant of frustration. We must come to see with the distinguished jurist of yesterday that "justice too long delayed is justice denied." We have waited for more than three hundred and forty years for our constitutional and God-given rights. The nations of Asia and Africa are mov-ing with jet-like speed toward the goal of political independence, and we still creep at horse and buggy pace toward the gaining of a cup of coffee at a lunch counter.

I guess it is easy for those who have never felt the stinging darts of segrega-tion to say wait. But when you have seen vicious mobs lynch your mothers and fathers at will and drown your sisters and brothers at whim; when you have seen hate-filled policemen curse, kick, brutalize, and even kill your black brothers and sisters with impunity; when you see the vast majority of your twenty million

Negro brothers smothering in an airtight cage of poverty in the midst of an afflu-
ent society; when you suddenly find your tongue twisted and your speech stam-
mering as you seek to explain to your six-year-old daughter why she can't go to
the public amusement park that has just been advertized on television, and see
tears welling up in her little eyes when she is told that Funtown is closed to colored children, and see the depressing clouds of inferiority begin to form in her little mental sky, and see her begin to distort her little personality by unconsciously
developing a bitterness toward white people; when you have to concoct an
answer for a five-year-old son asking in agonizing pathos: "Daddy, why do white
people treat colored people so mean?"; when you take a cross-country drive and
find it necessary to sleep night after night in the uncomfortable corners of your
automobile because no motel will accept you; when you are humiliated day in
and day out by nagging signs reading "white" men and "colored"; when your
first name becomes "nigger" and your middle name becomes "boy" (however old
you are) and your last name becomes "John," and when your wife and mother are
never given the respected title "Mrs."; when you are harried by day and haunted
by night by the fact that you are a Negro, living constantly a tiptoe stance never
quite knowing what to expect next, and plagued with inner fears and outer resentments; when you are forever fighting a degenerating sense of "nobodiness";—
then you will understand why we find it difficult to wait. There comes a time
when the cup of endurance runs over, and men are no longer willing to be
plunged into an abyss of injustice where they experience the bleakness of corrod-
ing despair. I hope, sirs, you can understand our legitimate and unavoidable
impatience.

You express a great deal of anxiety over our willingness to break laws.
This is certainly a legitimate concern. Since we so diligently urge people to obey
the Supreme Court's decision of 1954 outlawing segregation in the public
schools, it is rather strange and paradoxical to find us consciously breaking laws.
One may well ask, "How can you advocate breaking some laws and obeying others?" The answer is found in the fact that there are two types of laws. There are
just laws and there are *unjust* laws. I would be the first to advocate obeying just
laws. One has not only a legal but moral responsibility to obey just laws. Con-
versely, one has a moral responsibility to disobey unjust laws. I would agree
with Saint Augustine that "An unjust law is no law at all."

Now what is the difference between the two? How does one determine
when a law is just or unjust? A just law is a man-made code that squares with the
moral law or the law of God. An unjust law is a code that is out of harmony with
the moral law. To put it in the terms of Saint Thomas Aquinas, an unjust law is a
human law that is not rooted in eternal and natural law. Any law that uplifts
human personality is just. Any law that degrades human personality is unjust.
All segregation statutes are unjust because segregation distorts the soul and damages the personality. It gives the segregator a false sense of superiority and the
segregated a false sense of inferiority. To use the words of Martin Buber, the
great Jewish philosopher, segregation substitutes an "I-it" relationship for the "I-

thou" relationship, and ends up relegating persons to the status of things. So segregation is not only politically, economically, and sociologically unsound, but it is morally wrong and sinful. Paul Tillich has said that sin is separation. Isn't segregation an existential expression of man's tragic separation, an expression of his awful estrangement, his terrible sinfulness? So I can urge men to obey the 1954 decision of the Supreme Court because it is morally right, and I can urge them to disobey segregation ordinances because they are morally wrong.

Let us turn to a more concrete example of just and unjust laws. An unjust law is a code that a majority inflicts on a minority that is not binding on itself. This is *difference* made legal. On the other hand a just law is a code that a majority compels a minority to follow that it is willing to follow itself. This is *sameness* made legal.

Let me give another explanation. An unjust law is a code inflicted upon a minority which that minority had no part in enacting or creating because they did not have the unhampered right to vote. Who can say the legislature of Alabama which set up the segregation laws was democratically elected? Throughout the state of Alabama all types of conniving methods are used to prevent Negroes from becoming registered voters and there are some counties without a single Negro registered to vote despite the fact that the Negro constitutes a majority of the population. Can any law set up in such a state be considered democratically structured?

These are just a few examples of unjust and just laws. There are some instances when a law is just on its face but unjust in its application. For instance, I was arrested Friday on a charge of parading without a permit. Now there is nothing wrong with an ordinance which requires a permit for a parade, but when the ordinance is used to preserve segregation and to deny citizens the First Amendment privilege of peaceful assembly and peaceful protest, then it becomes unjust.

I hope you can see the distinction I am trying to point out. In no sense do I advocate evading or defying the law as the rabid segregationist would do. This would lead to anarchy. One who breaks an unjust law must do it *openly, lovingly* (not hatefully as the white mothers did in New Orleans when they were seen on television screaming "nigger, nigger, nigger") and with a willingness to accept the penalty. I submit that an individual who breaks a law that conscience tells him is unjust, and willingly accepts the penalty by staying in jail to arouse the conscience of the community over its injustice, is in reality expressing the very highest respect for the law.

Of course there is nothing new about this kind of civil disobedience. It was seen sublimely in the refusal of Shadrach, Meshach, and Abednego to obey the laws of Nebuchadnezzar because a higher moral law was involved. It was practiced superbly by the early Christians who were willing to face hungry lions and the excruciating pain of chopping blocks, before submitting to certain unjust laws of the Roman Empire. To a degree academic freedom is a reality today because Socrates practiced civil disobedience.

We can never forget that everything Hitler did in Germany was "legal" and everything the Hungarian freedom fighters did in Hungary was "illegal." It was "illegal" to aid and comfort a Jew in Hitler's Germany. But I am sure that, if I had lived in Germany during that time, I would have aided and comforted my Jewish brothers even though it was illegal. If I lived in a communist country today where certain principles dear to the Christian faith are suppressed, I believe I would openly advocate disobeying these antireligious laws.

I must make two honest confessions to you, my Christian and Jewish brothers. First I must confess that over the last few years I have been gravely disappointed with the white moderate. I have almost reached the regrettable conclusion that the Negroes' great stumbling block in the stride toward freedom is not the White Citizens' "Counciler" or the Klu Klux Klanner, but the white moderate who is more devoted to "order" than to justice; who prefers a negative peace which is the absence of tension to a positive peace which is the presence of justice; who constantly says "I agree with you in the goal you seek, but I can't agree with your methods of direct action"; who paternalistically feels that he can set the time-table for another man's freedom; who lives by the myth of time and who constantly advises the Negro to wait until a "more convenient season." Shallow understanding from people of good will is more frustrating than absolute misunderstanding from people of ill will. Lukewarm acceptance is much more bewildering than outright rejection.

I had hoped that the white moderate would understand that law and order exist for the purpose of establishing justice, and that when they fail to do this they become the dangerously structured dams that block the flow of social progress. I had hoped that the white moderate would understand the present tension in the South is merely a necessary phase of the transition from an obnoxious negative peace, where the Negro passively accepted his unjust plight, to a substance-filled positive peace, where all men will respect the dignity and worth of human personality. Actually, we who engage in nonviolent direct action are not the creators of tension. We merely bring to the surface the hidden tension that is already alive. We bring it out in the open where it can be seen and dealt with. Like a boil that can never be cured as long as it is covered up but must be opened with all its pus-flowing ugliness to the natural medicines of air and light, injustice must likewise be exposed, with all of the tension its exposing creates, to the light of human conscience and the air of national opinion before it can be cured.

In your statement you asserted that our actions, even though peaceful, must be condemned because they precipitate violence. But can this assertion be logically made? Isn't this like condemning the robbed man because his possession of money precipitated the evil act of robbery? Isn't this like condemning Socrates because his unswerving commitment to truth and his philosophical delvings precipitated the misguided popular mind to make him drink hemlock? Isn't this like condemning Jesus because His unique God consciousness and never-ceasing devotion to His will precipitated the evil act of crucifixtion? We must come to see, as federal courts have consistently affirmed, that it is immoral to urge an individual to withdraw his efforts to gain his basic constitutional rights because the quest precipitates violence. Society must protect the robbed and punish the robber.

I had also hoped that the white moderate would reject the myth of time. I received a letter this morning from a white brother in Texas which said: "All Christians know that the colored people will receive equal rights eventually, but is it possible that you are in too great of a religious hurry? It has taken Christianity almost 2000 years to accomplish what it has. The teachings of Christ take time to come to earth." All that is said here grows out of a tragic misconception of time. It is the strangely irrational notion that there is something in the very flow of time that will inevitably cure all ills. Actually time is neutral. It can be used either destructively or constructively. I am coming to feel that the people of ill will have used time much more effectively than the people of good will. We will have to repent in this generation not merely for the vitriolic words and actions of the bad people, but for the appalling silence of the good people. We must come to see that human progress never rolls in on wheels of inevitability. It comes through the tireless efforts and persistent work of men willing to be co-workers with God, and without this hard work time itself becomes an ally of the forces of social stagnation.

We must use time creatively, and forever realize that the time is always ripe to do right. Now is the time to make real the promise of democracy, and transform our pending national elegy into a creative psalm of brotherhood. Now is the time to lift our national policy from the quicksand of racial injustice to the solid rock of human dignity.

You spoke of our activity in Birmingham as extreme. At first I was rather disappointed that fellow clergymen would see my nonviolent efforts as those of the extremist. I started thinking about the fact that I stand in the middle of two opposing forces in the Negro community. One is a force of complacency made up of Negroes who, as a result of long years of oppression, have been so completely drained of self-respect and a sense of "somebodiness" that they have adjusted to segregation, and of a few Negroes in the middle class who, because of a degree of academic and economic security, and because at points they profit by segregation, have unconsciously become insensitive to the problems of the masses. The other force is one of bitterness and hatred and comes perilously close to advocating violence. It is expressed in the various black nationalist groups that are springing up over the nation, the largest and best known being Elijah Muhammad's Muslim movement. This movement is nourished by the contemporary frustration over the continued existence of racial discrimination. It is made up of people who have lost faith in America, who have absolutely repudiated Christianity, and who have concluded that the white man is an incurable "devil." I have tried to stand between these two forces saying that we need not follow the "do-nothingism" of the complacent or the hatred and despair of the black nationalist. There is the more excellent way of love and nonviolent protest. I'm grateful to God that, through the Negro church, the dimension of nonviolence entered our struggle. If this philosophy had not emerged I am convinced that by now many streets of the South would be flowing with floods of blood. And I am further convinced that if our white brothers dismiss us as "rabble rousers" and "outside agitators"—those of us who are working through the channels of nonviolent direct action—and refuse to support our nonviolent efforts, millions of Negroes, out of frustration and despair, will seek solace and security in black nationalist ideologies, a development that will lead inevitably to a frightening racial nightmare.

Oppressed people cannot remain oppressed forever. The urge for freedom will eventually come. This is what has happened to the American Negro. Something within has reminded him of his birthright of freedom; something without has reminded him that he can gain it. Consciously and unconsciously, he has been swept in by what the Germans called the *Zeitgeist,* and with his black brothers of Africa, and his brown and yellow brothers of Asia, South America, and the Caribbean, he is moving with a sense of cosmic energy toward the promised land of racial justice. Recognizing this vital urge that has engulfed the Negro community, one should readily understand public demonstrations. The Negro has many pent-up resentments and latent frustrations. He has to get them out. So let him march sometime; let him have his prayer pilgrimages to the city hall; understand why he must have sit-ins and freedom rides. If his repressed emotions do not come out in these nonviolent ways, they will come out in ominous expressions of violence. This is not a threat; it is a fact of history. So I have not said to my people, "Get rid of your discontent." But I have tried to say that this normal and healthy discontent can be channeled through the creative outlet of nonviolent direct action. Now this approach is being dismissed as extremist. I must admit that I was initially disappointed in being so categorized.

But as I continued to think about the matter I gradually gained a bit of satisfaction from being considered an extremist. Was not Jesus an extremist in love? "Love your enemies, bless them that curse you, pray for them that despitefully use you." Was not Amos an extremist for justice—"Let justice roll down like waters and righteousness like a mighty stream." Was not Paul an extremist for the Gospel of Jesus Christ—"I bear in my body the marks of the Lord Jesus." Was not Martin Luther an extremist—"Here I stand; I can do none other so help me God." Was not John Bunyan an extremist—"I will stay in jail to the end of my days before I make butchery of my conscience." Was not Abraham Lincoln an extremist—"This nation cannot survive half slave and half free." Was not Thomas Jefferson an extremist—"We hold these truths to be self-evident that all men are created equal." So the question is not whether we will be extremists but what kind of extremist will we be. Will we be extremists for hate or will we be extremists for love? Will we be extremists for the preservation of injustice—or will we be extremists for the cause of justice? In that dramatic scene on Calvary's hill three men were crucified. We must never forget that all three were crucified for the same crime—the crime of extremism. Two were extremists for immorality, and thus fell below their environment. The other, Jesus Christ, was an extremist for love, truth, and goodness, and thereby rose above His environment. So, after all, maybe the South, the nation, and the world are in dire need of creative extremists.

I had hoped that the white moderate would see this. Maybe I was too optimistic. Maybe I expected too much. I guess I should have realized that few members of a race that has oppressed another race can understand or appreciate the deep groans and passionate yearnings of those that have been oppressed, and still fewer have the vision to see that injustice must be rooted out by strong, persistent, and determined action. I am thankful, however, that some of our white brothers have grasped the meaning of this social revolution and committed themselves to it. They are still all too small in quantity, but they are big in quality. Some like Ralph McGill, Lillian Smith, Harry Golden, and James Dabbs have written about our struggle in eloquent, prophetic, and understanding terms. Others have marched with us down nameless streets of the South. They have languished in filthy, roach-infested jails, suffering the abuse and brutality of angry policemen who see them as "dirty nigger lovers." They, unlike so many of their moderate brothers and sisters, have recognized the urgency of the moment and sensed the need for powerful "action" antidotes to combat the disease of segregation.

Let me rush on to mention my other disappointment. I have been so greatly disappointed with the white Church and its leadership. Of course there are some notable exceptions. I am not unmindful of the fact that each of you has taken some significant stands on this issue. I commend you, Rev. Stalligs, for your Christian stand on this past Sunday, in welcoming Negroes to your worship service on a non-segregated basis. I commend the Catholic leaders of this state for integrating Springhill College several years ago.

But despite these notable exceptions I must honestly reiterate that I have been disappointed with the Church. I do not say that as one of those negative critics who can always find something wrong with the Church. I say it as a minister of the gospel, who loves the Church; who was nurtured in its bosom; who has been sustained by its spiritual blessings and who will remain true to it as long as the cord of life shall lengthen.

I had the strange feeling when I was suddenly catapulted into the leadership of the bus protest in Montgomery several years ago that we would have the support of the white Church. I felt that the white ministers, priests, and rabbis of the South would be some of our strongest allies. Instead, some have been outright opponents, refusing to understand the freedom movement and misrepresenting its leaders; all too many others have been more cautious than courageous and have remained silent behind the anesthetizing security of stained glass windows.

In spite of my shattered dreams of the past, I came to Birmingham with the hope that the white religious leadership of this community would see the justice of our cause and, with deep moral concern, serve as the channel through which our just grievances could get to the power structure. I had hoped that each of you would understand. But again I have been disappointed.

I have heard numerous religious leaders of the South call upon their worshippers to comply with a desegregation decision because it is the law, but I have longed to hear white ministers say follow this decree because integration is morally right and the Negro is your brother. In the midst of blatant injustices inflicted upon the Negro, I have watched white churches stand on the sideline and merely mouth pious irrelevancies and sanctimonious trivialities. In the midst of a mighty struggle to rid our nation of racial and economic injustice, I have heard so many ministers say, "Those are social issues with which the Gospel has no real concern," and I have watched so many churches commit themselves to a completely other-worldly religion which made a strange distinction between body and soul, the sacred and the secular.

So here we are moving toward the exit of the twentieth century with a religious community largely adjusted to the status quo, standing as a tail light behind other community agencies rather than a headlight leading men to higher levels of justice.

I have travelled the length and breadth of Alabama, Mississippi, and all the other Southern states. On sweltering summer days and crisp autumn mornings I have looked at their beautiful churches with their spires pointing heavenward. I have beheld the impressive outlay of her massive religious education buildings. Over and over again I have found myself asking: "Who worships here? Who is their God? Where were their voices when the lips of Governor Barnett dripped with words of interposition and nullification? Where were they when Governor Wallace gave the clarion call for defiance and hatred? Where were their voices of support when tired, bruised, and weary Negro men and women decided to rise from the dark dungeons of complacency to the bright hills of creative protest?"

Yes, these questions are still in my mind. In deep disappointment, I have wept over the laxity of the Church. But be assured that my tears have been tears of love. These can be no deep disappointment where there is not deep love. Yes, I love the Church; I love her sacred walls. How could I do otherwise? I am in the rather unique position of being the son, the grandson, and the great grandson of preachers. Yes, I see the Church as the body of Christ. But, oh! How we have blemished and scarred that body through social neglect and fear of being nonconformist.

There was a time when the Church was very powerful. It was during that period when the early Christians rejoiced when they were deemed worthy to suffer for what they believed. In those days the Church was not merely a thermometer that recorded the ideas and principles of popular opinion; it was a thermostat that transformed the mores of society. Wherever the early Christians entered a town the power structure got disturbed and immediately sought to convict them for being "disturbers of the peace" and "outside agitators." But they went on with the conviction that they were a "colony of heaven" and had to obey God rather than man. They were small in number but big in commitment. They were too God-intoxicated to be "astronomically intimidated." They brought an end to such ancient evils as infanticide and gladiatorial contests.

Things are different now. The contemporary Church is so often a weak, ineffectual voice with an uncertain sound. It is so often the arch-supporter of the status quo. Far from being disturbed by the presence of the Church, the power structure of the average community is consoled by the Church's silent and often vocal sanction of things as they are.

But the judgement of God is upon the Church as never before. If the Church of today does not recapture the sacrificial spirit of the early Church, it will lose its authentic ring, forfeit the loyalty of millions, and be dismissed as an irrelevant social club with no meaning for the twentieth century. I am meeting young people every day whose disappointment with the Church has risen to outright disgust.

Maybe again I have been too optimistic. Is organized religion too inextricably bound to the status quo to save our nation and the world? Maybe I must turn my faith to the inner spiritual Church, the church within the Church, as the true *ecclesia* and the hope of the world. But again I am thankful to God that some noble souls from the ranks of organized religion have broken loose from the paralyzing chains of conformity and joined us as active partners in the struggle for freedom. They have left their secure congregations and walked the streets of Albany, Georgia, with us. They have gone through the highways of the South on torturous rides for freedom. Yes, they have gone to jail with us. Some have been kicked out of their churches and lost the support of their bishops and fellow ministers. But they have gone with the faith that right defeated is stronger than evil triumphant. These men have been the leaven in the lump of the race. Their witness has been the spiritual salt that has preserved the true meaning of the Gospel in these troubled times. They have carved a tunnel of hope through the dark mountain of disappointment.

I hope the Church as a whole will meet the challenge of this decisive hour. But even if the Church does not come to the aid of justice, I have no despair about the future. I have no fear about the outcome of our struggle in Birmingham, even if our motives are presently misunderstood. We will reach the goal of freedom in Birmingham and all over the nation, because the goal of America is freedom. Abused and scorned though we may be, our destiny is tied up with the destiny of America. Before the pilgrims landed at Plymouth, we were here. Before the pen of Jefferson etched across the pages of history the majestic words of the Declaration of Independence, we were here. For more than two centuries our foreparents labored in this country without wages; they made cotton "king"; and they built the homes of their masters in the midst of brutal injustice and shameful humiliation—and yet out of bottomless vitality they continued to thrive and develop. If the inexpressible cruelties of slavery could not stop us, the opposition we now face will surely fail. We will win our freedom because the sacred heritage of our nation and the eternal will of God are embodied in our echoing demands.

I must close now. But before closing I am impelled to mention one other point in your statement that troubled me profoundly. You warmly commended the Birmingham police force for keeping "order" and "preventing violence." I don't believe you would have so warmly commended the police force if you had seen its angry violent dogs literally biting six unarmed, nonviolent Negroes. I don't believe you would so quickly commend the policemen if you would observe their ugly and inhuman treatment of Negroes here in the city jail; if you would watch them push and curse old Negro women and young Negro girls; if you would see them slap and kick old Negro men and young Negro boys; if you will observe them, as they did on two occasions, refuse to give us food because we wanted to sing our grace together. I'm sorry that I can't join you in your praise for the police department.

It is true that they have been rather disciplined in their public handling of the demonstrators. In this sense they have been rather publicly "nonviolent." But for what purpose? To preserve the evil system of segregation. Over the last few years I have consistently preached that nonviolence demands that the means we use must be as pure as the ends we seek. So I have tried to make it clear that it is wrong to use immoral means to attain moral ends. But now I must affirm that it is just as wrong, or even more so, to use moral means to preserve immoral ends. Maybe Mr. Connor and his policemen have been rather publicly nonviolent, as Chief Prichett was in Albany, Georgia, but they have used the moral means of nonviolence to maintain the immoral end of flagrant racial injustice. T. S. Eliot has said that there is no greater treason than to do the right deed for the wrong reason.

I wish you had commended the Negro sit-inners and demonstrators of Birmingham for their sublime courage, their willingness to suffer, and their amazing discipline in the midst of the most inhuman provocation. One day the South will recognize its real heros. They will be the James Merediths, courageously and with a majestic sense of purpose, facing jeering and hostile mobs and the agonizing loneliness that characterizes the life of the pioneer. They will be old, oppressed, battered Negro women, symbolized in a seventy-two year old woman of Montgomery, Alabama, who rose up with a sense of dignity and with her people decided not to ride the segregated buses, and responded to one who inquired about her tiredness with ungrammatical profundity: "My feets is tired, but my soul is rested." They will be young high school and college students, young ministers of the gospel and a host of the elders, courageously and nonviolently sitting in at lunch counters and willingly going to jail for conscience sake. One day the South will know that when these disinherited children of God sat down at lunch counters they were in reality standing up for the best in the American dream and the most sacred values in our Judeo-Christian heritage, and thus carrying our whole nation back to great wells of democracy which were dug deep by the founding fathers in the formulation of the Constitution and the Declaration of Independence.

Never before have I written a letter this long (or should I say a book?). I'm afraid that it is much too long to take your precious time. I can assure that it would have been much shorter if I had been writing from a comfortable desk, but what else is there to do when you are alone for days in the dull monotony of a narrow jail cell other than write long letters, think strange thoughts, and pray long prayers?

If I have said anything in this letter that is an overstatement of the truth and is indicative of an unreasonable impatience, I beg you to forgive me. If I have said anything in this letter that is an understatement of the truth and is indicative of my having a patience that makes me patient with anything less than brotherhood, I beg God to forgive me.

I hope this letter finds you strong in the faith. I also hope that circumstances will soon make it possible for me to meet each of you, not as an integrationist or a civil rights leader, but as a fellow clergyman and a Christian brother. Let us all hope that the dark clouds of racial prejudice will soon pass away and the deep fog of misunderstanding will be lifted from our fear-drenched communities and in some not too distant tomorrow the radiant stars of love and brotherhood will shine over our great nation with all of their scintillating beauty.

> Yours for the cause of
> Peace and Brotherhood
>
> Martin Luther King, Jr.

NOTE

1. Martin Luther King Jr., *Why We Can't Wait*, Harper and Row, 1963, pp. 77-78.

Part III

Contemporary Voices
of Nonviolence

10

The Nobel Peace Prize Lecture

Dalai Lama

Tenzin Gyatso was born into a peasant family in Amdo, eastern Tibet, in 1935 and was recognized at the age of two by a government search party and eminent lamas as the fourteenth incarnation in the line of Dalai Lama. At the age of four he was taken to Lhasa and officially installed as the Dalai Lama. Following the Chinese invasion and occupation of Tibet in 1950 and the subsequent large-scale popular revolt against the Chinese invaders in 1959, the Dalai Lama along with 100,000 Tibetan refugees fled across the Himalayas to India and other neighboring countries. In India, he drafted a democratic constitution, formed a Tibetan government-in-exile, and began to establish the institutions that would form the basis for a new Tibetan society: schools, hospitals, orphanages, craft co-ops, farming communities, institutions for the preservation of traditional music and drama, and monastic institutions. Today, under his leadership, the Tibetans are one of the best-settled refugee groups that the world has known. Inside Tibet the Chinese have, according to the report of the International Commission of Jurists, carried out wholesale cultural genocide. In 1959 there were over 6,000 monasteries in Tibet. By 1980, only 12 remained intact. Over 1 million of Tibet's 6 million inhabitants have died as a direct result of the Chinese occupation, 87,000 alone in Lhasa (by Chinese count) during the popular uprising. In 1989 the Nobel Peace Prize was awarded to the fourteenth Dalai Lama, the religious and political leader of the Tibetan people. He emerges as a highly pragmatic man, dedicated to the establishment of nonviolent solutions to human problems in the personal, environmental, and political arenas.

Brothers and Sisters:
It is an honor and pleasure to be among you today. I am really happy to see so many old friends who have come from different corners of the world, and to make new friends, whom I hope to meet again in the future. When I meet people in different parts of the world, I am always reminded that we are all basically

alike: we are all human beings. Maybe we have different clothes, our skin is of a different color, or we speak different languages. This is on the surface. But basically, we are the same human beings. That is what binds us to each other. That is what makes it possible for us to understand each other and to develop friendship and closeness.

Thinking over what I might say today, I decided to share with you some of my thoughts concerning the common problems all of us face as members of the human family. Because we all share this small planet earth, we have to learn to live in harmony and peace with each other and with nature. That is not just a dream, but a necessity. We are dependent on each other in so many ways that we can no longer live in isolated communities and ignore what is happening outside those communities. We need to help each other when we have difficulties, and we must share the good fortune that we enjoy. I speak to you as just another human being, as a simple monk. If you find what I say useful, then I hope you will try to practice it.

I also wish to share with you today my feelings concerning the plight and aspirations of the people of Tibet. The Nobel Prize is a prize they well deserve for their courage and unfailing determination during the past forty years of foreign occupation. As a free spokesman for my captive countrymen and -women, I feel it is my duty to speak out on their behalf. I speak not with a feeling of anger or hatred towards those who are responsible for the immense suffering of our people and the destruction of our land, homes and culture. They too are human beings who struggle to find happiness and deserve our compassion. I speak to inform you of the sad situation in my country today and of the aspirations of my people, because in our struggle for freedom, truth is the only weapon we possess.

The realization that we are all basically the same human beings, who seek happiness and try to avoid suffering, is very helpful in developing a sense of brotherhood and sisterhood—a warm feeling of love and compassion for others. This, in turn, is essential if we are to survive in this ever-shrinking world we live in. For if we each selfishly pursue only what we believe to be in our own interest, without caring about the needs of others, we not only may end up harming others but also ourselves. This fact has become very clear during the course of this century. We know that to wage a nuclear war today, for example, would be a form of suicide; or that to pollute the air or the oceans, in order to achieve some short-term benefit, would be to destroy the very basis for our survival. As individuals and nations are becoming increasingly interdependent we have no other choice than to develop what I call a sense of universal responsibility.

Today, we are truly a global family. What happens in one part of the world may affect us all. This, of course, is not only true of the negative things that happen, but is equally valid for the positive developments. We not only know what happens elsewhere, thanks to the extraordinary modern communications technology, we are also directly affected by events that occur far away. We feel a sense of sadness when children are starving in Eastern Africa. Similarly, we feel a sense of joy when a family is reunited after decades of separation by the Berlin

Wall. Our crops and livestock are contaminated and our health and livelihood threatened when a nuclear accident happens miles away in another country. Our own security is enhanced when peace breaks out between warring parties in other continents.

But war or peace; the destruction or the protection of nature; the violation or promotion of human rights and democratic freedoms; poverty or material well being; the lack of moral and spiritual values or their existence and development; and the breakdown or development of human understanding, are not isolated phenomena that can be analyzed and tackled independently of one another. In fact, they are very much interrelated at all levels and need to be approached with that understanding.

Peace, in the sense of the absence of war, is of little value to someone who is dying of hunger or cold. It will not remove the pain of torture inflicted on a prisoner of conscience. It does not comfort those who have lost their loved ones in floods caused by senseless deforestation in a neighboring country. Peace can only last where human rights are respected, where the people are fed, and where individuals and nations are free. True peace with ourselves and with the world around us can only be achieved through the development of mental peace. The other phenomena mentioned above are similarly interrelated. Thus, for example, we see that a clean environment, wealth or democracy mean little in the face of war, especially nuclear war, and that material development is not sufficient to ensure human happiness.

Material progress is of course important for human advancement. In Tibet, we paid much too little attention to technological and economic development, and today we realize that this was a mistake. At the same time, material development without spiritual development can also cause serious problems. In some countries too much attention is paid to external things and very little importance is given to inner development. I believe both are important and must be developed side by side so as to achieve a good balance between them. Tibetans are always described by foreign visitors as being a happy, jovial people. This is part of our national character, formed by cultural and religious values that stress the importance of mental peace through the generation of love and kindness to all other living sentient beings, both human and animal. Inner peace is the key: if you have inner peace, the external problems do not affect your deep sense of peace and tranquility. In that state of mind you can deal with situations with calmness and reason, while keeping your inner happiness. That is very important. Without this inner peace, no matter how comfortable your life is materially, you may still be worried, disturbed or unhappy because of circumstances.

Clearly, it is of great importance, therefore, to understand the interrelationship among these and other phenomena, and to approach and attempt to solve problems in a balanced way that takes these different aspects into consideration. Of course it is not easy. But it is of little benefit to try to solve one problem if doing so creates an equally serious new one. So really we have no alternative: we must develop a sense of universal responsibility not only in the geographic sense, but also in respect to the different issues that confront our planet.

Responsibility does not only lie with the leaders of our countries or with those who have been appointed or elected to do a particular job. It lies with each of us individually. Peace, for example, starts within each one of us. When we have inner peace, we can be at peace with those around us. When our community is in a state of peace, it can share that peace with neighboring communities, and so on. When we feel love and kindness towards others, it not only makes others feel loved and cared for, but it helps us also to develop inner happiness and peace. And there are ways in which we can consciously work to develop feelings of love and kindness. For some of us, the most effective way to do so is through religious practice. For others it may be non-religious practices. What is important is that we each make a sincere effort to take seriously our responsibility for each other and for the natural environment.

I am very encouraged by the developments which are taking place around us. After the young people of many countries, particularly in northern Europe, have repeatedly called for an end to the dangerous destruction of the environment which was being conducted in the name of economic development, the world's political leaders are now starting to take meaningful steps to address this problem. The report to the United Nations Secretary General by the World Commission on the Environment and Development (the Brundtland report) was an important step in educating governments on the urgency of the issue. Serious efforts to bring peace to war-torn zones and to implement the right to self-determination of some peoples have resulted in the withdrawal of Soviet troops from Afghanistan and the establishment of independent Namibia. Through persistent non-violent popular efforts dramatic changes, bringing many countries closer to real democracy, have occurred in many places, from Manila in the Philippines to Berlin in East Germany. With the Cold War era apparently drawing to a close, people everywhere live with renewed hope. Sadly, the courageous efforts of the Chinese people to bring similar change to their country was brutally crushed last June. But their efforts too are a source of hope. The military might has not extinguished the desire for freedom and the determination of the Chinese people to achieve it. I particularly admire the fact that these young people, who have been taught that "power grows from the barrel of the gun," chose, instead, to use non-violence as their weapon.

What these positive changes indicate is that reason, courage, determination, and the inextinguishable desire for freedom can ultimately win. In the struggle between forces of war, violence and oppression on the one hand, and peace, reason and freedom on the other, the latter are gaining the upper hand. This realization fills us Tibetans with hope that some day we too will once again be free.

The awarding of the Nobel Prize to me, a simple monk from far-away Tibet, here in Norway, also fills us Tibetans with hope. It means that, despite the fact that we have not drawn attention to our plight by means of violence, we have not been forgotten. It also means that the values we cherish, in particular our respect for all forms of life and the belief in the power of truth, are today recognized and encouraged. It is also a tribute to my mentor, Mahatma Gandhi, whose example is an inspiration to so many of us. This year's award is an indication that this sense of universal responsibility is developing. I am deeply touched by the sincere concern shown by so many people in this part of the world for the suffering of the people of Tibet. That is a source of hope not only for us Tibetans, but for all oppressed peoples.

As you know, Tibet has, for forty years, been under foreign occupation. Today, more than a quarter of a million Chinese troops are stationed in Tibet. Some sources estimate the occupation army to be twice this strength. During this time, Tibetans have been deprived of their most basic human rights, including the right to life, movement, speech, worship, only to mention a few. More than one sixth of Tibet's population of six million died as a direct result of the Chinese invasion and occupation. Even before the Cultural Revolution started, many of Tibet's monasteries, temples and historic buildings were destroyed. Almost everything that remained was destroyed during the Cultural Revolution. I do not wish to dwell on this point, which is well documented. What is important to realize, however, is that despite the limited freedom granted after 1979 to rebuild parts of some monasteries and other such tokens of liberalization, the fundamental human rights of the Tibetan people are still today being systematically violated. In recent months this bad situation has become even worse.

If it were not for our community in exile, so generously sheltered and supported by the government and people of India and helped by organizations and individuals from many parts of the world, our nation would today be little more than a shattered remnant of a people. Our culture, religion and national identity would have been effectively eliminated. As it is, we have built schools and monasteries in exile and have created democratic institutions to serve our people and preserve the seeds of our civilization. With this experience, we intend to implement full democracy in a future free Tibet. Thus, as we develop our community in exile on modern lines, we also cherish and preserve our own identity and culture and bring hope to millions of our countrymen and women in Tibet.

The issue of most urgent concern at this time is the massive influx of Chinese settlers into Tibet. Although in the first decades of occupation a considerable number of Chinese were transferred into the eastern parts of Tibet—in the Tibetan provinces of Amdo (Chinghai) and Kham (most of which has been annexed by the neighboring Chinese province)—since 1983 an unprecedented number of Chinese have been encouraged by their government to migrate to all parts of Tibet, including central and western Tibet (which the People's Republic of China refers to as the so-called Tibet Autonomous Region). Tibetans are rapidly being reduced to an insignificant minority in their own country. This development, which threatens the very survival of the Tibetan nation, its culture and spiritual heritage, can still be stopped and reversed. But this must be done now, before it is too late.

The new cycle of protest and violent repression, which started in Tibet in September of 1987 and culminated in the imposition of martial law in the capital, Lhasa, in March of this year, was in large part a reaction to this tremendous Chinese influx. Information reaching us in exile indicates that the protest marches and other peaceful forms of protest are continuing in Lhasa and a number of other places in Tibet despite the severe punishment and inhumane treatment given to Tibetans detained for expressing their grievances. The number of Tibetans killed by security forces during the protest in March and of those who died in detention afterward is not known but is believed to be more than two hundred. Thousands have been detained or arrested and imprisoned, and torture is commonplace.

It was against the background of this worsening situation and in order to prevent further bloodshed, that I proposed what is generally referred to as the Five Point Peace Plan for the restoration of peace and human rights in Tibet. I elaborated on the plan in a speech in Strasbourg last year. I believe the plan provides a reasonable and realistic framework for negotiations with the People's Republic of China. So far, however, China's leaders have been unwilling to respond constructively. The brutal suppression of the Chinese democracy movement in June of this year, however, reinforced my view that any settlement of the Tibetan question will only be meaningful if it is supported by adequate international guarantees.

The Five Point Peace Plan addresses the principal and interrelated issues, which I referred to in the first part of this lecture. It calls for (1) Transformation of the whole of Tibet, including the eastern provinces of Kham and Amdo, into a Zone of *Ahimsa* (non-violence); (2) Abandonment of China's population transfer policy; (3) Respect for the Tibetan people's fundamental human rights and democratic freedoms; (4) Restoration and protection of Tibet's natural environment; and (5) Commencement of earnest negotiations on the future status of Tibet and of relations between the Tibetan and Chinese peoples. In the Strasbourg address I proposed that Tibet become a fully self-governing democratic political entity.

I would like to take this opportunity to explain the Zone of Ahimsa or peace sanctuary concept, which is the central element of the Five Point Peace Plan. I am convinced that it is of great importance not only for Tibet, but for peace and stability in Asia.

It is my dream that the entire Tibetan plateau should become a free refuge where humanity and nature can live in peace and in harmonious balance. It would be a place where people from all over the world could come to seek the true meaning of peace within themselves, away from the tensions and pressures of much of the rest of the world. Tibet could indeed become a creative center for the promotion and development of peace.

The following are key elements of the proposed Zone of Ahimsa:

•   the entire Tibetan plateau would be demilitarized;

- the manufacture, testing, and stockpiling of nuclear weapons and other armaments on the Tibetan plateau would be prohibited;
- the Tibetan plateau would be transformed into the world's largest natural park or biosphere. Strict laws would be enforced to protect wildlife and plant life; the exploitation of natural resources would be carefully regulated so as not to damage relevant ecosystems; and a policy of sustainable development would be adopted in populated areas;
- the manufacture and use of nuclear power and other technologies which produce hazardous waste would be prohibited;
- national resources and policy would be directed towards the active promotion of peace and environmental protection. Organizations dedicated to the furtherance of peace and to the protection of all forms of life would find a hospitable home in Tibet;
- the establishment of international and regional organizations for the promotion and protection of human rights would be encouraged in Tibet.

Tibet's height and size (the size of the European Community), as well as its unique history and profound spiritual heritage make it ideally suited to fulfill the role of a sanctuary of peace in the strategic heart of Asia. It would also be in keeping with Tibet's historical role as a peaceful Buddhist nation and buffer region separating the Asian continent's great and often rival powers.

In order to reduce existing tensions in Asia, the President of the Soviet Union, Mr. Gorbachev, proposed the demilitarization of Soviet-Chinese borders and their transformation into a "frontier of peace and good neighborliness." The Nepal government had earlier proposed that the Himalayan country of Nepal, bordering on Tibet, should become a zone of peace, although that proposal did not include demilitarization of the country.

For the stability and peace of Asia, it is essential to create peace zones to separate the continent's biggest powers and potential adversaries. President Gorbachev's proposal, which also included a complete Soviet troop withdrawal from Mongolia, would help to reduce tension and the potential for confrontation between the Soviet Union and China. A true peace zone must, clearly, also be created to separate the world's two most populous states, China and India.

The establishment of the Zone of Ahimsa would require the withdrawal of troops and military installations from Tibet, which would enable India and Nepal also to withdraw troops and military installations from the Himalayan regions bordering Tibet. This would have to be achieved by international agreements. It would be in the best interest of all states in Asia, particularly China and India, as it would enhance their security, while reducing the economic burden of maintaining high troop concentrations in remote areas.

Tibet would not be the first strategic area to be demilitarized. Parts of the Sinai peninsula, the Egyptian territory separating Israel and Egypt, have been demilitarized for some time. Of course, Costa Rica is the best example of an entirely demilitarized country.

Tibet would also not be the first area to be turned into a natural preserve or biosphere. Many parks have been created throughout the world. Some very strategic areas have been turned into natural "peace parks." Two examples are the La Amistad park, on the Costa Rica-Panama border and the Si A Paz project on the Costa Rica-Nicaragua border.

When I visited Costa Rica earlier this year, I saw how a country can develop successfully without an army, to become a stable democracy committed to peace and the protection of the natural environment. This confirmed my belief that my vision of Tibet in the future is a realistic plan, not merely a dream.

Let me end with a personal note of thanks to all of you and our friends who are not here today. The concern and support which you have expressed for the plight of the Tibetans have touched us all greatly, and continue to give us courage to struggle for freedom and justice; not through the use of arms, but with the powerful weapons of truth and determination. I know that I speak on behalf of all the people of Tibet when I thank you and ask you not to forget Tibet at this critical time in our country's history. We too hope to contribute to the development of a more peaceful, more humane and more beautiful world. A future free Tibet will seek to help those in need throughout the world, to protect nature, and to promote peace. I believe that our Tibetan ability to combine spiritual qualities with a realistic and practical attitude enables us to make a special contribution in however modest a way. This is my hope and prayer.

In conclusion, let me share with you a short prayer which gives me great inspiration and determination:

> For as long as space endures,
> And for as long as living beings remain,
> Until then may I, too, abide
> To dispel the misery of the world.

Thank you.

11

The Almond Tree in Your Front Yard

Thich Nhat Hanh

Thich Nhat Hanh is a living example of a person dedicated to nonviolence. He is a Zen master, poet and writer of numerous books such as *The Miracle of Mindfulness,* from which this selection is taken, as well as *A Guide to Walking Meditation, Being Peace,* and *Peace Is Every Step: The Path of Mindfulness in Everyday Life* and others. During the Vietnam War, Thich Nhat Hanh was chairman of the Vietnamese Buddhist Peace Delegation and was nominated by Martin Luther King, Jr. for the Nobel Peace Prize. Presently he lives in France but travels extensively working not only for reconciliation and peace among countries but also for that commitment to nonviolence which must begin with the individual.

I've spoken about the contemplation on interdependence. Of course all the methods in the search for truth should be looked on as means rather than as ends in themselves or as absolute truth. The meditation on interdependence is intended to remove the false barriers of discrimination so that one can enter into the universal harmony of life. It is not intended to produce a philosophical system, a philosophy of interdependence. Herman Hesse, in his novel *Siddartha,* did not yet see this and so his Siddhartha speaks about the philosophy of interdependence in words which strike us as somewhat naive. The author offers us a picture of interdependence in which everything is interrelated, a system in which no fault can be found: everything must fit into the foolproof system of mutual dependence, a system in which one cannot consider the problem of liberation in this world.
    According to an insight of our tradition, reality has three natures: imagination, interdependence, and the nature of ultimate perfection. One first considers interdependence. Because of forgetfulness and prejudices, we generally cloak reality with a veil of false views and opinions. This is seeing reality through imagination. Imagination is an illusion of reality which conceives of reality as an assembly of small pieces of separate entities and selves. In order to break

through, the practitioner meditates on the nature of interdependence or the inter-relatedness of phenomena in the processes of creation and destruction. The consideration is a way of contemplation, not the basis of a philosophic doctrine. If one clings merely to a system of concepts, one only becomes stuck. The meditation on interdependence is to help one penetrate reality in order to be one with it, not to become caught up in philosophical opinion or meditation methods. The raft is used to cross the river. It isn't to be carried around on your shoulders. The finger which points at the moon isn't the moon itself.

Finally one proceeds to the nature of ultimate perfection—reality freed from all false views produced by the imagination. Reality is reality. It transcends every concept. There is no concept which can adequately describe it, not even the concept of interdependence. To assure that one doesn't become attached to a philosophical concept, our teaching speaks of the three *non*-natures to prevent the individual from becoming caught up in the doctrine of the three natures. The essence of Mahayana Buddhist teaching lies in this.

When reality is perceived in its nature of ultimate perfection, the practitioner has reached a level of wisdom called non-discrimination mind—a wondrous communion in which there is no longer any distinction made between subject and object. This isn't some far-off, unattainable state. Any one of us—by persisting in practicing even a little—can at least taste of it. I have a pile of orphan applications for sponsorship on my desk.[1] I translate a few each day. Before I begin to translate a sheet, I look into the eyes of the child on the photograph, and look at the child's expression and features closely. I feel a deep link between myself and each child, which allows me to enter a special communion with them. While writing this to you, I see that during those moments and hours, the communion I have experienced while translating the simple lines in the applications has been a kind of non-discrimination mind. I no longer see an "I" who translates the sheets to help each child, I no longer see a child who received love and help. The child and I are one: no one pities; no one asks for help; no one helps. There is no task, no social work to be done, no compassion, no special wisdom. These are moments of non-discrimination mind.

When reality is experienced in its nature of ultimate perfection an almond tree that may be in your front yard reveals its nature in perfect wholeness. The almond tree is itself truth, reality, your own self. Of all the people who have passed by your yard, how many have really seen the almond tree? The heart of an artist may be more sensitive; hopefully, he or she will be able to see the tree in a deeper way than many others. Because of a more open heart, a certain communion already exists between the artist and the tree. What counts is your own heart. If your hear is not clouded by false views, you will be able to enter into a natural communion with the tree. The almond tree will be ready to reveal itself to you in complete wholeness. To see the almond tree is to see the way. One Zen Master, when asked to explain the wonder of reality, pointed to a cypress tree and said, "Look at the cypress tree over there."

THE VOICE OF THE RISING TIDE

When your mind is liberated your heart floods with compassion: compassion for yourself, for having undergone countless sufferings because you were not yet able to relieve yourself of false views, hatred, ignorance, and anger; and compassion for others because they do not yet see and so are still imprisoned by false views, hatred, and ignorance and continue to create suffering for themselves and for others. Now you look at yourself and at others with the eyes of compassion, like a saint who hears the cry of every creature in the universe and whose voice is the voice of every person who has seen reality in perfect wholeness. As a Buddhist Sutra hears the voice of the Bodhisattva of compassion:

The wondrous voice, the voice of the one
who attends to the cries of the world
The noble voice, the voice of the rising
tide surpassing all the sounds of the world
Let our mind be attuned to that voice.

Put aside all doubt and meditate on the
pure and holy nature of the regarder
of the cries of the world
Because that is our reliance in situations
of pain, distress, calamity, death.

Perfect in all merits, beholding all sentient
beings with compassionate eyes,
making the ocean of blessings limitless,
Before this one, we should incline.

Practice looking at all beings with the eyes of compassion: this is the meditation called "the meditation on compassion."

The meditation on compassion must be realized during the hours you sit and during every moment you carry out service for others. No matter where you go or where you sit, remember the sacred call: "Look at all beings with the eyes of compassion."

There are many subjects and methods for meditation, so many that I could never hope to write them all down for our friends. I've only mentioned a few, simple but basic methods here. A peace worker is like any one else. She or he must live her own life. Work is only a part of life. But work is life only when done in mindfulness. Otherwise, one becomes like the person "who lives as though dead." We need to light our own torch in order to carry on. But the life of each one of us is connected with the life of those around us. If we know how to live in mindfulness, if we know how to preserve and care for our own mind and heart, then thanks to that, our brothers and sisters will also know how to live in mindfulness.

MEDITATION REVEALS AND HEALS

Sitting in mindfulness, both our bodies and minds can be at peace and totally relaxed. But this state of peace and relaxation differs fundamentally from the lazy, semi-conscious state of mind that one gets while resting and dozing. Sitting in such lazy semi-consciousness, far from being mindfulness, is like sitting in a dark cave. In mindfulness one is not only restful and happy, but alert and awake. Meditation is not evasion; it is a serene encounter with reality. The person who practices mindfulness should be no less awake than the driver of a car; if the practitioner isn't awake he will be possessed by dispersion and forgetfulness, just as the drowsy driver is likely to cause a grave accident. Be as awake as a person walking on high stilts—any mis-step could cause the walker to fall. Be like a medieval knight walking weaponless in a forest of swords. Be like a lion, going forward with slow, gentle, and firm steps. Only with this kind of vigilance can you realize total awakening.

For beginners, I recommend the method of pure recognition: recognition without judgment. Feelings, whether of compassion or irritation, should be welcomed, recognized, and treated on an absolutely equal basis; because both are ourselves. The tangerine I am eating is me. The mustard greens I am planting are me. I plant with all my heart and mind. I clean this teapot with the kind of attention I would have were I giving the baby Buddha or Jesus a bath. Nothing should be treated more carefully than anything else. In mindfulness, compassion, irritation, mustard green plant, and teapot are all sacred.

When possessed by a sadness, an anxiety, a hatred, or a passion or whatever, the method of pure observation and recognition may seem difficult to practice. If so, turn to meditation on a fixed object, using your own state of mind as meditation's subject. Such meditation reveals and heals. The sadness or anxiety, hatred or passion, under the gaze of concentration and meditation reveals its own nature—a revelation that leads naturally to healing and emancipation. The sadness (or whatever has caused the pain) can be used as a means of liberation from torment and suffering, like using a thorn to remove a thorn. We should treat our anxiety, our pain, our hatred and passion gently, respectfully, not resisting it, but living with it, making peace with it, penetrating into its nature by meditation on interdependence. One quickly learns how to select subjects of meditation that fit the situation. Subjects of meditation—like interdependence, compassion, self, emptiness, non-attachment—all these belong to the categories of meditation which have the power to reveal and to heal.

Meditation on these subjects, however, can only be successful if we have built up a certain power of concentration, a power achieved by the practice of mindfulness in everyday life, in the observation and recognition of all that is going on. But the objects of meditation must be realities that have real roots in yourselves—not just subjects of philosophical speculation. Each should be like a kind of food that must be cooked for a long time over a hot fire. We put it in a pot, cover it, and light the fire. The pot is ourselves and the heat used to cook is the power of concentration. The fuel comes from the continuous practice of mindfulness. Without enough heat the food will never be cooked. But once cooked, the food reveals its true nature and helps lead us to liberation.

THE WATER CLEANER, THE GRASS GREENER

The Buddha once said that the problem of life and death is itself the problem of mindfulness. Whether or not one is alive depends on whether one is mindful. In the Samyutta Nikaya Sutra, the Buddha tells a story which took place in a small village:

A famous dancer had just come to the village and the people were swarming the streets to catch a glimpse of her. At that same moment, a condemned criminal was obliged to cross the village carrying a bowl of oil filled to the very brim. He had to concentrate with all his might on keeping the bowl steady, for even if one drop of oil were to spill from the bowl to the ground, the soldier directly behind him had orders to take out his sword and cut off the man's head. Having reached this point in the story, Gautama Buddha asked: "Now, do you think our prisoner was able to keep all his attention so focused on the bowl of oil that his mind did not stray to steal a glimpse of the famous dancer in town, or to look up at the throngs of villagers making such a commotion in the streets, any of whom could bump into him at any moment?"

Another time the Buddha recounted a story which made me suddenly see the supreme importance of practicing mindfulness of one's own self—that is, to protect and care for one's self, not being preoccupied about the way others look after themselves, a habit of mind which gives rise to resentment and anxiety.

The Buddha said, "There once were a couple of acrobats. The teacher was a poor widower and the student was a small girl named Meda. The two of them performed in the streets to earn enough to eat. They used a tall bamboo pole which the teacher balanced on the top of his head while the little girl slowly climbed to the top. There she remained while the teacher continued to walk along the ground.

Both of them had to devote all their attention to maintain perfect balance and to prevent any accident from occurring. One day the teacher instructed the pupil: "Listen, Meda, I will watch you and you watch me, so that we can help each other maintain concentration and balance and prevent an accident. Then we'll be sure to earn enough to eat." But the little girl was wise and answered, "Dear master, I think it would be better for each of us to watch ourself. To look after oneself means to look after both of us. That way I am sure we will avoid any accidents and will earn enough to eat."

The Buddha said: "The child spoke correctly."

In a family, if there is one person who practices mindfulness, the entire family will be more mindful. Because of the presence of one member who lives in mindfulness, the entire family is reminded to live in mindfulness. If in one class, one student lives in mindfulness, the entire class is influenced.

In peace-serving communities, we must follow the same principle. Don't worry if those around you aren't doing their best. Just worry about how to make yourself worthy. Doing your best is the surest way to remind those around you to do their best. But to be worthy requires the continuing practice of mindfulness. That is a certainty. Only by practicing mindfulness will we not lose ourselves but acquire a bright joy and peace. Only by practicing mindfulness, will we not lose ourselves but acquire a bright joy and peace. Only by practicing mindfulness will we be able to look at everyone else with the open mind and eyes of love.

I was just invited downstairs for a cup of tea, into an apartment where a friend who helps us has a piano. As Kirsten—who is from Holland—poured tea for me, I looked at her pile of work and said, "Why don't you stop translating orphan applications for a minute and play the piano for me?" Kirsten was glad to put down her work for a moment and sat down at the piano to play a selection of Chopin she has known since she was a child. The piece has several measures which are soft and melodic but others which are loud and quick. Her dog was lying beneath the tea table, and when the music became excited, it began to bark and whine. I knew that it felt uneasy and wanted the music to stop. Kirsten's dog is treated with the kindness one gives to a small child, and perhaps is more sensitive to music than most children. Or perhaps it responded this way because its ears pick up certain vibrations that human ears do not. Kirsten continued to play while trying to console the dog at the same time, but to no avail. She finished and began to play another piece by Mozart which was light and harmonious. Now the dog lay quietly and appeared to be at peace. When Kirsten had finished she came over and sat down beside me and said, "Often when I play a piece of Chopin that is the least bit loud, the dog comes and grabs hold of my pantsleg, trying to force me to leave the piano. Sometimes I have to put her outside before I can continued playing. But whenever I play Bach or Mozart, she is peaceful."

Kirsten mentioned a report that in Canada people tried playing Mozart for their plants during the night. The plants grew more quickly than normal, and the flowers inclined toward the direction of the music. Others played Mozart every day in wheat and rye fields and were able to measure that the wheat and rye in these fields grew more quickly than the wheat and rye in other fields.

As Kirsten spoke, I thought about conference rooms where people argue and debate, where angry and reproachful words are hurled back and forth. If one placed flowers and plants in such rooms, chances are they would cease to grow.

I thought about the garden tended by a monk living in mindfulness. His flowers are always fresh and green, nourished by the peace and joy which flow from his mindfulness. One of the ancients said,

When a great Master is born, the water in the rivers turns clearer and the plants grow greener.

We ought to listen to music or sit and practice breathing at the beginning of every meeting or discussion.

NOTE

1. The Vietnamese Buddhist Peace Delegation has carried on a program of raising financial support for families within Vietnam who took in orphans. In the United States the sponsor contributed $6 a month for the family of the orphan he or she was helping.

12

Selections from *Long Walk to Freedom*

Nelson Mandela

Mandela's words "The struggle is my life" are not to be taken lightly. Nelson Mandela personifies struggle. He has led the fight against apartheid with extraordinary vigor and resilience after spending nearly three decades of his life from 1962 behind bars. He has sacrificed his private life and his youth for his people and remains South Africa's best-known and best-loved hero. Mandela has held numerous positions in the African National Congress (ANC): African National Congress Youth League (ANCYL) secretary (1948), ANCYL president (1950), ANC Transvaal president (1952), deputy national president (1952), and ANC president (1991). He was born at Qunu, near Umtata on July 19, 1918. His father, Henry Mgadla Mandela, was chief councillor to Thembuland's acting paramount chief David Dalindyebo. When his father died, Mandela became the chief's ward and was groomed for the chieftainship. Mandela matriculated at Healdtown Methodist Boarding School and then began studying for his B.A. degree at Fort Hare. As an SRC member he participated in a student strike and was expelled, along with the late Oliver Tambo, in 1940. He completed his degree by correspondence from Johannesburg, did articles of clerkship and enrolled for an L.L.B. at the University of the Witwatersrand. In 1944 he helped found the ANC Youth League, whose Programme of Action was adopted by the ANC in 1949. Mandela was elected national volunteer-in-chief of the 1952 Defiance Campaign. He travelled the country organizing resistance to discriminatory legislation. He was given a suspended sentence for his part in the campaign. Shortly afterward a banning order confined him to Johannesburg for six months. During this period he formulated the "M Plan," in terms of which ANC branches were broken down into underground cells. By 1952 Mandela and Tambo had opened the first black legal firm in the country, and Mandela was both Transvaal president of the ANC and deputy national president. A petition by the Transvaal Law Society to strike Mandela off the roll of attorneys was refused by the Supreme Court. In the 1950s, after being forced through constant bannings to resign officially from the ANC, Mandela analyzed the Bantustan policy as a political swindle. He predicted mass removals, political persecutions, and police terror. For the second half of the 1950s, he was one of the accused in the "Treason Trial." With Duma Nokwe, he conducted the defense. When the ANC was banned after the Sharpeville massacre in 1960, he was detained until 1961, when he went underground to lead a campaign for a new national convention. Umkhonto we Sizwe (MK), the military wing of the ANC, was born the same year. Under his leadership it launched a campaign of sabotage against government and economic installations. In 1962 Mandela left the country for military training in Algeria and to arrange training for other MK members. On his return he was arrested for leaving the country illegally and for incitement to strike. He conducted his own defense. He was convicted and jailed for five years in November 1962. While serving his sentence, he was charged, in the Rivonia trial, with sabotage and sentenced to life imprisonment. A decade before being imprisoned, Mandela had spoken out against the introduction of Bantu education, recommending that community activists "make every home, every shack or rickety structure a centre of learning." Robben Island, where he was imprisoned, became a center for learning, and Mandela was a central figure in the organized political education classes. In prison Mandela never compromised his political principles and was always a source of strength for the other prisoners. During the 1970s he refused the offer of a remission of sentence if he recognized Transkei and settled there. In 1982 Mandela was removed to Pollsmoor Maximum Security prison in Cape Town. In the 1980s he again rejected P.W. Botha's offer of freedom if he renounced violence. It is significant that shortly after his release on Sunday, February 11, 1990, Mandela and his delegation agreed to the suspension of armed struggle. Mandela has honorary degrees from more than fifty international universities and is chancellor of the University of the North. He was the first democratically elected state president of South Africa, May 10, 1994–June 1999. Nelson Mandela retired from public life in June 1999. He currently resides in his birthplace—Qunu, Transkei. The following selection is excerpted from his autobiography, *Long Walk to Freedom*.

Africans could not vote, but that did not mean that we did not care who won elections. The white general election of 1948 matched the ruling United Party, led by General Smuts, then at the height of his international regard, against the revived National Party. While Smuts had enlisted South Africa on the side of the Allies in World War II, the National Party refused to support Great Britain and publicly sympathized with Nazi Germany. The National Party's campaign centered around the *swart gevaar* (the black danger), and they fought the election on the twin slogans of *Die kaffer op sy plek* (The nigger in his place) and *Die koelies uit die land* (The coolies out of the country)—*coolies* being the Afrikaner's derogatory term for Indians.

The Nationalists, led by Dr. Daniel Malan, a former minister of the Dutch Reform Church and a newspaper editor, were a party animated by bitterness—bitterness toward the English, who had treated them as inferiors for decades, and bitterness toward the African, who the Nationalists believed was threatening the prosperity and purity of Afrikaner culture. Africans had no loyalty to General Smuts, but we had even less for the National Party.

Malan's platform was known as apartheid. *Apartheid* was new term but an old idea. It literally means "apartness" and it represented the codification in one oppressive system of all the laws and regulations that had kept Africans in an inferior position to whites for centuries. What had been more or less de facto was to become relentlessly de jure. The often haphazard segregation of the past three hundred years was to be consolidated into a monolithic system that was diabolical in its detail, inescapable in its reach, and overwhelming in its power. The premise of apartheid was that whites were superior to Africans, Coloureds, and Indians, and the function of it was to entrench white supremacy forever. As the Nationalists put it, *"Die wit man moet altyd baas wees"* (The white man must always remain boss). Their platform rested on the term *baasskap*, literally bossship, a freighted word that stood for white supremacy in all its harshness. The policy was supported by the Dutch Reform Church, which furnished apartheid with its religious underpinnings by suggesting that Afrikaners were God's chosen people and that blacks were a subservient species. In the Afrikaner's worldview, apartheid and the church went hand in hand.

The Nationalists' victory was the beginning of the end of the domination of the Afrikaner by the Englishman. English would now take second place to Afrikaans as an official language. The Nationalist slogan encapsulated their mission: *"Eie volk, eie taal, eie land"*—Our own people, our own language, our own land. In the distorted cosmology of the Afrikaner, the Nationalist victory was like the Israelites' journey to the Promised Land. This was the fulfillment of God's promise, and the justification for their view that South Africa should be a white man's country forever.

The victory was a shock. The United Party and General Smuts had beaten the Nazis, and surely they would defeat the National Party. On election day, I attended a meeting in Johannesburg with Oliver Tambo and several others. We barely discussed the question of a Nationalist government because we did not expect one. The meeting went on all night and we emerged at dawn and found a newspaper vendor selling the *Rand Daily Mail*: the Nationalists had triumphed. I was stunned and dismayed, but Oliver took a more considered line. "I like this," he said. "I like this." I could not imagine why. He explained, "Now we will know exactly who our enemies are and where we stand."

Even General Smuts realized the dangers of this harsh ideology, decrying apartheid as "a crazy concept, born of prejudice and fear." From the moment of the Nationalists' election, we knew that our land would henceforth be a place of tension and strife. For the first time in South African history, an exclusively Afrikaner party led the government. "South Africa belongs to us once more," Malan proclaimed in his victory speech.

Mass action was perilous in South Africa, where it was a criminal offense for an African to strike, and where the rights of free speech and movement were unmercifully curtailed. By striking, an African worker stood not only to lose his job but his entire livelihood and his right to stay in the area in which he was living. In my experience, a political strike is always riskier than an economic one. A strike based on a political grievance rather than on clear-cut issues like higher wages or shorter hours is a more precarious form of protest and demands particularly efficient organization. The Day of Protest was a political rather than an economic strike.

In preparation for June 26, Walter traveled around the country consulting local leaders. In his absence, I took charge of the bustling ANC office, the hub of a complicated national action. Every day, various leaders looked in to see that matters were going according to plan: Moses Kotane, Dr. Dadoo, Diliza Mji, J. B. Marks, president of the Transvaal ANC, Yusuf Cachalia and his brother Maulvi, Gaur Radebe, secretary of the Council of Action, Michael Harmel, Peter Raboroko, Nthatho Motlana. I was coordinating the actions in different parts of the country, and talking by phone with regional leaders. We had left ourselves little time, and the planning was hastily done.

The Day of Protest was the ANC's first attempt to hold a political strike on a national scale and it was a moderate success. In the cities, the majority of workers stayed home and black businesses did not open. In Bethal, Gert Sibande, who later became president of the Transvaal ANC, led a demonstration of five thousand people, which received headlines in major papers all across the country. The Day of Protest boosted our morale, made us realize our strength, and sent a warning to the Malan government that we would not remain passive in the face of apartheid. June 26 has since become a landmark day in the freedom struggle and within the liberation movement it is observed as Freedom Day.

It was the first time I had taken a significant part in a national campaign, and I felt the exhilaration that springs from the success of a well-planned battle against the enemy and the sense of comradeship that is born of fighting against formidable odds.

The struggle, I was learning, was all-consuming. A man involved in the struggle was man without a home life. It was in the midst of the Day of Protest that my second son, Makgatho Lewanika, was born. I was with Evelyn at the hospital when he came into the world, but it was only a brief respite from my activities. He was named for Sefako Mapogo Makgatho, the second president of the ANC, from 1917 until 1924, and Lewanika, a leading chief in Zambia Makgatho, the son of a Pedi chief, had led volunteers to defy the color bar that did not permit Africans to walk on the sidewalks of Pretoria, and his name for me was an emblem of indominability and courage.

One day, during this same time, my wife informed me that my elder son, Thembi, then five, had asked her, "Where does Daddy live?" I had been returning home late at night, long after he had gone to sleep, and departing early in the morning before he woke. I did not relish being deprived of the company of my children. I missed them a great deal during those days, long before I had any inkling that I would spend decades apart from them.

I was far more certain those days of what I was against than what I was for. My long-standing opposition to communism was breaking down. Moses Kotane, the general-secretary of the party and a member of the executive of the ANC, often came to my house late at night and we would debate until morning. Clear-thinking and self-taught, Kotane was the son of peasant farmers in the Transvaal. "Nelson," he would say, "what do you have against us? We are all fighting the same enemy. We do not seek to dominate the ANC; we are working within the context of African nationalism." In the end, I had no good response to his arguments.

Because of my friendships with Kotane, Ismail Meer, and Ruth First, and my observation of their own sacrifices, I was finding it more and more difficult to justify my prejudice against the party. Within the ANC, party members J. B. Marks, Edwin Mofutsanyana, Dan Tloome, and David Bopape, among others, were devoted and hardworking, and left nothing to gainsay as freedom fighters. Dr. Dadoo, one of the leaders of the 1946 resistance, was a well-known Marxist whose role as a fighter for human rights had made him a hero to all groups. I could not, and no longer did, question the bona fides of such men and women.

If I could not challenge their dedication, I could still question the philosophical and practical underpinnings of Marxism. But I had little knowledge of Marxism, and in political discussions with my Communist friends I found myself handicapped by my ignorance of Marxist philosophy. I decided to remedy this.

I acquired the complete works of Marx and Engels, Lenin, Stalin, Mao Tse-tung, and others and probed into the philosophy of dialectical and historical materialism. I had little time to study these works properly. While I was stimulated by the *Communist Manifesto*, I was exhausted by *Das Kapital*. But I found myself strongly drawn to the idea of a classless society, which, to my mind, was similar to traditional African culture where life was shared and communal. I subscribed to Marx's basic dictum, which has the simplicity and generosity of the Golden Rule: "From each according to this ability; to each according to his needs."

Dialectical materialism seemed to offer both a searchlight illuminating the dark night of racial oppression and a tool that could be used to end it. It helped me to see the situation other than through the prism of black and white relations, for if our struggle was to succeed, we had to transcend black and white. I was attracted to the scientific underpinnings of dialectical materialism, for I am always inclined to trust what I can verify. Its materialistic analysis of economics rang true to me. The idea that the value of goods was based on the amount of labor that went into them seemed particularly appropriate for South Africa. The ruling class paid African labor a subsistence wage and then added value to the cost of the goods, which they retained for themselves.

Marxism's call to revolutionary action was music to the ears of a freedom fighter. The idea that history progresses through struggle and change occurs in revolutionary jumps was similarly appealing. In my reading of Marxist works, I found a great deal of information that bore on the type of problems that face a practical politician. Marxists gave serious attention to national liberation movements and the Soviet Union in particular supported the national struggles of many colonial peoples. This was another reason why I amended my view of Communists and accepted the ANC position of welcoming Marxists into its ranks.

A friend once asked me how I could reconcile my creed of African nationalism with a belief in dialectical materialism. For me, there was no contradiction. I was first and foremost an African nationalist fighting for our emancipation from minority rule and the right to control our own destiny. But at the same time, South Africa and the African continent were part of the larger world. Our problems, while distinctive and special, were not entirely unique, and a philosophy that placed those problems in an international and historical context of the greater world and the course of history was valuable. I was prepared to use whatever means to speed up the erasure of human prejudice and the end of chauvinistic and violent nationalism. I did not need to become a Communist in order to work with them. I found that African nationalists and African Communists generally had far more uniting them than dividing them. The cynical have always suggested that the Communists were using us. But who is to say that we were not using them?

Within a few months, our life settled into a pattern. Prison life is about routine: each day like the one before; each week like the one before it, so that the months and years blend into each other. Anything that departs from this pattern upsets the authorities, for routine is the sign of a well-run prison.

Routine is also comforting for the prisoner, which is why it can be a trap. Routine can be a pleasant mistress whom it is hard to resist, for routine makes the time go faster. Watches and timepieces of any kind were barred on Robben Island, so we never knew precisely what time it was. We were dependent on bells and warders' whistles and shouts. With each week resembling the one before, one must make an effort to recall what day and month it is. One of the first things I did was to make a calendar on the wall of my cell. Losing a sense of time is an easy way to lose one's grip and even one's sanity.

Time slows down in prison; the days seem endless. The cliche of time passing slowly usually has to do with idleness and inactivity. But this was not the case on Robben Island. We were busy almost all the time, with work, study, resolving disputes. Yet, time nevertheless moved glacially. This is partially because things that took a few hours or days outside would take months or years in prison. A request for a new toothbrush might take six months or a year to be filled. Ahmed Kathrada once said that in prison the minutes can seem like years, but the years go by like minutes. An afternoon pounding rocks in the courtyard might seem like forever, but suddenly it is the end of the year, and you do not know where all the months went.

The challenge for every prisoner, particularly every political prisoner, is how to survive prison intact, how to emerge from prison undiminished, how to conserve and even replenish one's beliefs. The first task in accomplishing that is learning exactly what one must do to survive. To that end, one must know the enemy's purpose before adopting a strategy to undermine it. Prison is designed to break one's spirit and destroy one's resolve. To do this, the authorities attempt to exploit every weakness, demolish every initiative, negate all signs of individuality—all with the idea of stamping out that spark that makes each of us human and each of us who we are.

Our survival depended on understanding what the authorities were attempting to do to us, and sharing that understanding with each other. It would be very hard if not impossible for one man alone to resist. I do not know that I could have done it had I been alone. But the authorities' greatest mistake was keeping us together, for together our determination was reinforced. We supported each other and gained strength from each other. Whatever we knew, whatever we learned, we shared, and by sharing we multiplied whatever courage we had individually. That is not to say that we were all alike in our responses to the hardships we suffered. Men have different capacities and react differently to stress. But the stronger ones raised up the weaker ones, and both became stronger in the process. Ultimately, we had to create our own lives in prison. In a way that even the authorities acknowledged, order in prison was preserved not by the warders but by ourselves.

As a leader, one must sometimes take actions that are unpopular, or whose results will not be known for years to come. There are victories whose glory lies only in the fact that they are known to those who win them. This is particularly true of prison, where one must find consolation in being true to one's ideals, even if no one else knows of it.

I was now on the sidelines, but I also knew that I would not give up the fight. I was in a different and smaller arena, an arena for whom the only audience was ourselves and our oppressors. We regarded the struggle in prison as a microcosm of the struggle as a whole. We would fight inside as we had fought outside. The racism and repression were the same; I would simply have to fight on different terms.

Prison and the authorities conspire to rob each man of his dignity. In and of itself, that assured that I would survive, for any man or institution that tries to rob me of my dignity will lose because I will not part with it at any price or under any pressure. I never seriously considered the possibility that I would not emerge from prison one day. I never thought that a life sentence truly meant life and that I would die behind bars. Perhaps I was denying this prospect because it was too unpleasant to contemplate. But I always knew that someday I would once again feel the grass under my feet and walk in the sunshine as a free man.

I am fundamentally an optimist. Whether that comes from nature or nurture, I cannot say. Part of being optimistic is keeping one's head pointed toward the sun, one's feet moving forward. There were many dark moments when my faith in humanity was sorely tested, but I would not and could not give myself up to despair. That way lay defeat and death.

It would be hard to say what we did more of at the quarry: mine lime or talk. By 1966, the warders had adopted a laissez-faire attitude: we could talk as much as we wanted as long as we worked. We would cluster in small groups, four or five men in a rough circle, and talk all day long, about every subject under the sun. We were in a perpetual conversation with each other on topics both solemn and trifling.

There is no prospect about prison which pleases—with the possible exception of one. One has time to think. In the vortex of the struggle, when one is constantly reacting to changing circumstances, one rarely has the chance to carefully consider all the ramifications of one's decisions or policies. Prison provided the time—much more than enough time—to reflect on what one had done and not done.

We were constantly engaged in political debates. Some were dispatched in a day, others were disputed for years. I have always enjoyed the cut-and-thrust of debating, and was a ready participant. One of our earliest and longest debates concerned the relationship between the ANC and the Communist Party. Some of the men, especially those MK soldiers who had been trained in socialist countries, believed that the ANC and the party were one and the same. Even some very senior ANC colleagues, such as Govan Mbeki and Harry Gwala, subscribed to this theory.

The party did not exist as a separate entity on Robben Island. In prison, there was no point in making the distinction between the ANC and the party that existed on the outside. My own views on the subject had not altered in many years. The ANC was a mass liberation movement that welcomed all those with the same objectives.

Over time, the debate concerning the ANC and the party grew progressively acrimonious. A number of us proposed one way to resolve it: we would write to the ANC in exile in Lusaka. We prepared a secret twenty-two-page document on the subject with a covering letter from myself to be sent to Lusaka. It was a risky maneuver to prepare and smuggle out such a document. In the end, Lusaka confirmed the separation of the ANC and the party and the argument eventually withered away.

Another recurrent political discussion was whether or not the ANC leadership should come exclusively from the working class. Some argued that because the ANC was a mass organization made up mainly of ordinary workers, the leadership should come from those same ranks. My argument was that it was as undemocratic to specify that the leaders had to be from the working class as to declare that they should be bourgeois intellectuals. If the movement had insisted on such a rule, most of its leaders, men such as Chief Luthuli, Moses Kotane, Dr. Dadoo, would have been ineligible. Revolutionaries are drawn from every class.

At Pollsmor, we were more connected to outside events. We were aware that the struggle was intensifying, and that the efforts of the enemy were similarly increasing. In 1981, the South African Defense Force launched a raid on ANC offices in Maputo, Mozambique, killing thirteen of our people, including women and children. In December 1982, MK set off explosions at the unfinished Koeberg nuclear power plant outside Cape Town and placed bombs at many other military and apartheid targets around the country. That same month, the South African military again attacked an ANC outpost in Maseru, Lesotho, killing forty-two people, including a dozen women and children.

In August of 1982, activist Ruth First was opening her mail in Maputo, where she was living in exile, when she was murdered by a letter bomb. Ruth, the wife of Joe Slovo, was a brave anti-apartheid activist who had spent a number of months in prison. She was a forceful, engaging woman whom I first met when I was studying at Wits, and her death revealed the extent of the state's cruelty in combating our struggle.

MK's first car bomb attack took place in May of 1983, and was aimed at an air force and military intelligence office in the heart of Pretoria. This was an effort to retaliate for the unprovoked attacks the military had launched on the ANC in Maseru and elsewhere and was a clear escalation of the armed struggle. Nineteen people were killed and more than two hundred injured.

The killing of civilians was a tragic accident, and I felt a profound horror at the death toll. But as disturbed as I was by these casualties, I knew that such accidents were the inevitable consequence of the decision to embark on a military struggle. Human fallibility is always a part of war, and the price for it is always high. It was precisely because we knew that such incidents would occur that our decision to take up arms had been so grave and reluctant. But as Oliver said at the time of the bombing, the armed struggle was imposed upon us by the violence of the apartheid regime.

Both the government and the ANC were working on two tracks: military and political. On the political front, the government was pursuing its standard divide-and-rule strategy in attempting to separate Africans from Coloureds and Indians. In a referendum of November 1983, the white electorate endorsed P. W. Botha's plan to create a so-called tricameral Parliament, with Indian and Coloured chambers in addition to the white Parliament. This was an effort to lure Indians and Coloureds into the system, and divide them from Africans. But the offer was merely a "toy telephone," as all parliamentary action by Indians and Coloureds was subject to a white veto. It was also a way of fooling the outside world into thinking that the government was reforming apartheid. Botha's ruse did not fool the people, as more than 80 percent of eligible Indian and Coloured voters boycotted the election to the new houses of Parliament in 1984.

Powerful grassroots political movements were being formed inside the country that had firm links to the ANC, the principal one being the United Democratic Front [UDF], of which I was named a patron. The UDF had been created to coordinate protest against the new apartheid constitution in 1983, and the first elections to the segregated tricameral Parliament in 1984. The UDF soon blossomed into a powerful organization that united over six hundred anti-apartheid organizations—trade unions, community groups, church groups, student associations.

The ANC was experiencing a new birth of popularity. Opinion polls showed that the Congress was far and away the most popular political organization among Africans even though it had been banned for a quarter of a century. The anti-apartheid struggle as a whole had captured the attention of the world; in 1984, Bishop Desmond Tutu was awarded the Nobel Peace Prize. (The authorities refused to send Bishop Tutu my letter of congratulations.) The South African government was under growing international pressure, as nations all across the globe began to impose economic sanctions on Pretoria.

The government had sent "feelers" to me over the years, beginning with Minister Kruger's efforts to persuade me to move to the Transkei. These were not efforts to negotiate, but attempts to isolate me from my organization. On several other occasions, Kruger said to me: "Mandela, we can work with you, but not your colleagues. Be reasonable." Although I did not respond to these overtures, the mere fact that they were talking rather than attacking could be seen as a prelude to genuine negotiations.

The government was testing the waters. In late 1984 and early 1985, I had visits from two prominent Western statesmen, Lord Nicholas Bethell, a member of the British House of Lords and the European Parliament, and Samuel Dash, a professor of law at Georgetown University and a former counsel to the U. S. Senate Watergate Committee. Both visits were authorized by the new minister of justice, Kobie Coetsee, who appeared to be a new sort of Afrikaner leader.

I met Lord Bethell in the prison commander's office, which was dominated by a large photograph of a glowering President Botha. Bethell was a jovial, rotund man and when I first met him, I teased him about his stoutness. "You look like you are related to Winston Churchill," I said as we shook hands, and he laughed.

Lord Bethell wanted to know about our conditions at Pollsmoor and I told him. We discussed the armed struggle and I explained to him it was not up to us to renounce violence, but the government. I reaffirmed that we aimed for hard military targets, not people. "I would not want our men to assassinate, for instance, the major here," I said, pointing to Major Fritz van Sittert, who was monitoring the talks. Van Sittert was a good-natured fellow who did not say much, but he started at my remark.

In my visit with Professor Dash, which quickly followed that of Lord Bethell, I laid out what I saw as the minimum for a future nonracial South Africa: a unitary state without homelands; nonracial elections for the central Parliament; and one-person-one-vote. Professor Dash asked me whether I took any encouragement from the government's stated intention of repealing the mixed-marriage laws and certain other apartheid statutes. "This is a pinprick," I said. "It is not my ambition to marry a white woman or swim in a white pool. It is political equality that we want." I told Dash quite candidly that at the moment we could not defeat the government on the battlefield, but could make governing difficult for them.

I had one not-so-pleasant visit from two Americans, editors of the conservative newspaper the *Washington Times*. They seemed less intent on finding out my views than on proving that I was a Communist and a terrorist. All of their questions were slanted in that direction, and when I reiterated that I was neither a Communist nor a terrorist, they attempted to show that I was not a Christian either by asserting that the Reverend Martin Luther King never resorted to violence. I told them that the conditions in which Martin Luther King struggled were totally different from my own: the United States was a democracy with constitutional guarantees of equal rights that protected nonviolent protest (though there was still prejudice against blacks); South Africa was a police state with a constitution that enshrined inequality and an army that responded to nonviolence with force. I told them that I was a Christian and had always been a Christian. Even Christ, I said, when he was left with no alternative, used force to expel the moneylenders from the temple. He was not a man of violence, but had no choice but to use force against evil. I do not think I persuaded them.

Faced with trouble at home and pressure from abroad, P. W. Botha offered a tepid, halfway measure. On January 31, 1985, in a debate in Parliament, the state president publicly offered me my freedom if I "unconditionally rejected violence as a political instrument." This offer was extended to all political prisoners. Then, as if he were staking me to a public challenge, he added, "It is therefore not the South Africa government which now stands in the way of Mr. Mandela's freedom. It is he himself."

I had been warned by the authorities that the government was going to make a proposal involving my freedom, but I had not been prepared for the fact that it would be made in Parliament by the state president. By my reckoning, it was the sixth conditional offer the government had made for my release in the past ten years. After I listened to the speech on radio, I made a request to the commander of the prison for an urgent visit by my wife and my lawyer, Ismail Ayob, so that I could dictate my response to the state president's offer.

Winnie and Ismail were not given permission to visit for a week, and in the meantime I wrote a letter to the foreign minister, Pik Botha, rejecting the conditions for my release, while also preparing a public response. I was keen to do a number of things in this response, because Botha's offer was an attempt to drive a wedge between me and my colleagues by tempting me to accept a policy the ANC rejected. I wanted to reassure the ANC in general and Oliver in particular that my loyalty to the organization was beyond question. I also wished to send a message to the government that while I rejected its offer because of the conditions attached to it, I nevertheless thought negotiation, not war, was the path to a solution.

Botha wanted the onus of violence to rest on my shoulders and I wanted to reaffirm to the world that we were only responding to the violence done to us. I intended to make it clear that if I emerged from prison into the same circumstances in which I was arrested, I would be forced to resume the same activities for which I was arrested.

I met with Winnie and Ismail on a Friday; on Sunday, a UDF rally was to be held in Soweto's Jabulani Stadium, where my response would be made public.

Some guards with whom I was not familiar supervised the visit, and as we began discussing my response to the state president, one of the warders, a relatively young fellow, interrupted to say that only family matters were permitted to be discussed. I ignored him, and he returned minutes later with a senior warder whom I barely knew. This warder said that I must cease discussing politics, and I told him that I was dealing with a matter of national importance involving an offer from the state president. I warned him that if he wanted to halt the discussion he must get direct orders from the state president himself. "If you are not willing to telephone the state president to get these orders," I said coldly, "then kindly do not interrupt us again." He did not.

I gave Ismail and Winnie the speech I had prepared. In addition to responding to the government, I wanted to thank publicly the UDF for its fine work and to congratulate Bishop Tutu on his prize, adding that this award belonged to all the people. On Sunday, February 10, 1985, my daughter Zindzi read my response to a cheering crowd of people who had not been able to hear my word legally anywhere in South Africa for more than twenty years.

Zindzi was a dynamic speaker like her mother, and said that her father should be at the stadium to speak the words himself. I was proud to know that it was she who spoke my words.

I am a member of the African National Congress. I have always been a member of the African National Congress and will remain a member of the African National Congress until the day I die. Oliver Tambo is more than a brother to me. He is my greatest friend and comrade for nearly fifty years. If there is any one amongst you who cherishes my freedom, Oliver Tambo cherishes it more, and I know that he would give his life to see me free. . . .

I am surprised at the conditions that the government wants to impose on me. I am not a violent man. . . . It was only then, when all other forms of resistance were not longer open to us, that we turned to armed struggle. Let Botha show that he is different to Malan, Strijdom and Verwoerd. Let him renounce violence. Let him say that he will dismantle apartheid. Let him unban the people's organization, the African National Congress. Let him free all who have been imprisoned, banished or exiled for their opposition to apartheid. Let him guarantee free political activity so that people may decide who will govern them.

I cherish my own freedom dearly, but I care even more for your freedom. Too many have died since I went to prison. Too many have suffered for the love of freedom. I owe it to their widows, to their orphans, to their mothers, and to their fathers who have grieved and wept for them. Not only I have suffered during these long, lonely, wasted years. I am not less life-loving than you are. But I cannot sell my birthright, nor am I prepared to sell the birthright of the people to be free. . . .

What freedom am I being offered while the organization of the people remains banned? What freedom am I being offered when I may be arrested on a pass offense? What freedom am I being offered to live my life as a family with my dear wife who remains in banishment in Brandfort? What freedom am I being

offered when I must ask for permission to live in an urban area? . . .What freedom am I being offered when my very South African citizenship is not
respected?

Only free men can negotiate. Prisoners cannot enter into contracts . . . I cannot and will not give any undertaking at a time when I and you, the people, are
not free. Your freedom and mine cannot be separated. I will return.

At the meeting between myself and the Eminent Persons Group, we were
joined by two significant observers: Kobie Coetsee and Lieutenant General W. H.
Willemse, the commissioner of prisons. Like the tailor, these two men were there
to take my measure. But, curiously, they left shortly after the session started. I
pressed them to remain, saying I had nothing to hide, but they left anyway.
Before they took their leave, I told them the time had come for negotiations, not
fighting, and that the government and the ANC should sit down and talk.

The Eminent Persons Group had come with many questions involving the
issues of violence, negotiations, and international sanctions. At the outset, I set
the ground rules for our discussions. "I am not the head of the movement," I told
them. "The head of the movement is Oliver Tambo in Lusaka. You must go and
see him. You can tell him what my views are, but they are my personal views
alone. They don't even represent the views of my colleagues here in prison. All
that being said, I favor the ANC beginning discussions with the government."

Various members of the group had concerns about my political ideology
and what a South Africa under ANC leadership might look like. I told them I was
a South African nationalist, not a Communist, that nationalists came in every hue
and color, and that I was firmly committed to a nonracial society. I told them I
believed in the Freedom Charter, that the charter embodied principles of democracy and human rights, and that it was not a blueprint for socialism. I spoke of my
concern that the white minority feel a sense of security in any new South Africa.
I told them I thought many of our problems were a result of lack of communication between the government and the ANC and that some of these could be
resolved through actual talks.

They questioned me extensively on the issue of violence, and while I was
not yet willing to renounce violence, I affirmed in the strongest possible terms
that violence could never be the ultimate solution to the situation in South Africa
and that men and women by their very nature required some kind of negotiated
understanding. While I once again reiterated that these were my views and not
those of the ANC, I suggested that if the government withdrew the army and the
police from the townships, the ANC might agree to a suspension of the armed
struggle as a prelude to talks. I told them that my release alone would not stem
the violence in the country or stimulate negotiations.

After the group finished with me, they planned to see both Oliver in Lusaka
and government officials in Pretoria. In my remarks, I had sent messages to both
places. I wanted the government to see that under the right circumstances we
would talk and I wanted Oliver to know that my position and his were the same.

In May, the Eminent Persons Group was scheduled to see me one last time. I was optimistic as they had been to both Lusaka and Pretoria, and I hoped that the seed of negotiations had been planted. But the day before we were to meet, the South African government took a step that sabotaged whatever goodwill had been engendered by the Commonwealth visitors. On the day the Eminent Persons Group was scheduled to meet with cabinet ministers, the South African Defense Force, under the orders of President Botha, launched air raids and commando attacks on ANC bases in Botswana, Zambia, and Zimbabwe. This utterly poisoned the talks, and the Eminent Persons Group immediately left South Africa. Once again, I felt my efforts to move negotiations forward had stalled.

Oliver Tambo and the ANC had called for the people of South Africa to render the country ungovernable, and the people were obliging. The state of unrest and political violence was reaching new heights. The anger of the masses was unrestrained; the townships were in upheaval. International pressure was growing stronger every day. On June 12, 1986, the government imposed a State of Emergency in an attempt to keep a lid on protest. In every outward way, the time seemed inauspicious for negotiations. But often, the most discouraging moments are precisely the time to launch an initiative. At such times people are searching for a way out of their dilemma. That month I wrote a very simple letter to General Willemse, the commissioner of prisons. In it, I merely said, "I wish to see you on a matter of national importance." I handed the letter to Brigadier Munro on a Wednesday.

That weekend, I was told by the commanding officer to be prepared to see General Willemse, who was coming down from Pretoria. This meeting was not treated in the usual fashion. Instead of conferring with the general in the visiting area, I was taken to his residence on the grounds of Pollsmoor itself.

Willemse is a direct fellow and we got down to business immediately. I told him I wanted to see Kobie Coetsee, the minister of justice. He asked me why. I hesitated for a moment, reluctant to discuss political matters with a prison official. But I responded with frankness: "I want to see the minister in order to raise the question of talks between the government and the ANC."

He pondered this for a moment, and then said, "Mandela, as you know, I am not a politician. I cannot discuss such issues myself, for they are beyond my authority." He then paused, as if something had just occurred to him. "It just so happens," he said, "that the minister of justice is in Cape Town. Perhaps you can see him. I will find out."

The general then telephoned the minister and the two spoke for a few moments. After putting down the phone, the general turned to me and said, "The minister said, 'Bring him round.'" Minutes later, we left the general's residence in his car bound for the minister's house in Cape Town. Security was light; only one other car accompanied the general's vehicle. The ease and rapidity with which this meeting was set up made me suspect that the government might have planned this rendezvous ahead of time. Whether they had or not was immaterial; it was an opportunity to take the first step toward negotiations.

At his official residence in the city, Coetsee greeted me warmly and we settled down on comfortable chairs in his lounge. He apologized that I had not had a chance to change out of my prison clothes. I spent three hours in conversation with him and was struck by his sophistication and willingness to listen. He asked knowledgeable and relevant questions—questions that reflected a familiarity with the issues that divided the government and the ANC. He asked me under what circumstances would we suspend the armed struggle; whether or not I spoke for the ANC as a whole; whether I envisioned any constitutional guarantees for minorities in a new South Africa. His questions went to the heart of the issues dividing the government and the ANC.

After responding in much the same way as I did to the Eminent Persons Group, I sensed that Coetsee wanted some resolution. What is the next step? he asked. I told him I wanted to see the state president and the foreign minister, Pik Botha. Coetsee noted this on a small pad he had kept beside him, and said he would send my request through the proper channels. We then shook hands, and I was driven back to my solitary cell on the ground floor of Pollsmoor prison.

I was greatly encouraged. I sensed the government was anxious to overcome the impasse in the country, that they were now convinced they had to depart from their old positions. In ghostly outline, I saw the beginnings of a compromise.

I told no one of my encounter. I wanted the process to be under way before I informed anyone. Sometimes it is necessary to present one's colleagues with a policy that is already a fait accompli. I knew that once they examined the situation carefully, my colleagues at Pollsmoor and in Lusaka would support me. But again, after this promising start, nothing happened. Weeks and then months passed without a word from Coetsee. In some frustration, I wrote him another letter.

May 10 dawned bright and clear. For the past few days, I had been pleasantly besieged by arriving dignitaries and world leaders who were coming to pay their respects before the inauguration. The inauguration would be the largest gathering ever of international leaders on South African soil.

The ceremonies took place in the lovely sandstone amphitheater formed by the Union Buildings in Pretoria. For decades, this had been the seat of white supremacy, and now it was the site of a rainbow gathering of different colors and nations for the installation of South Africa's first democratic, nonracial government.

On that lovely autumn day I was accompanied by my daughter Zenani. On the podium, Mr. de Klerk was first sworn in as second deputy president. Then Thabo Mbeki was sworn in as first deputy president. When it was my turn, I pledged to obey and uphold the constitution and to devote myself to the well-being of the republic and its people. To the assembled guests and the watching world, I said:

Today, all of us do, by our presence here . . . confer glory and hope to newborn liberty. Out of the experience of an extraordinary human disaster that lasted too long, must be born a society of which all humanity will be proud.

. . . We, who were outlaws not so long ago, have today been given the rare privilege to be host to the nations of the world on our own soil. We thank all of our distinguished international guests for having come to take possession with the people of our country of what is, after all, a common victory for justice, for peace, for human dignity.

We have, at last, achieved our political emancipation. We pledge ourselves to liberate all our people from the continuing bondage of poverty, deprivation, suffering, gender, and other discrimination.

Never, never, and never again shall it be that this beautiful land will again experience the oppression of one by another . . . . The sun shall never set on so glorious a human achievement.

Let freedom reign. God bless Africa!

The policy of apartheid created a deep and lasting wound in my country and my people. All of us will spend many years, if not generations, recovering from that profound hurt. But the decades of oppression and brutality had another, unintended effect, and that was that it produced the Oliver Tambos, the Walter Sisulus, the Chief Luthulis, the Yusuf Dadoos, the Bram Fischers, the Robert Sobukwes of our time—men of such extraordinary courage, wisdom, and generosity that their like may never be known again. Perhaps it requires such depth of oppression to create such heights of character. My country is rich in the minerals and gems that lie beneath its soil, but I have always known that its greatest wealth is its people, finer and truer than the purest diamonds.

It is from these comrades in the struggle that I learned the meaning of courage. Time and again, I have seen men and women risk and give their lives for an idea. I have seen men stand up to attacks and torture without breaking, showing a strength and resiliency that defies the imagination. I learned that courage was not the absence of fear, but the triumph over it. I felt fear myself more times than I can remember, but I hid it behind a mask of boldness. The brave man is not he who does not feel afraid, but he who conquers that fear.

In life, every man has twin obligations—obligations to his family, to his parents, to his wife and children; and he has an obligation to his people, his community, his country. In a civil and humane society, each man is able to fulfill those obligations according to his own inclinations and abilities. But in a country like South Africa, it was almost impossible for a man of my birth and color to fulfill both of these obligations. In South Africa, a man of color who attempted to live as a human being was punished and isolated. In South Africa, a man who tried to fulfill his duty to his people was inevitably ripped from his family and his home and was forced to live life apart, a twilight existence of secrecy and rebellion. I did not in the beginning choose to place my people above my family, but in attempting to serve my people, I found that I was prevented from fulfilling my obligations as a son, a brother, a father, and a husband . . . .

I was not born with a hunger to be free. I was born free—free in every way that I could know. Free to run in the fields near my mother's hut, free to swim in the clear stream that ran through my village, free to roast mealies under the stars and ride the broad backs of slow-moving bulls. As long as I obeyed my father and abided by the customs of my tribe, I was not troubled by the laws of man or God.

It was only when I began to learn that my boyhood freedom was an illusion, when I discovered as a young man that my freedom had already been taken from me, that I began to hunger for it. At first, as a student, I wanted freedom only for myself, the transitory freedoms of being able to stay out at night, read what I pleased, and go where I chose. Later, as a young man in Johannesburg, I yearned for the basic and honorable freedoms of achieving my potential, of earning my keep, of marrying and having a family—the freedom not to be obstructed in a lawful life.

But then I slowly saw that not only was I not free, but my brothers and sisters were not free. I saw that it was not just my freedom that was curtailed, but the freedom of everyone who looked like I did. That is when I joined the African National Congress, and that is when the hunger for my own freedom became the greater hunger for the freedom of my people. It was this desire for the freedom of my people to live their lives with dignity and self-respect that animated my life, that transformed a frightened young man into a bold one, that drove a law-abiding attorney to become a criminal, that turned a family-loving husband into a man without a home, that forced a life-loving man to live like a monk. I am no more virtuous or self-sacrificing than the next man, but I found that I could not even enjoy the poor and limited freedoms I was allowed when I knew my people were not free. Freedom is indivisible; the chains on any one of my people were the chains on all of them, the chains on all of my people were the chains on me.

It was during those long and lonely years that my hunger for the freedom of my own people became a hunger for the freedom of all people, white and black. I knew as well as I knew anything that the oppressor must be liberated just as surely as the oppressed. A man who takes away another man's freedom is a prisoner of hatred; he is locked behind the bars of prejudice and narrow-mindedness. I am not truly free if I am taking away someone else's freedom, just as surely as I am not free when my freedom is taken from me. The oppressed and the oppressor alike are robbed of their humanity.

When I walked out of prison, that was my mission, to liberate the oppressed and the oppressor both. Some say that has now been achieved. But I know that that is not the case. The truth is that we are not yet free; we have merely achieved the freedom to be free, the right not to be oppressed. We have not taken the final step of our journey, but the first step on a longer and even more difficult road. For to be free is not merely to cast off one's chains, but to live in a way that respects and enhances the freedom of others. The true test of our devotion to freedom is just beginning.

I have walked that long road to freedom. I have tried not to falter; I have made missteps along the way. But I have discovered the secret that after climbing a great hill, one only finds that there are many more hills to climb. I have taken a moment here to rest, to steal a view of the glorious vista that surrounds me, to look back on the distance I have come. But I can rest only for a moment, for with freedom come responsibilities, and I dare not linger, for my long walk is not yet ended.

IV

Contemporary Issues and Women's Voices of Nonviolence

13

Speciesism Today

Peter Singer

Since its original publication in 1975, the groundbreaking book *Animal Liberation* has awakened millions of concerned men and women to the shocking abuse of animals everywhere—inspiring a worldwide movement to eliminate much of the cruel and unnecessary laboratory animal experimentation of years past. Author Peter Singer exposes the chilling realities of today's "factory farms" and product-testing procedures—offering sound, humane solutions to what has become a profound environmental and social as well as moral issue. The following selection is taken from the concluding chapter of the new, revised edition of *Animal Liberation*. Animal rights is a controversial contemporary issue that leads people to take different standpoints. The author brings out the issue of using animals for food, for experiments and so on within the context of speciesism.

defenses, rationalizations,
and objections to Animal Liberation
and the progress made in overcoming them.

We have seen how, in violation of the fundamental moral principle of equality of consideration of interests that ought to govern our relations with all beings, humans inflict suffering on non-humans for trivial purposes; and we have seen how generation after generation of Western thinkers has sought to defend the right of human beings to do this. In this final chapter I shall look at some of the ways in which speciesist practices are maintained and promoted today, and at the various arguments and excuses that are still used in defense of animal slavery. Some of these defenses have been raised against the position taken in this book, and so this chapter provides an opportunity to answer some of the objections most often made to the case for Animal Liberation; but the chapter is also intended as an extension of the previous one, revealing the continued existence of the ideology whose history we have traced back to the Bible and the ancient

Greeks. It is important to expose and criticize this ideology, because although contemporary attitudes to animals are sufficiently benevolent—on a very selective basis—to allow some improvements in the conditions of animals to be made without challenging basic attitudes to animals, these improvements will always be in danger of erosion unless we alter the underlying position that sanctions the ruthless exploitation of non-humans for human ends. Only by making a radical break with more than two thousand years of Western thought about animals can we build a solid foundation for the abolition of this exploitation.

Our attitudes to animals begin to form when we are very young, and they are dominated by the fact that we begin to eat meat at an early age. Interestingly enough, many children at first refuse to eat animal flesh, and only become accustomed to it after strenuous efforts by their parents, who mistakenly believe that it is necessary for good health. Whatever the child's initial reaction, though, the point to notice is that we eat animal flesh long before we are capable of understanding that what we are eating is the dead body of an animal. Thus we never make a conscious, informed decision, free from the bias that accompanies any long-established habit, reinforced by all the pressures of social conformity, to eat animal flesh. At the same time children have a natural love of animals, and our society encourages them to be affectionate toward animals such as dogs and cats and toward cuddly, stuffed toy animals. These facts help to explain the most distinctive characteristic of the attitudes of children in our society to animals— namely, that rather than having one unified attitude to animals, the child has two conflicting attitudes that coexist, carefully segregated so that the inherent contradiction between them rarely causes trouble.

Not so long ago children were brought up on fairy tales in which animals, especially wolves, were pictured as cunning enemies of man. A characteristic happy ending would leave the wolf drowning in a pond, weighed down by stones which the ingenious hero had sewn into its belly while it was asleep. . . . Today, however, such stories and rhymes have gone out of fashion, and on the surface all is sweetness and light, so far as children's attitudes to animals are concerned. Thereby a problem has arisen: What about the animals we eat?

One response to this problem is simple evasion. The child's affection for animals is directed toward animals that are not eaten: dogs, cats, and other companion animals. These are the animals that an urban or suburban child is most likely to see. Cuddly, stuffed toy animals are more likely to be bears or lions than pigs or cows. When farm animals are mentioned in picture books, stories, and on children's television shows, however, evasion may become a deliberate attempt to mislead children about the nature of modern farms, and so to screen them from the reality. . . . An example of this is the popular Hallmark book *Farm Animals,* which presents the child with pictures of hens, turkeys, cows, and pigs, all surrounded by their young, with not a cage, shed, or stall in sight. The text tells us that pigs "enjoy a good meal, then roll in the mud and let out a squeal!" while "Cows don't have a thing to do, but switch their tails, eat grass and moo."[1] British books, like *The Farm* in the best-selling Ladybird series, convey the same impression of rural simplicity, showing the hen running freely in an orchard with her chicks, and all the other animals living with their offspring in spacious quarters.[2] With this kind of early reading it is not surprising that children grow up believing that even if animals "must" die to provide human beings with food, they live happily until that time comes.

Recognizing the importance of the attitudes we form when young, the feminist movement has succeeded in fostering the growth of a new children's literature, in which brave princesses occasionally rescue helpless princes, and girls play the central, active roles that used to be reserved for boys. To alter the stories about animals that we read to our children will not be so easy, since cruelty is not an ideal subject for children's stories. Yet it should be possible to avoid the most gruesome details, and still give children picture books and stories that encourage respect for animals as independent beings, and not as cute little objects that exist for our amusement and table; and as children grow older, they can be made aware that most animals live under conditions that are not very pleasant....

Nor do the mass media educate the public on this topic. American television broadcasts programs on animals in the wild (or supposedly in the wild—sometimes the animals have been captured and released in a more limited space to make filming easier) almost every night of the week; but film of intensive farms is limited to the briefest of glimpses as part of infrequent "specials" on agriculture or food production. The average viewer must know more about the lives of cheetahs and sharks than he or she knows about the lives of chickens or veal calves. The result is that most of the "information" about farm animals to be gained from watching television is in the form of paid advertising, which ranges from ridiculous cartoons of pigs who want to be made into sausages and tuna trying to get themselves canned, to straightforward lies about the conditions in which broiler chickens are reared. The newspapers do little better. Their coverage of nonhuman animals is dominated by "human interest" events like the birth of a baby gorilla at the zoo, or by threats to endangered species; but developments in farming techniques that deprive millions of animals of freedom of movement go unreported.

Before the recent successes of the Animal Liberation movement in exposing one or two notorious laboratories, what went on in research with animals was no better known than what goes on down on the farm. The public, of course, does not have access to laboratories. Although researchers publish their reports in professional journals, researchers only release news of their work to the media when they can claim to have discovered something of special importance. Thus, until the Animal Liberation movement was able to attract national media attention, the public had no idea that most experiments performed on animals are never published at all, and that most of those published are trivial anyway....

Ignorance, then, is the speciesist's first line of defense. Yet it is easily breached by anyone with time and determination to find out the truth. Ignorance has prevailed so long only because people do not want to find out the truth. "Don't tell me, you'll spoil my dinner" is the usual reply to an attempt to tell someone just how that dinner was produced. Even people who are aware that the traditional family farm has been taken over by big business interests, and that some questionable experiments go on in laboratories, cling to a vague belief that conditions cannot be too bad, or else the government or the animal welfare societies would have done something about it. Some years ago Dr. Bernhard Grzimek, director of the Frankfurt Zoo and one of West Germany's most outspoken opponents of intensive farming, likened the ignorance of Germans about these farms to the ignorance of an earlier generation of Germans to another form of atrocity, also hidden away from most eyes;[3] and in both cases, no doubt, it is not the inability to find out what is going on as much as a desire not to know about facts that may lie heavy on one's conscience that is responsible for the lack of awareness—as well as, of course, the comforting thought that, after all, the victims of whatever it is that goes on in those places are not members of one's own group.

The thought that we can rely on the animal welfare societies to see that animals are not cruelly treated is a reassuring one. Most countries now have at least one large, well-established animal protection society; in the United States there are the American Society for the Prevention of Cruelty to Animals [ASPCA], the American Humane Association, and the Humane Society of the United States; in Britain the Royal Society for the Prevention of Cruelty to Animals [RSPCA] remains unchallenged as the largest group. It is reasonable to ask: Why have these associations not been able to prevent the clear cruelties described in Chapters 2 and 3 of this book?

There are several reasons for the failure of the animal welfare establishment to take action against the most important kinds of cruelty. One is historical. When first founded, the RSPCA and ASPCA were radical groups to all forms of cruelty to animals, including cruelty to farm animals, who then, as now, were the victims of many of the worst abuses. Gradually, however, as these organizations grew in wealth, membership, and respectability, they lost their radical commitment and became part of the "establishment." They built up close contacts with members of the government, and with businessmen and scientists. They tried to use these contacts to improve the conditions of animals, and some minor improvements resulted; but at the same time contacts with those whose basic interests are in the use of animals for food or research purposes blunted the radical criticism of the exploitation of animals that had inspired the founders. Again and again the societies compromised their fundamental principles for the sale of trivial reforms. Better some progress now than nothing at all, they said; but often the reforms proved ineffective in improving the conditions of the animals, and functioned rather to reassure the public that nothing further needed to be done.[4]

As their wealth increased, another consideration became important. The animal welfare societies had been set up as registered charities. This status brought them substantial tax savings; but it is a condition of being registered as a charity, in both Great Britain and United States, that the charitable organization does not engage in political activities. Political action, unfortunately, is sometimes the only way to improve the conditions of animals (especially if an organization is too cautious to call for public boycotts of animal products), but most of the large groups kept well clear of anything that might endanger their charitable status. This has led them to emphasize safe activities like collecting stray dogs and prosecuting individual acts of wanton cruelty, instead of broad campaigns against systematic cruelty.

Finally, at some point during the last hundred years the major animal welfare societies lost interest in farm animals. Perhaps this was because the supporters and officials of the societies came from the cities and knew more and cared more about dogs and cats than about pigs and calves. . . .

Among the factors that make it difficult to arouse public concern about animals perhaps the hardest to overcome is the assumption that "human beings come first" and that any problem about animals cannot be comparable, as a serious moral or political issue, to problems about humans. A number of things can be said about this assumption. First, it is in itself an indication of speciesism. How can anyone who has not made a thorough study of the topic possibly know that the problem is less serious than problems of human suffering? One can claim to know this only if one assumes that animals really do not matter, and that however much they suffer, their suffering is less important than the suffering of humans. But pain is pain, and the importance of preventing unnecessary pain and suffering does not diminish that being that suffers is not a member of our species. What would we think of someone who said that "whites come first" and that therefore poverty in Africa does not pose as serious a problem as poverty in Europe?

It is true that many problems in the world deserve our time and energy. Famine and poverty, racism, war and the threat of nuclear annihilation, sexism, unemployment, preservation of our fragile environment—all are major issues, and who can say which is the most important? Yet once we put aside speciesist biases we can see that the oppression of nonhumans by humans ranks somewhere along with these issues. The suffering that we inflict on nonhuman beings can be extreme, and the numbers involved are gigantic: more that 100 million pigs, cattle, and sheep go through the processes each year, in the United States alone; billions of chickens do the same; and at least 25 million animals are experimented upon annually. If a thousand human being s were forced to undergo the kind of tests that animals undergo to test the toxicity of household products, there would be a national uproar. The use of millions of animals for this purpose should cause at least as much concern, especially since this suffering is so unnecessary and could be stopped if we wanted to stop it. . . .

In any case, the idea that "humans come first" is more often used as an excuse for not doing anything about either human or nonhuman animals than as a genuine choice between incompatible alternatives. For the truth is that there is no incompatibility here. Granted, everyone has a limited amount of time and energy, and time taken in active work for one cause reduces the time available for another cause; but there is nothing to stop those who devote their time and energy to human problems from joining the boycott of the products of agribusiness cruelty. . . .

Speceisism is so pervasive and widespread an attitude that those who attack one or two of its manifestations—like the slaughter of wild animals by hunters, or cruel experimentation, or bullfighting—often participate in other speceisist practices themselves. This allows those attacked to accuse their opponents of inconsistency. "You say we are cruel because we shoot deer," the hunters say, "but you eat meat. What is the difference, except that you pay someone else to do the killing for you?" "You object to killing animals to clothe ourselves in their skins," say the furriers, "but you are wearing leather shoes." The experimenters plausibly ask why, if people accept the killing of animals to please their palates, they should object to the killing of animals to advance knowledge; and if the objection is just to suffering, they can point out that animals killed for food do not live without suffering either. Even the bullfight enthusiast can argue that the death of the bull in the ring gives pleasure to thousands of spectators, while the death of the steer in the slaughterhouse gives pleasure only to the few people who eat some part of it; and while in the end the bull may suffer more acute pain than the steer, for most of his life it is the bull who is better treated.

The charge of inconsistency really gives no logical support to the defenders of cruel practices. As Brigid Brophy has put it, it remains true that it is cruel to break people's legs, even if the statement is made by someone in the habit of breaking people's arms.[5] Yet people whose conduct is inconsistent with their professed beliefs will find it difficult to persuade others that their beliefs are right; and they will find it even more difficult to persuade others to act on those beliefs. Of course, it is always possible to find some reason for distinguishing between, say, wearing furs and wearing leather: many fur-bearing animals die only after hours or even days spent with a leg caught in a steel-toothed trap, while the animals from whose skins leather is made are spared this agony.[6] There is a tendency, however, for these fine distinctions to blunt the force of the original criticism; and in some cases, I do not think distinctions can validly be drawn at all. Why, for instance, is the hunter who shoots a deer for venison subject to more criticism than the person who buys a ham at the supermarket? Overall, it is probably the intensively reared pig who has suffered more . . . .

For all practical purposes as far as urban and suburban inhabitants of the industrialized nations are concerned, following the principle of equal consideration of interests requires us to be vegetarians. This is the most important step, and the one to which I have given most attention; but we should also, to be consistent, stop using other animal products for which animals have been killed or made to suffer. We should not wear furs. We should not buy leather products either, since the sale of hides for leather plays a significant role in the profitability of the meat industry. . . .

Up to this point we have been examining, in this chapter, attitudes that are shared by many people in Western societies, and the strategies and arguments that are commonly used to defend these attitudes. We have seen that from a log-

ical point of view these strategies and arguments are very weak. They are rationalizations and excuses rather than arguments. It might be thought, however,
that their weaknesses is due to some lack of expert knowledge that ordinary people have in discussing ethical questions. . . .

Philosophy ought to question the basic assumptions of the age. Thinking
through, critically and carefully, what most of us take for granted is, I believe, the
chief task of philosophy, and the task that makes philosophy a worthwhile activity. Regrettably, philosophy does not always live up to its historic role. Aristotle's defense of slavery will always stand as a reminder that philosophers are
human beings and are subject to all the preconceptions of the society to which
they belong. Sometimes they succeed in breaking free of the prevailing ideology; more often they become its most sophisticated defenders.

Philosophers later on did not challenge anyone's preconceptions about our
relations with other species. By their writings, most philosophers who tackled
problems that touched upon the issue revealed that they made the same unques-
tioned assumptions as most other human beings, and what they said tended to
confirm readers in their comfortable speciesist habits.

At that time, discussions of equality and rights in moral and political philosophy were almost always formulated as problems of human equality and human
rights. The effect of this was that the issue of the equality of animals never confronted philosophers or their students as an issue in itself—already an indication
of the failure of philosophy up to that time to probe accepted beliefs. . . .

For philosophers of the 1950s and 1960s, the problem was to interpret the
idea that all human beings are equal in a manner that does not make it plainly
false. In most ways, human beings are not equal; and if we seek some characteristic that all of them possess, then this characteristic must be a kind of lowest
common denominator, pitched so low that no human being lacks it. The catch is
that any such characteristic that is possessed by all human beings will not be possessed only by human beings. For example, all human beings, but not only
human beings, are capable of feeling pain; and while only human beings are
capable of solving complex mathematical problems, not all humans can do this.
So it turns out that in the only sense in which we can truly say, as an assertion of
fact, that all humans are equal, at least some members of other species are also
"equal"—equal, that is, to some humans.

If, on the other hand, we decide that, as I argued, these characteristics are
really irrelevant to the problem of equality, and equality must be based on the
moral principle of equal consideration of interests rather than on the possession
of some characteristic, it is even more difficult to find some basis for excluding
animals from the sphere of equality.

This result is not what the egalitarian philosophers of that period originally
intended to assert. Instead of accepting the outcome to which their own reason-
ings naturally pointed, however, they tried to reconcile their beliefs in human
equality and animal inequality by arguments that are either devious or myopic.
For instance, one philosopher prominent in philosophical discussions of equality

at the time was Richard Wasserstrom, then professor of philosophy and law at the University of California, Los Angeles. In his article "Rights, Human Rights and Racial Discrimination," Wasserstrom defined "human rights" as those rights that human beings have and nonhumans do not have. He then argued that there are human rights to well-being and to freedom. In defending the idea of a human right to well-being, Wasserstrom said that to deny someone relief from acute physical pain makes it impossible for that person to live a full or satisfying life. He then went on: "In a real sense, the enjoyment of these goods differentiates human from non-human entities."[7] The problem is that when we look back to find to what the expression "these goods" refers, the only example given is relief from acute physical pain—something that nonhumans may appreciate as well as humans. So if human beings have a right to relief from acute physical pain, it would not be a specifically human right, in the sense Wasserstrom had defined. Animals would have it too.

Faced with a situation in which they saw a need for some basis for the moral gulf that is still commonly thought to separate human beings and animals, but unable to find any concrete difference between human beings and animals that would do this without undermining the equality of human beings, philosophers tended to waffle. They resorted to high-sounding phrases like "the intrinsic dignity of the human individual."[8] They talked of "the intrinsic worth of all men" (sexism was as little questioned as speciesism) as if all men (humans?) had some unspecified worth that other beings do not have.[9] Or they would say that human beings, and only human beings, are "ends in themselves" while "everything other than a person can only have value for a person."[10] . . .

The truth is that the appeal to the intrinsic dignity of human beings appears to solve the egalitarian philosopher's problems only as long as it goes unchallenged. Once we ask why it should be that all human beings—including infants, the intellectually disabled, criminal psychopaths, Hitler, Stalin, and the rest—have some kind of dignity or worth that no elephant, pig, or chimpanzee can ever achieve, we see that this question is as difficult to answer as our original request for some relevant fact that justifies the inequality of humans and other animals. In fact, these two questions are really one: talk of intrinsic dignity or moral worth does not help, because any satisfactory defense of the claim that all and only human beings have intrinsic dignity would need to refer to some relevant capacities or characteristics that only human beings have, in virtue of which they have this unique dignity or worth. To introduce ideas of dignity and worth as a substitute for other reasons for distinguishing humans and animals is not good enough. Fine phrases are the last resource of those who have run out of arguments.

In case anyone still thinks it may be possible to find some relevant characteristic that distinguishes all human beings from all members of other species, let us consider again the fact that there are some human beings who quite clearly are below the level of awareness, self-consciousness, intelligence, and sentience of many nonhuman beings. I am thinking of human beings with severe and irreparable brain damage, and also of infant human beings; to avoid the complication of the potential of infants, however, I shall concentrate on permanently and profoundly retarded human beings.

Philosophers who set out to find a characteristic that would distinguish human beings from other animals rarely took the course of abandoning these groups of human beings by lumping them in with other animals. It is easy to see why they did not do so; to take this line without rethinking our attitudes to other animals would mean we have the right to perform painful experiments on retarded humans for trivial reasons; similarly it would follow that we have the right to rear and kill them for food.

For philosophers discussing the problem of equality, the easiest way out of the difficulty posed by the experience of human beings who are profoundly and permanently disabled intellectually was to ignore it. The Harvard philosopher John Rawls, in his long book *A Theory of Justice*, came up against this problem when trying to explain why we owe justice to human beings but not to other animals, but he brushed it aside with the remark, "I cannot examine this problem here, but I assume that the account of equality would not be materially affected."[11] This is an extraordinary way of handling the issue of equal treatment: it would appear to imply either that we may treat people who are profoundly and permanently disabled intellectually as we now treat animals, or that, contrary to Rawls's own statements, we do owe justice to animals.

What else could philosophers do? If they honestly confronted the problem posed by the existence of human beings with no morally relevant characteristics not also possessed by nonhuman beings, it would be impossible to cling to the equality of human beings without suggesting a radical revision in the status of nonhumans. In a desperate attempt to save the usually accepted views, it was even argued that we should treat beings according to what is "normal for the species" rather than according to their actual characteristics.[12] To see how outrageous this is, imagine that at some future date evidence were to be found that, even in the absence of any cultural conditioning, it was normal for more females than males in a society to stay at home looking after the children instead of going out to work. This finding would, of course, be perfectly compatible with the obvious fact that there are some women who are less well suited to looking after children, and better suited to going out to work, than some men. Would any philosopher then claim that these exceptional women should be treated in accordance with what is "normal for the sex"—and therefore, say, not be admitted to medical school—rather than in accordance with their actual characteristics? I do not think so. I find it hard to see anything in this argument except a defense of preferring the interests of members of our own species because they are members of our own species.

Like the other philosophical arguments common before the idea of equality for animals was taken seriously by philosophers, this one stands as a warning of the ease with which not only ordinary people, but also those most skilled in moral reasoning, can fall victim to a prevailing ideology. Now, however, I am truly delighted to report that philosophy has thrown off its ideological blinkers. Many of today's university courses in ethics really do challenge their students to rethink their attitudes on a range of ethical issues, and the moral status of nonhuman animals is prominent among them. Fifteen years ago I had to search hard to find a handful of references by academic philosophers on the issue of the status of animals; today I could have filled this entire book with an account of what has been written on this topic during the past fifteen years. Articles on how we ought to treat animals are included in virtually all the standard collections of readings used in applied ethics courses. It is the complacent, unargued assumptions of the moral insignificance of nonhuman animals which have become scarce. . . .

Of course, philosophers are not unanimous in support of vegetarianism and Animal Liberation—when were they ever unanimous about anything? But even those philosophers who have been critical of claims made by their colleagues on behalf of animals have accepted important elements of the case for change. For example R. G. Frey of Bowling Green State University, Ohio, who has written more in opposition to my views on animals than any other philosopher, begins one of his articles by stating flatly: "I am not an antivivisectionist . . . " But he then acknowledges that:

I have and know of nothing which enables me to say, a priori, that a human life of any quality, however low, is more valuable than an animal life of any quality, however high.

As a result, Frey recognizes that "the case for antivivisectionism is far stronger than most people allow." He concludes that if one seeks to justify experimenting on nonhuman animals by the benefits they produce (which is, in his view, the only way in which the practice can be justified), there is no intrinsic reason why such benefits would not also justify experiments on "humans whose quality of life is exceeded by or equal to that of animals." Hence he accepts experiments on animals where the benefits are sufficiently important, but only at the price of accepting the possibility of similar experiments on humans.[13]

More dramatic still was the change of heart shown by the Canadian philosopher Michael Allen Fox. In 1986 the publication of his book *The Case for Animal Experimentation* seemed sure to earn him a prominent spot at scholarly conferences as the chief philosophical defender of the animal research industry. The drug companies and lobbyists for animal experiments who thought they had, at last, a tame philosopher they could use to defend themselves against ethical criticism must have been dismayed, however, when Fox suddenly disavowed his own book. In a response to a highly critical review in *The Scientist*, Fox wrote a letter to the editor saying that he agreed with the reviewer; he had come to see that the arguments of his book were mistaken, and it was not possible to justify animal experimentation on ethical grounds. Later Fox followed through on his courageous change of mind by becoming a vegetarian.[14]

The rise of the Animal Liberation movement may be unique among modern social causes in the extent to which it has been linked with the development of the issue as a topic of discussion in the circles of academic philosophy. In considering the status of nonhuman animals, philosophy itself has undergone a remarkable transformation: it has abandoned the comfortable conformism of accepted dogma and returned to its ancient Socratic role.

The core of this book is the claim that to discriminate against beings solely on account of their species is a form of prejudice, immoral and indefensible in the same way that discrimination on the basis of race is immoral and indefensible. I have not been content to put forward this claim as a bare assertion or as a statement of my own personal view, which others may or may not choose to accept. I have argued for it, appealing to reason rather than to emotion or sentiment. I have chosen this path, not because I am unaware of the importance of kind feelings and sentiments of respect toward other creatures, but because reason is more universal and more compelling in its appeal. Greatly as I admire those who have eliminated speciesism from their lives purely because their sympathetic concern for others reaches out to all sentient creatures, I do not think that an appeal to sympathy and good-heartedness alone will convince most people of the wrongness of speciesism. Even where other human beings are concerned, people are surprisingly adept at limiting their sympathies to those of their own nation or race. Almost everyone, however, is at least nominally prepared to listen to reason. Admittedly, there are some who flirt with an excessive subjectivism in morality, saying that any morality is as good as any other; but when these same people are pressed to say if they think the morality of Hitler, or of the slave traders, is as good as the morality of Albert Schweitzer or Martin Luther King, they find that, after all, they believe some moralities are better than others.

So throughout this book I have relied on rational argument. Unless you can refute the central argument of this book, you should now recognize that speciesism is wrong, and this means that, if you take morality seriously, you should try to eliminate speciesist practices from your own life, and oppose them elsewhere. Otherwise no basis remains from which you can, without hypocrisy, criticize racism or sexism . . . .

I believe that the case for Animal Liberation is logically cogent, and cannot be refuted; but the task of overthrowing speciesism in practice is a formidable one. We have seen that speciesism has historical roots that go deep into the consciousness of Western society. We have seen that the elimination of speciesist practices would threaten the vested interests of the giant agribusiness corporations, and the professional associations of research workers and veterinarians. When necessary, these corporations and organizations are prepared to spend millions of dollars in defense of their interests, and the public will then be bombarded with advertisements denying allegations of cruelty. Moreover the public has—or thinks it has—an interest in the continuance of the speciesist practice of raising and killing animals for food and this makes people ready to accept reassurances that, in this respect at least, there is little cruelty. As we have seen, people are also ready to accept fallacious forms of reasoning, of the type we have examined in this chapter, which they would never entertain for a moment were it not for the fact that these fallacies appear to justify their preferred diet. . . .

We have noted some of the gains for animals as they arose in our discussion of particular topics, but they are worth bringing together. They include the prohibition of veal crates in Britain and the phasing out of battery cages in Switzerland and the Netherlands, as well as the more far-reaching legislation in Sweden which will eliminate veal crates, battery cages, sow stalls, and all other devices that prevent animals from moving about freely. It will also make it illegal to keep cattle without allowing them to graze in pastures during the warmer months. The worldwide campaign against the fur trade has succeeded in greatly reducing the quantity of fur sold, especially in Europe. In Britain the House of Fraser, a leading chain of department stores, was the target of protests against fur. In December 1989, it announced that it was closing the fur salons in fifty-nine of its sixty stores, leaving only one remaining in the famous London store, Harrods.

In the United States there have been no gains for farm animals yet, but several particularly objectionable series of experiments have been brought to a halt. The first success was achieved in 1977, when a campaign led by Henry Spira persuaded the American Museum of Natural History to stop a pointless series of experiments that involved mutilating cats in order to investigate the effect this had on their sex lives.[15] In 1981 came exposure by the Animal Liberation activist Alex Pacheco of the appalling conditions of seventeen monkeys at Edward Taub's Institute for Behavioral Research, in Silver Springs, Maryland. The National Institutes of Health cut off Taub's funding, and Taub became the first in the United States to be convicted of cruelty—although the conviction was later reversed on the technical ground that animal experimenters receiving federal tax funding do not have to obey state anticruelty laws.[16] Meanwhile the case gave national prominence to a fledgling group called People for the Ethical Treatment of Animals, which in 1984 led efforts to stop Dr. Thomas Gennarelli's head injury experiments on monkeys at the University of Pennsylvania. These efforts were triggered by extraordinary videotapes of animal abuse, shot by the experimenters themselves and stolen from the laboratory in a night raid carried out by the Animal Liberation Front. Gennarelli's grant was withdrawn.[17] In 1988, after months of picketing by Trans-Species Unlimited, a researcher at Cornell University gave up a $530,000 grant to study barbiturate addiction using cats.[18] Around the same time Benetton, the Italian fashion chain, announced that it would no longer perform safety tests for new cosmetics and toiletries on animals. Benetton had been the target of an international campaign, coordinated by People for the Ethical Treatment of Animals, that involved Animal Liberationists in seven countries. Noxell Corporation, an American cosmetics manufacturer, had not been the object of such a campaign; but it made its own decision to rely on tissue culture instead of performing Draize tests on rabbits to determine whether its products can damage the human eye. Noxell's decision was part of a steady movement toward alternatives by major cosmetics, toiletries, and pharmaceutical corporations, initiated and constantly spurred on by the Coalition to Abolish the

LD50 and Draize Tests.[19] Years of hard work paid off in 1989 when Avon, Revlon, Faberge, Mary Kay, Amway, Elizabeth Arden, Max Factor, Christian Dior, and several small companies announced that they were ending, or at least suspending, all animal experimentation. In the same year the European Commission, which is responsible for safety testing in ten nations of the European Community, announced that it would accept alternatives to the LD50 and Draize tests, and invited all OECD [Organization for Economic Cooperation and Development] nations (a group which includes the U.S. and Japan) to work toward developing common alternative safety tests. Both the LD50 and the Draize test have now been banned by government regulation in Victoria and New South Wales, Australia's most populous states and the states in which most animal experimentation has been carried out.[20]

In the United States, momentum is also building on the issue of dissection in high schools. The stubborn resistance to dissection of one Californian high school student, Jennifer Graham—and her insistence on not losing marks for her conscientious objection—led to the passage, in 1988, of the California Students' Rights Bill, which gives students in California primary and secondary schools the right to refuse to dissect without suffering a penalty. Similar bills are now being introduced in New Jersey, Massachusetts, Maine, Hawaii, and several other states.

As the movement gains increased visibility and support, the groundswell of people doing their part gathers momentum. Rock musicians have helped to circulate the Animal Liberation message. Movie stars, models, and dress designers have pledged to avoid furs. The international success of the Body Shop chain has made cruelty-free cosmetics more attractive and readily available. Vegetarian restaurants are proliferating and even nonvegetarian restaurants are offering vegetarian dishes. All this makes it easier for newcomers to join those already doing what they can to limit cruelty to animals in their daily lives.

Nevertheless, Animal Liberation will require greater altruism on the part of human beings than any other liberation movement. The animals themselves are incapable of demanding their own liberation or of protesting against their condition with votes, demonstrations, or boycotts. Human beings have the power to continue to oppress other species forever, or until we make this planet unsuitable for living beings. Will our tyranny continue, proving that morality counts for nothing when it clashes with self-interest, as the most cynical of poets and philosophers have always said? Or will we rise to the challenge and prove our capacity for genuine altruism by ending our ruthless exploitation of the species in our power, not because we are forced to do so by rebels or terrorists, but because we recognize that our position is morally indefensible?

The way in which we answer this question depends on the way in which each one of us, individually, answers it.

NOTES

1. Dean Walley and Frieda Staake, *Farm Animals* (Kansas City: Hallmark Children's Editions, no date).

2. M. E. Gagg and C. F. Tunnicliffe, *The Farm* (Loughborough, England: Ladybird Books, 1958).

3. Bernhard Grzimek, "Gequalte Tierre: Ungluck fur die Landwirtschaft," in *Das Tier* (Bern, Switzerland), special supplement.

4. Examples are the 1876 British Cruelty to Animals Act and the 1966–1970 Animal Welfare Act in the United States, both of which were enacted in response to concern about animals being used in experiments but have done little to benefit those animals.

5. Brigid Brophy, "In Pursuit of a Fantasy," in Stanley and Roslind Godlovitch and John Harris, eds., *Animals, Men and Morals* (New York: Taplinger, 1972), p. 132.

6. See Cleveland Amory, *Man Kind?* (New York: Harper and Row, 1974), p. 237.

7. In A. I. Melden, ed., *Human Rights* (Belmont, Calif.: Wadsworth, 1970), p. 106.

8. W. Frankena, "The Concept of Social Justice," in R. Brandt, ed., *Social Justice* (Englewood Cliffs, N. J.: Prentice-Hall, 1962).

9. H. A. Bedau, "Egalitarianism and the Idea of Equality," in J. R. Pennock and J. W. Chapman, eds., *Nomos IX: Equality* (New York. Atherton Press, 1967).

10. G. Vlastos, "Justice and Equality," in *Social Justice*, p. 48.

11. J. Rawls, *A Theory of Justice* (Harvard University Press, Cambridge: Belknap Press, 1972), p. 510. For another example, see Bernard Williams, "The Idea of Equality," in P. Laslett and W. Runciman, eds., *Philosophy, Politics and Society*, second series (Oxford: Blackwell, 1962), p. 118.

12. For an example, see Stanley Benn's "Egalitarianism and Equal Consideration of Interests," *Nomos IX: Equality*, pp. 62ff.

13. R. G. Frey, "Vivisection, Morals and Medicine," *Journal of Medical Ethics* 9: 95-104 (1983). Frey's major critique of my work is *Rights, Killing and Suffering* (Oxford: Blackwell, 1983), but see also his *Interests and Rights: The Case against Animals* (Oxford: Clarendon Press, 1980). I respond (too briefly) to these books in "Ten Years of Animal Liberation," *The New York Review of Books*, April 25, 1985.

14. See M. A. Fox, *The Case for Animal Experimentation* (Berkeley: University of California Press, 1986) and Fox's letter in *The Scientist*, December 15, 1986; see also Fox's "Animal Experimentation: A Philosopher's Changing Views," *Between the Species* 3: 55–60 (1987), and the interview with Fox in *Animals' Agenda*, March 1988.

15. See Henry Spira, "Fighting to Win," in Peter Singer, ed., *In Defense of Animals* (Oxford: Blackwell, 1985), pp. 194–208.

16. See Alex Pacheco with Anna Francione, "The Silver Spring Monkeys," Peter Singer, ed., *In Defense of Animals*, pp. 135-147.

17. See Chapter 2, note 118 of *Animal Liberation*.

18. *Newsweek*, December 26, 1988, pp. 50–51.

19. Barnaby J. Feder, "Research Looks Away from Laboratory Animals," *The New York Times*, January 29, 1989, p. 24; for an earlier picture of the work of the Coalition to Abolish the LD50 and Draize Tests, see Henry Spira, "Fighting to Win" in Peter Singer, ed., *In Defense of Animals*.

20. Government of Victoria, *Prevention of Cruelty to Animals Regulations*, 1986, no. 24. The regulation covers the testing of any chemical cosmetic, toilet, household, or industrial preparation. It prohibits the use of the conjunctival sac of rabbits for that purpose, and also prohibits any test in which animals are subjected to a range of increasing doses and the number of fatalities is used for the purpose of producing a statistically valid result. On New South Wales, see *Animal Liberation: The Magazine* (Melbourne) 27: 23 (January-March 1989).

14

Selections from *Race Matters*

Cornel West

This selection is the Introduction of Cornel West's book *Race Matters*. This book addresses some of today's most urgent issues for black Americans—from discrimination to despair, from leadership to the legacy of Malcolm X. West has the courage to break taboos of silence in the black community, while always acknowledging the realities of race in America. The grandson of a Baptist minister, he has fused the love ethic of the African American religious tradition with the political insights of the Black Panthers. Philosopher, theologian, and activist, West is described by the *New York Times* as "a cosmopolitan public intellectual among academic specialists . . . . (West) makes the life of the mind exciting." Racial hierarchy, he warns, dooms us as a nation to collective paranoia and hysteria—the unmaking of any democratic order. Some of his well-known books are *The African-American Century: How Black Americans Have Shaped Our Country* and *The Cornel West Reader,* which he edited. He has written many articles.

What happened in Los Angeles in April of 1992 was neither a race riot nor a class rebellion. Rather, this monumental upheaval was a multiracial, trans-class, and largely male display of justified social rage. For all its ugly, xenophobic resentment, its air of adolescent carnival, and its downright barbaric behavior, it signified the sense of powerlessness in American society. Glib attempts to reduce its meaning to the pathologies of the black underclass, the criminal actions of hoodlums, or the political revolt of the oppressed urban masses miss the mark. Of those arrested, only 36 percent were black, more than a third had full-time jobs, and most claimed to shun political affiliation. What we witnessed in Los Angeles was the consequence of a lethal linkage of economic decline, cultural decay, and political lethargy in American life. Race was the visible catalyst, not the underlying cause.

The meaning of the earthshaking events in Los Angeles is difficult to grasp because most of us remain trapped in the narrow framework of the dominant liberal and conservative views of race in America, which with its worn-out vocabulary leaves us intellectually debilitated, morally disempowered, and personally depressed. The astonishing disappearance of the event from public dialogue is testimony to just how painful and distressing a serious engagement with race is. Our truncated public discussions of race suppress the best of who and what we are as a people because they fail to confront the complexity of the issue in a candid and critical manner. The predictable pitting of liberals against conservatives, Great Society Democrats against self-help Republicans, reinforces intellectual parochialism and political paralysis.

The liberal notion that more government programs can solve racial problems is simplistic—precisely because it focuses *solely* on the economic dimension. And the conservative idea that what is needed is a change in the moral behavior of poor black urban dwellers (especially poor black men, who, they say, should stay married, support their children, and stop committing so much crime) highlights immoral actions while ignoring public responsibility for the immoral circumstances that haunt our fellow citizens.

The common denominator of these views of race is that each still sees black people as a "problem people," in the words of Dorothy I. Height, president of the National Council of Negro Women, rather than as fellow American citizens with problems. Her words echo the poignant "unasked question" of W.E.B. Du Bois, who, in *The Souls of Black Folk* (1903), wrote:

> They approach me in a half-hesitant sort of way, eye me curiously or compassionately, and then instead of saying directly, How does it feel to be a problem? they say, I know an excellent colored man in my town . . . . Do not these Southern outrages make your blood boil? At these I smile, or am interested, or reduce the boiling to a simmer, as the occasion may require. To the real question, How does it feel to be a problem? I answer seldom a word.

Nearly a century later, we confine discussions about race in America to the "problems" black people pose for whites rather than consider what this way of viewing black people reveals about us as a nation.

This paralyzing framework encourages liberals to relieve their guilty consciences by supporting public funds directed at "the problems"; but at the same time, reluctant to exercise principled criticism of black people, liberals deny them the freedom to err. Similarly, conservatives blame the "problems" on black people themselves—and thereby render black social misery invisible or unworthy of public attention.

Hence, for liberals, black people are to be "included" and "integrated" into "our" society and culture, while for conservatives they are to be "well behaved" and "worthy of acceptance" by "our" way of life. Both fail to see that the presence and predicaments of black people are neither additions to nor defections from American life, but rather *constitutive elements of that life*.

To engage in a serious discussion of race in America, we must begin not with the problems of black people but with the flaws of American society—flaws rooted in historic inequalities and longstanding cultural stereotypes. How we set up the terms for discussing racial issues shapes our perception and response to these issues. As long as black people are viewed as a "them," the burden falls on blacks to do all the "cultural" and "moral" work necessary for healthy race relations. The implication is that only certain Americans can define what it means to be American—and the rest must simply "fit in."

The emergence of strong black-nationalist sentiments among blacks, especially among young people, is a revolt against this sense of having to "fit in." The variety of black-nationalist ideologies, from the moderate views of Supreme Court Justice Clarence Thomas in his youth to those of Louis Farrakhan today, rest upon a fundamental truth: white America has been historically weak-willed in ensuring racial justice and has continued to resist fully accepting the humanity of blacks. As long as double standards and differential treatment abound—as long as the rap performer Ice-T is harshly condemned while former Los Angeles Police Chief Daryl F. Gates's antiblack comments are received in polite silence, as long as Dr. Leonard Jeffries's anti-Semitic statements are met with vitriolic outrage while presidential candidate Patrick J. Buchanan's anti-Semitism receives a genteel response—black nationalisms will thrive.

Afrocentrism, a contemporary species of black nationalism, is a gallant yet misguided attempt to define an African identity in a white society perceived to be hostile. It is gallant because it puts black doings and sufferings, not white anxieties and fears, at the center of discussion. It is misguided because—out of fear of cultural hybridization and through silence on the issue of class, retrograde views on black women, gay men, and lesbians, and a reluctance to link race to the common good—it reinforces the narrow discussions about race.

To establish a new framework, we need to begin with a frank acknowledgment of the basic humanness and Americanness of each of us. And we must acknowledge that as a people—*E Pluribus Unum*—we are on a slippery slope toward economic strife, social turmoil, and cultural chaos. If we go down, we go down together. The Los Angeles upheaval forced us to see not only that we are not connected in ways we would like to be but also, in a more profound sense, that this failure to connect binds us even more tightly together. The paradox of race in America is that our common destiny is more pronounced and imperiled precisely when our divisions are deeper. The Civil War and its legacy speak loudly here. And our divisions are growing deeper. Today, eighty-six percent of white suburban Americans live in neighborhoods that are less than 1 percent black, meaning that the prospects for the country depend largely on how its cities fare in the hands of a suburban electorate. There is no escape from our interracial interdependence, yet enforced racial hierarchy dooms us as a nation to collective paranoia and hysteria—the unmaking of any democratic order.

The verdict in the Rodney King case which sparked the incidents in Los Angeles was perceived to be wrong by the vast majority of Americans. But whites have often failed to acknowledge the widespread mistreatment of black people, especially black men, by law enforcement agencies, which helped ignite the spark. The verdict was merely the occasion for deep-seated rage to come to the surface. This rage is fed by the "silent" depression ravaging the country—in which real weekly wages of all American workers since 1973 have declined nearly 20 percent, while at the same time wealth has been upwardly distributed.

The exodus of stable industrial jobs from urban centers to cheaper labor markets here and abroad, housing policies that have created "chocolate cities and vanilla suburbs" (to use the popular musical artist George Clinton's memorable phrase), white fear of black crime, and the urban influx of poor Spanish-speaking and Asian immigrants—all have helped erode the tax base of American cities just as the federal government has cut its supports and programs. The result is unemployment, hunger, homelessness, and sickness for millions.

And a pervasive spiritual impoverishment grows. The collapse of meaning in life—the eclipse of hope and absence of love of self and others, the breakdown of family and neighborhood bonds—leads to the social deracination and cultural denudement of urban dwellers, especially children. We have created rootless, dangling people with little link to the supportive networks—family, friends, school—that sustain some sense of purpose in life. We have witnessed the collapse of the spiritual communities that in the past helped Americans face despair, disease, and death and that transmit through the generations dignity and decency, excellence and elegance.

The result is lives of what we might call "random nows," of fortuitous and fleeting moments preoccupied with "getting over"—with acquiring pleasure, property, and power by any means necessary. (This is not what Malcolm X meant by this famous phrase.) Post-modern culture is more and more a market culture dominated by gangster mentalities and self-destructive wantonness. This culture engulfs all of us—yet its impact on the disadvantaged is devastating, resulting in extreme violence in everyday life. Sexual violence against women and homicidal assaults by young black men on one another are only the most obvious signs of this empty quest for pleasure, property, and power.

Last, this rage is fueled by a political atmosphere in which images, not ideas, dominate, where politicians spend more time raising money than debating issues. The functions of parties have been displaced by public polls, and politicians behave less as thermostats that determine the climate of opinion than as thermometers registering the public mood. American politics has been rocked by an unleashing of greed among opportunistic public officials—who have followed the lead of their counterparts in the private sphere, where, as of 1989, 1 percent of the population owned 37 percent of the wealth and 10 percent of the population owned 86 percent of the wealth—leading to a profound cynicism and pessimism among the citizenry.

And given the way in which the Republican Party since 1968 has appealed to popular xenophobic images—playing the black, female, and homophobic cards to realign the electorate along race, sex, and sexual-orientation lines—it is no surprise that the notion that we are all part of one garment of destiny is discredited. Appeals to special interests rather than to public interests reinforce this polarization. The Los Angeles upheaval was an expression of utter fragmentation by a powerless citizenry that includes not just the poor but all of us.

What is to be done? How do we capture a new spirit and vision to meet the challenges of the post-industrial city, post-modern culture, and post-party politics?

First, we must admit that the most valuable sources for help, hope, and power consist of ourselves and our common history. As in the ages of Lincoln, Roosevelt, and King, we must look to new frameworks and languages to understand our multilayered crisis and overcome our deep malaise.

Second, we must focus our attention on the public square—the common good that undergirds our national and global destinies. The vitality of any public square ultimately depends on how much we *care* about the quality of our lives together. The neglect of our public infrastructure, for example—our water and sewage systems, bridges, tunnels, highways, subways, and streets—reflects not only our myopic economic policies, which impede productivity, but also the low priority we place on our common life.

The tragic plight of our children clearly reveals our deep disregard for public well-being. About one out of every five children in this country lives in poverty, including one out of every two black children and two out of every five Hispanic children. Most of our children—neglected by overburdened parents and bombarded by the market values of profit-hungry corporations—are ill-equipped to live lives of spiritual and cultural quality. Faced with these facts, how do we expect ever to constitute a vibrant society?

One essential step is some form of large-scale public intervention to ensure access to basic social goods—housing, food, health care, education, child care, and jobs. We must invigorate the common good with a mixture of government, business, and labor that does not follow any existing blueprint. After a period in which the private sphere has been sacralized and the public square gutted, the temptation is to make a fetish of the public square. We need to resist such dogmatic swings.

Last, the major challenge is to meet the need to generate new leadership. The paucity of courageous leaders—so apparent in the response to the events in Los Angeles—requires that we look beyond the same elites and voices that recycle the older frameworks. We need leaders—neither saints nor sparkling television personalities—who can situate themselves within a larger historical narrative of this country and our world, who can grasp the complex dynamics of our peoplehood and imagine a future grounded in the best of our past, yet who are attuned to the frightening obstacles that now perplex us. Our ideals of freedom, democracy, and equality must be invoked to invigorate all of us, especially the landless, propertyless, and luckless. Only a visionary leadership that can motivate "the better angels of our nature," as Lincoln said, and activate possibilities for a freer, more efficient, and stable America—only that leadership deserves cultivation and support.

This new leadership must be grounded in grass-roots organizing that high-lights democratic accountability. Whoever *our* leaders will be as we approach the twenty-first century, their challenge will be to help Americans determine whether a genuine multiracial democracy can be created and sustained in an era of global economy and a moment of xenophobic frenzy.

Let us hope and pray that the vast intelligence, imagination, humor, and courage of Americans will not fail us. Either we learn a new language of empathy and compassion, or the fire this time will consume us all.

15

Draft of a Global Program

Jeremy Brecher, Tim Costello, and Brendan Smith

The emergence of a worldwide social movement for globalization from below changes the conditions of human action. It opens new possibilities for addressing not only globalization from above but also long-standing problems of poverty, oppression, war, and environmental destruction. In their book *Globalization from Below: The Power of Solidarity,* from which the following selection has been taken, the authors contribute to the international dialogue on the new possibilities and how to utilize them. In the following selection, the authors state one possible version of the emerging common program of globalization from below.

We wrote in Chapter 1 that participants in the movements for globalization from below have varied goals, but the movement's unifying goal is "to bring about sufficient democratic control over states, markets, and corporations to permit people and the planet to survive and begin to shape a viable future." In this chapter we present the draft of a program to impose such democratic control. It proposes institutions and practices designed to turn global norms into enforceable rules.

This draft program is offered as a contribution to the ongoing process of constructing a program for globalization from below. It is not derived from an underlying political philosophy, but rather is synthesized from the solutions that diverse constituencies have proposed on their itineraries to globalization from below. It represents a work in progress, based on elements that have been percolating through the movement. Similar approaches have been formulated in previous programs presented by transitional groupings of various kinds.[1] Many of these elements have been included in the Global Sustainable Development Resolution cosponsored by a group of progressive members of the U.S. Congress.[2]

This synthesis is guided by Chapter 1's analysis of the conflict between globalization from above and globalization from below; Chapter 2's concept of social movements imposing norms; Chapter 3's emphasis on addressing the different levels from the local to the global; Chapter 4's approach to integrating the needs of people and nature and of North and South; and Chapter 5's delineation of the origins and functions of a program.

This program is not the design for a utopia or a plan to fix all the world's ills. Its purpose is to provide a win-win framework for the many constituencies converging into globalization from below. It seeks ways that their needs, concerns, and interests can be complementary rather than contradictory.[3] Rather than treating trade, finance, development, labor, environment, agriculture, and other aspects of globalization as separate, unrelated compartments, this draft program addresses the global economy holistically. While each element also requires detailed elaboration, all are presented here as parts of an integrated project.

While this program aims to change the global economy, it is designed to be fought for and implemented as much in local arenas as in Washington or Geneva. For example, local struggles over the right to organize unions and control over corporate waste disposal can help level labor and environmental conditions upward, especially if they receive solidarity support from a broad coalition around the world. Reducing the volatility of the global economy involves local economic development protected from the gyrations of the global casino. While this program ultimately envisions new rules and institutions for the global economy, many of its objectives can be implemented piecemeal through pressure on particular corporations, governments, and institutions.

The goals of globalization from below are often expressed in broad language advocating just and sustainable development. One formulation describes the movement's goal as "a new economy based on fairness and justice, on a sound ecology and a healthy environment, one that protects human rights and serves freedom."[4] Another calls for a "sustainable, socially just and democratically accountable" system.[5] Our sketch of a program for globalization from below is organized around seven basic principles:

1. Level labor, environmental, social, and human rights conditions upward.
2. Democratize institutions at every level from local to global.
3. Make decisions as close as possible to those they affect.
4. Equalize global wealth and power.
5. Convert the global economy to environmental sustainability.
6. Create prosperity by meeting human and environmental needs.
7. Protect against global boom and bust.

LEVEL LABOR, ENVIRONMENTAL, SOCIAL, AND HUMAN RIGHTS CONDITIONS UPWARD

Globalization from above is creating a race to the bottom, an economic war of all against all in which each workforce, community, and country is forced to compete by offering lower labor, social, environmental, and human rights conditions. The result is impoverishment, inequality, volatility, degradation of democracy, and environmental destruction. Halting the race to the bottom requires raising labor, environmental, social, and human rights conditions for those at the bottom. Such upward leveling can start with specific struggles to raise conditions for those who are being driven downward. Ultimately, minimum environmental, labor, social and human rights standards must be incorporated in national and international law. Such standards protect communities and countries from the pressure to compete by sacrificing their rights and environment. Rising conditions for those at the bottom can also expand employment and markets and generate a virtuous circle of economic growth.

Raise labor, environmental, social, and human rights conditions locally: The fight to reverse the race to the bottom can begin at home. For example, living wage campaigns in local communities can be part of the process of upward leveling for wages. Organizing unions, ensuring the right to organize, establishing rights for workers in contingent jobs, and creating an adequate social safety net all establish rights and raise standards for those threatened by the downward pressures of the global economy. Campaigns for environmental justice and the protection of local environments similarly resist the environmental race to the bottom.[6]

Force standards on corporations: Workers and other citizens, acting in civil society, should pressure global corporations to negotiate minimum global standards for labor and environment.[7] National governments should be pressured to incorporate such standards in national trade laws and international financial and trade organizations.

Incorporate global standards in national law: Internationally recognized labor rights are regularly violated not only in the third world but also in the U.S. Every country's law should enforce those rights at home and require their corporations to meet international labor standards throughout the world.

Put floors, not ceilings, in international trade agreements: NAFTA [the North American Free Trade Agreement], the WTO [World Trade Organization], and other trade agreements often forbid labor, environmental, health, and other regulations that exceed the agreement's own standards. Such ceilings should be eliminated to allow communities and countries to set their own minimum standards.

Negotiate agreements to protect minimum standards for labor, environment, and human rights: Such agreements can be implemented by established institutions such as international trade organizations or the UN [United Nations], or by new ones established for the purpose.[8]

DEMOCRATIZE INSTITUTIONS AT EVERY LEVEL FROM LOCAL TO GLOBAL

Globalization from above has restricted the power of self-government for people all over the world. At the heart of globalization from below lies democratization—making institutions accountable to those they affect.

Open the dialogue on the future of the global economy to all: The movement has already initiated a participatory global dialogue on democratizing the global economy. That dialogue should be expanded in every local community, in every country, and worldwide. A model here is the movement in Canada, which organized community forums across the country to discuss a people's alternative to the MAI.[9]

Establish a Global Economy Truth Commission: Globalization has been conducted behind the back of the world's people. A truth commission can provide citizens of the world with the information they need to monitor the results, impacts, and failures of economic institutions and policy at every level. The Truth Commission's inquest should be given the powers to investigate, publicize and refer abuses in the use of international funds and the powers of international financial institutions to other authorities.

Democratize international trade and financial institutions: It is unacceptable that a few rich countries monopolize decision making regarding the global economy's future through the control of the IMF [International Monetary Fund], World Bank, and WTO [World Trade Organization] and through the control of major policy decisions by the G-7. Voting in international financial and trade institutions must move toward the standard of equal representation for the world's people.[10] International economic policy making must move from the rich men's club of the G-7 to forums where poor countries are fairly represented. International economic institutions must be made transparent in all their operations.

Let those affected by international economic policies participate in making them: Instead of closed negotiations with top government and corporate officials, decisions about international economic agreements and loans should require participation by labor unions, environmental groups, women's organizations, development organizations, and other major sectors of civil society in each country.

Establish an enforceable code of conduct for global corporations: Corporations that operate in more than one country should be subject to a global code of conduct with minimum requirements for disclosure of activities and compliance with labor and environmental standards. The UN Center of Transnational Corporations was in the process of developing such a code, but it was stopped by U.S. opposition.[11]

Make corporations legally accountable: Corporations should be held legally liable for harms caused abroad and be subject to actions for relief in home-country courts. They should be required to disclose their use, emission, and accidental discharge of toxic substances and the names and addresses of their fully or partially owned facilities, contractors, and subcontractors.

End the domination of politics by big money: Ending "crony capitalism" means reducing the domination of political systems and media by economic oligarchs and increasing the capacity of people to organize themselves at the grassroots. This is as necessary in the United States as in Indonesia, Mexico, or Russia.[12]

MAKE DECISIONS AS CLOSE AS POSSIBLE TO THOSE THEY AFFECT

The movement for globalization from below should aim to construct a multilevel global economy. In accordance with the subsidiary principle, power and initiative should be concentrated at as low a level as possible, with higher-level regulation established where and only where necessary. This approach envisions relatively self-reliant, self-governing communities, states, provinces, countries, and regions, with global regulation only sufficient to protect the environment, redistribute resources, block the race to the bottom, and perform other essential functions.

Build a community-controlled economic sector: A key strategy for protecting local communities from the vagaries of the global economy is to create an economic sector that is partially insulated from global markets. This sector needs to be rooted in and controlled by local people and based on meeting local needs. Creating such a sector involves initiating local projects, such as worker and community-owned businesses, cooperatives, development banks, and loan funds. It also involves supportive public policies, such as government procurement and funding policies that support sustainable local development.

Make corporations locally accountable: Local labor unions, community groups, and governments should pressure corporations to negotiate with them regarding acceptable norms of behavior.

Establish local control of local environment: In accord with the principle of subsidiarity, any activity with potential impact on the local environment should require the informed consent of the people in that community.[13]

Protect local and national economic development capacity: Current trade agreements often interfere with the right of countries and communities to pursue local economic development objectives, such as job creation and targeting development for needy groups. International agreements should instead protect that right.

Establish regional "no raiding" pacts: States and provinces should agree not to complete to provide subsidies to lure companies to relocate. No-raiding rules exist in the EU [European Union], and corporations have been heavily fined for taking state and provincial subsidies to relocate. Unions in the northeastern U.S. have proposed a multistate agreement that would block the regional race to the bottom by punishing companies that relocate to areas with lower standards.[14]

EQUALIZE GLOBAL WEALTH AND POWER

The current gap between the global rich and poor is unacceptable; it is unconscionable to act as if it can be a permanent feature of the global economy. It is equally unacceptable to assume that the rich countries of the world can call all the shots regarding the global economy's future. Policy at every level should prioritize economic advancement of the most oppressed and exploited people, including women, immigrants, racial and ethnic minorities, and indigenous peoples. It should increase power, capability, resources, and income for those at the bottom.

Shop and invest ethically: Individual consumers, institutions, and governments should use their buying power to purchase goods, services, and investments that support acceptable labor, environmental, and social conditions. Consumer power is already being used in such areas as the boycott of companies that invest in Burma and of World Bank bonds. Consumer purchasing power is also being harnessed to support fair trade—for example, through the Rugmark consumer seal for rugs produced without child labor; the creation of organizations to certify that garments and other products are not produced under sweatshop conditions; and the marketing of crafts and coffee from fairly paid workers and employee-owned cooperatives.

Revive the North-South Dialogue: In the 1970's, the rich and poor countries of the world initiated the North-South Dialogue, a series of ongoing UN discussions designed to establish a New International Economic Order that would support third world development. This dialogue, terminated by Ronald Reagan, should be revived as a step toward providing poor countries with a greater voice in global policies.

End global debt slavery: Today poor countries are forced to run their economies to pay debts promoted by foreign investors and taken on by corrupt governments that did not represent their people. The wealthy countries and the international financial institutions should immediately cancel the debts of the poorest countries. Repayment requirements should be limited for all underdeveloped countries.[15] No poor country should be required to use more than a small proportion of its income for debt repayment.

Make global markets work for developing economies: Rather than promoting indiscriminate free trade, trade policy should specifically encourage development of poor countries by providing them with preferential access to first world markets. (This is already done in a modest way with the Generalized System of Preferences, which reduces tariffs for developing countries.) To reverse the fall in commodity prices that has devastated third world producers and to prevent a global race to the bottom in commodities, commodity agreements to promote stability in price and production levels should be encouraged.

Provide developing countries access to technical knowledge: International trade agreements have enormously expanded the so-called intellectual property rights of corporations. This blocks poor countries from the knowledge they need to develop and become more self-reliant. Often this causes terrible hardship, such as the murderous drug company policy of using their "intellectual property rights" to price lifesaving drugs out of reach of the world's ordinary citizens. Global policy should encourage rapid and inexpensive access to all forms of technical knowledge to aid sustainable development. Those with access to such knowledge should, when necessary, commit "intellectual civil disobedience" by helping make it available to those who need it.

Invest in sustainable development: Global investment should be redirected from private financial speculation to one or more public international investment funds. The primary purpose of these funds should be to meet human and environmental needs by channeling money into locally controlled, environmentally sustainable, long-term investment. Sources for funding could include a Tobin Tax on international currency transactions; a global tax on carbon use designed to reduce greenhouse gas emissions; reductions in military spending; and public and private investment.[16] Such funds could also counter global economic cycles by appropriate expansion and contradiction of their activities.

CONVERT THE GLOBAL ECONOMY TO ENVIRONMENTAL SUSTAINABILITY.

The world is in the midst of a global environment catastrophe. Ill-conceived economic activity is disrupting the basic balances of climate and ecology on which human life depends. Globalization is rapidly accelerating that ongoing catastrophe. The sources of environmental destruction lie primarily in the wrongly developed countries to the North and in the activities of global corporations in the South. The only way to reverse this catastrophe is to halt the present dynamic of globalization and meet human needs by technologies and social practices that progressively reduce the negative impact of the economy on the environment.

Transform the production and consumption patterns of wrongly developed countries: The so-called developed or industrialized countries of the North produce the lion's share of the world's pollution and climate-changing carbon emissions. The technological and social means to change their destructive patterns exist but are not being utilized. Public policy, including taxation, regulation, planning, and investment, must be directed to completely rebuilding these wrongly developed economies on an environmentally sustainable basis.

Make international environmental agreements enforceable: International agreements have been developed to combat global warming, protect endangered species, and restrict foreign dumping of toxic waste. But these agreements have little provision for enforcement. For example, many countries have ignored the agreements they signed at the Rio conference on environment and development. Such agreements should now be made enforceable by incorporating sanctions like those for protection of international property rights in the WTO.[17]

Incorporate environmental protections in trade agreements: The WTO, NAFTA, and other trade agreements should discourage environmentally destructive practices. Countries should be free to ban import of goods produced under conditions that violate environmental principles.

End the despoiling of natural resources for export: Countries should not be required by the IMF, World Bank, or global investors to chop down their forests, overfarm their lands, and overfish their waters to service their debts or increase investor profit.

Encourage sustainable development: Establish sustainable development plans at local and national levels. Pursue "conservation-based development" that combines good gobs and income with environmental enhancement. Focus international aid on helping to implement sustainable development plans.

CREATE PROSPERITY BY MEETING HUMAN AND ENVIRONMENTAL NEEDS

Today, an estimated 1 billion people are unemployed. Millions are forced to leave rural areas and migrate to cities or around the world seeking work. Meanwhile, the world's vast need for goods and services to alleviate poverty and to reconstruct society on an environmentally sustainable basis goes unmet. A goal of economic policy at every level must be to create a new kind of full employment based on meeting those needs.

Encourage development, not austerity: Neoliberalism, the IMF, and the World Bank have imposed austerity policies on much of the world, leading to massive unemployment and the destruction of small businesses and farms. Instead, local, national, and global policies should aim to ensure livable wages. They should make credit available for small and medium-sized locally owned businesses and farms. They should pursue a progressive tax policy that reduces the burden on the poor. This will help reverse the destructive competition that is promoted by globalization from above.

Promote local food production for local needs: Today's global economy subsidizes corporate food exports while forcing countries to open up to foreign food imports, thereby driving millions of small-scale farmers off the land. Instead, global policy should promote small-scale, environmentally sound farming for local markets. It should end agricultural export dumping. It should encourage countries to provide basic food security for their people.[18]

Utilize development planning techniques: Governments should revive the development planning techniques that have been forbidden by neoliberalism and its institutions. Such tools include reserving some economic sectors for public, state, or national ownership. They also include performance requirements designed to achieve local, regional, or national economic objectives, such as requirements for local inputs and local hiring preferences.

Promote long-term investment: Short-term foreign investment that just skims off speculative profits does little or nothing for economic development.

Only long-term investment that builds economic capacity and protects the environment is likely to benefit poorer countries. Public policy should encourage investment that leads to genuine sustainable development, not exploitation of people and resources for short-term gain.

Reestablish national full employment policies: Neoliberal economic policies have used mass unemployment to keep wages low, allegedly to fight inflation. National governments should instead use tax, budget, and monetary policies to ensure full employment.

PROTECT AGAINST GLOBAL BOOM AND BUST

The era of globalization has been an era of volatility. Its repeated crises have destroyed local and national economies overnight and driven hundreds of millions of people into poverty. An unregulated global economy has led to huge flows of speculative funds that can swamp national economies. No one country can control these forces on its own. Yet neoliberal economics and the major economic powers have resisted any changes that might restrict the freedom of capital. Economic security for ordinary people requires just such restrictions.

Utilize capital controls: Under the articles of the IMF, countries have the power to impose controls on the movement of capital across their borders. This power, which was used regularly by most countries for many decades, helps protect against wild rushes of money into and out of a country. But the current policies of the IMF and other institutions and the pressures of globalization have largely undermined the capacity of individual countries to use such controls effectively. Countries and international institutions should cooperate to restore their effectiveness.

Establish a "hot money" tax: A global tax on short-term hot money transactions—known as a Tobin Tax—will reduce global speculation, as well as provide resources for world development and environmental protection.

Coordinate demand in the major economies: The maintenance of property worldwide requires cooperation of the major economic powers working in parallel to ensure demand adequate to help all economies grow.[19]

Assure global liquidity: Financial crises have been a regular part of globalization. When such crises occur, short-term lack of liquidity can cause long-term economic devastation. Provisions should be made in advance to reduce the effects of such liquid crises, especially on poorer countries. In the 1970's, for example, a system of Special Drawing Rights was established to protect the global economy from liquidity squeezes. The expansion of this or an equivalent system is required today.

Stabilize exchange rates: An effective system to prevent wild fluctuations in currency exchange rates existed for decades under the original design of the Bretton Woods agreement, but it was abandoned in the early 1970's. Such a system should be revived through international cooperation. It should aim to help countries adjust to changing conditions without drastic devaluations and massive increases in exports.[20]

Make speculations pay for their losses: International bailouts have insulated large banks and investors from the consequences of their high-risk speculations. This leads to what economists call moral hazard—encouraging more such speculative ventures. The result is even more international volatility. Assistance provided for economies in trouble must go to benefit the people, not to line the pockets of the international investors who lured them into trouble in the first place.

Establish a permanent insolvency mechanism for indebted countries: Such a mechanism can draw on the experience of other bankruptcy procedures for governments, such as the municipal insolvency provisions of Chapter 9 of U.S. bankruptcy law. Arbitration panels should represent both debtors and creditors, and should establish the debtor country's capacity to pay, taking into account necessary expenditures for social safety nets to protect a minimum of human dignity of the poor and the debtor's economic future.[21]

Develop international monetary regulation: Over the course of centuries, nations developed central banks to regulate private banks, control the supply of money, and counter booms and busts. But globalization has undermined their capacity to do so, creating a global monetary system that is wildly out of control. That makes it necessary to develop international institutions to perform or assist with functions of monetary regulation currently performed inadequately by national central banks. Regulating global banks, for example, requires international cooperation. Equally important, the non-bank financial services companies that have grown explosively in the past decades need to be brought under national and international regulation. And, since money has become global, an international equivalent to the national regulation of interest rates and money supply is needed.[22] Such regulation must support basic objectives of just and sustainable development.

The movement for globalization from below is indeed developing an alternative vision for the global economy. It is not just a nostalgic desire to return to the past, nor a fearful rejection of a wider world, nor a laundry list of wishes and hopes. It is a program for the transformation of the global economy. Its elements are concrete enough to implement. They fit together well enough to be synergistic. They address the needs of the overwhelming majority of the world's people.

People can begin to implement these elements wherever and whenever they have the power to do so. As some elements are implemented, that can help strengthen the capacity to implement others.

That doesn't mean that the program presented here is adequate or final. On the contrary, it represents only an early attempt to put the proposals of different parts of the movement together into a common whole. The next step is to review this and other such syntheses in the light of the problems and concerns of different constituencies and to revise the whole in the light of the various needs to which it must respond. That is a work for many hands.

NOTES

1. For such a common program for the Americas, see "Alternatives for the Americas: Building a People's Hemispheric Agreement," which is available on-line at http://www.web.net/comfront/alts4americas/eng/eng.html; summary in Anderson et al., *Field Guide to the Global Economy*, pp. 130ff. For a synthesis from the Asian-Pacific network PP21, see Muto Ichiyo, "For an Alliance of Hope," in Brecher et al., *Global Visions*, pp. 147ff. For trade issues, see "WTO—Shrink or Sink!: The Turn Around Agenda" (http://www.trade-watch.org). For financial issues, see "From Speculation to the Real Economy: An Emerging North-South Labor-Citizens Agenda on Global Finance," the summary of recommendations from the 1998 conference "Toward a Progressive International Economy," sponsored by Friends of the Earth, the International Forum on Globalization, and the Third World Network, in Anderson et al., *Field Guide to the Global Economy*, pp. 128ff. Similar ideas are spelled out more fully in Sarah Anderson and John Cavanagh, *Bearing the Burden: The Impact of Global Financial Crisis on Workers and Alternative Agendas for the IMF and Other Institutions* (Washington: Institute for Policy Studies, April 2000). Many similar proposals are presented in UNDP [United Nations Development Program], *Human Development Report* 1999, and in its previous annual editions. Many significant labor proposals regarding reform of the global economy are available on-line at the AFL-CIO [American Federation of Labor and Congress of Industrial Organizations] web site: http//www.aflcio.org. Several valuable recent articles on alternatives for the global economy are collected in "Section Four: Ways to Restructure the Global Economy" in Burbach and Danaher, *Globalize This!* See also the wide-ranging synthesis of proposals for reform on the global economy presented by William Greider in a series of articles in *The Nation*: "Global Agenda" (January 31, 2000), "Shopping Till We Drop" (April 10, 2000), and "Time to Rein in Global Finance" (April 24, 2000). For ongoing coverage of third world proposals relating to international negotiations, see the magazine *Third World Resurgence*.

2. H. Res. 479, text available on-line through the U.S. House of Representatives web site: http://thomas.loc.gov/.

For additional information visit Representative Bernie Sanders' (I-VT) web site: http://bernie.house.gov/imf/global.asp. See also "Whose Globalization?" *The Nation*, March 22, 1999, and Ellen Frank, "Bye Bye IMF?: A New Blueprint for the Global Economy," in *Dollars and Sense* 224 (July-August 1999).

3. It is often assumed that these interests are inherently contradictory. For example, it is assumed that rising living standards in the South necessitate lowered living standards in the North or that protection and restoration of the environment imply worse living standards for some or all of the world's people. While neither poverty nor environmental destruction can be reversed without major change worldwide, such change does not require the impoverishment of ordinary citizens of the North. Ending wasteful and destructive use of the world's resources and putting its unused and poorly used resources, particularly its one billion unemployed, to work could largely eliminate poverty and environmental degradation without reducing the real quality of life in the North. Change in consumption patterns will be necessary—for example, reduced depen-

dence on fossil fuels—and the lifestyles of the rich will no doubt need to take a hit, but this does not imply a reduction in overall quality of life for the majority in the North.

4. Starhawk, "How We Really Shut Down the WTO," in Burbach and Danaher, *Globalize This!* pp. 39-40.

5. "WTO—Shrink or Sink!" (http://www.tradewatch.org).

6. See Jeremy Brecher, Tim Costello, and Brandan Smith, *Fight Where You Stand! Why Globalization in Your Community and Workplace and How to Address It at the Grassroots* (Boston: Campaign on Contingent Work/Common-work, 2000).

7. Professor Andy Banks of the George Meany Center has proposed that international law mandate that companies recognize and bargain with global union structures composed of unions representing all their workers worldwide. The law would mandate a minimum standard agreement which those structures would have the power to enforce through legally protected local monitoring committees. Personal communication, May 18, 2000. See also Andy Banks, "Monitoring Trade Union Perspective" (unpublished paper).

8. There has been considerable debate regarding the appropriate venues for such standards. The international trade union movement, for example, has strongly advocated that such standards be included in the WTO, while third world governments and many NGOs [Nongovernmental Organizations] have opposed that proposal and have argued that such issues belong instead in the ILO[International Labor Organization]. In fact, this question is currently moot, since the opposition to incorporating such standards in any international agreement is overwhelming. For the time being, labor rights will have to be imposed on corporations primarily by direct pressure in civil society. As other means for imposing them, such as national policy or international agreement open up, those opportunities should be seized without regard to preconceptions about appropriate venues.

As we argued in Chapter 4, the emerging structures regulating the global economy tend to be multiple and overlapping. And, as Waldon Bello has argued, such pluralism is desirable. "Trade, development, and environmental issues must be formulated and interpreted by a wider body of global organizations (than the WTO), including UNCTAD [United Nations Conference on Trade and Development], the International Labor Organization (ILO), the implementing bodies of multilateral environmental agreements, and regional economic blocs" ("UNCTAD: Time to Lead, Time to Challenge the WTO," in Burbach and Danaher, *Globalize This!* p. 172). Steven Shrybman similarly argues that environmental regulations should be embodied both within trade organizations like the WTO and in international environmental agreements ("Trade Now, Pay Later," in Burbach and Danaher, *Globalize This!* p. 162). Ultimately, such standards should be incorporated in a wide range of rule-making structures. For an extended discussion of issues regarding implementation of labor rights requirements, see Pharis J. Harvey and Terry Collingsworth, "Developing Effective Mechanisms for Implementing Labor Rights in the Global Economy" (Discussion Draft, International Labor Rights Fund, March 9, 1998).

9. "Economic Forum: MAI Foes to Hold Inquiry to View Alternatives," *Vancouver Sun*, September 11, 1998. A discussion paper about this process and its

results, "Towards a Citizen's MAI: An Alternative Approach to Developing a Global Investment Treaty Based on Citizens' Rights and Democratic Control" (1998), was prepared by the Polaris Institute in Canada with input from scholars and activists around the world.

10. Proposals include restoring the original Bretton Woods conception that the UN Economic and Social Council (ECOSOC) oversee and coordinate the work of international trade and financial institutions; changing the weighted voting in international financial institutions to correspond to population rather than just investment; adding additional countries to international institution governing boards; establishing elected regional boards of directors; and creating a directly elected Global People's Assembly within the UN system.

11. For the UN Center on Transnational Corporations corporate code of conduct efforts, see Walter A. Chudson, "An Impressionistic Tour of International Investment Codes, 1948–1994," in Orin Kirshner, ed., *The Bretton Woods-GATT System* (Armonk, New York: M. E. Sharpe, 1996), p. 177.

12. For detailed suggestions for reclaiming popular control of national governments, see "Democratic Governance," a working paper prepared by Tony Clarke of the Polaris Institute in Canada for the International Forum on Globalization.

13. See Vandana Shiva, "The Greening of the Global Reach," in Brecher et al., *Global Visions*, p. 59.

14. Regional efforts can themselves be transnational. The Great Lakes Regional Compact brings together U.S. states and Canadian provinces for economic development and environmental protection. PP21 has established regional networks of grassroots organizations across national boundaries in several major Asian river valleys.

15. See, for example, Rev. Dr. Robert W. Edgar, "Jubilee 2000: Paying Our Debts," *The Nation*, April 24, 2000, pp. 20–21.

16. For a detailed proposal for such an international investment fund, see Jane D'Arista, "Financial Regulation in a Liberalized Global Environment," paper prepared for the Conference on International Capital Markets and Future of Economic Policy, Queens' College, University of Cambridge, April 16–17, 1998. For D'Arista's proposals and related work, see the Financial Markets Center web site at http://www.fmcenter.org. As discussed below, the purpose of the Tobin Tax is not simply to raise revenue, but also to put "speed bumps" in the flow of speculative capital. For information on the Tobin Tax and on the campaign promoting it, visit the web site of the Tobin Tax Initiative USA at http://www.tobintax.org. The United Nations Conference on Trade and Development (UNCTAD) predicts that a .25 percent transaction tax would reduce global foreign-exchange transactions by up to 30 percent, while generating around $300 billion in tax revenues. ("Financial Globalization vs. Free Trade: The Case for the Tobin Tax," *UNCTAD Bulletin*, January-March 1996.) For a discussion of issues around global taxation, also see Howard M. Wachtel, "The Mosaic of Global Taxes," in Pieterse, ed., *Global Futures*, pp. 83ff. The Association for the Taxation of Financial Transactions for the Aid of Citizens (ATTAC), an international effort initiated in France, has drawn tens of thousands of people into discussion of the Tobin Tax and related issues. Visit the association's web site on-line at http://www.attaac.org.

Peter Dorman has suggested that such funds could provide a transition to a generally more democratic global economy in which securities

> would pass progressively into the ownership of a class of financial intermediaries chartered on condition of extensive public input. Competition between these institutions and transparency in their operations would preserve incentives for efficient investment, but governments or other agents of the public would increasingly find it in their power to loosely guide or set limits to portfolio choice. This leverage would mitigate pressures toward financial instability and the excessive power of financial markets over democratic institutions. . . . (and) the intermediaries themselves would acquire global scope, providing a venue for democratic processes across national borders.

Peter Dorman, "Actually Existing Globalization," in Peter Aulakh and Michael Schechter, eds., *Rethinking Globalization(s): From Corporate Transnationalism in Local Interventions* (New York: St. Martin's Press, 2000).

17. See Steven Shrybman, "Trade Now, Pay Later," in Burbach and Danaher, *Globalize This!*

18. For background on global agricultural issues, see Mark Ritchie, "Rural-Urban Cooperation: Our Populist History and Future," in Brecher and Costello, *Building Bridges*. See also Peter Rosset, "A New Food Movement Comes of Age in Seattle," in Danaher and Burbach, *Globalize This!*

19. See, for example, Oskar Lafontaine, "The Future of German Social Democracy," extract of the text of a speech to the SPD Conference, Hannover, December 2–4, 1997, in *New Left Review* 227 (January–February 1998): 72ff. Lafontaine tried to develop cooperative international policies along these lines during his brief tenure as Germany's finance minister.

20. See the various proposals in Jo Marie Griesgraber and Bernhard G. Gunter eds., *The World's Monetary System: Toward Stability and Sustainability in the Twenty-First Century* (London: Pluto Press, 1996).

21. Proposals for an insolvency mechanism have been developed by Prof. Kunibert Raffer. See Kunibert Raffer, "Applying Chapter 9 Insolvency to International Debts: An Economically Efficient Solution with a Human Face," *World Development* 18: 2 (February 1990): 301ff.

22. Jane D'Arista has proposed one valuable model for such regulation. It involves the regulation of banks and all other financial institutions by national and international regulatory authorities; internationally coordinated minimum reserve requirements on the consolidated global balance sheets of all financial firms; and utilization of reserve requirements to counter cyclical variations in global growth rates. See D'Arista, "Financial Regulation in a Liberalized Global Environment." For D'Arista's proposals and related work, see the Financial Markets Center web site at http://www.fmcenter.org. For more establishment-oriented advocacy of expanded global financial regulation, see John Eatwell and Lance Taylor, "International Capital Markets and the Future of Economic Policy," Center for Economic Policy Analysis, August 1998, and Jeffrey E. Garten, "Needed: A Fed for the World," *New York Times*, September 23, 1998.

16

It Is All about Human/Civil Rights

Doris Hunter

Doris Hunter received her graduate degrees from Boston University in theology and in philosophy of religion. She has taught courses in World Religions, Introduction to Philosophy and Aesthetics, and Humanities at Boston University, Northeastern University, Tufts University, and Bentley College in Massachusetts. In 1975, she was ordained as a Unitarian Universalist Minister. During her ministry and her teaching, she has written several books on nonviolence and violence with her colleagues, including Dr. Krishna Mallick. This original article reveals her commitment to civil/human rights and the necessity for violence to end in regard to the issue of homophobia.

In his book *One Nation, After All,* Alan Wolfe, professor of sociology at Boston University, describes the hundreds of interviews he conducted in middle class communities outside four metropolitan areas—Boston, Atlanta, Tulsa and San Diego—asking questions about morality, diversity, work and family issues. Instead of finding deep divisions and disagreements, he found Americans tolerant of diversity, pragmatic in their morality, focused on their work and families generally minding their own business except for one issue, the issue of homosexuality. Here is where the "one nation" construct breaks down. Alan Wolfe tells us that is the one area where people use words like sinful, hateful, wrong, immoral . . . the kind of words they never used on any other subject.

Did you hear that . . . middle class Americans? And isn't that the focus for the major issues of human and civil rights, the issues of marriage, children, living the suburban life? We who have the automatic, natural rights given by a marriage license, the protection of our children within marriage, and the safety nets of insurance, mortgages, last will and testaments forget, can't imagine or do not even entertain in our waking consciousness what it means to be deprived of these basic rights and privileges because of a sexual orientation. Yet listen again to Wolfe's remarks, "It's not hatred, it's fear, and it has much to do with the 'sexuality' as with the 'homo' part of the word." Was it fear that made Congress in

1996 pass the Defense of Marriage Act signed by President Clinton which bars federal benefits to spouses in same-sex marriages and allows states to ignore gay and lesbian marriages legalized in other states? Was it fear that cause the State of Maine to repeal a law banning discrimination against gays and lesbians in housing and employment? Was it fear that resulted in a ruling by a Florida court that custody of a child should be given to a father who was a convicted murderer rather than a lesbian mother? Is it fear that promotes the "Don't Ask, Don't Tell" policy regarding gays and lesbians in the military? If it is fear and that fear has to do with sexuality, then what is *this* fear of sexuality?

To begin to answer this question we should acknowledge that our society has a deep ambivalence about sexuality. In one sense we flaunt it in advertisements, in political life, in power relationships, in pornography while we moralize about it in terms of family values and the institution of marriage. We X rate it in the movies when we P13 violence and hatred. Isn't a gun more sexy than a kiss? Our culture glamorizes sexuality on one hand while on the other hand it condemns it. We live in a Puritan culture that advises "Just Say No!" while a hedonistic culture promotes "Yes! Yes! Yes!" It is no wonder our children are confused and sometimes tragically sexually abused by confused adults.

Why? Isn't it because sexuality is the major tool, a device for manipulation and power? Look at the people in power—-in politics, in business, in education, in the media, in the ministry, in marriage, in all aspects of life. The most intimate tender expression of love can become the harsh and brutal expression of dominance and abuse. Traditionally heterosexual marriage made no excuses for its pattern of male dominance over the female. It was and is the socially acceptable pattern for acting out the masculine characteristics of being the provider while the woman was/is the sustainer. She gave birth to his children within the confines of a legal relationship of ownership, the DNA security of past ages. It is no wonder in our present age with women working outside the home that the traditional roles of provider/sustainer are confused along with the traditional patterns of marriage. We see evidence of this in the divorce statistics in our society. 50% of marriages end in divorce. Congress should rethink its reason for passing the Defense of Marriage Act.

It is obvious we need to examine the sexual roles in heterosexual marriage. Oh, but we are whether we like it or not. Hear the cries for equality in marriage, sharing the tasks of homemaking and child care, being partners in every way. No more dominance, violence, abuse. No more submission, passivity, acquiescence. Yet it has been over three thousand years of patriarchy which produced not only the role of male dominance but also the ideas of democracy, individualism and liberty. Now suddenly upon the civilized stage of Western masculine thought comes feminism with its demand for equality, nurturing of the earth and human relationships, and the interdependent web of all existence. It is no wonder we are in such an upheaval and it is no wonder there is this fear of homosexuality. When men and women confuse the roles of masculine and feminine sexuality, especially men, there is a fear that the solid walls of patriarchy will crumble. I suppose we could imagine a modern-day Jericho not with Joshua and his army marching around its walls but a parade of gays, lesbians, bisexuals, straights demanding that these walls come tumbling down.

We should not be surprised, therefore, that the forces of the religious right hold up the Bible as the final authority against homosexuality. And yet as Peter Gomes, Harvard University's pastor, preacher, Christian, homosexual, points out in his new book, *The Good Book: Reading the Bible with Mind and Heart*, the Bible has little to say about homosexuality. It is not mentioned in the Ten Commandments, no prophet discourses on it as a major sin of Israel, Jesus doesn't mention it. In fact, the word itself is an invention of the late nineteenth century and does not occur in any of the original manuscripts from which came the translations of the English Bible. The first use of the word homosexual is found in the Revised Standard Edition published in 1946.

But the homosexual act is there in the Bible if not the word. Right? Peter Gomes meets this challenge by showing us the references used by the seekers for Biblical authority. Some of us may not rely on Biblical authority for truth but we should be ready to answer with our own challenge when others use the Bible as grounds for their homophobia. Briefly, the references used are (1) the Creation Story which is about Adam and Eve and not Adam and Steve; therefore homosexuality is the only God-given way for human beings. Yet what an assumption when this is a creation story written by men explaining the biological beginning of humanity. "The creation story is the basis and not the end of human diversity, and thus to regard it as excluding everything it does not mention is to place too great a burden on the text and its writers and too little responsibility upon the intelligence of the readers and on varieties of human experience" (Gomes, p. 150). (2) There is the reference to the Sodom and Gomorrah story in Genesis 19 which is not about homosexuality but the lack of hospitality, a greater sin in the early history of Israel than any sexual misconduct. (3) Next there is the reference in Leviticus which includes the Holiness Code listing items of ritual impurity no longer relevant to modern cultures. Homosexuality is ritually impure along with inbreeding of cattle, sowing fields with two kinds of seeds, wearing garments made of two different kinds of material—also round haircuts, tattoos and consultations with mediums and wizards. (4) Finally, what St. Paul said about the sin of unnatural acts in the New Testament indicates a judgment upon all sexuality which is absorbed with self for egoistical, exploited, possessive reasons.

Even when it is difficult for persons to take seriously arguments from the Bible as justification for homophobia, it is important for us to remember that it is not the Bible but the people who read it and interpret isolated passages for such justification without acknowledging careful Biblical criticism of these passages. So if the Bible is a shield for homophobia, what is the fear behind this shield? It is a fear of sexuality promoted by centuries of Christian belief which honored celibacy as the highest virtue, marriage as a concession to human weakness and as a necessity for continuing the human race. What was the original sin in the Garden of Eden? It was not disobedience but the discovery of sexual shame, according to the early Christian theologians. "In sin did my mother conceive me" (Psalm 51:5). The obvious conclusion followed . . . all sexual activity outside marriage especially any that did not result in procreation was sinful. Thus homosexuality was/is a sin, a crime, an illness. But wait! Is the sole natural function of sex procreation?

"How ridiculous, of course not." We are liberated from those old fashioned Jewish/Christian notions which proclaim that the one and only one essential function of sexuality is the reproduction of the human race. Are we not liberated from the shame of St. Augustine's theology of sexuality? Do we not act like we are liberated from St. Thomas Aquinas' teachings that sexual activity outside marriage is a threat to the moral order? Do we not question the Roman Catholic doctrine which requires clergy to be celibate? So are we liberated enough to understand sexuality as an important aspect of the spiritual life for everyone? If that is true, do not same-sex relationships have the same potential for sacramental meaning and power as heterosexual relationships? If sex in any relationship has the potential for the expression of love, depth of spiritual oneness, then we all have a responsibility to live up to this potential. This is the ideal for all sexual relationships.

The temptations, however, for both the heterosexual and homosexual are real. We despair and react to this loss of faith in our sexual lives by engaging in the fleeting liberation of anonymous sex or secret affairs, by the quick fix of substance abuse, by our acts of deception. We flaunt ourselves in the worst possible way. Heterosexuals have been doing this for centuries. Isn't it time for all of us to model a fully integrated sexual and spiritual life? I am convinced that we need models to help us especially models of homosexual love to help with this integration.

What a demand this is to make but we need help to change our cultural notions of restricted love. How can we make love only straight? Impossible! How can we make marriage only straight? We desperately need models of love relationships between women and between men to correct this cultural prejudice. We are fortunate to have such models as members of our communities. Now inspired by their lives together, we should integrate our efforts to make possible for them all the human/civil rights heterosexuals possess. No more silence. No more jokes. No more acquiescence to middle American fear. Listen to these statements from gay men and lesbians:

How we act is more important than who we are and if we get harassed it's our problem and if we get attacked we provoked it and if we raise our voices we're flaunting ourselves and if we enjoy sex we're perverts and if we have AIDS we deserve it and if we march with pride we're recruiting children and if we want or have children we're unfit parents and if we stand up for our rights we're overstepping our boundaries. We are forced constantly to question our own worth as human beings. If we don't have a relationship with someone of the opposite sex, we haven't given it a chance. If we have a relationship with someone of the same sex, it is not recognized and we are told our love is not "real" and if we come out of the closet we're just going through a phase.

We need to turn this old world of fear and hate upside down. After all, it is a matter of human/civil rights!

REFERENCES

Peter Gomes, *The Good Book: Reading the Bible with Mind and Heart,* New York, N.Y.: William Morrow, 1996.

John McNeill, *Freedom, Glorious Freedom: The Spiritual Journey to the Fullness of Life for Gays, Lesbians and Everyone Else,* Boston: Beacon Press, 1995.

17

Taking Empirical Data Seriously: An Ecofeminist Philosophical Perspective

Karen J. Warren

This article explores real-life, experiential concerns that have motivated ecofeminism as a grassroots, women-initiated movement around the globe. It considers topics such as trees and forests, water, food production, toxins, the U. S. military, environmental racism, classism, ageism, and language to motivate the ecofeminist analysis of environmental problems and solutions. Karen Warren argues that any development project or environmental philosophy that fails to take seriously the connections between these issues and women will be grossly inadequate. Her scholarly interests are in feminist philosophy, environmental philosophy, and critical thinking. She has published numerous articles, edited and coedited many books and produced an award winning video *Thinking Out Loud*. She teaches philosophy at Macalester College in St. Paul, Minnesota. This selection is taken from the book that she edited, *Ecofeminism: Women, Culture, Nature*.

Trees, forests, and deforestation. Water, drought, and desertification. Food production, poverty, and toxic wastes. Environmental destruction and women. And women? What do these environmental issues have to do with women?[1]

According to ecological feminists ("ecofeminists"), important connections exist between the treatment of women, people of color, and the underclass on one hand and the treatment of nonhuman nature on the other. Ecological feminists claim that any feminism, environmentalism, or environmental ethic which fails to take these connections seriously is grossly inadequate.[2] Establishing the nature of these connections, particularly what I call women-nature connections, and determining which are potentially liberating for both women and nonhuman nature is a major project of ecofeminist philosophy.[3]

In this chapter I focus on empirical women-nature connections. I suggest that from an ecofeminist philosophical perspective, it is important for all of us interested in finding solutions to the problems of environmental destruction and the unjustified subordination of women and other subdominant groups to take these connections seriously. By doing so, I hope to motivate and establish the practical significance of ecofeminist philosophy.[4]

FEMINISM AND FEMINIST ISSUES

As I understand feminism, it is a movement committed to the elimination of male-gender power and privilege, or sexism. Despite differences among feminists, all feminists agree that sexism exists, is wrong, and ought to be changed. But while feminism was initially conceived as a movement to end sexist oppression, academic feminists have come to see that liberation of women cannot be achieved until *all* women are liberated from the multiple oppressions that structure our gender identities: women of color from racism, poor women from classism, lesbian women from heterosexism, young and older women from ageism, Jewish women from anti-Semitism, women of the South from ethnocentrism. Thus feminism is intrinsically a movement to end racism, classism, heterosexism, ageism, anti-Semitism, ethnocentrism.

Something is a feminist issue if an understanding of it helps one understand the oppression or subordination of women. Issues involving equal rights, comparable pay for comparable work, and day-care centers are feminist because understanding them sheds light on the subordination of women. Racism, classism, ableism, anti-Semitism raise feminist issues because understanding them helps one understand the subordination of women. According to ecofeminists, trees, water, animals, toxics, and nature language are feminist issues because understanding them helps one understand the status and plight of women cross-culturally. At least, that's what I hope to suggest in this chapter.

ECOFEMINISM

Just as there is not one feminism, there is not one ecofeminism or one ecofeminist philosophy. Ecological feminism has roots in the wide variety of feminisms (e.g., liberal feminism, Marxist feminism, radical and socialist feminisms, black and Third World feminisms). What makes ecofeminism distinct is its insistence that nonhuman nature and naturism (i.e., the unjustified domination of nature) are feminist issues. Ecofeminist philosophy extends familiar feminist critiques of social isms of domination (e.g., sexism, racism, classism, heterosexism, ageism, anti-Semitism) to nature (i.e., naturism). According to ecofeminists, nature is a feminist issue. In fact, an understanding of the overlapping and intersecting nature of isms of domination is so important to feminism, science, and local community life that I have found it helpful to visualize ecofeminist philosophy as the intersection of three spheres at * in the drawing [see Figure]. According to this way of visualizing ecofeminist philosophy, it arises out of and builds on the mutually supportive insights of feminism, of science, development and technology, and of local perspectives. Ecofeminist philosophy brings all the

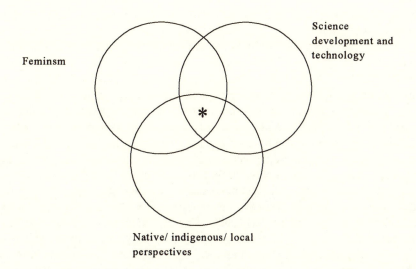

Feminsm

Science
development and
technology

*

Native/ indigenous/ local
perspectives

tools of feminist philosophy to bear on issues which are at *. Those contributions which fall outside * would not be distinctively ecofeminist philosophy.

TREES, FORESTS, FORESTRY

Consider next why nature is a feminist issue. This will show why ecofeminist philosophers take empirical data on women-nature connections very seriously.

In 1974, twenty-seven women of Reni in northern India took simple but effective action to stop tree felling. They threatened to hug the trees if the lumberjacks attempted to fell them. The women's protest, known as the Chipko (Hindi for "to embrace" or "hug") movement, saved 12,000 square kilometers of sensitive watershed.[5] This grassroots, nonviolent, women-initiated movement also gave visibility to two basic complaints of local women: commercial felling by contractors damages a large number of unfelled trees, and the teak and eucalyptus monoculture plantations are replacing valuable indigenous forests.[6]

The Chipko movement is ostensibly about saving trees, especially indigenous forests.[7] But it is also about important women-nature connections: trees and forests are inextricably connected to rural and household economies governed by women, especially in Third World countries, so tree shortages are about women, too. As a result of First World development decisions in India, multiculture species of trees have been replaced by monocultural species, primarily eucalyptus. But eucalyptus is very unpopular among local women.[8] The reasons why local women dislike eucalyptus plantations show four crucial respects in which trees, forests, and forestry are a feminist issue, i.e., how understanding the empirical connections between women and trees improves one's understanding of the subordination of women.

First, in developing countries women are more dependent than men on tree and forest products.[9] Trees provide five essential elements in these household economies: food, fuel, fodder, products for the home (including building materials, household utensils, gardens, dyes, medicines), and income.[10]

Second, women are the primary sufferers of environmental degradation and forest resource depletion.[11] This is because it is women who must walk farther for fuelwood and fodder and who must carry it all back themselves (e.g., without the help of animals). According to one estimate, women in New Delhi walk an average of ten kilometers every three or four days for an average of seven hours each time just to obtain firewood.[12] As more and more men seek employment in towns and cities, women must carry out men's former jobs plus the laborious tasks of collecting and processing forest products on degraded soils. It is women whom the reduced availability of forest products used as a source of income leaves without income-producing alternatives. And it is the household technology needs of women which new development projects have failed to adequately address.

Third, women face customs, taboos, and legal and time constraints that men do not face. For example, among the Ibo, men own timber trees and women control the use of food trees; women cannot inherit economic trees, although they have a right to be maintained from the proceeds of trees owned by their parents.[13]

Fourth, trees, forests, and forestry are a feminist issue for conceptual reasons: some key assumptions of orthodox forestry are male-biased. Consider three such assumptions.

One assumption of orthodox forestry is that the outsider knows best: the outsider has the requisite technical expertise to solve the problem of the lack of trees in Third World countries. But this assumption is false or problematic. It is the insider most inside the culture—the Chipko women of India, for example—who are the experts, who have what feminist foresters call indigenous technical knowledge (ITK) and feminist philosophers call epistemic privilege around forestry production.[14] Because local women are the primary users of forest commodities in most developing countries, Louise P. Fortmann and Sally K. Fairfax state that their "day-to-day, hands-on involvement with forestry goes far beyond that of many professionally trained foresters."[15] Women in a Sierra Leone village were able to identify thirty-one products from nearby bushes and trees, whereas men could identify only eight.[16] Women's ITK grows out of their daily felt and lived experiences as managers of trees and tree products.

A second assumption of orthodox forestry is that activities which fall outside the boundaries of commercial fiber production are of lesser importance.[17] Yet these activities are precisely those which women engage in on a daily basis. Conceptually, the seeming invisibility of what women do accounts for the mistaken assumption that management and production policies of orthodox forestry are not gender-biased. It also explains why, as Fortmann and Fairfax report, many foresters "literally do not see trees that are used as hedgerows or living fence poles; trees that provide materials for basketry, dyes, medicines, or decorations; trees that provide sites for honey barrels; trees that provide shade; or trees that provide human food."[18] And because these foresters literally do not see these multiple uses of trees, they also often do not see a lot more, e.g., that multiculture tree species are useful, that men and women may have very different uses for the same tree or may use different trees for different purposes. This inability to see women's contributions has been called a "patriarchal conceptual trap" of orthodox forestry.[19]

A third assumption of orthodox forestry is that it usually is better to have large-scale production using a small number of tree species than small-scale, community-based forestry using a wide variety of species. The Chipko movement challenges this assumption.[20] Since small-scale production reflects local priorities, involves multiple uses of many species of trees, and is responsive to the social reality of women's importance in agriculture and forest production, to threaten small-scale production is to threaten the livelihood and well-being of women.

WATER

Without doubt, then, trees, forests, and forestry are ecofeminist issues. Let us next consider other empirical examples.[21]

Only 8 percent of the world's water supply is fresh or potable.[22] Millions of humans have difficulty getting the water necessary for their survival, about five liters a day. In more than half of the so-called developing countries, less than 50 percent of the population has a source of potable water or facilities for sewage disposal. The World Health Organization estimates that approximately 85 percent of all sickness and disease in countries in the southern hemisphere is attributable to inadequate water or sanitation and as many as 25 million deaths a year are due to water-related illnesses. Some fifteen million children die every year before they are five years old; four million of them die from diarrhea and associated water-related diseases.[23]

In the southern hemisphere, women and children perform most of the water-collection work.[24] Because of natural resource depletion, women also must walk further for water (e.g., one to fifteen kilometers daily through rough terrain in Uttarkhand, India). Since it is typically women and children who perform the water-collection work, it is women and children who experience disproportionately higher health risks in the presence of unsanitary water. Each year millions of people, predominately women, are affected by major illnesses acquired while drawing water—300 million people with malaria, 20-30 million with river blindness, and 270 million with elephantiasis.[25] Drinking water is often drawn from public bathing and laundering places, and the same places frequently are used as public toilets.[26]

Contaminated water is not just a problem of countries of the southern hemisphere. In 1980, the United States produced 125 billion pounds of hazardous waste, enough to fill approximately 3,000 Love Canals. In the mid-1970's, 90 percent of hazardous wastes were being disposed of improperly. "These wastes have contributed to groundwater contamination on a local basis in all parts of the nation and on a regional basis in some heavily populated and industrialized areas," the *New York Times* reported in 1980, adding that the U.S. House Subcommittee on Environment, Energy, and Natural Resources listed 250 dump sites that "present a great potential threat to drinking water supplies."[27] Groundwater is the drinking water source for nearly half of the population of the United States.[28] Yet, according to 1991 estimates, one in six persons in the United States drinks water contaminated by lead, a known cause of I.Q. impairment in children. Water, then, is an ecofeminist issue.

FOOD AND FARMING

It is estimated that women farmers grow at least 59 percent of the world's food, perhaps as much as 80 percent. Between one-third and one-half of the agricultural laborers in the Third World are women. Yet the gender division of labor typically puts men in charge of cash crops while the women manage food crops. Women in Africa produce more than 70 percent of Africa's food, typically without tractors, oxen, or even plows.[29] According to Mayra Buvinic and Sally Yudelman,

As a rule, women farmers work longer hours, have fewer assets and lower incomes than men farmers do, and have almost as many dependents to support. The disparity is not due to lack of education or competence. Women farmers are poorer because their access to credit is limited. Without credit they cannot acquire productive assets, such as cattle, fertilizer or improved seeds, to improve the productivity of their labor.[30]

Consider the root crop cassava. Cassava is critically important in parts of Africa in times of scarcity. Women do 70 to 80 percent of the growing and harvesting of cassava and 100 percent of the processing, which includes washing out the natural cyanide found in it (a process which takes eighteen five-hour days). Little money has been devoted to research on cassava or on the development of technologies that would increase the productivity of women farmers and the demand and price of cassava.[31]

Women's agricultural roles are many. Women are farm owners and farm managers (with major decision-making responsibilities about production and most agricultural tasks), farm partners (who share responsibility for agricultural production, typically with another household member), farm workers (unpaid family laborers), and wage laborers (who work for a daily wage or are paid by output).[32] Historically, a failure to realize the extent of women's contribution to agriculture (e.g., by First World development policies and practices) has contributed to the "invisibility of women" in all aspects of agricultural work (e.g., in plowing, planting, caring for livestock, harvesting, weeding, processing and the storing of crops.)[33]

TECHNOLOGIES

Often the technologies exported from northern to southern countries only exacerbate the problem of tree, water, and food shortages for women. In forestry, men are the primary recipients of training in urban pulp and commodity production plants, and are the major decision makers about forest management, even though local women often know more about trees than local men or outsiders. In agriculture, men are the primary recipients of training and access to machines, tractors, plows, and irrigation systems, even though women are the major food producers. In water systems, men are the primary recipients of training in the construction and use of water pumps, wells, filtering systems, and faucets, even though women are responsible for water collection and distribution.

Here is a striking example of a so-called appropriate technology, i.e., a small-scale, simple, inexpensive, intermediate technology made from local materials and labor, which is totally inappropriate for women in Africa:

> In Africa where sunshine is abundant but oil, coal and wood are scarce and expensive, a solar stove should really mean utmost happiness to women—or so some eager development theoreticians thought. Field tests then showed what every experienced expert [or local woman] could have predicted: in the African bush, meals are prepared in the morning or in the evening when the sun has not yet risen or has already set. Furthermore: which cook wants to stand in the scorching sun? Finally: the nightly fire also has a group and therefore social function.[34]

"Appropriate technology," when developed and carried out by men and women who lack a basic understanding of women's lives and work, results in the creation not only of solar stoves for women who cook before dawn and after dusk but also of maize shellers which take longer to do the job than women do when shelling themselves and pedal-driven grinding mills in areas where women are forbidden to sit astride.[35] Technology is an ecofeminist issue.

TOXINS

While neither sex is naturally more resistant to toxic agents, and resistance often appears to depend on the substance in question,[36] there is strong evidence for the existence of gender-related differences in reactions to environmental toxic substances. Persistent toxic chemicals, largely because of their ability to cross the placenta, to bioaccumulate, and to occur as mixtures, pose serious health threats disproportionately to infants, mothers and the elderly.

The household is an important locus of environmental health hazards for women.[37] Woman-headed households are a growing worldwide phenomenon, making up over 20 percent of all households in Africa, the developed regions, Latin America, and the Caribbean.[38] Edward Calabrese and Michael Dorsey state that "most workplace health standards tend to be based on criteria derived from the assessment of how *men* have responded in the historical past to pollutants."[39] Toxins are a gender issue; they are also a race and class issue.

ENVIRONMENTAL RACISM

In the United States, Native American women face unique health risks because of the presence of uranium mining on or near reservations. (The uranium is used for nuclear energy.) According to Lance Hughes, director of Native Americans for a Clean Environment, the Navajo, Zuni, Laguna, Cheyenne, Arapahoe, Utes, and Cree all report health problems from uranium mining on their land.[40] According to one report,

A survey of households and hospitals on the Pine Ridge Reservation in South Dakota revealed that in one month in 1979, 38 percent of the pregnant women on the reservation suffered miscarriages, compared to the normal rate of between 10 and 20 percent. . . . [There were] extremely high rates of cleft palate and other birth defects, as well as hepatitis, jaundice, and serious diarrhea. Health officials confirmed that their reservation had higher than average rates of bone and gynecological cancers.[41]

Navajo Indians are the primary work force in the mining of uranium in the United States. According to a 1986 report, "Toxics and Minority Communities," by the Center for Third World Organizing in Oakland, California, two million tons of radioactive uranium trailings have been dumped on Native American lands. Reservations of the Kaibab Paiutes (northern Arizona) and other tribes across the United States are targeted sites for hazardous waste incinerators, disposal, and storage facilities.[42] Many tribes, states the *Christian Science Monitor*, "faced with unemployment rates of 80 percent or higher, are desperate for both jobs and capital."[43]

The issues facing women and men of color raise serious concerns about environmental racism. In 1987 the United Church of Christ Commission for Racial Justice did a study entitled "Toxic Waste and Race in the United States."[44] The study concluded that race is a major factor in the location of hazardous waste in the United States: three out of every five African and Hispanic Americans (more than 15 million of the nation's 26 million African Americans and over 8 million of the 15 million Hispanics) and over half of all Asian Pacific Islanders and American Indians live in communities with one or more uncontrolled toxic waste sites. Seventy-five percent of residents in the rural Southwest, mostly Hispanic, drink pesticide-contaminated water. The nation's largest hazardous-waste landfill, receiving toxins from forty-five states, is in Emelle, Alabama, which is 79.9 percent African American. Probably the greatest concentration of hazardous waste sites in the United States is on the predominantly African American and Hispanic South Side of Chicago. In Houston, Texas, six of eight municipal incinerators and all five city landfills are located in predominantly African American neighborhoods.[45]

There are hundreds of grassroots environmental organizations and actions initiated by women and low-income minorities throughout the world. As Cynthia Hamilton claims,

> Women often play a primary role in community action because it is about things they know best. They also tend to use organizing strategies and methods that are the antithesis of those of the traditional environmental movement. Minority women in several urban areas [of the United States] have found themselves part of a new radical core of environmental activists, motivated by the irrationalities of capital-intensive growth. These individuals are responding not to "nature" in the abstract but to their homes and the health of their children. . . . Women are more likely to take on these issues than men precisely because the home has been defined as a woman's domain.[46]

Environmental racism is an ecofeminist issue.

ENVIRONMENTAL AGEISM: CHILDREN

As Hamilton suggests, the health of children is also a feminist environmental issue. The federal Centers for Disease Control in Atlanta document that lead poisoning endangers the health of nearly eight million inner-city, largely African American and Hispanic children. Countless more live with crumbling asbestos in housing projects and schools.[47] In the United States, over 700,000 inner-city children are suffering from lead poisoning (and the learning disabilities which result); 50 percent of them are African, Hispanic and Asian American.[48] In the United States, the National Resources Defense Council estimates that more than half of the lifetime risk of cancer associated with pesticides on fruit is incurred before age six.[49] Reproductive organ cancer among Navajo teenagers is seventeen times the national average.

Furthermore, women and children are seriously affected by poverty. In the United States, 78 percent of all people living in poverty are women or children under the age of eighteen. In Australia, the proportion is 75 percent. Worldwide, the largest poverty group is women-headed households.[50] The three elements which make up the major part of Third World disasters are deforestation, desertification, and soil erosion. The rural poor, a disproportionate number of whom are women and children, are the primary victims of these disasters. The living conditions of women, people of color, the poor, and children, then, are an ecofeminist issue.

SEXIST-NATURIST LANGUAGE

Many philosophers (e.g. Wittgenstein) have argued that the language we use mirrors and reflects our conception of ourselves and our world. When language is sexist or naturist, it mirrors and reflects conceptions of women and non-human nature as inferior to, having less prestige or status than, that which is identified as male, masculine, or "human" (i.e., male).

The language used to describe women, nature, and nuclear weaponry often is sexist and naturist. Women are described in animal terms as pets, cows, sows, foxes, chicks, serpents, bitches, beavers, old bats, old hens, mother hens, pussy-cats, cats, cheetahs, birdbrains, and harebrains. Animalizing or naturalizing women in a (patriarchal) culture where animals are seen as inferior to humans (men) thereby reinforces and authorizes women's inferior status. Similarly, language which feminizes nature in a (patriarchal) culture where women are viewed as subordinate and inferior reinforces and authorizes the domination of nature: "Mother Nature" is raped, mastered, conquered, mined; her secrets are "penetrated" and her "womb" is to be put into service of the "man of science." Virgin timber is felled, cut down; fertile soil is tilled, and land that lies "fallow" is "barren," useless. The exploitation of nature and animals is justified by feminizing them; the exploitation of women is justified by naturalizing them.

In a startling essay called "Sex and Death in the Rational World of Defense Intellectuals," Carol Cohn describes how sexist-naturist language pervades nuclear parlance. Nuclear missiles are in "silos" on "farms." That part of the submarine where twenty-four multiple warhead nuclear missiles are lined up, ready for launching, is called "the Christmas tree farm." BAMBI is the acronym developed for an early version of an antiballistic missile system (for Ballistic Missile Boost Intercept). Cohn describes a linguistic world of vertical erector launchers, thrust-to-weight ratios, soft laydowns, deep penetration, penetration aids (familiarly known as "penaids": devices that help bombers or missiles get past the "enemy's" defensive systems), and "the comparative advances of pro-tracted versus spasm attacks"—or what one military advisor to the National Security Council called "releasing 70 to 80 percent of our megatonnage in one orgasmic whump." It is a world where missiles are "patted" like pets (how can pets be harmful?), where India's explosion of a nuclear bomb is spoken of as "losing her virginity," and where New Zealand's refusal to allow nuclear arms or nuclear-powered warships into its ports is described as "nuclear virginity."[51] Such sexist-naturist language creates, reinforces, and justifies nuclear weapons as a kind of sexual dominance.

Lest one suppose that use of such language is a philosophical oxymoron, consider the language used routinely by philosophers to describe that which "we" value most: reason. Since Aristotle, reason, or rationality, has been taken not only as the hallmark of humanness (allegedly, humans alone are rational animals) but also as what makes humans superior to (some) other humans and to nonhuman animals and nature. Yet, as Vance Cope-Kasten shows in an article entitled "A Portrait of Dominating Rationality," domination metaphors and sexist language pervade philosophical descriptions of reason, rationality, and good reasoning: good reasoners knock down arguments; they tear, rip, chew, cut them up, attack them, try to beat, destroy, or annihilate them, preferably by "nailing them to the wall." Good arguers are sharp, incisive, cutting, relentless, intimidating, brutal. Those not good at giving arguments are wimpy, touchy, quarrelsome, irritable, nagging. Good arguments have a thrust to them; they are compelling, binding, air-tight, steel-trap, knock-down, dynamite, smashing and devastating bits of reasoning which lay things out and pin them down, overcoming any resistance. Bad arguments are described in metaphors of the dominated and powerless: they "fall flat on their face," are limp, lame, soft, fuzzy, silly, and "full of holes."[52]

So even if in some sense the concepts of reason and rationality are gender-neutral, certainly historically both their distribution and characterization have been gender-biased and nature-biased: women and animals are less rational or nonrational (respectively), and "bad reasoning" is described in sexist and domination metaphors. Therefore, sexist-naturist language is an ecofeminist issue.

TAKING EMPIRICAL DATA SERIOUSLY

The empirical and linguistic data provided by ecofeminism are significant philosophically. These data suggest (1) the historical and causal significance of ways in which environmental destruction disproportionately affects women and children; (2) the epistemological significance of the "invisibility of women," especially of what women know (e.g., about trees), for policies which affect both women's livelihood and ecological sustainability; (3) the methodological significance of omitting, neglecting, or overlooking issues about gender, race, class, and age in framing environmental policies and theories; (4) the conceptual significance of mainstream assumptions, e.g., about rationality and the environment, which may inadvertently, unconsciously, and unintentionally sanction or perpetuate environmental activities, with disproportionately adverse effects on women, children, people of color, and the poor; (5) the political and practical significance of women-initiated protests and grassroots organizing activities for both women and the natural environment; (6) the ethical significance of empirical data for theories and theorizing about women, people of color, children, and nature; (7) the theoretical significance of ecofeminist insights for any politics, policy, or philosophy; and (8) the linguistic and symbolic significance of language used to conceptualize and describe women and nonhuman nature.

I hope these remarks will motivate and establish the need for feminists, environmentalists, philosophers—indeed, all of us—to think deeply about empirical connections between women and nature, and also between people of color, children, the poor, and nature. I also hope they will suggest why, from an ecofeminist philosophical perspective, one should take this sort of empirical data very seriously.

NOTES

1. This essay was given at a conference on Human Values and the Environment in October 1992 at the University of Wisconsin-Madison and appeared in the Proceedings of that conference, published by the University of Wisconsin-Madison.   An expanded version appears as chap.1 in my forthcoming book, *Quilting Feminist Philosophies* (Boulder: Westview Press).   Sections of the essay have also appeared in "Toward an Ecofeminist Ethic," *Studies in the Humanities* 15, no. 2 (December 1988): 140-56, and "Women, Nature, and Technology: An Ecofeminist Philosophical Perspective," *Research in Philosophy and Technology,* Special Issue on Technology and Feminism (1993).

2. For a selected bibliography of ecfeminist literature, see Carol J. Adams and Karen J. Warren, "Feminism and the Environment: A Selected Bibliography," *Newsletter on Feminism and Philosophy* (American Philosophical Association, Fall 1991): 148-57.

3. For a discussion of a variety of women-nature connections, see Karen J. Warren, "Feminism and the Environment: An Overview of the Issues," *Newsletter on Feminism and Philosophy* (American Philosophical Association, Fall 1991): 108-16.

4. Two caveats are in order. First, the examples offered here provide only a glimpse of the range and diversity of contemporary women-nature issues which motivate, document, and inspire ecofeminism as a political movement and set of theoretical positions. These examples also provide only a pigeonhole view of the sorts of philosophically significant things one could say about empirical women-nature connections. Second, although my focus is on women, I do not intend to suggest that men are not affected by these issues or that all men are affected in similar ways (any more than I intend to suggest that all women are affected in similar ways). I intend that the empirical considerations offered here to be read as just that: empirical considerations that illustrate and motivate the need to take seriously women-nature connections. This is true even if, as I believe, these connections also illustrate the need to take seriously other connections (e.g., connections between nature and old persons/young persons, race/ethnicity).

5. This discussion of the Chipko movement as an ecofeminist concern is taken from my article "Toward an Ecofeminist Ethic" (see n.1).

6. See *The State of India's Environment: 1984-1985,* The *Second Citizens' Report* (New Delhi: Center for Science and Environment, 1985), 94.   The Chipko movement is especially noteworthy for its distinctively ecological sensitivity. This is clearly seen in the slogan of the movement, which points out that the main products of the forests are not timber or resin, but "soil, water, and oxygen"; cited in Jayanta Badyopadhyay and Vandana Shiva, "Chipko: Rekindling India's Forest Culture," *Ecologist* 17, no.1 (1987):35. According to Bandyopadhyay and Shiva,

> The new concern to save and protect forests through Chipko satyagraha did not arise from resentment against further encroachment on the people's access to forest resources. It arose from the alarming signals of rapid ecological destabilisation in the hills. . . . It has now evolved to the demand for ecological rehabilitation. Since the Chipko movement is based upon the perception of forests in their ecological context, it exposes the social and ecological costs of short-term growth-orientated forest management.

For an excellent discussion of the Chipko movement and its effectiveness as a resistance strategy to what Shiva calls Western maldevelopment (First World development policies and practices aimed primarily at increasing productivity, capital accumulation, and the commercialization of Third World economies for surplus and profit), see Vandana Shiva, *Staying Alive: Women, Ecology and Development* (London: Zed Books, 1988).

7. India is losing 1.3 million hectares of forests a year, nearly eight times the annual rate admitted by forest departments. Wood shortages are great and wood prices are high (*The State of India's Environment,* 49).

8. The replacement of natural forests in India with eucalyptus plantations has been justified on the grounds of increased productivity. But the productivity is in the area of pulpwood only:

What has been called the "Eucalyptus controversy" is in reality a conflict of paradigms, between an ecological approach to forestry on the one hand, and a reductionist, partisan approach which only responds to industrial requirements on the other. While the former views natural forests and many indigenous tree species more productive than eucalyptus, the reverse is true according to the paradigm of Commercial Forestry. The scientific conflict is in fact an economic conflict over which needs and whose needs are important. (*The State of India's Environment,* 33)

9. See *Restoring the Balance: Women and Forest Resources* (Rome: Food and Culture Organization and Swedish International Development Authority, 1987), 4.

10. Ibid., 104.

11. Louise Fortmann and Dianne Rocheleau, "Women and Agroforestry: Four Myths and Three Case Studies," *Agroforestry Systems* 9, no. 2 (1985):37.

12. Marilyn Waring, *If Women Counted: A New Feminist Economics* (New York: Harper and Row, 1988), 263.

13. Louise P. Formann and Sally K. Fairfax, "American Forestry Professionalism in the Third World: Some Preliminary Observations on Effects," in *Women Creating Wealth: Transforming Economic Development,* Selected Papers and Speeches from the Association of Women in Development Conference (Washington, D.C., 1988), 107. Formann and Fairfax take their information from S.N.C. Obi, *The Law of Property* (London: Butterworths, 1963), 97.

14. See e.g., Fortmann and Fairfax, "American Forestry Professionalism"; Fortmann and Rocheleau, "Women and Agroforestry"; *Linking Energy with Survival: A Guide to Energy, Environment, and Rural Women's Work* (Geneva: International Labor Office, 1987); *Restoring the Balance*; Irene Tinker, "Women and Energy: Program Implications," Equity Policy Center, Washington, D.C., 1980; *Women and the World Conservation Strategy* (Gland: International Union for the Conservancy of Nature, 1987).

15. Fortmann and Fairfax, "American Forestry Professionalism," 105.

16. Marilyn Hoskins, "Observations on Indigenous and Modern Agroforestry Activities in West Africa," in *Problems of Agroforestry* (University of Freiburg, 1982); cited in Fortmann and Fairfax, 105.

17. See Fortmann and Fairfax, "American Forestry Professionalism," 106.

18. Ibid.

19. This term is used by Elizabeth Dodson Gray, *Patriarchy as a Conceptual Trap* (Wellesley, Mass: Roundtable Press, 1982).

20. In developing countries, women, as heads of households, have become increasingly involved in nontraditional roles in both agriculture and forestry.

21. Unlike the preceding discussion of women and trees, the data in this section are given without critical commentary. The philosophical and feminist significance of the data will be given generically at the end.

22. Waring, *If Women Counted*, 258.

23. See ibid., 257, and Lloyd Timberlake and Laura Thomas, *When the Bough Breaks; Our Children, Our Environment* (London; Earthscan, 1990) 128. According to Waring, half of these children could be saved if they had access to safe drinking water.

24. Small-scale studies in Asia and Africa indicate that women and girls spend on average five to seventeen hours per week collecting and carrying water (e.g., in Africa: 17.5 hours in Senegal, 5.5 hours in rural areas of Botswana, and 43.5 hours on northern farms in Ghana; in Asia: 7 hours in the Baroda region of India, 1.5-4.9 hours in Nepal villages depending on the ages of the girls, and 3.5 hours in Pakistan). See *The World's Women*, 1970-1990: *Trends and Statistics* (New York: United Nations, 1991),75.

25. Ann Olson and Joni Seager, *Women in the World: An International Atlas* (New York: Simon and Schuster, 1986), sec. 25.

26. The war in the Persian Gulf drew attention to and exacerbated the problem of unpotable water. "The Tigris River has been used as a well, as a bathing place, and, increasingly, as a latrine," according to Richard Reid of the United Nation's Children's Fund (*Minneapolis Star/Tribune*, March 2, 1991, 11A). Reid worries about the "burning urgency to make sure that kids and pregnant women do not fall victim to" this environmental disaster.

27. *New York Times*, September 20,1980, 45, cited in Nicholas Freudenberg and Ellen Zalzberg, "From Grassroots Activism to Political Power: Women Organizing against Environmental Hazards," in *Double Exposure*, ed. Wendy Chavkin (New York: Monthly Review Press, 1984), 253.

28. Waring, ibid., 259.

29. Jane Perlez, "Inequalities Plague African Women," *Minneapolis Star/Tribune*, March 4, 1991, 4A.

30. Mayra Buvinic and Sally Yudelman, *Women, Poverty and Progress in the Third World* (New York: Foreign Policy Association, 1989),24.

31. Ibid., 30. According to Buvinic and Yudelman, cassava illustrates four issues critical to understanding women's role in agriculture: the extent of women's participation in food production and their contributions to food security; the heavy demands farming places on women's time and labor; the willingness of women to grow crops which have little or no economic payoff but enable poor families to eat during periods of food scarcity; and the general tendency to assign fewer resources to crops grown by women.

32. Buvinic and Yudelman, 24-26.

33. See *Handbook on Women in Africa*, United Nations Economic Commissions for Africa, 1975. Cited in *The World's Women: 1970-1990*, 17.

34. Helmut Mylenbusch, "Appropriate Technology—Fashionable Term, Practical Necessity, or New Social Philosophy?" *Development and Cooperation* 3 (1979):18.

35. Cited in Karl, ibid., 90.

36. See *Health Risks*, 318.

37. In "The Home Is the Workplace: Hazards, Stress, and Pollutants in the Household" (in *Double Exposure*, 219-24), Harriet Rosenberg claims that a rigid sexual division of labor in the household contributes to significant health and safety hazards for women who work in the home. (The data are based on United States households.) Health hazards exist in most home cleaning products (e.g., drain and oven cleaners containing lye, toilet bowl and window cleaners containing ammonia, scouring powders, chlorine bleach, disinfectants, detergents, furniture polishes) and in appliances (e.g., gas stoves which emit carbon monoxide, radiation leakage from microwave ovens, fluorescent lights). Furthermore, according to Rosenberg, the average household has about 250 chemicals which, if ingested, could send a child to the hospital. And the home has a full range of problematic substances (e.g., lead, asbestos, PCBs, formaldehyde) used in household construction and insulation as well as insecticides, pesticides, and herbicides used outdoors.

38. *The World's Women*, 17.

39. Edward Calabrese and Michael Dorsey, *Healthy Living in an Unhealthy World* (New York: Simon and Schuster, 1984), 3.

40. Lance Hughes, "American Indians and the Energy Crisis: Interview with Lance Hughes," *Race, Poverty, and the Environment* 2, no. 2 (Summer 1992): 5, 17.

41. Freudenberg and Zalzberg, 249.

42. On July 4, 1990, the *Minneapolis Star/Tribune* reported that members of the Kaibab Paiute reservation in northern Arizona were negotiating to bring about 70,000 tons of hazardous waste each year to the Kaibab Paiute reservation. An incinerator would burn the waste, and the ash would be buried on tribal land. The Paiutes stand to reap $1 million a year from the waste-burning operation. The Kaibab Paiutes and other tribes are torn between accepting the economic gains and giving up the integrity of their land and traditional ways.

43. *Christian Science Monitor*, February 14, 1991, 18.

44. "Toxic Waste and Race in the United States: A National Report on the Racial and Socioeconomic Characteristics of Communities with Hazardous Waste Sites," 1987, Commission for Racial Justice, United Church of Christ, 105 Madison Avenue, New York, NY 10016.

45. Mainstream media attention within the United States and Canada to what is called environmental racism was the topic of an important groundbreaking essay in 1970 by Nathan Hare, "Black Ecology." Hare argued that environmental problems are different for black Americans, since black and white environments differ in degree and nature. Hare presented alarming empirical data. There is a greater degree of all varieties of pollutants in the black ghetto (e.g., smoke, soot, dust, fly ash, fumes, gases, stench, carbon monoxide) and a heavier preponderance of rats and cockroaches (disease-spreading rodents and insects). Blacks are exposed to more harmful and diverse sorts of environmental handicaps: black Americans suffer disproportionately the effects of overcrowding (e.g., increased noise levels, loss of individual space, greater probability of hearing loss, more exposure to unsanitary debris), polluted housing (e.g., three out of ten units are without hot water, toilet, or bath), lack of "climate control" (e.g., of temperature and humidity) contributing to a higher proportional incidence of communicable

diseases (e.g., pneumonia and influenza), shorter life expectancy, and poor nutrition during pregnancy. Hare argued that some of these ecological differentials between blacks and whites were due to racism.

46. Cynthia Hamilton, "Women, Home, and Community," *Woman of Power*, no. 20 (Spring 1991): 43.

47. There are four specific areas in which children are physically more vulnerable than adults: food and water, home, schools, outdoor play areas. Furthermore, characteristics unique to children, especially poor children and children of color, make them particularly vulnerable to environmental hazards. Poor children are more likely to live in neighborhoods with environmental hazards; poor families lack the financial resources to remove hazards from their home or purchase alternative, nonhazardous products; poor children are less likely to have access to health care for treatment; the families of poor children often lack the necessary political clout to insist on the cleanup of hazards in the neighborhood. In homes and schools, hazardous products (e.g., cleaning products) and exposure to lead, radon, asbestos, and indoor air pollution (e.g., tobacco smoke, formaldehyde found in some carpeting, wallboard, and insulation) are particularly harmful to children, since the same amount of exposure is believed to produce higher concentrations in the smaller bodies of children than in adults. Outdoors, pesticides, harmful sun exposure, air pollution, and play in unsafe areas can result in serious health conditions in children (e.g., breathing certain kinds of asbestos fibers can increase the chance of developing chronic diseases; ground-level, ozone-caused air pollution can cause respiratory problems, such as shortness of breath and coughing). See Dana Hughes, "What's Gotten into Our Children," published 1990 by Children Now, 10951 West Pico Boulevard, Los Angeles, CA 90064.

48. Hamilton, "Women, Home, and Community," 42.

49. Hughes, "What's Gotten into Our Children," 6.

50. Olson and Seager, *Women in the World*, 114.

51. Carol Cohn, "Sex and Death in the Rational World of Defense Intellectuals," in *Exposing Nuclear Fallacies*, ed. Diana E. H. Russell (New York: Pergamon Press, 1989), 133-37.

52. Vance Cope-Kasten, "A Portrait of Dominating Rationality," *Newsletter on Feminism and Philosophy* (American Philosophical Association, March 1989): 29-34. Of course, suggesting the significance of these empirical connections and defending their significance are two different activities. I have suggested elsewhere (Warren, "Feminism and Ecology: Making Connections," *Environmental Ethics* 9, no. 3 (Winter 1987): 3-20; "The Power and Promise of Ecological Feminism," *Environmental Ethics* 12, no. 2 (Winter 1990): 125-46) that one main source of the philosophical significance of empirical women-nature connections is conceptual: it is traceable to oppressive patriarchal conceptual frameworks and the behaviors they sanction. An oppressive conceptual framework is characterized by five features: (1) value-hierarchical thinking, i.e., "up-down" thinking which attributes greater value to that which is higher or "up" than to that which is lower or "down;" (2) value dualisms, i.e., disjunctive pairs in which the disjuncts are seen as exclusive (rather than inclusive) and oppositional (rather than complementary); (3) power-over conceptions of power; (4) conceptions of privilege which serve to maintain and justify the dominance

of those who are "up" over those who are "down"; and (5) a logic of domination, i.e., a structure of argumentation which provides the moral justification of subordination, viz., that superiority justifies subordination. It is the last condition, the logic of domination, which is conceptually fundamental. Without it, difference would just be glorious diversity. With it, difference becomes grounds for domination and subordination, inferiorization and marginalization. Bona fide and respected cultural diversity or cultural pluralism in any system whose basic relationships are structured by a logic of domination is not possible. We must all oppose the way this logic of domination has functioned historically within different cultural contexts to justify the domination of groups deemed inferior—women, people of color, Jews, gays and lesbians, the differently abled. An ecofeminist philosophical perspective on empirical women-nature connections extends this sort of feminist critique of oppressive conceptual frameworks, and the behaviors of domination they give rise to, to nonhuman nature. Making visible oppressive conceptual frameworks and the logic of domination which undergirds them, wherever and whenever they occur, is a central project of ecofeminist philosophy.

18

Let Us Survive: Women, Ecology, and Development

Vandana Shiva

Vandana Shiva is a physicist, ecologist, activist, editor, and author of *Staying Alive: Women, Ecology and Development* and *Biopiracy: The Plunder of Nature and Knowledge,* among many other books. She is the director of the Research Foundation for Science, Technology, and Ecology in New Delhi, India. She has established Navdanya, a movement for the biodiversity conservation of farmers' rights and Diverse Women for Diversity, a movement that echoes women's voices from the local and grassroots level to global fora and international negotiations. It seeks to strengthen women's grassroots movements and provide women with a common international platform to air their views. This article considers the meaning of ecotheological issues in the context of India. Shiva's reflections on ecological themes are rooted in life-and-death matters, not in theory nor statistics. She shows how the violation of nature is linked with the violation and marginalization of women in the Third World.

"Development" was to have been a liberating project—a project for removal of poverty and levelling of socio-economic inequalities, based on class, ethnicity and gender. While the dominant image of "development" persists as a class and gender neutral model of progress for all, the experience of "development" has been the opposite, polarizing the dichotomizing society, creating new forms of affluence for the powerful, and the new forms of deprivation and dispossession for the weak.

DEVELOPMENT AS A PATRIARCHAL PROJECT

The U.N. [United Nations] Decade of Women was based on the assumption that the improvement of women's economic position would automatically flow from an expansion and diffusion of the development process. Yet, by the end of the Decade, it was becoming clear that development itself was the problem. Insufficient and inadequate "participation" in "development" was not the cause for women's increasing under-development; it was, rather, their enforced but asymmetric participation in it by which they bore the costs but were excluded from the benefits. Development exclusivity and dispossession aggravated and deepened the colonial process of ecological degradation and the loss of political control over nature's sustenance base. Economic growth was a new colonialism, draining resources away from those who need them most. The discontinuity lay in the fact that it was now new national elites, not colonial powers, who master-minded the exploitation on grounds of "national interest" and growing GNPs [gross national product], and it was accomplished with more powerful technologies of appropriation and destruction.

Ester Boserup has documented how women's impoverishment increased during colonial rule; those rulers who had spent a few centuries in subjugating and crippling their own women into de-skilled, de-intellectualized appendages, disfavored the women of the colonies on matters of access to land, technology and employment.[1] The economic and political processes of colonial under-development bore the clear mark of modern Western patriarchy, and while large numbers of women and men were impoverished by these processes, women tended to lose more. The privatization of land for revenue generation displaced women more critically, eroding their traditional land use rights. The expansion of cash crops undermined food production, and women were often left with meager resources to feed and care for children, the aged and the infirm when men migrated or were conscripted into forced labor by the colonizers. As a collective document by women activists, organizers and researchers stated at the end of the U.N. Decade for Women:

> The almost uniform conclusion of the Decade's research is that, with a few exceptions, women's relative access to economic resources, incomes and employment has worsened, their burden of work has increased, and their relative and even absolute health, nutritional and educational status has declined.

The displacement of women from productive activity by the expansion of development was rooted largely in the manner in which development projects appropriated or destroyed the natural resource base for the production of sustenance and survival. It destroyed women's productivity both by removing land, water and forests from their management and control, as well as through the ecological destruction of soil, water and vegetation systems so that nature's productivity and renewability were impaired. While gender subordination and patriarchy are the oldest of oppressions, they have taken on new and more violent forms through the project of development. Patriarchal categories which understand destruction as "production" and regeneration of life as "passivity" have generated a crisis of survival. Passivity, as an assumed category of the "nature" of nature and of women, denies the activity of nature and life. Fragmentation and uniformity as assumed categories of progress and development destroy the living forces which arise from relationships within the "web of life" and the diversity in the elements and patterns of these relationships.

We perceive development as a patriarchal project because it has emerged from centers of western capitalist patriarchy, and it reproduces these patriarchal structures within the family, in community and throughout the fabric of Third World societies. Patriarchal prejudice colors the structures of knowledge as well as the structures of production and work that shape and are in turn shaped by "development" activity. Women's knowledge and work as integrally linked to nature are marginalized or displaced, and in their place are introduced patterns of thought and patterns of work that devalue the worth of women's knowledge and women's activities. This fragments both nature and society.

Productivity, viewed from the perspective of survival, differs sharply from the dominant view of the productivity of labor as defined for processes of capital accumulation. "Man's" production of commodities by using some of nature's wealth and women's work as raw material and dispensing with the rest as waste, becomes the only legitimate category of work, wealth and production. Nature and women working to produce and reproduce life are declared "unproductive."

With Adam Smith, the wealth created by nature and women's work was made invisible. Labor, and especially male labor, became the fund which originally supplies humans with all the necessities and conveniences of life. As this assumption spread to all human communities, it introduced dualities within society, and between nature and man. No more was nature a source of wealth and sustenance; no more was women's work in sustenance "productive" work; no more were peasant and tribal societies creative and productive. They were all marginal to the framework of industrial society, except as resources and inputs. The transforming, productive power was associated only with male Western labor, and economic development became a design for remodeling the world on that assumption. The devaluation and derecognition of nature's work and productivity have led to the ecological crises; the devaluation and derecognition of women's work have created sexism and inequality between men and women. The devaluation of subsistence, or rather sustenance economies, based on harmony between nature's work and human's work has created the various forms of ethnic and cultural crises that plague our world today.

MODERN SCIENCE AS PATRIARCHY'S PROJECT

Modern science is projected as a universal, value-free system of knowledge that has displaced all other belief and knowledge systems by its universality and value neutrality, and by the logic of its method to arrive at objective claims about nature. Yet the dominant stream of modern science, the reductionist or mechanical paradigm, is a particular response of a particular group of people. It is a specific project of Western man which came into being during the fifteenth to seventeenth centuries as the much-acclaimed Scientific Revolution. During the last few years, feminist scholarship has begun to recognize that the dominant science system emerged as a liberating force, not for humanity as a whole (though it legitimized itself in terms of universal betterment of the species), but as a masculine and patriarchal project which necessarily entailed the subjugation of both nature and women. Harding has called it a "Western, bourgeois, masculine project," and according to Keller:

> Science has been produced by a particular sub-set of the human race, that is, almost entirely by white, middle-class males. For the founding fathers of modern science, the reliance on the language of gender was explicit; they sought a philosophy that deserved to be called "masculine," that could be distinguished from its ineffective predecessors by its "virile" powers, its capacity to bind Nature to man's service and make her his slave.[2]

Bacon (1561–1626) was the father of modern science, the originator of the concept of the modern research institute and industrial science, and the inspiration behind the Royal Society. His contribution to modern science and its organization is critical. From the point of view of nature, women and marginal groups, however, Bacon's program was not humanly inclusive. It was a special program benefiting the middle-class European male entrepreneur through the conjunction of human knowledge and power in science.

In Bacon's experimental method, which was central to this masculine project, there was a dichotomizing between male and female, mind and matter, objective and subjective, rational and emotional, and a conjunction of masculine and scientific domination over nature, women and the non-West. His was not a "neutral," "objective," "scientific" method—it was a masculine mode of aggression against nature and domination over women. The severe testing of hypothesis through controlled manipulations, if experiments are to be repeatable, is here formulated in clearly sexist metaphors. Both nature and inquiry appear conceptualized in ways modeled on rape and torture—on man's most violent and misogynous relationships with women—and this modeling is advanced as a reason to value science. According to Bacon:

> The nature of things betrays itself more readily under the vexations of art than in its natural freedom. The discipline of scientific knowledge, and the mechanical inventions it leads to, do not merely exert a gentle guidance over nature's course; they have the power to conquer and subdue her, to shake her to her foundations.[3]

In *Tempores Partus Masculus,* or *The Masculine Birth of Time,* translated by Farrington in 1951, Bacon promised to create "a blessed race of heroes and supermen" who would dominate both nature and society. The title is interpreted by Farrington as suggesting a shift from the older science, represented as female—passive and weak—to a new masculine science of the Scientific Revolution which Bacon saw himself as heralding. In *New Atlantis*, Bacon's Bensalem was administered from Solomon's House, a scientific research institute, from which male scientists ruled over and made decisions for society and decided which secrets should be revealed and which remain the private property of the institute.[4]

Science-dominated society has evolved very much in the pattern of Bacon's Bensalem, with nature being transformed and mutilated in modern Solomon's Houses—corporate labs and the university programs they sponsor. With the new biotechnologies, Bacon's vision of controlling reproduction for the sake of production is being realized, while the green revolution and the bio-revolution have realized what in *New Atlantis* was only a utopia.

Biotechnologies project themselves as ecologically benign, but the biohazards they will unleash threaten life on this planet more than all earlier technologies. The biotechnology era is the ultimate fragmentation and control of life itself. That it does not undo the disruption of nature of the mechanical and chemical phases of industrialization was dramatized most brutally in the Bhopal disaster; rather it aggravates and accelerates the disruption of life by engineering it into a reductionist mold. Biotechnologies are reductionist, centralized, exclusive and homogenistic.

By contrast, the approach to life needed for ecological stability is holistic, decentered, participatory, and respectful of diversity. Genetic engineering as a whole is a women's issue, and not just when it directly controls women's bodies through reproductive technologies. Biotechnologies in agriculture are also a threat to the health and safety of women. But, most significantly, the underlying assumptions of genetic engineering are anti-nature and anti-women, wanting to control and engineer both on the basis of patriarchal values of "improvement" and designing the "best." As argued powerfully by Linda Bullard, this exercise is, however, inherently eugenic in that it always requires someone to decide what is a good and a bad gene. It is also inherently disruptive of ecological processes, because in trying to control nature's inner workings it creates a nature totally out of control.

Modern science was a consciously gendered, patriarchal activity. As nature came to be seen more like a woman to be raped, gender too was recreated. Science as a male venture, based on the subjugation of female nature and female sex, provided support for the polarization of gender. Patriarchy as the new scientific and technological power was a political need of emerging industrial capitalism. While, on the one hand, the ideology of science sanctioned the denudation of nature, on the other it legitimized the dependency of women and the authority of men. Science and masculinity were associated in domination over nature and all that is seen as feminine; the ideologies of science and gender reinforced each other. The witch-hunting hysteria, which was aimed at annihilating women in Europe as knowers and experts, was contemporaneous with two centuries of Scientific Revolution. Witch-hunting reached its peak at the time of Galileo's *Dialogue concerning the Two Chief World Systems* and faded during the founding of the Royal Society of London and the Paris Academy of Sciences.

Systems of knowledge on which development activity in the contemporary Third World are based are historically and intellectually rooted in the emergence of the "masculine" science of the Scientific Revolution. These knowledge systems are characterized by the fragmentation of nature into discrete, unrelated, atomistic, uniform and homogeneous parts, and dichotomize society into experts and non-experts. Women's holistic knowledge of forestry, agriculture, food processing, soil, and water systems is thus delegitimized and displaced by reductionist knowledge. The ecological destruction of nature thus goes hand in hand with the intellectual destruction of women's knowledge and expertise.

WOMEN AND ECOLOGY MOVEMENTS

To say that women and nature are intimately associated is not to say anything revolutionary. After all, it was precisely just such an assumption that allowed the domination of both women and nature. The new insight provided by rural women in the Third World is that women and nature are associated, not in passivity but in creativity and in the maintenance of life.

This analysis differs from most conventional analyses of environmentalists and feminists. Most work on women and environment in the Third World has focused on women as special victims of environmental degradation. Yet the women who participate in and lead ecology movements in countries like India are not speaking merely as victims. Their voices are the voices of liberation and transformation which provide new categories of thought in new exploratory directions. In this sense, this is a post-victimology study. It is an articulation of the challenge that women in ecology movements are creating in the Third World. The women and environmental issues can be approached either from these categories of challenge that have been thrown up by women in the struggle for life, or they can be approached through an extension of conventional categories of patriarchy and reductionism. In the perspective of women engaged in survival struggles, which are simultaneously struggles for the protection of nature, women and nature are intimately related, and their domination and liberation similarly linked. The women's movement and the ecology movement are therefore one and are primarily counter-trends to patriarchal maldevelopment.

Contemporary development activity in the Third World superimposes the scientific and economic paradigms created by Western, gender-based ideology on communities in other cultures. Ecological destruction and the marginalization of women, we know now, have been the inevitable results of most development programs and projects based on such paradigms; they violate the integrity of one and destroy the productivity of the other. Women, as victims of the violence of patriarchal forms of development, have risen against it to protect nature and preserve their survival and sustenance. They have been in the forefront of ecological struggles to conserve forests, land and water. They have challenged the Western concept of nature as an object of exploitation and have protected her, the living force that supports life. They have challenged the Western concept of economics and production of profits and capital accumulation with their own concept of economics as production of sustenance and needs satisfaction.

A science that does not respect nature's needs and a development that does not respect people's needs inevitably threaten survival. In their fight to survive the onslaughts of both, women have begun a struggle that challenges the most fundamental categories of Western patriarchy—its concepts of nature and women, and of science and development. Their ecological struggles are aimed simultaneously at liberating nature from ceaseless exploitation and themselves from limitless marginalization. They are creating a feminist ideology that transcends gender and a political practice that is humanly inclusive; they are challenging patriarchy's ideological claim to universalism not with another universalizing tendency but, rather, with diversity; and they are challenging the dominant concept of power as violence with the alternative concept of non-violence as power.

It is, of course, not stated here that *all* women are ecologically rooted nor that *only* women are challenging the industrial system both on grounds of its reductionist philosophy as well as its destructive impact. Such a belief would be biologism, against which feminists have been struggling everywhere. We see the categories of "masculine" and "feminine" as socially and culturally constructed, not biologically determined, and the relationship of Third World women and nature as historically conditioned.

The violation of nature is linked with the violation and marginalization of women, especially in the Third World. Women produce and reproduce life not merely biologically, but also through their social role in providing sustenance. All ecological societies of forest dwellers and peasants, whose life is organized on the principle of sustainability and the reproduction of life in all its richness, embody the feminine principle. Historically, however, when such societies have been colonized and broken up, the men have had to migrate; the women, meanwhile, usually continue to be linked to life and nature through their role as providers of sustenance, food and water. The privileged access of women to the sustaining principle thus has a historical and cultural, not merely biological, basis.

The principle of creating and conserving life is lost to the ecologically alienated, consumerist elite women of the Third World and the over-consuming West, just as much as it is conserved in the lifestyle of the male and female forest dwellers and peasants in small pockets of the Third World. It would be inaccurate to gloss over the class and cultural differences among women or to ignore the strands of the ecology movement which do not converge with the feminist response.

What is needed is a new concept responsive to commonality, one that roots itself in the concreteness and complexity of our multiple identities that have been subjugated, distorted and fractured in different ways by the same sources of domination.

LINKS BETWEEN ECOLOGICAL CRISIS AND CULTURAL CRISIS

Since diversity characterizes nature and society in our part of the world, the attempt to homogenize nature creates social and cultural dislocations and the homogenization of nature also gets linked to the homogenization of society. Ethnic and communal conflicts, which are in part a response to cultural homogenization, are further aggravated with the process of development which alienates control over resources, dispossesses people, and degrades eco-systems.

The accelerated Mahaweli Development program in Sri Lanka is an example of development policies that ignore both human and environmental factors from a long-term perspective. Building dams across Sri Lanka's longest river deforested and changed the contour of vast areas of land, at the same time displacing thousands of families, mostly peasants. These peasants were then resettled in parts of the north-central and eastern provinces. This resettlement policy led to a dramatic change in demographic patterns of the Eastern Province in particular, altering a previously balanced ethnic composition in favor of the majority Sinhalese community, and thereby created a situation which influenced ethnic tensions.

The recent communalization of the Punjab problem seems to have a similar basis. The Green Revolution, a "development" strategy for linking Third World agriculture into the global markets of fertilizers, pesticides and seeds, has generated severe economic vulnerabilities for both small and large farmers in Punjab. The farming community in Punjab also happens to be Jat Sikh, and economic tension between the Centre (Delhi) and Punjab farmers, and between farmers and traders, has been ethnicized easily first by the Centre and later by the people of Punjab.

In May 1984, the farmer's agitation was at its height in Punjab. For a week farmers surrounded the Punjab Raj Bhavan—from May 10 to 18. By conservative estimates at any time more than 15–20 thousand farmers were present in Chandigarh during the gherao. Earlier, from May 1 to 7, the farmers had decided to boycott the grain markets to register their protest against the central government procurement policy. On May 23, 1984, Harchand Singh Longowal, the Akali Dal president, announced that the next phase of the agitation would include attempts to stop the sale of food grain to the Food Corporation of India. Since Punjab provides the bulk of the reserves of grain, which are used to sustain the government distribution system and thus keep prices down, a successful grain blockade implied a serious national crisis and would have given Punjab a powerful bargaining tool for its demands for greater state autonomy. On June 3, Mrs. Gandhi called out the army in Punjab and on June 5, the Golden Temple was attacked; for the Sikhs, this was an attack on the Sikh faith and Sikh dignity and honor. After Operation Blue Star the Sikhs as a farming community have been forgotten; only Sikhs as a religious community remain in national consciousness. Nothing after that could be read without the "communal" stamp on it. Thus in the resolution passed at the Sarbat Khalsa in April 1986, the Sikh extremists talked of the need to "defeat the communal Brahmin-Bania combine that controls the Delhi Darbar." This, according to the extremists, was the only way of "establishing hegemony of Sikhism in this country."

The Punjab conflicts are at another level a genuine cultural upsurge as a corrective to the commercial culture spread by the Green Revolution. The Green Revolution, and the spread of capitalist agriculture created new inequalities, disrupted community ties, dislocated old forms of life and fractured the moral and ethical fabric that had provided social norms. Alcoholism, smoking, and drug addiction spread as more money circulated in the villages. Religious revivalism became a moral corrective to these trends. In the early phase, when Bhindranwale preached from this ground, his most ardent followers were women and children because they suffered most with a drunken or drug-addicted father/brother/husband in the family. During this phase, Bhindranwale made no anti-Hindu statements. He was popular because he was seen as transforming society into a "good" society. Even today, rural people in Punjab remember him only in his capacity as a preacher and a social and religious reformer.

What began as economic demands and a recovery of ethical order was thus transformed in Punjab into a war between two hegemonic tendencies—one of the State, the other of the extremists. What began as a recovery for diversity, a search for economic security and cultural identity, has been forced to turn into ethnic chauvinism embroiling ever larger numbers, ever larger regions into violence.

We see the spread of violence as a way of life, as the culmination of patriarchal projects which have made death-risking the paradigmatically human act in place of the reproduction of our species. Capitalist patriarchy has substituted the sacredness of life with the sacredness of science and development. Patriarchal responses to this destruction of life and liberty have been characterized by the rise of fundamentalism, terrorism and communalism, which further threaten life and peace. The feminist response to violence against women, against nature and against people in general, attempts to make the maintenance and nurturance of life the organizing principle of society and economic activity. Since violence is legitimized by both patriarchal science and patriarchal religion, Third World women are engaged simultaneously in a struggle against the patriarchal culture of both science and religion. Whether it is the technological terrorism of Union Carbide in Bhopal or the terrorism of fundamentalism and communism in Pakistan, India and Sri Lanka, we see a culture of violence and death extinguishing a culture of the generation, protection and renewal of life. It is in reclaiming life and recovering its sanctity that women of our region search for their liberation and the liberation of their societies.[5]

NOTES

1. Ester Boserup. *Women's Role in Economic Development*. London: Allen and Urwin, 1970.

2. Susan Harding. *The Science Questions in Feminism*. Ithaca, NY: Cornell University Press, 1986; Evelyn F. Keller. *Reflections on Gender and Science*. New Haven, CT: Yale University Press, 1985, p. 7.

3. F. H. Anderson (ed). *Francis Bacon: The New Organon and Related Writings*. Indianapolis, IN: Bobbs-Merrill, 1960.

4. See Vandana Shiva. *Staying Alive: Women, Ecology and Development*. London: Zed, 1989, pp. 16–17.

5. Based on "Staying Alive: Women, Ecology and Survival in India," Kali for Women, 1988, as well as on conversations during the FAO/FFHC Workshop on "South Asian Feminist Theory" in Bangalore, January, 1989.

Part V

Application
of Nonviolence

19

The Importance of Strategic Planning in Nonviolent Struggle

Gene Sharp

Gene Sharp, who has been called "the Clausewitz of nonviolent warfare," emphasized the "technique approach" to nonviolent action. He argued that nonviolent action is a means of wielding power in a conflict and is more often used for pragmatic reasons than for religious or ethical ones. In 1953, during the Korean War, Sharp was imprisoned for his stand as a conscientious objector. He lived for ten years in England and Norway. He did advanced studies at Oxford University, and in Norway he held positions at the University of Oslo and the Institute for Social Research. In 1983, Dr. Sharp founded two organizations to promote research, policy studies, and education concerning the strategic use of nonviolent action in acute conflicts: the Program on Nonviolent Sanctions at Harvard University's Center for International Affairs and the Albert Einstein Institution. He is the author of various books on nonviolent struggle, power, political problems, dictatorships, and defense policy. He is best known for his three-volume work *The Politics of Nonviolent Action* (1973). This book was immediately hailed as a landmark study of nonviolent struggle. His writings have been published in English in several countries and in twenty-seven other languages, and his nonviolent civilian defense has been taken up by several national governments. He is Senior Scholar at the Albert Einstein Institution in Boston. This selection is taken from *Nonviolent Sanctions*, Spring 1995, newsletter of the Albert Einstein Institution.

The use of strategy is best known in military conflict. For centuries military officers have engaged in strategic planning for military campaigns, and important thinkers such as Sun Tzu, Clausewitz, and Liddell Hart have analyzed and refined military strategy. In conventional military warfare and in guerrilla warfare, the use of sophisticated strategy is a basic requirement for effectiveness.

Just as effective military struggle requires wise strategies, planning, and implementation, nonviolent action will be most effective when it also operates on the basis of sound strategic planning. The formulation and adoption of wise strategies can greatly increase the power of nonviolent struggle.

THE IMPORTANCE OF STRATEGY

If one wishes to accomplish something, the chances of achieving that goal will be greatest if one uses one's available resources and leverage to maximum effectiveness. That means having a strategic plan which is designed to move from the present (in which the goal is not achieved) to the future (in which it is achieved). Strategy pertains to charting the course of action which makes it most likely to get from the present to a desired situation in the future.

For example, if one wants to travel from one place to another, one needs to plan in advance how to do so. Will one walk? Take a train? Drive a car? Fly? Even then the plan is far from complete. Does one have the money to pay for the cost of the trip and other expenses? If the trip is a long one, where will one sleep and eat? Are travel documents, passports, or visas required, and if so how will one obtain them? Are there matters to be arranged to cover one's absence during the trip?

This type of thinking and planning, which some individuals undertake for ordinary purposes in daily life, should be undertaken by leaders of social and political movements. Unfortunately, however, strategic planning is rarely given the attention it deserves within such movements.

Some people naively think that if they simply assert their goal strongly and firmly enough, long enough, it will somehow come to pass. Others assume that if they remain true to their principles and ideals and witness to them in the face of adversity, then they are doing all they can to help to achieve them. Assertion of desirable goals and remaining loyal to ideals are admirable, but are in themselves grossly inadequate to change the status quo and bring into being designated goals.

Of course, seeking to change a society, or to prevent changes in a society, or to remove a foreign occupation, or to defend a society from attack, are all far more complicated tasks than planning a trip. Yet only rarely do people seeking such objectives fully recognize the extreme importance of preparing a comprehensive strategic plan before they act.

Very often in social and political movements, the individuals and groups involved recognize that they need to plan how they are to act, but do so only on a very limited, short-term, or tactical, basis. They do not attempt to formulate a broader, longer-term or strategic plan of action. They may not see it to be necessary. They may at the time be unable to think and analyze in those terms. Or, they may allow themselves to be repeatedly distracted from their larger goal by focusing continually on small issues, repeatedly responding to the opponents' initiatives, and acting feverishly on short-term activities. They may not allocate time and energy to planning a strategy, or exploring several alternative strategies, which could guide their overall efforts toward achieving their goal.

Sometimes, too, it must be admitted, people do not attempt to chart a strategy to achieve their goal, because deep down they do not really believe that achieving their goal is possible. They see themselves as weak, as helpless victims of overpowering forces, so the best they can do, they believe, is to assert and witness, or even die, in the faith that they are right. Consequently, they do not attempt to think and plan strategically to accomplish their objective.

The result of such failures to plan strategically is that the chances of success are drastically reduced, and at times eliminated. One's strength is dissipated. One's actions are ineffective. Sacrifices are wasted and one's cause is not well served. The failure to plan strategically is likely to result in the failure to achieve one's objectives.

Without the formulation of a careful strategic plan of action,

* one's energy can be deflected to minor issues and applied ineffectively,
* opportunities for advancing one's cause will go unutilized,
* the opponents' initiatives will determine the course of events,
* the weaknesses of one's own side will grow and have detrimental effects on the attempt to achieve the goal, and
* the efforts to reach the goal will have very little chance of being successful

On the contrary, the formulation and adoption of brilliant strategies increase the chances of success. Directed action in accordance with a strategic plan enables one to concentrate one's strengths and actions to move in a determined direction toward the desired goal. They can be focused to serve the main objectives and to aggravate the opponents' weaknesses. Casualties and other costs may be reduced and the sacrifices may serve the main goal more effectively. The chances of the nonviolent campaign succeeding are increased.

FORMULATING WISE STRATEGIES

The selection, or formulation, of a wise strategy requires:

* an accurate sense of the whole context in which the struggle is to be waged,
* identification of the nature of the difference between where one is and where one wants to be,
* assessment of the impediments to achieving the goal and the factors which may facilitate the task,
* assessment of the strengths and weaknesses of one's opponents, of one's own group, and of third parties which may assist or hinder the campaign,
* evaluation of the merits and limitations of several potential courses of action one might follow,
* selection of a viable course among existing options or the charting of a completely new one, and

- identification of an overall plan of action which determines what smaller (tactical) plans and specific methods of action should be used in pursuit of the main goal (i.e., what specific localized or shorter-term activities or steps should be taken to implement the overall strategic plan).

LEVELS OF PLANNING AND ACTION

In developing a strategic plan one needs to understand that there are different levels of planning and action. At the highest level is grand strategy. Then there is strategy itself, followed by tactics and methods.

Grand strategy is the overall conception which serves to coordinate and direct all appropriate and available resources (economic, human, moral, political, organizational, etc.) of the nation or other group to attain its objectives in a conflict.

Grand strategy includes consideration of the rightness of the cause, assessment of other influences in the situation, and selection of the technique of action to be used (for example, nonviolent struggle, conventional politics, guerrilla warfare, or conventional warfare), how the objective will be achieved, and long-term consequences.

Grand strategy sets the basic framework for the selection of more limited strategies for waging the struggle. Grand strategy also includes the allocation of general tasks to particular groups and the distribution of resources to them for use in the struggle.

Strategy is the conception of how best to achieve objectives in a conflict (violent or nonviolent). Strategy is concerned with whether, when, or how to fight, and how to achieve maximum effectiveness in order to gain certain ends. Strategy is the plan for the practical distribution, adaptation, and application of the available means to attain desired objectives.

Strategy may also include efforts to develop a strategic situation so advantageous that it may bring success without open struggle. Applied to the struggle itself, strategy is the basic idea of how the campaign shall develop, and how its separate components shall be fitted together most advantageously to achieve its objectives.

Strategy involves consideration of the results likely to follow from particular actions; the skillful determination of the deployment of conflict groups in smaller actions; consideration of the requirements for success in the operation of the chosen technique; and making good use of success.

Strategy operates within the scope of grand strategy. Tactics and methods of action are used to implement the strategy. To be most effective, the tactics and methods must be chosen and applied so that they really assist the application of the strategy and contribute to achieving the requirements for success.

In formulating strategy in nonviolent struggle, the following aspects are to be taken into account: one's own objectives, resources, and strength; the opponents' objectives, resources, and strength; the actual and possible roles of third parties; the opponents' various possible courses and means of action; and one's own various possible courses and means of action—both offensive and defensive; the requirements for success with this technique, its dynamics of action, and its mechanisms of change.

A *tactic* is a limited plan of action, based on a conception of how best to utilize the available means of fighting to achieve a restricted objective as part of the wider strategy. A tactic is concerned with a limited course of action which fits within the broad strategy, just as a strategy fits within the grand strategy. A particular tactic can only be understood as part of the overall strategy of a battle or a campaign.

Tactics deal with how particular methods of action are applied, or how particular groups of combatants shall act in a specific situation. Tactics are applied for shorter periods of time than strategies, or in smaller areas (geographical, institutional, etc.), or by a more limited number of people, or for more limited objectives, or in some combination of these.

Method refers to the specific means of action within the technique of nonviolent struggle. These include dozens of particular forms of action, such as the many kinds of strikes, boycotts, political noncooperation, and the like.

The development of a responsible and effective strategic plan for a nonviolent struggle depends upon the careful formulation and selection of grand strategy, strategies, tactics, and methods.

SOME KEY ELEMENTS OF NONVIOLENT STRATEGY

There is no single strategy for the use of nonviolent struggle that is appropriate for all occasions. Indeed, the technique of nonviolent action makes possible the development of a variety of strategies for meeting various types of conflict situations. Additionally, nonviolent struggle may often need to be combined in a grand strategy with the use of other means of action.

This does not mean that nonviolent struggle is compatible with all other techniques of action. For example, the use of violence along with nonviolent struggle destroys various of the processes by which nonviolent struggle operates, and thereby contributes to its ineffectiveness at best and its collapse or defeat at worst.

However, it is fairly obvious that such means as fact-finding, publicity, public education, appeals to the opponents, negotiations, and the like could beneficially in many situations be used in connection with the use of nonviolent struggle. These means are often used in connection with economic boycotts and labor strikes, for example.

Essential to the planning of nonviolent struggle campaigns is a basic principle: Plan your struggle so that the success of the conflict becomes possible by reliance on yourselves alone. This was Charles Stewart Parnell's message to Irish peasants during a rent strike of 1879–1880: "rely on yourselves," and not on anyone else.

Assuming that a strong nonviolent struggle is planned and being waged, it is fine to seek limited and nonviolent assistance from others, but winning the struggle must depend on one's own group. Then, if no one else provides help, assuming that the strategic planning has been sound, one still has a chance to succeed. However, if the responsibility for success and failure has been given to others, when they do not come forward the struggle will fail. In any case, responsible external support is more likely to be forthcoming when a strong nonviolent struggle is being conducted by the aggrieved population, acting correctly as though success or failure will be determined by its efforts only.

The formulation of wise strategies and tactics for nonviolent struggles requires a thorough understanding of the dynamics and mechanisms of nonviolent struggle, such as is presented in *The Politics of Nonviolent Action*. It is necessary to be attentive to the selection of those plans and actions which facilitate their operation and to the need to reject those which if implemented would disrupt the very factors which can contribute to effectiveness. The most advanced study of strategy in nonviolent struggle is *Strategic Nonviolent Conflict*, by Peter Ackerman and Christopher Kruegler.

Attention will also be needed to such additional factors as psychological elements and morale, geographical and physical elements, timing, numbers and strength, the relation between the issue and the concentration of strength, the maintenance of the initiative, and the choice of specific methods of action which can contribute to achieving the objectives of the strategy and tactics.

The importance of strategic planning for nonviolent struggle cannot be over-emphasized. It is the key to making social and political movements more effective. It may not guarantee that a movement will achieve its objectives, but it will certainly make the possibility of success more likely.

20

The Eight Essential Steps to Conflict Resolution

Dudley Weeks

Dudley Weeks is well known as one of the world's leading facilitators in conflict resolution. He has worked with conflict parties in over sixty countries and has counseled thousands of families, businesses, and communities in the United States. He has taught conflict resolution at several universities and presents training workshops and serves as a facilitator/mediator throughout the world. With the eight essential steps to conflict resolution, the author presents an innovative and proven method to resolve personal and professional differences of any magnitude in any situation by achieving results that are mutually beneficial and truly lasting. Most of the following pages summarize the skills (he has named them the Partnership Life Skills) in his *Conflict Partnership Process for Conflict Resolution and Relationship-Building*.

CREATE AN EFFECTIVE ATMOSPHERE

Rather than jumping into an intense conflict resolution process prematurely, do some groundwork:

- Choose a time that is long enough and free enough from outside distractions to allow for effective interaction.
- Choose a time that maximizes the positive skills of all parties.
- Choose a place that is nonthreatening to all parties, one that helps all parties feel positively empowered to work effectively on the conflict.
- Choose a place that promotes a relationship of being connected in a partnership rather than being divided in an I-versus-you battle.
- In conflicts involving differing cultural or socioeconomic parties, choose a place that does not offend cultural mores or favor one party over the other.

Opening comments should establish a partnership atmosphere:

- Let your conflict partner know that you are interested in improving the overall relationship while dealing with the particular conflict at hand.

- Try to affirm the belief that options and feasible steps to improvement can be generated through a shared effort, and that you are open to suggestions.
- Let your conflict partner know that you believe it is both possible and healthy for people in a relationship to agree to disagree on certain points, and that there are other parts of the relationship that can remain strong.

CLARIFYING PERCEPTIONS

The *Conflict Partnership* process focuses on clarifying perceptions in four critical areas: perceptions of the relationship, perceptions of the conflict, of the self, and of the conflict partner:

- What does the relationship need, not just what do I want out of this conflict?
- Is the conflict over one rather isolated event, or is it but the latest in a series of conflicts revealing problems within the relationship as a whole?
- Am I sure this is a conflict with the other party and not a conflict within myself?
- What do I think the conflict is about? What is it not about?
- Is the conflict over values or just preferences?
- Is the conflict really over needs or desires?
- Is the conflict over goals or methods?
- What are the components of the conflict? Which do I feel most strongly about? Which parts should be dealt with first, and which can be addressed more effectively if we consider them after dealing with other parts first?

By sorting the components of a conflict we can: find starting points to use in the conflict resolution process; attempt to identify parts that one or all parties feel are priorities; we attempt to identify parts in need of clarification; we attempt to identify parts that will need to be dealt with eventually, but not at first; we are attempting to identify what might be primarily an internal conflict within one of the parties but that is being perceived (or selfishly used) as a conflict between parties.

In value conflicts, clarify how important the value is to you and how important it is to the worth of the relationship.

- Clarify how important the value in conflict is to your partner.
- Three options in value conflicts: do battle until one changes position; agree to disagree, and end the relationship; agree to disagree and focus on other parts of the relationship.
- How am I perceiving the conflict and its resolution? What are my needs? What are most vital and immediate? If I don't get what I say I'm needing, how will I be damaged? How will the relationship be damaged? Do any of my perceived needs obstruct some of the needs of the relationship?
- What does the relationship need if it is to be improved?
- What are my goals for the relationship, and how do my goals for this particular conflict affect them?

- Are my expectations positive yet realistic?
- What have I done to contribute to the cause and perpetuation of the conflict?
- What are my "buttons" and how might I recognize them and deal with them effectively?
- In what ways do I need the other party?
- What misperceptions might the other party have of me, and how has my behavior contributed to those misperceptions?
- Am I dealing with the conflict only in a power role, or using the partnership model?

Clarifying perceptions of the other party involves: avoiding stereotyping; trying to understand your conflict partners (their needs, reasons for their behavior, their positive potential); using well the communication skills of listening, sensing, and asking clarifying questions; recognizing the buttons and vulnerabilities in yourself and your conflict partners; and avoiding using them as weapons.

FOCUS ON INDIVIDUAL AND SHARED NEEDS

- Looking at the current conflict, are any of my needs being ignored or obstructed? If those needs were being met, would there still be a conflict?
- What do I need to feel positive in this relationship? Are those needs being met? Does the current conflict have anything to do with those relationship needs? Does this particular need help promote the goals I have for this relationship?
- Have I made my conflict partner aware of my needs, and have I clarified those needs so that they can be understood?
- What can be done specifically to get those needs met?
- What will your life or the relationship be like during the next week, month or year if you do not have what you say you are needing?
- Ask your conflict partners: What do you need our relationship to provide? What do you need as an outcome of this process to make you feel strengthened and that the relationship has improved?
- Ask yourself: If I were in their place, what would I need?
- If they secure this particular need, will I really be damaged?
- Will their getting this particular need I perceive them as having promote their positive power, and thus the health of our relationship?
- Pay attention to the needs of the overall relationship.
- Sometimes particular personal wants, or even needs, may not seem as critical when the needs of the overall relationship are considered.
- Shared needs: At what points do your needs intersect? How do you need each other in order for you and your relationship to be strengthened and improved?

BUILD SHARED POSITIVE POWER

- Positive power energizes a "power with"[1] process rather than a "power over" pattern.

- Positive self-power involves having a clear self-image; a clear understanding of our values and a consistency between our values and our behavior; being in charge of yourself.
- Positive self-power involves learning and applying effective relationship and conflict resolution skills.
- Keep reaching for the partner's positive potential and power.
- Don't define the other party only by their negative power and behavior.
- Realize and act on the principle that you need the other party to be positively powerful and to use that positive power.
- Help create a process that leaves options open for the partner to use positive power.
- Shared positive power constructs the process and moves it toward effective conflict resolution. "Our" power is stronger than individual power.

LOOK TO THE FUTURE, THEN LEARN FROM THE PAST

- People sometimes allow the past to hold present and future possibilities prisoner by thinking that because they did not deal well with a conflict in the past, they cannot deal effectively with a current conflict.
- People sometimes see only the past negative behavior of their conflict partner, refusing to see the positive potential.
- People sometimes blame themselves for what they were or did at some time in the past and continue to punish their own lives and their relationships in a subconscious attempt at penance.
- People are sometimes unwilling to let go of a particular demand or behavior they expressed in the past, even though that demand or behavior is no longer relevant or helpful in the present.
- People sometimes assume that because something has always been done a certain way, it somehow means it's the best way.
- People sometimes romanticize or glorify the past to such a degree that present behavior or relationships can never compare favorably with that past behavior or that past relationship.
- We need to try to focus on what we can do now and tomorrow, no matter what has occurred in the past.
- We need to understand the part that past events have played in creating a particular conflict. What positive things gave your relationship strength and meaning in the past? What specific acts and events played a part in creating the current conflict?
- What do you and your conflict partner need done about that past event in order to move beyond it?
- We need to develop and use skills that can help us learn from the past so that the way we deal with our differences and our relationships in the future will be improved.
- Forgiving past behavior can provide a strong foundation on which to build positive steps in the present and future.
- Engage your conflict partner in an imaging exercise to get a mental picture and a feeling of what the relationship will be like if you deal with the current conflict effectively.

GENERATE OPTIONS

- Ask yourselves what options you may have left unexplored as the conflict increased step by step.
- Spend some time envisioning new possibilities.
- Come prepared with several specific options you have determined meet some shared needs, require shared power to be implemented, and can probably become specific steps toward dealing with the conflict and improving the relationship.
- Remind yourself that the options you are identifying are but possible starting points for the process of generating options you and your partner will do together.
- Beware of preconceived answers.
- Look more deeply to see if there might be some commonalities hidden within seemingly incompatible options.
- If no commonalities appear, clarify where the disagreements are and then set aside those options and work together to generate other options around other parts of the relationship or conflict.
- Engage in a cooperative effort in which parties in conflict creatively suggest and imagine a wide range of possibilities. List at least four or five new ideas before exploring the feasibility and pros and cons of any of them.
- Identify the most possible options. These meet one or more shared needs; meet one or more individual needs that are not incompatible with the other party's needs; require mutual positive power to be implemented; have the potential of improving future relationship patterns; is "doable"; can at least be accepted or, better, enthusiastically supported by all parties.

DEVELOP "DOABLES"[2]: THE STEPPING-STONES TO ACTION

A doable is an action that embodies the following:

- It stands a good chance of being accomplished.
- It does not favor one party at the expense of other parties.
- It usually requires the participation of all parties involved in the conflict in order to be implemented successfully.
- It meets one or more shared needs.
- It meets one or more individual needs that are not incompatible with another party's individual needs.
- It uses the positive power of the conflict partners, ideally involving shared positive power, in which the partners need each other to make the process work.
- It helps build trust, momentum, and confidence in working together.
- It adds another stepping-stone along the pathway to improving the overall relationship and reaching mutual-benefit outcomes of particular conflicts within the relationship.
- Make sure that the doable is not just a temporary quick-fix Band-Aid.
- Make sure that the doable is not a delaying tactic favoring only one of the parties.

- Doables are not ends in themselves. They are steps that can move conflict partners closer to mutually healthy decisions on major issues.
- A conflict is not completely resolved just because a temporary agreement is reached.

MAKE MUTUAL-BENEFIT AGREEMENTS

Instead of demands, with mutual-benefit agreements the parties focus on developing agreements that can meet some of each party's needs, accomplish some shared goals, and establish a precedent in which power is defined as positive mutual action through which disagreements can be dealt with constructively.

- Mutual-benefit proposals usually deal with the most difficult issues and combine steps of improvement into a comprehensive agreement.
- Mutual-benefit agreements clarify all parties' specific responsibilities in the future.
- Mutual-benefit agreements begin an improved *Conflict Partnership* process, rather than end it.

THE *CONFLICT-PARTNERSHIP* PATHWAY TO EFFECTIVE CONFLICT RESOLUTION

Table 1

Conflict Partner A	The Relationship	Conflict Partner B
needs	conflicts	needs
values	commonalities	values
perceptions	differences	perceptions
goals	shared needs	goals
feelings		feelings
interests		interests

1. Create an effective atmosphere.
2. Clarify perceptions.
3. Focus on individual and shared needs.
4. Build shared positive power.
5. Look to the future, then learn from the past.
6. Generate options.
7. Develop "doables"—stepping-stones to action.
8. Make mutual-benefit agreement.

Table 2

Conflict Partner A	Improved relationships patterns in which differences and conflicts are dealt with in ways that nurture development.	Conflict Partner B

Table 3

From	To
An I-versus-you battle for victory and/or advantage over adversaries	A shared *we* responsibility and opportunity to clarify and improve the relationship while resolving, with mutual benefit, particular conflicts arising within the relationship
Solely a rescue-squad reaction aimed at putting out conflict fires or temporarily fixing them	Both a proactive process through which healthy relationships can be built and strengthened *and* a process to deal effectively with conflicts once they occur
An event that begins when parties in conflict sit down to negotiate and ends when a temporary agreement is reached on a conflict	A process consisting of skills and steps taken both alone and with the other party before, during, and after working out a mutually, beneficial resolution to a conflict
A way of dealing with conflicts that focuses on making demands and then on trading portions of those demands to gain advantage.	A process based on needs, both individual and shared, on clarified perceptions, on improving the relationship, and on mutual benefits, not domination

A CASE OF CONFLICT[3]

The Downtown Improvement Commission (DIC) is a group established by the Office of the Mayor to bring improvements to the crowded downtown section of a city of 300,000 citizens. The two most powerful members of the DIC, Mary

Rolf and John Allen, have worked hard to obtain a large grant from the local Odal Foundation. Odal has just awarded the grant to the DIC with the stipulation that all of the grant be used for a single project so as to maximize quality rather than quantity.

Mary and her supporters on the DIC are arguing strongly for a daycare center to accommodate the working parents in the many office buildings downtown. John and his supporters are pushing just as hard for a small urban park to provide an attractive relief from the concrete jungle and an ideal place for the office workers to spend their lunch hour. Heated debates between the two factions have so monopolized and polarized the recent meetings of the DIC that the city newspapers have had a field day with the controversy. With all of the bad publicity, the DIC is on the verge of falling apart internally, the mayor is considering disbanning the DIC, and the entire city seems angry at the DIC for fomenting dissention rather than much-needed community unity in a city already troubled with severe factionalism.

The director of the DIC explodes during one meting and tells Mary and John to get together and work out their conflict or there won't be a DIC to continue the generally acknowledged excellent work so far accomplished on other downtown projects. John and Mary meet one evening and follow their usual conquest style of dealing with conflict. We will eavesdrop on a portion of this first meeting.

John: If you weren't so bull-headed all the time, we could work this thing out.

Mary: Me bull-headed? *You're* the one hell-bent on sacrificing the needs of our young children just so you can have a nice place to eat lunch!

John: I am not going to agree to spend this grant I worked so hard to get on a daycare center! And that's final!

Mary: Well, I refuse to use the money for some fancy park! And *that's* final!

(John stomps to the window and looks out. He decides he will come closer to getting what he wants if he tries to win Mary over with smooth talk, promising her something in the future, which, of course, it is not in his power to give. He turns back to Mary.)

John: (smiling) Look, Mary. You are a reasonable person. In fact, you are one of the most capable people I know. Let's talk sensibly about this. I'll make a compromise. You want your daycare center and I want my park. Let's build the park now and make the mayor happy, and I'll promise to get you another grant next year for the daycare center. Now I think that's a reasonable compromise, don't you?

Mary: You know, John, you're some piece of work, you really are. What do you take me for? But if you want to play that game, then let's do the daycare center now and I'll get you a grant for the park next year.

(Needless to say, John and Mary are getting nowhere fast. Urged on by one of you readers who is a good friend to Mary, Mary goes home and reads a book on the *conflict partnership* approach. When she and John meet again the next day, Mary uses the new approach. Let's see how she does.)

1. Mary: John, you and I have worked hard to make the DIC an excellent group. You and I have cooperated on numerous worthwhile projects in the past, and I believe we can do it again. We need each other if we are to keep DIC alive and effective in contributing to what I know we both have said many times is our major goal: improving the downtown area. Do you still agree that is our major goal?

John: Of course I do. And the park is the best way to achieve that goal.

2. Mary: I accept the fact that you believe in the park, John. The park is a good idea and the daycare center is a good idea. But we don't have enough money to do both to the degree each of us thinks is needed. We've both stated that. So, since I am not willing to spend the grant for the park,

3. and you're not willing to spend the grant for the daycare center, maybe we can stop fighting and generate some other options.

4. John You mean both of us should give up what we want? Look, Mary, I don't know what you're trying to pull, but it won't work. I want that park and the mayor wants it. It's the best way to spend the grant.

5. Mary: What indication do you have that the mayor favors either plan?

John: Well . . . . I just know she wants the park.

6. Mary: C'mon, John. Let's stick with what the mayor has actually said. Remember what she said to the two of us last week?

John: She said that she's leaving it up to us. But I'm sure she favors the park.

7. Mary: And I'm sure she doesn't. So we can sit here and try to speak for the mayor, or we can realize that this is our decision to make and that we need to work together to keep the DIC viable.

John: Okay, okay. So I don't really know what the mayor wants.

Mary: Nor do I. What we *do* know is that I think the city needs the daycare center and you think the city needs the park. The city probably needs both. But we won't get the grant if we don't come up with one, just one project we agree on, and the DIC will probably fall apart if we mess

8. up on this opportunity to show we can work together. Maybe we should put the park and the daycare center aside

9. for tonight and focus on the thing we both share as a crucial goal: the DIC and the improvement of the downtown area.

John: I guess that is our common goal, alright.

10. *Mary:* There's something else we need each other for. We need to demonstrate that the DIC isn't made up of a bunch of people who can't get along.

John: You're right about that. The papers are crucifying us and so is the mayor.

11. *Mary:* Maybe we ought to find something the two of us can cooperate on, something the DIC already has the money to fund. That way we can prove to each other that we really *can* work together, and everybody will see that the DIC isn't always bickering internally.

12. *John:* Well, how about the Citizen of the Month idea that anonymous letter to the DIC suggested last week?

Mary: That's a good idea. Maybe we could coauthor a proposal and get the papers to interview both of us together?

John: Let's do the proposal now.

13. (Mary and John work for an hour drafting the Citizen of the Month proposal.)

Mary: That's a great proposal, John. I can't believe I'm saying this, but (grinning) you aren't half bad to work with.

John: (laughing) Thanks . . . I think. We did do well, didn't we?

14. *Mary:* Now let's see if we can do as well on the Odal grant.

John: Uh oh. Round two of the fight, huh?

15. *Mary:* It doesn't have to be. Let's keep focusing on the other options besides the daycare center and the park. What are some other possibilities for the Odal grant?

John: Well, I guess we could resurface that idea we talked about last year but didn't have any money for. Remember? The shelter for the homeless? The homeless population has increased a lot in the past year.

John: That's an idea. Or how about a really attractive parking garage, with a lot of trees and flowers around it. People are screaming about the parking problems.

John: Then there's the renovation of some of the older and really quite dangerous buildings. But that may be opening a hornet's nest since there's so many of them. (pause) But I don't like any of these ideas as much as the park.

16. Mary: And I still like the daycare center better. But at least now we know there *are* other possibilities. We don't have to always see it as an "either yours or mine" issue. If we can come up with these ideas, we both see as important and could work on together, then we don't have to accept the misperception that we are at an impasse. And we cranked out a dynamite proposal together on the Citizen of the Month thing.

17. John: You know, you're right. That helped. (John suddenly snaps his fingers.) Hey! I just thought of something! One of the reasons Odal is willing to give DIC this grant is because they want the DIC to show internal cooperation and to be a model for other cooperative community endeavors. I wonder what would happen if we developed a plan for putting a really fantastic daycare center in the middle of the park area I've been talking about and then went to Odal *together* and asked for whatever additional monies might be needed?

18. Mary: That's a great idea! And if they wouldn't be willing

19. to give any more money, I'll bet we could merge our ideas for what I wanted the daycare center to be and what you wanted the park to be and still come up with a quality daycare center and a park around it that would fit into the existing grant.

John: It would knock their socks off if the two major combatants came up with this plan together and made a joint presentation. The newspapers would give it wide coverage and the DIC would benefit enormously.

20. Mary: And the city would get a daycare center, a park, and a model for future cooperation. I like this!

21. John: You know, it feels good to work *with* you for a change. I was beginning to think we would always be at each other's throats.

22. Mary: Well now we know we can use a process that yields mutual benefits. When do you want to start working on our joint presentation?

John: Let's go for it tonight. I had set aside four hours because I thought it would take that long to do battle with you and win you over. Now, because of the way we've done this, we've still got a lot of time left tonight.

ANALYSIS OF THE CONFLICT

The following paragraphs correspond to the numbers found in the dialogue.

1. Mary's new opening stresses the technique of learning from the past as she reminds John that they have been able to work together well in the past and can again. She also focuses on the important fact that conflict partners need each other to resolve conflicts effectively and to reach shared needs and goals.

2. Mary acknowledges the other party's beliefs and even affirms that John's idea has merit. She also states her own strong beliefs. She then clarifies the givens by stating that there is not enough money to do both the park and the daycare center to the degree envisioned and that neither Mary nor John is willing to support the other's pet idea.

3. Mary makes the critical point that because they have reached an impasse of their pet ideas, they should generate other options. Although John continues to follow his old patterns, Mary has at least focused on the need to generate other options, a skill they will eventually use to great mutual advantage.

4. John clings tightly to the conquest pattern. When only one party is using the *conflict partnership* approach, we often find that the other party resists at first. The one using *conflict partnership* needs to keep trusting in the process and continue to demonstrate its effectiveness for *all* parties.

5. Mary clarifies perceptions by asking John what indication he has of the mayor's position. In the second number 5 marginal note, she urges John to stick with the facts and not complicate matters by issue proliferation or misrepresented statements. She then gets John to clarify what the mayor had actually said at a recent meeting.

6. Mary keeps using "we" and stresses the mutual positive power she and John have as the people responsible for working together for the shared value of keeping the DIC viable.

7. Mary again clarifies the givens when she reminds John that the DIC is in trouble if they fail to work *together* on their problem ("we" again).

8. Here Mary makes a crucial contribution: she suggests that they put the two pet ideas aside because they are, at least for the present, creating an impasse, and once again suggests that together they generate options. Please note that she suggests basing the options on the shared value and goal of the DIC and improving the downtown area. She also keeps reaching for the positive potential in John, an approach that will eventually bear fruit for both parties.

9. Mary mentions another shared need and goal, the internal unity of the DIC.

10. Developing doables is managed effectively by Mary. She realizes that she and John need to lay at least one stepping-stone before they can build a pathway to an effective resolution of the current conflict *and* improve their relationship. She bases the prospect of a doable on the shared needs of the DIC and on their own need to earn each other's trust.

11. John finally begins to see the value of the process and comes up with an excellent doable. In the dialogue between margin notes 11 and 12, Mary affirms John's good idea (his positive power), thereby nurturing the belief that they don't have to use the old adversarial patterns to obtain mutual benefits.

12. The doable is accomplished and makes the important contributions for which doables are designed: creating positive momentum, mutual trust, and a stepping-stone along the pathway to dealing with the more troublesome issues.

13. Mary stresses the power of the doable they have just completed by expressing the need to use the newfound cooperation in dealing with the Odal grant.

14. Mary stays in charge of herself and perseveres in her confidence in the *conflict partnership* process even though John's old patterns are still hovering in the air. She then urges them to generate options again. John has now realized the value of the *conflict partnership* process, and contributes some options.

15. Mary affirms their mutual positive power.

16. John can no longer doubt the value and power of the process. He has experienced it firsthand. He comes up with a mutual benefit proposal incorporating all of the things such a proposal should contain: mutual positive power, shared needs and goals, and mutual benefits.

17. Once again, Mary affirms John's positive power, something he probably needs because he is so accustomed to employing *negative* power. Throughout the discussion, Mary has consistently kept reaching for John's positive power until she and John both find it and use it to mutual benefit.

18. Mary realizes that Odal may not be willing to give additional funds, and therefore suggests another mutual-benefit proposal based on their steadily improving relationship: cutting back on the original preconceived answer each brought to the discussion and working together to design a project that would still meet shared needs and goals with quality.

19. Mary reinforces the shared needs and goals and the mutual benefits of the plan they have worked out together.

20. John has obviously learned from the *conflict partnership* process as applied to one conflict situation and sees hope for an improved future relationship.

21. Mary reaffirms that they now have the capability of using an effective process to deal with their relationship and conflicts therein. They get to work on putting the mutual-benefit proposal into action.

NOTES

1. "Power-with" is a term coined by Dudley Weeks.
2. "Doables" is a term coined by Dudley Weeks in conflict resolution literature.
3. The following case is taken from *Eight Essential Steps to Conflict Resolution,* pp. 277–285.

21

The Interfaith Movement: The Present Reality

Marcus Braybrooke

Reverend Marcus Braybrooke is an Anglican vicar near Oxford. He has consider-
able experience in interfaith work. A former executive director of the Council of
Christians and Jews, he is joint president of the World Congress of Faiths, an
International Peace councillor, a patron of the International Interfaith Center at
Oxford, and a member of the International Association of Religious Freedom
(IARF). He has written several books, including *Pilgrimage of Hope: One Hun-
dred Years of Global Interfaith Dialogue; A Wider Vision: A History of the
World Congress of Faiths; Time to Meet; How to Understand Judaism; Faith
and Interfaith in a Global Age,* and others. The following selection is taken from
Visions of an Interfaith Future.

Stage 1: PREPARATORY ASSESSMENT OF THE PRESENT REALITY
OF RELIGIOUS COOPERATION

Hans Kung ends his book, *Global Responsibility*, with these words:

No human life together without a world ethic for the nations.
No peace among the nations without peace among the religions.
No peace among the religions without dialogue among the religions.

One hundred years ago Charles Bonney who presided at the World's Parliament of Religions in Chicago ended his closing address like this: "Henceforth the
religions of the world will make war, not on each other, but on the giant evils that
afflict mankind." Sadly, religions have failed to fulfil that hope, but after a century of catastrophic wars, these words are still a challenge to all believers.

Often rivalry between religions has made matters worse: but all the great
faiths inspire love and respect for other people. The continuing question for the
interfaith movement is how to encourage such respect. There are many problems
of prejudice and exclusivism still to be overcome.

Many people believe that the survival of life on this planet depends upon humanity realizing its oneness. The problems of war, poverty, homelessness and the environment have to be tackled on a global scale. This is the message of the "Year of Inter-religious Understanding and Co-operation," being held to mark the centenary of the World's Parliament of Religions.

THE WORLD'S PARLIAMENT OF RELIGIONS, CHICAGO, 1893

The World's Parliament of Religions was held as part of the World Fair or Columbian Exposition which marked the four hundredth anniversary of Columbus' "discovery" of America.

The word "Parliament" was chosen to emphasize that participants of all religions were equal, but the body had no executive or legislative authority. It reflected the optimism and self-confidence characteristic of the U.S.A. towards the end of the nineteenth century. Most of the participants were Christian and their presuppositions permeated the gathering. Yet the Christians themselves represented a very wide spectrum of denominations and the contribution made by those of other faiths, although their number was small, was very significant.

The World's Parliament of Religions gave much attention to the contribution of religion to peace and social issues. Women were encouraged to play quite a part at the Parliament—more so that at most subsequent interfaith gatherings.

THE STUDY OF WORLD RELIGIONS

The World's Parliament of Religions gave an impetus to the emerging study of world religions. Whilst such study is an academic discipline in its own right, it has greatly increased awareness of the teachings and practices of world religions at every level. This century [twentieth] has seen an enormous increase in knowledge about world religions. Books, films and videos are widely available. This study has helped to provide accurate information about the religions of the world. Even so, much ignorance and prejudice still exist.

Initially the study was confined to university departments devoted to the "Science of Religions" or "the Comparative Study of Religions"—although such departments were very unevenly spread across the world. Slowly, in some countries, the teaching of world religions has spread to schools, although the situation and law in every country is different.

For some time many scholars of the subject stood apart from the interfaith movement partly because they felt that their study should be objective or neutral and partly because they concentrated on the study of the texts and the history of religions. Now, partly because there is more interest in the faith and practice of believers, far more scholars take part in interfaith discussions. This has enriched the interfaith movement.

Knowledge may not of itself create sympathy. Opportunities for personal meeting and friendship are important to dispel prejudice and to encourage real understanding. Many interfaith groups attach much importance to providing opportunities for young people to meet. Often they discover that they face similar problems and that in every society many young people are questioning all religions. They may also discover how much people of all faiths can do together to work for a better world.

ORGANIZATIONS FOR INTERFAITH UNDERSTANDING

No continuing organization emerged from the World's Parliament of Religions. At first slowly and recently more rapidly, interfaith groups have been established in many places. Some are quite small, meeting in a home. Members get to know each other and learn about each other's beliefs and practices. Sometimes members pray together or share in social or peace work. Other interfaith organizations are national bodies and some are international, seeking to co-ordinate global interfaith concern. The leading international interfaith organizations are the International Association for Religious Freedom, the World Congress of Faiths, and the Temple of Understanding, together with the World Conference on Religion and Peace, which is discussed in the next section.

Those who take part in interfaith bodies seek for a bond between religious believers, despite the differences of belief and practice between and within the great religions. The interfaith organizations all reject "syncretism," which implies an artificial mixing of religions, and "indifferentism," which suggests that it does not matter what you believe. None of these organizations are trying to create one new world religion, although some other groups have that hope.

The interfaith organizations accept that most of their members will be loyal and committed members of a particular faith community. Respect for the integrity of other people's faith commitment and religious practices is essential. A few members of interfaith organizations may have no specific allegiance and describe themselves as "seekers."

Aware of the distinctiveness of the world religions, members of interfaith organizations hope that some basis of unity exists or may be discovered, although the nature of the relationship of religions to each other is still much debated. For some people the unity rests upon our common humanity; for others there is an essential agreement between religions on moral values; for others there is a mystical unity, by which they mean that religious experience is ultimately the same and that differences are a matter of culture and language; others hope that through dialogue religions will come closer together and grow in their understanding of the Truth; others stress the need of religious people to work together for peace and justice and the relief of human suffering; for some, it is enough that there should be tolerance and respect, without bothering about questions of truth.

All these shades of opinion and many more are reflected within the interfaith organizations, which have avoided trying to define the relationship of religions. For them, the search for understanding and co-operation is urgent in itself.

In their early years all three organizations tended to stress what united religious believers. Now, with greater trust and knowledge, equal emphasis is given to appreciating the distinctive contribution each faith— and the various traditions within each faith—make to human awareness of the Divine. Increasingly those who occupy leadership roles in the various religious communities have begun to take an active part in the interfaith organizations, whereas at first the initiative lay with inspired individuals. It has taken a long time to erode the traditional suspicion and competition between religions—and it still persists, especially in the problems created by aggressive missionary work. The main brake on the growth of interfaith understanding has been the conservatism of religious communities. Happily now in many religious traditions at the leadership level there is a recognition of the vital importance of inter-religious co-operation.

PEACE THROUGH RELIGION

Whilst all efforts for interfaith understanding promote a climate of peace, some interfaith organizations, especially the World Conference on Religion and Peace, have concentrated on encouraging religious people to be active in peace work. Attempts to bring together people of different religions to promote peace date back to the early part of this century. Even so, the first Assembly of the World Conference on Religion and Peace did not meet until 1970.

It is hard to assess the impact that religious people can have on political processes, especially as politicians seldom acknowledge those who have influenced them. Modern communications have given added weight to popular opinion. Religious leaders may play an important role in forming public opinion. They can insist on the relevance of spiritual and moral considerations. They have helped to maintain public alarm at the enormous stockpile of nuclear weapons and other means of mass destruction. They have voiced public outrage at the starvation of millions of people, as a result of hunger, war, injustice and an unfair pattern of international trade. They have upheld human dignity and protested against torture and racism. They have underpinned efforts to develop internationally agreed standards of human rights and have helped to monitor their application. Inter-religious conferences have been among the first to warn of threats to the environment. In local areas of conflict, religious people have often maintained contact across boundaries and divisions. Yet often, too, religious people have used religious loyalties to enflame conflict and have allowed particular interests to outweigh common human and religious moral values. Some extremists stir up religious passions to gain support for their concerns.

It is even more difficult to evaluate the power of prayer, but certainly remarkable changes have recently taken place in the world scene, especially since the first World Day of Prayer for Peace at Assisi in 1986. Each year some people of all religions join in the Week of Prayer for World Peace. Special days of prayer are held to mark human rights anniversaries and for particular areas of conflict. Many people regularly repeat the Universal Prayer for Peace:

Lead me from death to life, from falsehood to truth.
Lead me from despair to hope, from fear to trust.
Lead me from hate to love, from war to peace.
Let peace fill our heart, our world, our universe.

RELIGIOUS INSTITUTIONS ENGAGE IN DIALOGUE

Often those who have pioneered the search for good relations between religions have faced misunderstanding and even hostility in their own faith community.   They have been accused of compromising or "watering down" the distinctive beliefs of their own religion. In fact, most witness that learning about other religions has helped them appreciate their own more deeply.

Slowly the value of interfaith dialogue has become more widely recognized. In the Christian world, in 1966, the Second Vatican Council's decree *Nostra Aetate* transformed the Catholic Church's attitude to people of other religions. A Secretariat for Non-Christians was established, which is now called the Pontifical Council for Inter-Religious Dialogue. At much the same time, the World Council of Churches established a Unit for Dialogue with People of Living Faiths, which has arranged various consultations. Some other religions now have agencies to encourage dialogue, such as the International Jewish Committee for Inter-Religious Consultations or the World Muslim League's office for inter-religious affairs.

Clearly, official dialogue has a character of its own. Participants have some representative role. Much of the work is to remove misunderstanding and build up good relations, as well as encouraging practical co-operation on moral issues and social concerns. More speculative discussion about questions of "truth" may be inappropriate. Further, whilst most organizations fully respect the freedom of all who participate in consultations, the host organization may have its own agenda. This means that official inter-religious discussions need to be distinguished from "inter-faith" organizations, where ultimate control rests with a board or executive which is itself inter-faith in composition and where funding comes from several religious communities. The growth of discussions between representatives of religious communities is, however, a sign that the importance of harmony between religions is now seen as urgent by the leaders and members of religious communities themselves. This is in part due to the pioneering work of interfaith organizations.

BILATERAL CONVERSATIONS

As in a family, there are times when the whole family wishes to be together and times when two members of the family want to talk by themselves, so there are times when members of just two religions wish to engage in dialogue. A particular example of this is Jewish-Christian dialogue and a major international organization. The International Council of Christians and Jews was formed in 1975 to foster good relations between the two religions. Other examples are the growing Christian-Muslim dialogue, some Muslim-Jewish dialogue and considerable Christian-Buddhist dialogue both in North America and in Japan. There are now many study and conference centres in different parts of the world which promote dialogue between members of two or three religions.

THE PRACTICAL IMPORTANCE OF INTERFAITH UNDERSTANDING

The Gulf War and the Salmon Rushdie Affair have emphasized the practical importance and urgency of interfaith understanding. No longer can anyone dismiss religion as obsolescent or irrelevant to world affairs. But many wonder whether the future belongs to the interfaith movement or whether we are likely to see increasing religious rivalry. Some indeed have an apocalyptic vision of the next century being dominated by renewed conflict between Christendom and the world of Islam. The interfaith movement has serious problems to overcome if it is to achieve its goals.

In all religions there is an increase of extremism, which also alienates others from any religious allegiance. Missionary groups in some religions make exclusive claims that theirs is the only way to truth and salvation. Elsewhere religious differences enflame political and economic divisions and sometimes religion is exploited by the powerful as an instrument of social control. Even India, of whose tolerance Swami Vivekananda boasted at the World's Parliament of Religions one hundred years ago, has seen the increase of "communalism" or rivalry between different religious and ethnic groups.

In Eastern Europe, the renewed nationalism is often closely linked to religious identity and has been accompanied by anti-Semitism and discrimination against religious minorities.

It is easy to deplore intolerance—especially in others. It is harder to understand its causes, which may be psychological or related to a group feeling politically, culturally or economically marginalized. Intolerance may be caused by fear or ignorance or it may be based on exclusive claims to truth.

Even dialogue itself may be misused. As it becomes more popular, it may be "hi-jacked" for "ideological" purposes—that is to say people may have hidden agendas such as wanting to change the views of their dialogue partners or seeking to gain their support for a political cause.

MUCH TO BE DONE

Despite all the problems, the interfaith movement has made progress, especially in recent years. Even so, it is still very weak. The initiative was often with "marginal" groups— to whom all credit is due. Gradually liberal members of the major religions began to take part. Now many religious leaders are committed to this work. Yet the religious communities are still reluctant to fund interfaith work, most of which is semi-voluntary. Co-operation between interfaith organizations is still only on an *ad hoc* basis. Adequate structures for greater coordination and co-operation are required. There is an urgent need too for a centre of information about world-wide interfaith work. There is also much popular ignorance.

The "Year of Inter-religious Understanding and Co-operation" in 1993 is intended to increase public awareness of the need for interfaith co-operation and to encourage those involved self-critically to assess progress and to determine priorities for future work.

The educational task is still far from complete. The growth of religious studies has helped to dispel ignorance about the world religions, but ignorance is still widespread. Theologians have helped their communities rethink traditional attitudes to other faiths, yet exclusive attitudes are still common. All religions claim insights into "Truth." There needs therefore, to be continuing dialogue so that religions may share their insights and together come to a deeper understanding of Ultimate Reality. This dialogue includes both intellectual discussion and efforts to appreciate each other's patterns of prayer and meditation.

Yet in many cases the thinkers are remote from religious leaders. Meanwhile religious rivalries destroy lives. Religious people are reluctant to make clear that their commitment to the search for truth and the defence of human rights is stronger than their group loyalty—costly as this may be.

Increasingly the interfaith movement is becoming more practical with an emphasis on ways of co-operating to face urgent problems and to seek a "global ethic" or consensus on moral values. The discovery of those who attended the first meeting of the World Conference on Religion and Peace in Kyoto, Japan in 1970 was that "the things which unite us are more important than the things which divide us." The interfaith organizations have shown that people of many religions can agree on the importance of peace and justice and on action to relieve suffering and to save the planet.

The Year of Inter-Religious Understanding and Co-operation in 1993 provides a chance to make the vital importance of interfaith work far more widely known, not only in combatting extremism and communalism but in harnessing the energies of all people of faith and of good will to tackle the urgent problems of the world. Only together will the dreams of 1893 be realized. Only together will prejudice and discrimination be removed, violence and injustice ended, poverty relieved and the planet preserved.

22

The 1989 Democratic Uprising in China: A Nonviolent Perspective

Michael True

Michael True is professor emeritus of English at Assumption College. He wrote *An Energy Field More Intense than War: The Nonviolent Tradition and American Literature* (1995), *To Construct Peace: Thirty More Justice Seekers, Peace Makers* (1992), and other books and articles. He is the president of the International Peace Research Association (IPRA) foundation. He is a peace activist and was arrested for civil disobedience for resisting the making and deployment of nuclear weapons at Raytheon Electronic Systems and GTE. He has received the Courage of Conscience award from Peace Abbey in Sherborn, Massachusetts. He has taught at Nanjing University in China from 1984 to 1985 and in 1989 during the uprising in Tiananmen Square. In this article, taken from *Legacy and Future of Nonviolence*, edited by Mahendra Kumar and Peter Low, Professor True looks at the uprising in China, Tiananmen Square, within the context of Chinese history and culture and in relation to nonviolent theory and strategy.

Political Analysts and historians generally agree that the democratic uprising in China was both memorable and significant, particularly those events prompted by the unexpected death on April 15 of Hu Yaobang, reform leader and once party secretary, and continuing through mid-June 1989.[1] Although some commentators regard the uprising as "unprecedented, not only since the Communist Party took over in 1949, but also in the entire history of China,"[2] few agree on the overall success of the campaign and its significance in the history of nonviolence. Even six years after the government's murderous assault on the demonstrators, the full implications of the events, particularly beyond the confines of Tiananmen Square, often go unrecognized.[3]

In an effort to correct what seems to me a deficiency in most accounts and evaluations—or at least to argue for factors not always included—I have chosen to look at the uprising within the context of Chinese history and culture and in relation to essential elements regarding nonviolent theory and strategy. In doing so, I emphasize what seem to me to be obvious truths: first, that the students' ability to sustain a concerted, though often improvised, national campaign for as long as they did was a major achievement (one is tempted to say "a miracle") in Chinese history; second, that a fuller understanding of that achievement among researchers and activists is crucial, if we are to make nonviolent alternatives accessible to those who daily risk their lives for justice in particular settings around the world.

Since 1989, several commentators—most notably Gene Sharp and Bruce Jenkins—have asked important questions about the uprising, including possible alternative strategies.[4] Might the killings have been averted, for example, if student leaders had held to their original plan of vacating the square earlier? What might have been offered by more experienced nonviolent theorists and activists to students at the time? Were there means of containing the violence, the weapons and Molotov cocktails employed by some demonstrators (provocateurs planted by the government?) that legitimized, to some extent, a violent response? Why did the government move so vehemently against workers, in its unnecessarily brutal response to the uprising?

Such questions are difficult to pose, in the midst of ongoing repression, imprisonment, and exile of dissidents in China, but anyone seriously concerned about the nature of nonviolence must attempt, nonetheless, to address them. Gandhi asked and addressed such questions, as he pushed forward, then retreated, in the face of massive violence by the British in India; so did Martin Luther King, amid death threats and killings during the civil rights campaign in the south; so have other activists during recent justice struggles in the Philippines, Korea, Thailand, and South Africa. Anyone who makes judgements about the dynamics of nonviolent movements, in fact, must face these complex, demanding questions.

The Chinese uprising is important for another, broader reason, as well, particularly as we face the challenges of a changing world order. In speaking about this condition, Richard Falk of Princeton University accurately described the choice before us as being between "globalization from above" and "globalization from below."[5] By the first, he meant "a terrifying mixture of global apartheid and eco-fascism" and by the second, "an ethos of nonviolence, democracy, and eco-feminism." The third alternative, "a future shaped by democratic forces without significant resistance from entrenched market/state forces," which Professor Falk thought an unlikely choice, a sentiment that anyone familiar with recent developments in the U.S., Russia, China, and elsewhere, is likely to agree with. Whatever the limitations of the campaign initiated by the students in China, its consequences were generally salutary for nonviolent, democratic social change, and its long-term effects are everywhere evident.

In the history of nonviolence, the uprising offers a number of insights into how reformers might proceed in the future. As with any effective nonviolent campaign, it also provided, for anyone paying attention, new information not only about the limitations of the present government, but also about possible strategies for people involved in necessary reform in that country and in similar settings.

As a nation embodying a fourth of the world's population, China will remain a powerful influence on choices at every level between "globalization from above" and "globalization from below." Few countries dramatize more powerfully the spread of free-market practices and the effects, some disastrous, in the alliance between local power and global wealth. Economic changes in China since 1985,[6] brought on by inflation and a "get rich quick" ethic resemble, in fact, growing disparities between rich and poor in the United States, particularly during the Reagan and Bush administrations.

One might say, also, that the political fall-out from recent administrations in the U.S.—lying and corruption among high-ranking officials, government control of the press during the Gulf war, increases in violent crime—are mirrored, even magnified, in China during the same period. Whatever the case, any movement for social change as massive as the uprising of 1989, involving almost every university and millions of people throughout provincial capitals and other urban centers, carries special meaning for all of us. And details about the way it was conducted and about how nonviolent strategy worked (or did not work) at a particular moment deserve careful study.

Commenting on a country as large as China or a campaign as multifaceted and complex as the 1989 uprising, one must begin, nonetheless, with this disclaimer: at some given moment, all things that have been reported about the country and the movement were probably true. And one generalizes about the uprising while thinking of all contrary evidence. In Chinese history and culture, conflicting ideas or truths live side by side, so it is best to acknowledge them, even as one moves towards a judgement or conclusion. For that reason, it is well to keep in mind many elements across a wide cultural spectrum, including the randomness or incompleteness of data. Even the popular opinion that peasants neither supported nor involved themselves in the uprising, for example, deserves much careful examination. Although probably not among the "June 4" students and workers, peasants demonstrated in Beijing at the time, complaining that the party that "wants our tax money, grain, and unborn children," had not come across with cash payments for goods and services.

An initial and important point in evaluating the uprising is to regard it as part of a process, both violent and nonviolent, in a century-long effort rightly described by Jonathan Spence "the search for modern China."[7] Without reviewing all the cultural elements that influenced the democratic uprising, three conditions seem to me essential in judging it from it from a nonviolent perspective: (i) that the uprising is best seen as one in a series of efforts—not unique, but certainly special—for fundamental social change, from the late nineteenth century to the present; (ii) that it effectively addressed cultural power, to use Johan Galtung's useful identification of the various forces that must be addressed in "making peace"[8]; and (iii) that it was a truly national movement, with rather different configurations in major cities and regions beyond the capital city.

Although China has a tradition of student protest, even of organized dissent, it has no tradition of nonviolence, in the sense that some imperial cultures and countries do—from Quakers in Pennsylvania to Adin Ballou, Martin Luther King, and Catholic Workers in the U.S.; from Tolstoy and the Christian anarchists to the recent nonviolent response to the coup in Russia; and from Gandhi and Vinoba Bhave to campaigns for land reform in India. The absence of a tradition of nonviolence, in the philosophic as opposed to strategic sense, was reflected not only in the students' lack of knowledge about concept and praxis—including how to conduct a fast—but also in the way the government responded to them. That ongoing conversation between the state and nonviolent activists (over conscientious objection to military service and war taxes, for example) which began centuries ago in England and the U.S. seems, at least, to have no parallel in China.

There, as among some of the warring tribes in Europe, the victor in struggles for power or with dissenters often simply annihilates the opponent. In an ancient rivalry between Beijing (northern capital) and Nanjing (southern capital), in several dynasties, for example, northern conquerors levelled the "defeated" city. In the 1920's, Chiang Kai-shek and the Kuomintang, after agreeing to an alliance, murdered the Communists, who retaliated in kind once they came to power in 1949.

Transitions—even within institutions—or sharing of power between one regime and the next is seldom orderly in modern Chinese history, from the perspective of most Westerners, at least. And the compromise that one hoped for (which the students allowed for and Zhao Ziyang, the relatively liberal party secretary, apparently argued for, at one point) seems never to have occurred to Deng Xiaoping and "the Gang of Old," who ordered the repression, and Li Peng, the premier, who carried it out. In crushing the rebellion, Deng reverted to tactics that he had used against the Hundred Flowers Campaign in 1957, against those who called for democratic reform in 1979, and against Hu Yaobang and student demonstrations in 1986–87.

After the latter "democracy" campaign, the party bragged about the wisdom of suppressing "bourgeois liberalization"—a reference to student pro-democracy demonstrations the previous fall—much as it did later, in "re-writing" (or attempting to rewrite) the history of the 1989 uprising. A government publication giving the party line in 1987, for example, said that "facts" showed its policies towards "bourgeois liberalization" were "correct, in keeping the struggle strictly inside the Communist Party, of carrying it out mainly in the political and ideological spheres, of directing the efforts at solving problems of political principle and orientation, of not turning it into a political movement and not linking the struggle to economic reforms or extending it to involve the countryside, and of conducting only positive education in enterprises, government offices and army units."[9]

Having escaped harsh criticism by the international community in 1987, Deng Xiaoping perhaps did not expect it two years later, particularly from countries such as France and Australia. In 1989, remorseless attempts to re-write the history of the uprising, which began even before June 4 on television, failed miserably, not only among the international community, but also among a surprisingly large percentage of the Chinese people. In a representative incident after June 4, reported by Liu Binyan—a famous journalist, now in exile—a movie audience, viewing scenes of the Kuomintang police using water cannons against demonstrating students in the 1930s, shouted out, "they were not nearly as bad as the People's Liberation Army!"

One of the many "victories" of the uprising, in fact, was the united front with which workers, merchants, journalists, and intellectuals resisted the extensive efforts at political propaganda and re-education by the party ever since. Persistence reports about labourers resisting the government continue, as in the case of Han Dongfang; "an ordinary railroad worker who never went to college," he was imprisoned after heading a workers' federation during the 1989 uprising, was infected with tuberculosis, then was released, to risk prison again by encouraging an independent workers' movement for reform.[10]

Deng's reasons for putting down the uprising (though not for murdering participants) are understandable, if not convincing. Terrible chaos, if even a small percentage of the population decided to rebel, is likely, perhaps inevitable in China. (Ten percent of the population means 120,000,000 people or half the population of the U.S.). In addition, harsh measures for punishing wrong-doers are generally tolerated by the populace. Public executions occur still in some areas; and Amnesty International is still not allowed to investigate prison conditions throughout the country.

Having said this, I must also add that not a single Chinese I spoke with in Shanghai, Nanjing, and Harbin before and after June 4—or subsequently—expected the government to murder the demonstrators. The people I interviewed included Chinese citizens who were sympathetic to the party until 1985, if increasingly cynical about its policies after 1987.

When they joined the movement, students, faculty, and party members who signed wall posters or gave speeches on campuses and in the cities understood, nonetheless, that they would probably be disciplined in some way for the protests. Strong disciplinary action by the party has been common during political shifts since 1949 and indeed throughout China's history. Yet the intensity and immediacy of the repression shocked everyone. I will long remember, for example, the deep depression that overcame one of my closest friends—a congenital optimist—the morning after Li Peng's speech on May 20, which called for "resolute and powerful turmoil." Although he continued to support the movement openly, he anticipated something approaching the "powerful measures" launched on the early morning of June 4, "to put an end to such chaos," as Li Peng put it.[11] Similarly, the only time I have seen a Chinese man cry in public was the morning of June 4, as an American literature scholar from a major university in Shanghai, tears running down his cheeks, told me about his worries for his son in Beijing and for his country.

In the meantime, students throughout the country had initiated a remarkably effective challenge to the government and, by mid-May, had elicited an incredible response from thousands of potentially unsympathetic bystanders. Arriving in Shanghai on May 16, the same day as Gorbachev—the first Soviet head of state to meet with a Chinese head of state in thirty years—I was stunned to find so many townspeople among the students participating in and otherwise supporting the demonstrations throughout the city. Some merchants and particularly workers, as I observed when teaching in China in 1984–85 and again in 1987, can be rather contemptuous of the "elite," that is, the 1-2 percent of the population educated beyond high school.

Surely, I thought, observing or joining the crowds in Shanghai and Nanjing in late May, something very unusual has occurred: student organizers have succeeded in getting merchants and workers not only to sympathize with their protest, but actually to join them. How did that happen? In answering that question, I shall focus on events in regions of the country outside Beijing, especially capitals of two provinces that are among the richest in agriculture and industry: Nanjing, Jiangsu province on the Yangtze River, 200 miles west of Shanghai; and Harbin, Heilongjiang province, 700 hundred miles northeast of Beijing.

The day after my arrival in China, 1,000,000 protesters poured into Nanjing's Gu Lou Square (China's Times Square or at least its Chicago Loop), and taxi-cab drivers, including the driver I had counted on to take me from the railroad station to my residence, formed a protective cordon between the demonstrators and the city traffic. More surprisingly, people standing on the sidewalks in that city of 3.5 million applauded students who walked daily from the gates of the many colleges and universities to Gu Lou, for rallies and speeches; and sidewalk café owners gave food and drinks to the students, who eventually initiated a hunger strike, similar to the earlier one in Beijing. In communicating their message—criticizing corruption, nepotism, and political censorship—the students devised a variety of methods, some traditional, some new. The traditional ones were the handsomely lettered signs identifying the universities and organizations; other signs repeated statements used in the historic May 4, 1919, movement, which provoked a renaissance in literature and led to the birth of the Communist Party. The fact that the seventieth anniversary of that event fell during the 1989 campaign obviously gave resonance to the students' nationalistic slogans. This time, as in 1919, responding to the Versailles treaty, students throughout the country called government officials to judgement, while pledging themselves to nonviolence.

Similarly, wall posters, which had been used so effectively in the 1979 "Democracy Wall" movement, covered the bulletin boards at the university gates, many signed by faculty, with names added day by day. As Dru Gladney has said, the symbols employed by the students "called upon the revolutionary history of China from the May 4 movement of 1919 to the Cultural Revolution, by drawing upon texts that were immediately obvious to their audience."[12] While some used quotations from Martin Luther King ("I have a dream"), Lord Acton ("power corrupts, absolute power corrupts absolutely") or Henry David Thoreau (pleas for civil disobedience), most of them relied—wisely—on Chinese writers, including Chairman Mao, but particularly those associated with resistance to injustice, such as Lu Xun (1881–1936), the country's most famous short story writer, as well as a poet and essayist and Bei Dao (b. 1950). The students' nationalism was reflected as well, according to Andrew J. Nathan, in statements emphasizing the value of the state above their own lives: a tradition that goes back to Qu Yuan, "who had lived in the fourth century B.C. and who committed suicide to show his loyalty to the ruler who failed to heed his advice." That precedent may have influenced their choice of tactics, also, more than "the examples of Mahatma Gandhi, Martin Luther King, or Corazon Aquino, so often mentioned in the Western media." Bei Dao, a well-known contemporary author living in exile in England, was represented by quotations from his poem "The Answer or the Response." In that verse, a rebel speaks defiantly, in a final gesture of independence, before the court:

Before sentencing, I will speak my piece,
Announcing to the world, I accuse!
Although you trod a thousand resisters under foot,
I shall be the one thousand and first . . . .
And if a continent is to rise up
Let humanity choose a new path.
Glittering stars, like a good omen, decorate the sky,
Resembling 5000-year old Chinese characters,
And the gazing eyes of the young.

The argument and tone of the poem, characteristically Chinese, echo important cultural themes, particularly the confidence of a people who regard themselves as the centre of the world (Guongguo—"the middle kingdom") and the highly romantic impulse at the heart of their "democracy" cry.

Each morning, awakened by the romantic strains of the "Internationale" over the campus loudspeaker, I could not help wishing that students would choose the more pragmatic approach of the American colonists, with their slogan, "no taxation without representation," rather than the more abstract, emotionally charged slogan of the French revolutionists, "Liberty, Equality, and Fraternity."

In a similar way, the powerful symbolism of the "goddess of democracy" in Tiananmen Square may have antagonized those whom the students were trying to get to identify with them and to win over to their position. Although it obviously evoked strong sentiments from students, who posed for pictures in front of the statue, and from an international television audience, the "goddess," with its obvious similarities to the Statue of Liberty, may have further distanced the students from their elders and dissipated the nationalistic spirit that informed their movement.

As a nonviolent strategy, in other words, choosing the "goddess of democracy" as a key image may have been counterproductive in the long run. One wonders what might have happened if the artists had sculpted instead a statue of Lu Xun, a hero to party as well as to non-party members, though apparently "too much deified by the party," according to one young scholar, to serve as an appropriate symbol for students. Lu Xun's witty, yet powerful aphorisms on social justice are nonetheless part of the iconography of the country's agonizing accommodation to the twentieth century; and officials might think twice about ordering bulldozers in to crush a statue of him, as they did with the goddess of democracy, no matter the "rebellious" uses employed in remembering Lu Xun's legacy.

As the weeks went by, foreign observers and some Chinese criticized the demonstrators for not being specific about their goals and strategies—and with good reason. At that time and since, nonetheless, it is important to emphasize how much and how quickly the students learned about conducting a nonviolent campaign during the "China Spring" and over the previous ten years. I have often wondered, also, how many of their critics have been as faithful or as effective in addressing basic political issues and campaigning for justice in less threatening circumstances. And are we still expecting young people, rather than experienced, sophisticated people like ourselves, to provide the leadership for social change?

My point here is that, within a certain sphere of influence, young students were remarkably effective in moving their fellow citizens to resistance and along the rocky, sometimes circular, path to freedom of the press and democratic reform. In thinking about similar struggles in the West, we need to remember how long and multi-faceted that journey has been in our own tradition, from John Milton's essays to the publication of the Pentagon Papers. Chinese students chose nonviolence for practical reasons, as they said, in order to deal effectively with political and economic contradictions in Chinese society. Although they clearly moved from point to point without a carefully outlined plan for "victory," they achieved, consciously or unconsciously, more than anyone might have expected. Along the way, they gave new meaning and significance to old symbols, in language and image, and set a new standard for judging the government and upholding the common good.

Some of this was accomplished by liberating the press, that is, by drawing into the movement journalists, writers, and TV personalities who had been cautiously, if understandably, silent before. "The media enjoyed a short, limited freedom of speech," as one teacher said, "which was unprecedented, encouraging." The footage and newspaper accounts are replete with pictures of staff members from *China Daily*, the principal English-speaking newspaper, and the *People's Daily*, the party organ, marching under banners proclaiming their support. Journalists in Nanjing and other provincial capitals were similarly active and partisan. Television commentators openly supported the movement, in daily newscasts in late May.

After June 4, when TV announcers had to read official bulletins that pointedly conflicted with previous reports, they indicated their displeasure through their expression or tone of voice. Not surprisingly, they soon disappeared from view, to be replaced by printed announcements, as the repression accelerated.

One reason for the response of professional journalists was the students' sophistication in communicating their message and in maintaining contact with their contemporaries throughout the country. Students at national universities—including the teachers colleges, in Beijing, Nanjing, Shanghai, and elsewhere—form, after all, a kind of network; many come from similar backgrounds or are graduates from the same college-preparatory high schools. Students with contemporaries at universities in Beijing were in constant communication by phone; by late May, on several university campuses, loudspeakers provided daily bulletins from Tiananmen Square, and broadcast news from the BBC and recordings of movement speakers, to which cheering crowds responded. Similar contacts were maintained with supporters in Hong Kong and beyond, by fax machines. Some observers said that army troops sent into Beijing relied on these reports, which may have accounted for their reluctance to obey orders to shoot or to arrest their contemporaries occupying Tiananmen Square.

Even more surprising, for anyone familiar with Chinese society, was the students' success in winning support from workers, something that cannot be stressed enough in evaluating the campaign. Dismissing the uprising as "elitist," in fact, had led many to ignore the full political and cultural implications of this development, as I suggested earlier.

University students in China are an elite, to be sure, and the behavior of some student leaders, since their coming to the U.S,, betrays their impulse to ignore what a populist might regard as basic democratic values. A student's elite status, however, is an advantage as well as a disadvantage, and many made full use of the first and overcame the second. As creatures of advantage, they seized the opportunity to convince others of their seriousness by their very presence, their sacrifices during the hunger strike, and their standing up to the army. "In traditional Chinese hierarchy, it is the body of the scholar-officials who, under the Emperor, rank the highest in value. By extension, students occupy a special place of value."[13] In risking themselves, out of a sense of patriotism, they eventually won workers, merchants, and others to the campaign. No wonder that unexpected allies took similar, often even greater, risks. In the end, workers were the principal victims in the massacre in Beijing and later through execution and imprisonment.

The attitude and deportment of students in Nanjing and Harbin that I witnessed were anything but elitist. In Nanjing, for example, students remained persistent and disciplined in communicating their message to the broader populace, fanning out through the city to explain themselves and going daily into factories with leaflets about their campaign. As in Beijing, "they cast themselves not as dissidents but as loyal followers, appealing to the authorities to live up to the values they themselves had articulated."[14] The appearance of banners by various workers' organizations and unions, a turning point in the events at Gu Lou Square, was cheered by faculty and students directly involved in the movement. After Li Peng's speech on May 21, condemning the students, the posters and signs, with growing militancy, openly satirized and attacked him, and a leading party member and various workers spoke to a large public audience in support of the students.

In Harbin, similarly, where I attended an international conference of scholars and translators before, during, and after June 4, the student-led campaign was equally effective, with an extensive network of cooperation among local campuses and through ongoing communication with others in Beijing. When three students from the Harbin Technical University died at Tiananmen Square, students and local citizens poured out into the streets in mourning, many carrying memorial wreaths in the demonstrations. Later, students set up cordons throughout the city, when it appeared that the army might move in from the outskirts. Having to make our way through the cordons on our way to the train on June 6, I was again impressed by the skill and persistent dedication to nonviolence among student leaders.

During the 1500-mile train-ride from Harbin south to Nanjing, university students on their way home continued their efforts to acquaint everybody within reach with their movement, all along the way. Many who joined the train after the stop at Tianjin/Beijing moved through the passenger train with tape recording of speeches at Tiananmen Square and personal stories about their own involvement. Later, when our express train halted in Jinan for twelve hours (because of violence farther down the line), my colleagues and I jumped to a local, a real "slow train through Arkansas," where more students talked animatedly with peasants and others selling produce on the train and at stops along the route.

By the time we reached Nanjing, arriving on the north side of the Yangtze River, the provincial government, with encouragement from university officials, had already developed a number of strategies to avert violence. It apparently kept the People's Liberation Army at bay. Although rumors abounded that military divisions were in revolt or would take over the major cities, Nanjing remained relatively quiet—I saw only one small truck of soldiers along the main thoroughfare, for example. And the universities and colleges moved quickly to dismiss the students, to keep them from being rounded up, once the party moved to crush the uprising. Faculty and administrators sent buses out to retrieve students on "a long march" under way from Nanjing to Beijing, for example. Nonviolent resistance to the national government, nonetheless, did not end with the massacre in Beijing or, about the same time, in Chengdu.

Another major achievement of the movement became apparent later in the summer, in fact, as the party attempted to pursue its repressive policy of rounding up demonstrators and punishing others who merely supported them. Hundreds of workers were executed and many students were imprisoned, of course. And since the uprising, first-year students at major universities have had to endure a month to a year of military training. But passive resistance to non-cooperation with the government's repressive measures during and after the uprising contrasted dramatically with public response to similar measures since 1949, when neighbors informed on neighbors and family members were divided against one another.

A common response to inquiries in factories or organizations about activists during the days of "reflection" following June 4 was that "no one here was involved," as if huge crowds had simply disappeared from the face of the earth. Asked to report "rebels" to the police, people phoned in reports on themselves or listed hundreds of others, from ordinary workers to cadres, thereby blocking phone calls from "real" informers. A good deal of black humor went around; some people, for example, made fun of the incident by saying how "nice" the government was in not using jet-fighters against the students. Also, important leaders of the uprising, including Chai Ling, "Commander-in-Chief of Tiananmen Square," and her husband, managed to escape the country with support from party members or state employees.

But what about the consequences of the uprising over the past more than six years? What are the signs of success or failure? In the U.S., perhaps too much attention has been focused on the splintering, dissident groups and their leaders in exile. Not surprisingly, as with other young people (actors or rock stars) suddenly thrust into an international limelight, student leaders often fail to live up to the high expectations that they themselves or others place upon them. As in past history, attempts to conduct a campaign of resistance outside the country are fraught with difficulty, though some historians point to the positive example of sun Yat-sen and the earlier democratic revolution.

From the perspective of nonviolence, the more important questions have to do with ongoing plans and strategies and the ability of the movement to build on what the 1989 uprising accomplished inside China. Information on resistance there is scant, however, because of the political risks involved in giving testimony. It is also difficult to evaluate—given the dramatic changes taking place in China at this time—the rapid economic growth and recent power struggles within the party. The absence of any viable "lawful" alternative to the dominant party makes political organization and dramatic changes or reforms unlikely, at least until the death of Deng Xiaoping. After that, various economic factors may keep China on the road to reform, although basic "democratic" initiatives will probably have to arise from the grassroots.

Materially, life for many Chinese is better since 1979, with increasing access to commodities and comforts that citizens of industrial nations take for granted. Meanwhile, changes associated with private enterprise—as opposed to state-directed programmes—accelerate. The party espouses "Chinese learning as the essence, Western learning for utility" (*zhong xue wei ti, xi xue wei yong*), by which it means "no political or social change, to accompany the economic change." Whether party leaders believe it or not, they continue to assert that the political consequences of a free market in China will be different from those of a free market in other countries.[15] No other "free market" nation, however, has escaped the cultural fall-out of capitalism, has it? Is going capitalism "the Chinese way" likely to produce radically different results? Following the pattern of the imperial West, for example, China continues to finance "peacetime" projects at home by increasing weapons sales abroad; and reports of greater corruption in government, as well as a return to gambling, prostitution, and drugs increase.

As for citizens of other industrial, imperial nations on this fragile planet, life in urban China is increasingly hectic, even threatening, for many who earlier lived in relative security. At the same time, interest in the philosophy and strategies of nonviolence has increased, as peace researchers explore the history of previous dissent and think about the future. And further "experiments with truth" may offer the principal hope for defending themselves against, and building alternatives to, "globalization from above."

NOTES

1. In referring to the events of Spring 1989 as a "democratic uprising," rather than the "pro-democracy movement" (or the Chinese designation 6/4), I am aware of the inadequacy of both designations. Some of the leaders and participants obviously behaved more like Ming dynasty emperors than Jeffersonian democrats. The primary impulse of the campaign was, nonetheless, towards an extension of the franchise and against government corruption, nepotism, and censorship; it built on earlier resistance to top-down management and advocated participation and accountability.

2. Liu Binyan, Ruan Ming, and Xu Gang, *"Tell the World:" What Happened in China and Why,* tr. Henry L. Epstein (New York: Pantheon Books, 1989), p. 124.

3. Andrew J. Nathan provides useful political background in *Chinese Democracy* (Berkeley: University of California Press, 1986); and *China's Crisis: Dilemmas of Reform and Prospects of Democracy* (New York: Columbia University Press, 1990). See also *The Broken Mirror: China after Tiananmen,* ed., George Hicks (Chicago: St. James Press, 1990). An on-going record of information has been provided by Ruth Cremerius, Doris Fischer, and Peter Schier, *Studentenprotest and Repression in China, April-June 1989: Analyse, Chronologic, Dokumente,* 2nd ed. rev. (Hamburg: Mitteilungen des Institutes fur Asinkunde No. 192, 1991). Henry Rosenontu Jr., "China: The Morning After," *Z Magazine,* March 1990, 5–6ff, gives an excellent brief account and evaluation of Tiananmen Square; see also, *June Four: A Chronicle of the Chinese Democratic Uprising,* tr. Jin Jiang and Qin Zhou (Little Rock, University of Arkansas Press, 1989); Harrison E. Salisbury, *Tiananmen Diary: Thirteen Days in June* (Boston: Little, Brown, 1989); review/essays by journalists and scholars in the *New York Review of Books:* Orville Schell (June 29, 1989); Fang Lizhi, Simon Leys, Roderick MacFarquhar (July 20, 1989); John K. Fairbanks (September 28, 1989), Merle Goldman (November 9, 1989); Jonathan Mirsky, "The Empire Strikes Back" (February 1, 1990). Relevant documents appear in *Cries for*

Democracy: Writings and Speeches from the 1989 Chinese Democracy Movement (Princeton, NJ: Princeton University Press, 1990).

4. Gene Sharp and Bruce Jenkins, "Nonviolence Struggle in China: An Eyewitness Account," in *Nonviolent Sanctions: News from the Albert Einstein Institution,* Vol. I, No. 2 (Fall 1989), pp. 1, 3–7. See also Peter Ackerman and Christopher Kruegler, *Strategic Nonviolent Conflict: The Dynamics of Peoples's Power in the Twentieth Century* (Westport, CT: Praeger, 1994), pp. 342–43.

5. Richard Falk, "Challenges of a Changing Global Order," Fourteenth General Conference of International Peace Research Association (IPRA), July 27, 1992, Kyoto, Japan.

6. General accounts of changing economic conditions appear in Orville Schell, *Discos and Democracy: China in the Throes of Reform* (New York: Doubleday, 1989); and Fox Butterfield, *China: Alive in the Bitter Sea,* rev. ed. (New York: Random House, 1990) which adds a chapter on the uprising to his 1982 edition.

7. Jonathan D. Spence, *The Search for Modern China* (New York: W. W. Norton Co., 1990), as well as his invaluable cultural history, *The Gate of Heavenly Peace: The Chinese and Their Revolution, 1895–1980* (New York: Penguin Books, 1982).

8. Johan Galtung, "Visioning a Peaceful World," *Buddhism and Nonviolent Global Problem-Solving: Ulan Bator Explorations,* ed. Glenn D. Paige and Sarah Gilliat (Honolulu: Spark Matsunaga Institute for Peace, University of Hawaii, 1991).

9. *Beijing Review,* June 1987, p. 4.

10. Liu Binyan's "Conclusion" gives many examples of ongoing resistance to the government policy. Nicholas D. Kristof, "Defiant Chinese Dissident Tells of His Ordeal," *New York Times,* April 16, 1992, tells the story of Han Dongfang.

11. See "Appendix 2: Chronology (April 15–July 15, 1989)," in Chu-Yuan Cheng, *Behind the Tiananmen Massacre: Social, Political, and Econimic Ferment in China* (Boulder, CO: Westview Press, 1990), pp. 201–08.

12. Dru Gladney, "Symbolizing Nonviolent Protest in Tiananmen Square: Traditional and Post-Modern Challenges to the Chinese State," summarized in *Transforming Struggles: Strategy and the Global Experience of Nonviolent Direct Action* (Cambridge, MA: Committee on International Affairs, Harvard University, 1992), p. 99. Professor Gladney argued also that *The Yellow River Elegy,* a popular film that is critical of the establishment and widely circulated the previous summer and fall, prepared the way for the 1989 uprising. Although communist hard-liners had tried to suppress the film, Zhao Ziyang ordered it aired a second time, according to Harrison Salisbury; it ends with a statement that "the characteristic of democracy should be transparency, popular will, and scientism."

13. Ibid.

14. Andrew Nathan, *China's Crisis,* p. 183.

15. *China Reconstructs,* May 1987, p. 5, a government publication, put it this way: "The great majority of Chinese support this position—to carry on, but critically, our own historical tradition, while fully responding to the spirit of the

times, and to accept good things from the rest of the world to enhance and enliven, but not replace, our own culture."

23

The Global Spread of Active Nonviolence

Richard Deats

Richard Deats,editor, *Fellowship Magazine* and former executive director, Fellowship of Reconciliation, taught social ethics for eighteen years at Union Theological Seminary, Manila, the Philippines, before returning to the United .States. His books include *Martin Luther King, Jr.: Spirit-Led Prophet* (1999) and *How to Keep Laughing Even Though You've Considered All the Facts* (1999). The following selection shows how nonviolence has been applied by different countries of the world in a variety of ways.

In the last century Victor Hugo wrote, "An invasion of armies can be resisted, but not an idea whose time has come." Looking back over the twentieth century we see the growing influence and impact of nonviolence all over the world. While "nonviolence is as old as the hills," as Gandhi said, it is our century in which the philosophy and practice of nonviolence have grasped the human imagination and exploded in amazing and unexpected ways, as individuals, groups, and movements have developed creative, life-affirming ways to resolve conflict, overcome oppression, establish justice, protect the earth, and build democracy.

Mohandas Gandhi pioneered in developing the philosophy and practice of nonviolence. On the vast subcontinent of India he led a colonial people to freedom through satyagraha—soul force—defeating what was at the time the greatest empire on earth, the British Raj. Not long after Gandhi's death, Martin Luther King, Jr. found in the Mahatma's philosophy the key he was searching for. He moved individualistic religion toward a socially dynamic religious philosophy that propelled the civil rights movement into a nonviolent revolution, thus changing the course of U.S. history.

The Gandhian and Kingian movements have provided a seedbed for a social ferment and revolutionary change across the planet, providing a mighty impetus for human and ecological transformation. Many, perhaps most, still do not recognize the significance of this development and persist in thinking that in the final analysis it is lethal force, or the threat of it, that is the decisive arbiter of human affairs. Why else would we as a nation continue to pour hundreds of billions into weaponry even as we cut foreign aid, refuse to pay our United Nations dues, and send our armed forces abroad on peacekeeping missions without providing them with training in the way of peace and nonviolence?

We need to do a better job of bringing into the public consciousness an awareness of the nonviolent breakthroughs that have been occurring and that provide an alternative paradigm to the ancient belief in marching armies and bloody warfare as the stuff of human history. What follows are, in necessarily broad strokes, some of the highlights of how this alternative vision is developing even as it changes history.

THE PHILIPPINES

In 1986 millions of unarmed Filipinos surprised the world by nonviolently overthrowing the brutal dictatorship of Ferdinand Marcos, who was known at the time as "the Hitler of Southeast Asia." The movement they called "People Power" demonstrated in an astounding way the power of active nonviolence.

Beginning as a reaction to the assassination in 1983 of the popular opposition leader, Sen. Benigno Aquino, the movement against Marcos grew rapidly. Drawing on Aquino's own advocacy of nonviolence and aided by widespread workshops in active nonviolence, the people began to realize that armed rebellion was not the only way to overthrow the dictator.

In late 1985, when Marcos called a snap election, the divided opposition united behind Corazon Aquino, the widow of the slain senator. Despite fraud, intimidation, and violence employed by Marcos, the Aquino forces brilliantly used a nonviolent strategy employing marches, petitions, trained poll watchers, and an independent polling commission. When Marcos tried to steal the election and thwart the people's will, the country came to the brink of civil war. The Catholic cardinal called upon the contemplative orders of nuns to pray and fast for the country. Thirty computer operators tabulating the election results publicly denounced the official counting, exposing the fraud to the world. Corazon Aquino called for a nonviolent struggle of rallies, vigils, and civil disobedience to undermine the fraudulent claim of Marcos that he had won the election. Church leaders fully backed her call.

Crucial defections from the government by two key leaders and a few hundred troops became the occasion for millions of unarmed Filipinos to pour into the streets of Manila to protect the defectors and demand the resignation of the discredited government. Troops sent to attack the rebels were met by citizens massed in the streets, singing and praying, calling on the soldiers to join them. Clandestine radio broadcasts gave instructions in nonviolent resistance. When fighter planes were sent to bomb the rebel camp, the pilots saw it surrounded by the people and defected. A military man said, "This is something new. Soldiers are supposed to protect the civilians. In this particular case, you have civilians protecting the soldiers." Facing the collapse of his support, Marcos and his family fled the country. The dictatorship fell in four days.

Ending the dictatorship was only the first step in the long struggle for freedom. Widespread poverty, unjust distribution of the land, and an unreformed military remained, undercutting the completion of the revolution. Challenges to the further development of effective People Power continue, as a determined grass-roots movement works for the transformation of society.

CHILE

The Chileans, who like the Filipinos suffered under a brutal dictatorship, gained inspiration from the People Power movement as they built their own movement of nonviolent resistance to General Pinochet. They used the image of drops of water wearing away the stone of oppression.

In 1986 leftist guerrillas killed five bodyguards of Pinochet in an assassination attempt on the general. In retaliation, the military decided to take revenge by arresting five critics of the regime. A human rights lawyer alerted his neighbors to the danger of his being abducted, and they made plans to protect him. Cars arrived in the early morning hours carrying hooded men who tried to enter the house. Unable to break down reinforced doors and locks, they tried to force barred windows. The lawyer's family turned on all the lights and banged pots and blew whistles, awakening the neighbors, who then did the same. The attackers, unexpectedly blocked by united neighbors, fled the scene.

Groups formed to carefully locate sites of government torture and then, after prayer and reflection, found ways to expose the evil. Some padlocked themselves to iron railings near a targeted building; others proceeded to such a site during rush hour, then unfurled a banner saying, "Here they torture people." Sometimes they would disappear into the crowd; other times they would wait until they were arrested.

In October of 1988, the government called on the people to vote "accept" or "no" on continued military rule. Despite widespread intimidation against Pinochet's critics, the people were determined. Workshops were held to help them overcome their fear and to work to influence the election. Inspired and instructed by Filipino opposition to Marcos, voter registration drives and the training of poll watchers proceeded all over the country. The results exceeded the protesters' fondest expectations: 91% of all eligible voters registered and the opposition won 54.7% of all votes cast. Afterwards over a million people gathered in a Santiago park to celebrate their victory.

In the late 1980's, throughout Latin America, dictatorships fell like dominos. This came about not through armed uprisings, but through the determination of unarmed people—students, mothers, workers, religious groups— persisting in their witness against oppression and injustice, even in the face of torture and death. In Brazil the nonviolent movement for justice was called *firmeza permanente*, "relentless persistence." Base communities in the Brazilian countryside, for example, became organizing centers for the landless struggling to regain their land. In Argentina, "mothers of the disappeared" were unceasing in their agitation for an accounting of the "*desaparacidos*"—the disappeared—of the military regime. In Montevideo, a fast in the tiny office of Serpaj (Service for Justice & Peace) brought to the fore the first public opposition to Uruguay's rapacious junta and elicited widespread sympathy that turned the tide toward democracy.

HAITI

Nowhere has the struggle for democracy been more difficult than in Haiti, yet even there the people developed courageous and determined nonviolent resistance against all odds. The people's movement is called *Lavalas*, the flood washing away oppression. Defying governmental prohibitions and military abuse, the people demonstrated and marched and prayed. In 1986, when Fr. Jean Bertrand Aristide was silenced by his religious order and reassigned by the hierarchy to a church in a dangerous area dominated by the military, students from his church in the slums occupied the front rows of the national cathedral in Port-au-Prince. Seven students fasted at the altar, persisting for six days, until the bishops backed down and allowed Aristide to continue working in his parish. Then, in December 1990, Aristide was elected to the presidency. Driven from office and exiled abroad, he was able to return only after U.S. troops went into Haiti. The long-term building of a democratic society there faces enormous odds—but it can be built, given time and persistence and the strengthening of the popular movement out of which the first democratic elections were held.

CHINA

Stunning developments took place in China in the spring of 1989. What began as a memorial march for a deceased leader quickly led into a mass expression of the pent-up longings of the Chinese people. With slogans such as "People Power" and "We Shall Overcome," students—later joined by workers—called for democracy, an end to corruption, a free press, and other democratic reforms. Hundreds of thousands of Chinese joined the protesters in Tiananmen Square. Day after day, week after week, they peacefully called on their government to accede to their demands. First a few, then hundreds, joined in a fast. Growing numbers of citizens, including police, soldiers, even generals, expressed sympathy with the movement. The first soldiers sent to stop the demonstrators were disarmed with gifts and goodwill, just as the Filipinos had done in Manila. The top leaders of the government, in an important concession, met in a televised session with students. The movement spread, beyond control it seemed, to other cities. Finally, however, a confused and divided government resorted to brute force, and on June 4 the massacre of Tiananmen Square occurred.

This great tragedy was not necessarily the end of People Power in China, any more than the Amritsar massacre of unarmed Indians by the British was the end of the Indian revolution, nor the assassination of Benigno Aquino was the end of the democracy movement in the Philippines. Both of those tragedies proved to be beginnings rather than endings. Martin Luther King reminded us that "unearned suffering is redemptive." This can be true for a people as well as for an individual.

China has also brutally sought to destroy democratic rights in Tibet. The Tibetans' exiled leader and Nobel Prize laureate, the Dalai Lama, bravely persists in calling his people not to flag in their nonviolent efforts to gain their freedom from Chinese domination. He believes that these efforts will resonate with China's democracy movement, which was only temporarily set back by the Tiananmen Square massacre. He maintains that following the course of nonviolent resistance will in time bring political concessions from China that seem unimaginable at present.

BURMA

A movement remarkably parallel to China's occurred in Burma a year earlier. In Rangoon, the capital, a students' nonviolent movement was launched in summer of 1988 against the brutally repressive military rulers. Students began mass marches that increased week by week, as professionals, the middle class, and working people joined.

During this tumultuous period Aung San Suu Kyi quickly rose to prominence. The daughter of Aung San, the father of modern Burma, she had married an Oxford professor and moved to England. She had returned to Rangoon from abroad because of her mother's illness. Suu Kyi was drawn into the democracy movement and fearlessly spoke at mass rallies, once walking through a contingent of soldiers ready to fire on her.

Finally, as would occur in China a year later, the threatened leaders ordered a bloody crackdown, killing thousands of unarmed demonstrators, with thousands more fleeing into the jungle. In the May 1990 national elections, the people voted overwhelmingly for Aung San Suu Kyi's National League for Democracy [NLD], even though she and the other NLD leaders had been placed under house arrest months earlier. The government refused to recognize the results of the election and continued to govern, keeping Suu Kyi under house arrest for five years. Meanwhile she was awarded the Nobel Peace Prize in 1991. In one of her essays she wrote, " The well-spring of courage and endurance in the face of unbridled power is generally a firm belief in the sanctity of ethical principles, combined with a historical sense that despite all setbacks, the condition of man is set on an ultimate course for both spiritual and material advancement." Her quiet determination and courage continue as a tower of strength to the Burmese in their quest for freedom.

ISRAEL/PALESTINE

Prior to the start of the peace process in the Middle East, the predominant impression of the Palestinian/Israeli conflict, fed by media images, was one of rock-throwing Palestinian young men fighting well-armed Israeli soldiers. But since 1967 there had been two parts of the Palestinian resistance movement, the paramilitary and the civil. The *Intifada* (Arabic for "to shake off") was from its inception a multidimensional movement containing many nonviolent aspects:

- strikes by schools and businesses called to protest specific policies and actions of the occupying authorities
- agricultural projects, such as the planting of victory gardens and trees planted on disputed lands
- visiting committees for prisoners and the families of those who have been killed
- boycotts of all Israeli-made products
- tax refusal, as in the Palestinian village of Beit Sahour where the VAT [value added tax] and income taxes were not paid
- solidarity demonstrations, undertaken when villagers were unjustly arrested, by other residents who went to police stations asking to be arrested as well
- establishment of alternative institutions to build Palestinian self-sufficiency

Commenting on such developments, Labor Party leader Schlomo Avineri observed, "An army can beat an army, but an army cannot beat a people. . . . Iron can smash iron, it cannot smash an unarmed fist."

The just demands and nonviolent actions of the Intifada strengthened the voices of Israelis working to find a just and peaceful resolution of the conflict. And, despite grave legal risks, covert meetings between Palestinians and Israelis slowly built growing areas of understanding. In March 1989 the chairman of the Palestine National Council's political committee told a New York audience how secret friendships with Jewish leaders helped Palestinian leaders to publicly adopt a two-state solution. In the fall of 1992, Norway began hosting fourteen secret meetings between Palestinians and Israelis out of which the Declaration of Principles was forged that provided the basis of the Israeli-PLO [Palestine Liberation Organization] Accord signed on the White House lawn on September 13, 1993.

Extremists on both sides have been unrelenting in their efforts to undermine the peace process. The assassination of Prime Minister Rabin and the defeat of the peace forces in the May 1996 Israeli elections were grave blows to the Accord.

The forces of fairness and good will have an even more daunting task ahead of them. To those who say peace is now impossible, Gandhi reminds us, "Think of all the things that were thought impossible until they happened."

SOUTH AFRICA

Decades of resistance to apartheid and witness for a multiracial, democratic society slowly but surely wore away the adamant oppression dominating South Africa. The brutal policies of the government convinced many that apartheid would only end in a violent showdown, that nonviolence could not overcome such a racist regime. Nonetheless, the heart of the resistance movement was basically nonviolent: education, vigils, rallies, marches, petitions, boycotts, prayers, fasts, and acts of civil disobedience. Governmental attempts to stop the movement with massive detentions, bannings of organizations and individuals, intimidation and murder could not, in the end, stop it.

Even the establishment of emergency rule in 1988 failed: the churches responded with a nationwide program called "effective nonviolent action" that trained citizens for grass-roots campaigns to break racial barriers in housing and transportation, defend conscientious objectors, visit prisoners across racial lines, etc. Emergency rule, rather than strengthening the government, exposed its desperation and moral bankruptcy in the face of widespread nonviolent resistance.

An unexpected breakthrough came when President deKlerk began instituting reforms, eventually legalizing the African National Congress and releasing Nelson Mandela, who had been in prison twenty-nine years. The dramatic changes demonstrate a concept from the civil rights movement in the U.S., "top down/bottom up"—i.e., pressure for change from the grassroots is met by reforms accepted by or initiated from the top, creating a dynamic tension that fosters change.

In the midst of these changes, the government still carried out brutal policies—but the force for change was not to be denied. When the first open elections in South Africa's history were held, the world saw an amazing manifestation: a whole nation peacefully voting for revolutionary change, moving from a white racist regime to multiracial democratic rule under the presidency of Nelson Mandela. His passion for freedom and justice for all was expressed in a greatness of spirit that reached out to his former enemies. In his inaugural address, he held before the people a unifying vision "in which all South Africans . . . will be able to walk tall, without any fear in their hearts, sure of their inalienable right to human dignity—a rainbow nation at peace with itself and the world."

THE FORMER SOVIET BLOC

The same "top down/bottom up" process occurred in the unraveling of the Soviet bloc that followed the policies of *glasnost, perestroika,* and *democratsatsiya* (openness, restructuring and democracy) instituted by President Mikhail Gorbachev. Pressure from below—relentless persistence—helped to create a climate ripe for change. This ferment from below was long in building. On the one hand there was a small but determined band of human rights advocates such as

Andrei Sakharov and Yelena Bonner who were unrelenting in their call for the observance of universally accepted standards of human rights. Others—religious, peace, and environmental groups, artists and poets—refused to submit to totalitarian rule.

The crushing of Czechoslovakia's 1968 experiment to create "socialism with a human face" had strengthened the widely held assumption at that time that communism was incapable of peaceful change and democratic openness, that nonviolence might "work" in India or the U.S., but "never with the communists." This added fuel to the Cold War, the nuclear arms race, and the belief that World War III was a virtual certainty. Not many paid attention to those aspects of the Czech experiment that contained hints of the People Power revolutions that were to flower in the 1980s—but they were highly significant.

The 1968 invasion by the Warsaw Pact armies had been expected to crush all resistance in a few days. It took *eight months*. Czechoslovakia's large and well-trained army was ordered to stay in its barracks while the populace responded in unexpectedly creative, nonviolent ways. The Czech news agency refused to report the disinformation that said Czech leaders had requested the invasion. Highway and street signs were turned around to confuse the invading forces. Students sat in the path of incoming tanks; others climbed onto the tanks and talked to the crews. While the people did not physically fight the invaders, they refused to cooperate with them. Clandestine radio messages kept up the morale of the people, passing on vital information and instructions, such as the calling of one-hour general strikes. The Czech leaders were able to hold on to their offices and continue some of the reforms until the nonviolence finally began to erode, quite possibly through the work of *agents provocateurs*.

Twelve years later neighboring Poland took up the fallen nonviolent banner. Gdansk shipyard workers went on strike and, with prayer and rallies, *Solidarnosc* was born in August 1980—giving laborers an independent voice. Using strikes, sit-ins, and demonstrations, "Solidarity" began a grassroots movement for change that spread rapidly across Poland. The government responded with the brutal imposition of martial law in December 1981. But instead of destroying Solidarity, the people began the creation of an alternative society from the base, choosing to live "as if they were free." A new society began to be born in the shell of the old. When finally, in 1989, open elections were held, Solidarity won by a landslide.

The Polish elections were aided by the breathtaking changes occurring in the Soviet Union. Gorbachev's reforms, beginning in 1985, opened the floodgates of pent-up longing for change that were eventually to sweep away even Gorbachev and the USSR. One by one, the nations of Eastern Europe saw the overthrow of totalitarian rule by people armed with truth and courage. A critical mass had been reached: growing numbers of people were emboldened by such things as the writings of Vaclav Havel from a Czech prison and prayer meetings and discussion groups in Leipzig, East Germany. The symbol of these vast changes was the peaceful breaching of the Berlin Wall on November 9, 1989, as the established order collapsed and the old regimes were swept aside with remarkably little violence or loss of life.

The widespread assumption that totalitarian regimes could not be over-turned by unarmed people was decisively shown to be wrong. Governments ulti-mately derive their strength from the consent—either passive or active—of the governed. Once that consent disappears and resistance spreads, governments find their power to rule weakened and, under the right circumstances, destroyed.

What happened in Eastern Europe happened in the USSR as well. The reforms speeded up the stirrings for change, as thousands of grassroots groups sprang up to deal with a whole spectrum of social, economic, political, environ-mental, and cultural issues. In July 1990, 100,000 coal miners went out on a strike in Siberia that spread westward to Ukraine. Strongly disciplined, the min-ers policed themselves, closed down mining town liquor stores, and gathered for massive rallies.

From the local to the national level, elections became more democratic, bringing about the election of reform candidates. In the spring of 1989, 2,000 persons, including Andrei Sakharov, were elected to the Congress of Peoples' Deputies in the freest election since the revolution. Popularly elected legislatures came into office throughout the USSR, breaking the monopoly of the Communist Party. The leaders for these changes came from popular fronts established in republic after republic, beginning with Lativia (October 1988), Ukraine (Septem-ber 1989) and *Sajudis* in Lithuania, which won multi-party elections (February 1990). Respect for the language, history, and traditions of the various nationali-ties challenged the Russification that had undergirded Soviet power and control.

The Baltic state of Lithuania was the first of the Soviet republics to pro-claim outright independence—which it did on March 11, 1990. This most repressed of the republics started a "singing revolution," defying decades of cul-tural repression by reviving long-forbidden Lithuanian folk songs, festivals, reli-gious practices, and traditions. Trying to halt the dissolution of the Union, Moscow retaliated with a crippling blockade. The following January, crack Red Army troops moved on the capital of Vilnius, killing fourteen unarmed demon-strators who were protecting the nation's TV tower. Instead of surrendering or issuing a call to arms, Lithuania called on the citizenry to "hold to principles of nonviolent insubordinate resistance and political and social noncooperation." The Lithuanians did just that, continuing their nonviolent and independent course.

Then in August 1991, elements of the Communist Party, the KGB, and the Army tried to stage a coup in Moscow. Despite the arrest of Gorbachev and his family, resistance was widespread. People poured into the streets to protect the Russian parliament. Women and students called on the soldiers to join the peo-ple. Religious people knelt in the streets in prayer. Closed newspapers and radio stations quickly set up alternative media. The mayor of Leningrad told the mili-tary in his city not to follow the order of the plotters, and the head of the Russian Orthodox Church threatened excommunication to those who followed the coup.

Even some members of the KGB refused orders, risking death for their defiance. Eventually the coup attempt collapsed, opening the way for Lithuania and the other republics to begin an independent course.

The breakup of the Soviet empire will doubtless be followed by years of upheaval as its constituent parts find their place in a world reaching for democracy but often lacking the experience, patience, and vision to implement the hope. At this point in history we have learned a great deal about nonviolent resistance to evil and bringing down oppressors. We still have much to learn about the next steps needed to foster the democratic evolution of society characterized by justice, peace, and freedom.

Democracy is the institutionalization of nonviolent problem-solving in the social order. Education, conflict resolution, the struggle for justice, nonviolent direct action, organizing for special needs, voting on issues, adjudicating differences, framing laws for change and reform—these are all nonviolent in essence and help build what Martin Luther King, Jr. called "the beloved community." Democratic nations are truest to their values when they deal with other nation states nonviolently, through diplomacy, treaties, mutual respect, and fairness.

Nonviolent movements in the United States have a long and significant history, from the abolitionist struggle against slavery; the labor movement; the peace movement; the environmental movement; the movements for the rights of women, African-Americans, gays and lesbians, as well as other minorities and oppressed groups. Nonetheless, there is still far to go when one considers the degree of violence and the lack of justice in the national life and in the foreign policy of the United States.

At the time of the Philippine overthrow of the Marcos dictatorship, a Filipino writer said that whereas the past one hundred years were dominated by Karl Marx and the armed revolutionary, the next hundred years would be shaped by Gandhi and the unarmed *satyagrahi*, the votary of Truth. Gandhi said that "Truth is God" and that the Truth expressed in the unarmed struggle for justice, peace, and freedom is the greatest power in the world.

During Gandhi's lifetime, many looked upon him with contempt. Churchill dismissed him as a "half-naked fakir." Communists and other advocates of violent revolution branded his nonviolence as bourgeois and reactionary. Most advances in the human race have faced long years of ridicule and opposition. New insights of truth are often considered heresy; prophets are driven out, their followers persecuted. But half a century after his assassination, Gandhi's influence continues to grow with the amazing spread of nonviolent movements around the world. Martin Luther King built on the Gandhian legacy and at the time of his death was speaking increasingly of the radical and costly nature of revolutionary, nonviolent transformation.

If a global, democratic civilization is to come into being and endure, our challenge is to continue developing radical nonviolent alternatives to war and all forms of oppression, from individuals to groups, from nation-states to the peoples of the world. We must continue to challenge the age-old assumptions about the necessity of violence in overcoming injustice, resisting oppression, and establishing social well-being.

What if a writer in the pages of *Fellowship* fifteen years ago had predicted that unarmed Filipinos would overthrow the Marcos dictatorship in a four-day uprising; that military regimes across Latin America would be toppled by the relentless persistence of their unarmed opponents; that apartheid would end peacefully and that in a massive and peaceful plebescite, all races of South Africa would elect Nelson Mandela to the presidency; that the Berlin Wall would be peacefully brought down; and that Arafat and Rabin would shake hands at the White House at a ceremony establishing a peace accord between the PLO and Israel?

Such a writer would probably have been thought ridiculously naive and dismissed out of hand. *And yet these things happened.* Why do we so resist the potential in the "not yet" which is stirring in the present moment? Elise Boulding reminds us how deadly pessimism can be, eroding our determination to work for a better tomorrow. Hope infused in an apparently hopeless situation creates the possibility of change. This is the faith that can sing, in the face of police dogs and water cannons, "We Shall Overcome." Or as Joan of Arc muses in Shaw's *St. Joan*, "Some people see things as they are and ask 'Why?' I dream of things that never were and ask, 'Why not?'"

24

Gandhian Satyagraha and the Chipko Movement of India

Krishna Mallick

Krishna Mallick received her M.A. in philosophy from Calcutta University and Ph.D. in philosophy from Brandeis University and currently teaches in the Philosophy Department at Salem State College in Massachusetts. She has presented and published papers on the Chipko movement and sex-determination test in India and has coedited two books, *Business Ethics: A Philosophical Approach* with Edward Meagher and Kevin Funchion and *Nonviolence: A Reader in the Ethics of Action* with Dr. Doris Hunter. She is the coordinator of the Peace Institute at Salem State College. In this original article, the author traces the evolution of the Chipko (Hug the Trees) movement by showing how it has applied the Gandhian method of Satyagraha.

The Chipko movement or Hug the Trees movement, a protest against deforestation, began in the early 1970s in the Garhwal region of Uttar Pradesh, but now the philosophy of Chipko has spread to Himachal Pradesh in the north, to Karnataka in the south, to Rajasthan in the west, to Bihar in the east, and to the Vindhyas in Central India. The contemporary Chipko movement is the result of multidimensional conflicts over forest resources at the scientific, technical, economic and particularly at the ecological levels. The Chipko movement is not a conflict over the local distribution of forest resources. It is based on the perception of forest in the ecological context. This movement has been successful in forcing a 15-year ban on commercial green felling in the hills of Uttar Pradesh, in stopping clear felling in the Western Ghats and the Vindhyas, and in generating pressure for a national forest policy, which is more sensitive to the people's needs and to the ecological requirements of the country.

HISTORICAL EVOLUTION OF FOREST MOVEMENTS

In pre-independent India, colonial impact on forest management undermined conservation strategies in two ways:

First, changes in the system of land tenure through the introduction of the zamindari system transformed common village resources into the private property of newly created landlords. Prior to this zamindari (landlord) system, many people fulfilled their domestic needs from the collectively owned village forests but with the newly created landlords, these people had now to turn to natural forests.

Second, large-scale felling of trees in natural forests to satisfy non-local commercial needs, such as shipbuilding for the British navy and sleepers for the expanding railway network, resulted in the destruction of forest. For about fifty years this kind of uncontrolled exploitation continued, at which point it was felt that some kind of control over exploitation is necessary. The colonial response took two forms: first, vesting ownership in the state and second, setting up a forest bureaucracy to regulate commercial exploitation and to conserve forests. This typically colonial interpretation of conservation generated severe conflict on two levels. On the level of utilization, the new management system catered only to commercial demands and ignored local basic needs. People were denied their traditional rights for which there were frequent struggles due to which sometimes rights were granted as favors. On the level of conservation, since the new forest management was concerned solely with forest revenues, ecologically unsound silvicultural practices were introduced. This undermined biological productivity of forest areas and transformed renewable resources into non-renewable ones.

With the reservation of forests and the denial of the people's right of access to them, the villagers created resistance movements in all parts of the country. The Forest Act of 1927 sharpened the conflicts, and in 1930s people witnessed widespread forest satyagrahas as a mode of nonviolent resistance to the new forest laws and policies: Villagers ceremonially removed forest produce from the reserved forests to defy forest laws that denied them their right to forest products. These satyagrahas were specially successful in regions where survival of the local population was intimately linked with the access to the forests, for example, the Himalayan foothills, the Western Ghats and the Central Indian hills. These nonviolent protests were suppressed by armed forces. In Central India, Gond tribals were gunned down for participating in the satyagraha. In the Himalayan foothills dozens of unarmed villagers were killed and hundreds injured in Tilari village of Tehri Garhwal on May 30, 1930, when they gathered to protest against the forest laws. After enormous loss of lives, the satyagrahas were finally successful in regaining some of the traditional rights of the village communities to various forest produce. But the forest policy and its revenue-maximizing objective remained unchanged.

In independent India the same colonial forest-management policy was continued but with greater ruthlessness, which is justified in the name of "national interest" and "economic growth." The threat to survival of the poor people in the region became a major problem. Interestingly, the response of the people changed: sporadic protests became more organized and sustained movements. Chipko is the most spectacular of these movements. The link between the pre-independent and post-independent forms of this satyagraha has been provided by Gandhians, such as Sri Dev Suman, Mira Behn and Sarala Behn. Sri Dev Suman was initiated into Gandhian Satyagraha at the time of the Salt Satyagraha. He died as a martyr for the cause of Garhwali people's rights to survive with dignity and freedom. Both Mira Behn and Sarala Behn, both Englishwomen, were close associates of Gandhi. After Gandhi's death, they both moved to the interior of Himalaya and established ashrams. Sarala Behn settled in Kumaun and Mira Behn lived in Garhwal until her departure to Vienna due to ill health. Equipped with Gandhian world-view of development based upon justice and ecological stability, they contributed silently to the growth of women-power and ecological consciousness in the hill areas of Uttar Pradesh. The Chipko movement is direct action based on Gandhian Satyagraha. It tries to establish that steadiness and stability do not mean stagnation. As Vandana Shiva says, "Balance with nature's innate ecological processes is not technological backwardness but technological sophistication."[1] The Chipko movement gives a new dimension to nonviolent struggle. Its significance lies in the fact that it is taking place in the post-independent India.

Sunderlal Bahuguna, Gandhian activist, philosopher, is the most successful campaigner of the movement. Influenced by Sri Dev Suman, he joined the Independence movement at the age of 13. Now, at over 70, he is busy strengthening the philosophical base of the Chipko movement from the Gandhian view of nature. He fasted against the auction of Adwani forests in 1977 and a woman named Bachhni Devi headed other women in the village and was able to save the forest from being auctioned through their nonviolent ecological slogan "What do the forests bear? soil, water and pure air." This became the slogan of the Chipko movement. The late Prime Minister Indira Gandhi met with Bahuguna and issued a directive for a 15-year ban on commercial green felling in the Himalayan forests of Uttar Pradesh. Bahuguna's method of functioning is far removed from that of self-seeking politicians. A non-political person, he was able to strike a chord in the hearts of those who were totally dissatisfied with the hypocrisy of politicians and the electoral process. Gandhian methods of nonviolence and Bahuguna's asceticism were appreciatively responded to by the predominantly Hindu peasantry. The capacity of physical suffering and spirit of sacrifice in an age of selfishness were constantly marvelled at by villagers who read into these acts the renunciation of worldly ambition as stated in Hindu scriptures.

Bahuguna's philosophy is based on the ecological premise that the depletion of forests is entirely traceable to commercial exploitation and that it is desirable to establish in the Himalaya a pre-industrial agricultural economy. The present economic crisis can be solved only by directly addressing the ecological crises symptomized by the destabilization of the hydrological system and the disruption of nutrient cycles. Bahuguna calls for a complete cessation of all commercial fellings in the Himalaya. Ecological rehabilitation of the hill areas is the primary task, and this involves a temporary moratorium on green-felling for commercial objectives, both local and non-local, to facilitate regeneration. Economic development in this perspective can only be based on minimizing ecological costs of growth while maximizing the sustainable productivity of nature for the satisfaction of primary human needs.

Chandi Prasad Bhatt is another activist of this movement working in a different area, Chamoli district. The eco-development model of Bhatt acknowledges the role of rural demand in the depletion of forest wealth by attempting to see that their demands are fulfilled in such a fashion that damage to forests is mitigated by organizing the rural population in a positive endeavor to restore the forest wealth. He is not opposed to forest-based industry per se but argues that it must be so organized as to genuinely help the poor forest dweller. Poverty is seen by Bhatt as having a technological solution. He emphasizes the involvement of local population in revegetating the Himalaya and takes a conservationist stand with regard to ecology. But Bahuguna sees the solution to poverty in the ecological rebuilding of nature's productivity by taking a preservationist standpoint of ecology. For Bhatt, the development prescription is that with the help of modern scientific knowledge the instruments of production are improved and the standard of living is raised.[2] Co-operative felling and the use of trees by the local people can provide employment and thus regenerate the hill economy.

In the early 1960s 25% of India was covered with trees. At present, only 19% is forested. Deforestation has led to soil erosion which has severely disrupted the natural processes of water conservation in different parts of India. Because of this both floods and drought have increased significantly. In the study that was done by the National Remote Sensing Agency of India, statistics verifies the point that forest area has decreased from 1970s to 1980s but due to a variety of reasons, one of which is Chipko protest, the forest area has increased from 14.10% in 1980s to 19% in 1990.

CRITICISMS OF CHIPKO MOVEMENT

Some scholars believe that to say that the Chipko movement is based on Gandhian Satyagraha is not appropriate. As Ramachandra Guha says in his book *Unquiet Woods*, "Although Chipko, like many Gandhian movements, has an important ethical dimension, its underlying notions or morality and justice are intrinsic to a history of protest against state restrictions on peasant access to forest produce. Nor should superficial similarities in methods of protest lead one to designate Chipko as 'Gandhian', its 'non-violent' method being an inspired and highly original response to forest felling rather than ideologically motivated."[3]

In response to this criticism, I like to say that since all the characteristics of Gandhian Satyagraha are present in the Chipko movement, it can be argued that it is based on Satyagraha. It is true that this movement and the forest Satyagrahas which preceded this movement were not absolutely nonviolent in the sense that no violence was used at all but realistically that is not possible. As long as there is minimal violence, it can be considered as nonviolent. I think that Gandhian Satyagraha involves the following:

First, it is a response to someone who is doing injustice. In this case, it is quite clear that the system of forestry management is doing injustice to the poor people whose life is dependent on the forest by collecting woods from the forest and burning the woods for cooking and it is also leading to the destruction of the ecological system.

Second, in changing this injustice to justice one tries to persuade the other side by using the nonviolent means of non-co-operation. Satyagraha is based on the philosophy of persuasion. Again, the nonviolent method used by the Chipko activists and its members is to hug the tree and not allow commercial cutting of trees. Though initially the nonviolent method of hugging the trees by the Chipko members did not succeed in persuading the industries from cutting the trees for commercial purposes but by using this nonviolent method persistently, commercial tree cutters were persuaded to stop cutting the trees for commercial purposes in this particular Himalayan region of the state of the state of Uttar Pradesh.

Third, by using the nonviolent method, it should persuade the other side/ person to come to the realization of the injustice that is being done and then try to change it. The Chipko movement has been successful in making the Indian government to have a fifteen-year ban on commercial tree-felling.

Fourth, the practitioner of Satyagraha must be ready to go through the suffering and stick to the cause at any cost. Even to this day Sunderlal Bahuguna and others are fighting for the sake of justice at any cost. The Chipko activists went through much suffering as many of them were arrested by police but they did not give up their fight for justice.

Fifth, Satyagraha is the weapon of the strong, not the weak. It requires discipline and courage on the part of its practitioner. The Chipko activists were disciplined and gained courage collectively through the cause of justice. This characteristic is present among the members of the Chipko movement as their survival is threatened by the ecological disaster.

Sixth, Satyagraha excludes violence in any shape or form, whether in thought, speech or deed. With regard to this, one can argue that though there has not been an absolute exclusion of violence, yet it involved minimum violence. And that is what Gandhi meant by nonviolence.

Seventh, Satyagraha is described as an unending, relentless, dialectical quest for truth. It is holding on to truth, no matter what. In Indian cosmology, person and nature, i.e., Purusha and Prakriti are, a duality in unity. Every form of creation is an embodiment of dialectical unity of diversity within a unifying principle. They are two aspects of one being. What should be noted here is that the dualism of the Indian traditions is not the dichotomy of human against the non-human. Humans share in both realms of being—the soul-world and the world of nature. This cosmological viewpoint of duality in unity is the basis of the ecological movement of India.

Last, Satyagraha requires no physical assistance or material aid and is capable of being exercised by men, women and children. Though the leaders of the Chipko movement are men, most of its members are women.

My contention is that since the Chipko movement follows all the above characteristics of Satyagraha, it is not inappropriate to claim that Chipko is based on Gandhian Satyagraha and that Gandhian Satyagraha can be applied in the world that we live in today.

IDEOLOGY OF THE CHIPKO MOVEMENT

It is ecologically based on people's needs and rights and at the same time it can be translated into economic development. The over-exploitation of forest resources and the resulting threat to communities living in the forests evolved from concerns for distribution of material benefits to concern for distribution of ecologically generated material costs. Genuine development is based only on ecological stability which gives the assurance of sustainable supplies of vital resources. Economic development and ecological stability are not mutually exclusive. Only when ecological stability is kept in the focus, is there a guarantee of stable material basis of life.

Economic policies should be made not only by the elites but also by the public whose survival is threatened. Involvement of the public in economic policies generates new paradigms of science and development based on ecological principles which ensure sustainability and justice. It is only by generating new paradigms that environmental conflicts can be resolved.

Further, the Chipko movement displays that scientific knowledge is not universal, objective and neutral as believed by some. It is always a particular response to a particular interest. When there is commercial utilization of resources for maximizing exchanging value, the type of knowledge system that is created is reductionist. When nature is treated as if its parts are isolated and unrelated and the only components with economic value are those which can be transformed into commodities, the consequence is internalization of profits and externalization of costs. On the other hand, when the interest is sustainable livelihood of the people and the satisfaction of basic needs, ecological knowledge is the response. As Sunderlal Bahuguna says, "Legislation without a popular movement to build strong public opinion is like a tree with shallow roots. The storm can at any time uproot it. People's movements are digging a deep ditch for the roots of environmental legislation to go deeper. People's ecology movements are thus forerunners of a sustainable and equitable process of economic development."[4]

CONCLUSION

The ideology of the Chipko movement can be applied to any country though the circumstances of each country can be very different. As the common goal is equity and justice, it is applicable everywhere. I will conclude with a quote from the *Time* magazine article where Ted Gup says, "The U.S. will have to recognize that no society can have it at all times—unfettered harvesting of natural resources, full employment and a healthy and rich environment."[5]

NOTES

1. "Ecology Movements of India" by Vandana Shiva, p. 272.

2. See *The Chipko Experience,* Bhatt and Kanwar, India: Dasholi Gram Swarajya Mandal, Gopeshwar, 1982.

3. Ramachandra Guha, *Unquiet Woods*, Los Angeles, University of California Press, 1990, p. 176.

4. See *Ecosystem of the Central Himalaya*, Chandi Prasad Bhatt, India: Dasholi Gram Swarajya Mandal, Gopeshwar, 1980.

5. "Owl vs. Man," Ted Gup, *Time*, June 25, 1990, p. 65.

25

Silence in the Brandenburg Gate

Maria Diefenbach

The idea of creating a non-denominational Room of Silence in the middle of Berlin came about shortly after the Berlin Wall fell in 1989. A small "Action Group," consisting of citizens of Berlin was formed with the aim of creating a Room of Silence in a suitable building in the center of Berlin, near the former frontier between opposing military forces and hostile ideologies. The room was modelled on a similar room, which Dag Hammarskjold had commissioned for himself and his colleagues in 1954 in the United Nations building in New York. This room is still in use. Thanks to the help of the Berlin Senate the Room of Silence could be opened in the Brandenburg Gate in October 1994.

According to the sponsors the Room of Silence has a dual Purpose: Firstly it provides an opportunity for everyone, independent of background, colour, ideology, religion and physical condition to enter and remain in silence for a while to simply relax, to gain strength for the daily life, or to remember inside this historic place the dark but also hopeful events, to meditate and to feel gratitude for the achievements of recent years. As everyone is invited to remain in silence and peace for a while, the room itself acquires a symbolic meaning, the other purpose the sponsors had in mind. This room is a symbol, a continuous invitation to tolerance, the brotherhood of man embracing all nationalities and ideologies, a continuous reminder against violence and xenophobia—a contribution, a small step towards peace and spiritual unity, according to the prayer of the United Nations:

"Oh Lord, our planet Earth is only a small star in space. It is our duty, to transform it into a planet whose creatures are no longer tormented by war, hunger and fear, no longer senselessly divided by race, colour and ideology. Give us courage and strength to begin this task today so that our children and children's children shall one day carry the name of man with pride."

The Room of Silence is not dedicated to any ideology or any religion—every one may enter without fear of thus relating to any interests, programmes or institutions. This does not contradict the fact the sponsors and wardens who look after the room on a voluntary basis spring largely from religious communities, the different christian churches, the Jewish, Islamic, Buddhist, Hindu and Baha'i communities. All these persons of different ideological backgrounds had a common goal in creating a place in the middle of Berlin where one can meet in silence, leaving aside one's differences.

The room's Decoration reflects its non-denominational character, avoiding any religious, ideological or political symbolism, it is neutral and simple. Its only adornment is a woven wall hanging, which Hungarian artist Ritta Hager made for this room, abstractly symbolising light penetrating darkness. Paul Corazolla, Berlin, designed the blue wall in the vestibule, this verbal reference to the Room of Silence equals the figurative invitation to silence by the relief which P. Franz Prentke, Berlin, created.

The fact that the Room of Silence could be created inside the Brandenburg Gate is of special importance also concerning the gate itself. For this Brandenburg Gate, built by Langhans about 200 years ago, was designed as a gate of peace: On top of the gate Schadow's Quadriga with the Goddess of Peace enters the town, underneath there is an Attic Relievo by Schadow as well which shows the Goddess as a messenger of peace. Also the statue of Mars in the southern part of the gate is engaged to peace, for Mars sheaths his sword.

During it's history—especially under the Nazi-Regime—the Brandenburg Gate was often used and misused for political ends. For years the gate symbolized a divided city and a divided world. Through the fall of the Wall, it became once again a symbol for a united peaceful future in Germany and Europe.

The Room of Silence symbolizes the original idea of the Brandenburg Gate as a gate of peace and thus meets the sense of the genius loci.

As a place of thoughtfulness, brother and sisterhood it will—we hope—confer honour and blessings to our city and to its symbol as a representation of peace here and elsewhere in the world.

THE PRAYER OF THE UNITED NATIONS

Oh Lord, our planet Earth is only a small star in space. It is our duty, to transform it into a planet whose creatures are no longer tormented by war, hunger and fear, by race, colour and strength to begin this task today so that our children and children's children shall one day carry the name of "Man" with pride.

Selected Bibliography

NONVIOLENCE

Addams, Jane. *Bread and Peace in Time of War.* New Society Publishers, 1972.

Alonso, Harriet Hyman. *Peace as a Women's Issue: A History of the U.S. Movement for World Peace and Women's Rights.* Syracuse Studies on Peace and Conflict Resolution, 1993.

Boulding, Elise. *Cultures of Peace: The Hidden Side of History.* Syracuse University Press, 2000.

————. *Building a Global Civic Culture: Education for an Interdependent World.* Teachers College Press, Columbia University, 1988.

Brinton, William M., and Rinzler, Alan, eds. *Without Force or Lies.* Mercury House, Inc., 1990.

Brock-Utne, Birgit. *Educating for Peace: A Feminist Perspective.* Pergamon Press, 1985.

Brsheeth, Haim, and Yuval-Davis, Nira, eds. *The Gulf War and the New World Order.* Zed Books, Humanities Press International, 1992.

Bruyn, Severyn T., and Rayman, Paula M., eds. *Nonviolent Action and Social Change.* Irvington, 1979.

Chappell, David W., ed. *Buddhist Peacework: Creating Cultures of Peace.* Wisdom Publications, 2000.

Cooney, Robert, and Michalowski, Helen, eds. *The Power of the People: Active Nonviolence in the United States.* Peace Press, 1987.

Dalton, Dennis, ed. *Mahatma Gandhi: Selected Political Writings.* Hackett Publishing Company, 1996.

Day, Dorothy. *The Long Loneliness, Loaves and Fishes, and on Pilgrimage: The Sixties.* Curtis Books, 1972.

DeBenedetti, Charles, ed. *Peace Heroes in Twentieth Century America.* Indiana University Press, 1988.

————. *An American Ordeal: The Antiwar Movement of the Vietnam Era.* Syracuse University Press, 1990.

Dellinger, Charles. *Revolutionary Nonviolence.* Bobbs-Merrill, 1970.

Eck, Diana L., and Jain, Devaki, eds. *Speaking of Faith: Global Perspectives on Women, Religion and Social Change.* New Society, 1987.

Egan, Eileen. *Peace Be With You: Justified Warfare or the Way of Nonviolence*. Orbis Books, 1999.

Epstein, Barbara. *Political Protest and Cultural Revolution: Nonviolent Direct Action in the 1970s and 1980s*. University of California Press, 1991.

Fellman, Gordon. *Rambo and the Dalai Lama: The Compulsion to Win and Its Threat to Human Survival*. State University of New York Press, 1998.

Gage, Richard L., trans. and ed. *A Lifelong Quest for Peace: A Dialogue between Linus Pauling and Daisaku Ikeda*. Jones and Bartlett, 1992.

Gallen, David, ed. *Malcolm A to X: The Man and His Ideas*. Pathfinder, 1992.

Goldman, Emma. *Red Emma Speaks: Selected Writings and Speeches*. Compiled and edited by Alix Kates Shulman. Random House, 1972.

Harak, G. Simon, ed. *Nonviolence for the Third Millennium: Its Legacy and Future*. Mercer University Press, 2000.

Haring, Bernard. *The Healing Power of Peace and Nonviolence*. , Paulist Press, 1986.

Holmes, Robert L. *Nonviolence in Theory and Practice*. Wadsworth Publishing Company, 1990.

Hopkins, Jeffrey, ed. *The Art of Peace: Nobel Peace Laureates discuss Human Rights, Conflict and Reconciliation*. Snow Lions Publications, 2000.

Irwin, Robert A. *Building a Peace System*. ExPro Press, 1989.

King, Martin Luther, Jr. *Stride toward Freedom*. Harper & Row Publishers, 1958.

Lackey, Douglas P. *The Ethics of War and Peace*. Prentice-Hall, 1989.

Lens, Sidney. *Labor Wars: From the Molly McGuires to the Sitdowns*. Doubleday, 1974.

Lynd, Staughton, ed. *Nonviolence in America*. Bobbs Merrill, 1968.

Makhijani, Arjun. *From Global Capitalism to Economic Justice*. , The Apex Press, 1992.

Mandela, Nelson. *The Struggle Is My Life*. Pathfinder Press, 1986.

Marable, Manning. *The Crisis of Color and Democracy: Essays on Race, Class, and Power*. Common Courage Press, 1992.

McAllister, Pam, ed., *Reweaving the Web of Life: Feminism and Nonviolence*. New Society Publishers, 1982.

———. *This River of Courage: Generations of Women's Resistance and Action*. New Society Publishers, 1991.

Merton, Thomas, and Zahn, Gordon Charles, ed. *The Nonviolent Alternative*. Farrar, Straus, and Giroux, 1981.

Moulton, Phillips P. *Ammunition for Peacemakers: Answers for Activists*. The Pilgrim Press, 1986.

Mufson, Steven. *Fighting Years: Black Resistance and the Struggle for a New South Africa*. Beacon Press, 1990.

O'Gorman, Angie, ed. *The Universe Bends toward Justice: A Reader on Christian Nonviolence in the U.S.* New Society Publishers, 1990.

Ostergaard, Geoffrey. *Nonviolent Revolution in India*. Gandhi Peace Foundation, 1985.

Peacework: 20 Years of Nonviolent Social Change. Fortkamp Publishing Company, 1991.

Porpora, Douglas. *How Holocausts Happen: The United States in Central America*. Temple University Press, 1990.

Rummel, Randolph J. *Power Kills: Democracy as a Method of Nonviolence*. Transaction, 1997.

Sibley, Mulford Q. *The Quiet Battle: Writings on the Theory and Practice of Non-Violent Resistance*. Beacon Press, 1968.

Smoker, Paul, Davies, Ruth and Munske, Barbara, eds. *A Reader in Peace Studies*. Pergamon Press, 1990.

Smith-Christopher, Daniel L., ed. *Subverting Hatred: The Challenge of Nonviolence in Religious Traditions*. Orbis Books, 2000.

Tolstoi, Leo. *Law of Violence and Law of Love*. Concord Grove, 1983.

Weathering the Storm: Christian Pacifist Responses to War. Faith and Life Press, 1991.

Weber, David R., ed. *Civil Disobedience in America: A Documentary History*. Cornell University Press, 1978.

Westing, Arthur H., ed. *Environmental Hazards of War: Releasing Dangerous Forces in an Industrialized World*. Sage, 1990.

Yoder, John H. *Nevertheless: The Varieties and Shortcomings of Religious Pacifism*. Herald Press, 1992.

CONFLICT RESOLUTION

Ackerman, Peter and Kruegler, Christopher. *Strategic Nonviolent Conflict: The Dynamics of People Power in the Twentieth Century*. Praeger, 1994.

Boudreau,Thomas E. *Sheathing the Sword: The U.N. Secretary-General and the Prevention of International Conflict*. Greenwood Press, 1991.

Breslin, William J., and Rubin, Jeffrey, eds. *Negotiation Theory and Practice*. PON Books, 1991.

Cornelius, Helena, and Faire, Shoshana. *Everyone Can Win: How to Resolve Conflict*. Simon and Schuster, 1993.

Dauer, E. *Alternative Dispute Resolution in Health Care: Analysis, Guidelines and Commentary*. Center for Public Resources Health Care Program, 1992.

Duffy, Karen Grover, Grosch, James W. and Olczak, Paul V., eds. *Community Mediation: A Handbook for Practitioners and Researchers*. The Guilford Press, 1991.

Fisher, Roger and Brown, Scott. *Getting Together: Building Relationships That Gets to Yes*. Penguin Books, 1988.

Fisher, Roger and Ury, William. *Getting to Yes*. Penguin Books, 1991.

Goldberg, Stephen B., Rogers, Nancy and Sander, Frank E. A. *Dispute Resolution*. Little, Brown and Company, 1992.

Hocker, Joyce L., and Wilmot,William W. *Interpersonal Conflict*, 3rd ed. Wm. C. Brown, 1991.

Kriesberg, Louis, Northrup, Terrell A. and Thorson, Stuart J., eds. *Intractable Conflicts and Their Transformation*. Syracuse University Press, 1989.

Meyer, Aleta Lynn. *Promoting Nonviolence in Early Adolescence: Responding in Peaceful and Positive Ways*. Kluwer Academic/Plenum, 2000.

Myriam, Miedzian. *Boys Will Be Boys: Breaking the Link between Masculinity and Violence*. Doubleday, 1991.

Powers, Roger S., and Vogele, Willaim B., eds. *Protest, Power, and Change: An Encyclopedia of Nonviolence Action from ACT-UP to Women's Suffrage*. Garland, 1997.

Steger, Manfred B., and Lind, Nancy S., eds. *Violence and Its Alternatives: An Interdisciplinary Reader*. St. Martin's Press, 1999.

Ury, William. *Getting Past No: Negotiating with Difficult People*. Bantam Books, 1991.

Weber, Thomas. *Conflict Resolution and Gandhian Ethics*. Gandhi Peace Foundation, 221/223 Deen Dayal Upadhyaya Marg, New Delhi 110002, India, 1991.

Yankelovich, Daniel. *The Magic of Dialogue: Transforming Conflict into Cooperation.* Simon and Schuster, 1999.

JOURNALS/PERIODICALS AND NEWSLETTERS/ORGANIZATIONS

Conflict Management and Peace Science, Pennsylvania State University.
Conflict Studies, Research Institute for the Study of Conflict and Terrorism, England.
Conflict Resolution Notes, Conflict Resolution Center International, Inc. (Newsletter)
Gandhi Marg, Journal of the Gandhi Peace Foundation of New Delhi, India.
Gandhians in Action: International Quarterly, Sulabh Foundation, India.
Gandhian Perspectives, Gandhian Institute of Studies, India.
Global Justice, Center on Rights Development, Graduate School of International Studies, University of Denver, Denver.
Global Networks: A Journal of Transnational Affairs, Blackwell Publishers.
Journal of Conflict Resolution, University of Washington, Seattle, USA, SAGE Publications.
Martin Luther King, Jr., Center for Nonviolent Social Change, Center for Nonviolent Social Change. (Newsletter)
Martin Luther King, Jr. Memorial Studies in Religion and Social Development, Peter Lang Publishing.
Maryknoll, Maryknoll, NY.
Mediation Quarterly, Academy of Family Mediations.
Negotiation Journal: On the Process to Dispute Settlement, Plenum Publishing Corp., 233 Spring Street, New York, NY 10013
Nonviolent Activist, War Resisters League. (Newsletter)
Peace and Change: A Journal of Peace Research, Sage Periodicals Press.
Peace Chronicle: Consortium on Peace Research, Education and Development, Institute for Conflict Analysis and Resolution, George Mason University.
Peace and Freedom, Women's International League
Peace Education: IAEWP Journal of Peace Education Annual, International Association of Educators for World Peace.
Peace Magazine, Canadian Disarmament Information Service, Canada. Web site: www.peacemagazine.org
Peace News for Nonviolent Revolution, England. Web site: www.gn.apc.org/peacenews
Peace Newsletter, Syracuse Peace Council.
Peace Reporter, National Peace Foundation. Web site: www.nationalpeace.org
Peace Review: The International Quarterly of World Peace, Carfax. Web site: www.carfax.co.uk
Peacework, American Friends Service Committee (AFSC), Cambridge, MA.
Boston Research Center (BRC) in Cambridge, MA, is an international peace institute. Human rights, nonviolence, ecological harmony and economic justice are focal points of the center's work. Web site: http://www.brc21.org Address: 396 Harvard Street, Cambridge, MA 02138. Telephone: (617) 491-1090.

OTHER WEBSITES

www.gabn.net/hassan/malcolm9.htm

www.excelcenter.com
mama.indstate.edu/users/india/country/mahatma.html
www.nuvs.com/ashram/gallery/index.html
www.sscnet.ucla.edu/southasia/History/Gandhi/gandhi.html
www.tradewatch.org
www.web.net/comfront/alts4americas/eng/eng.html
www.etown.edu/vl/
www.iwpr.net
www.incore.ulst.ac.uk/cds/countries/index.html
www.usip.org/
students.vassar.edu/~vietnam/

Index

About the Editors

KRISHNA MALLICK is Associate Professor of Philosophy, Chairperson of the Philosophy Department and coordinator of the Peace Institute at Salem State College. She has coedited two books and published several scholarly articles and book chapters.

DORIS HUNTER is a Unitarian Universalist Minister in the Boston area. She has taught philosophy and religion at various institutions and has written extensively on the subjects of violence and nonviolence.